I0083812

Unexpected Voices in Imperial Parliaments

Empire's Other Histories

Series Editors: Victoria Haskins (University of Newcastle, Australia), Emily Manktelow (Royal Holloway, University of London, UK), Jonathan Saha (University of Leeds, UK) and Fae Dussart (University of Sussex, UK)

Editorial Board: Esme Cleall, (University of Sheffield, UK), Swapna Banerjee, (CUNY, USA), Lynette Russell, (Monash University, Australia), Tony Ballantyne, (University of Otago, New Zealand)

Empire's Other Histories is an innovative series devoted to the shared and diverse experiences of the marginalised, dispossessed and disenfranchised in modern imperial and colonial histories. It responds to an ever-growing academic and popular interest in the histories of those erased, dismissed, or ignored in traditional historiographies of empire. It will elaborate on and analyse new questions of perspective, identity, agency, motilities, intersectionality and power relations.

Forthcoming:

In the Service of Empire, Fae Dussart
Extreme Violence and the 'British Way' Michelle Gordon
Spiritual Colonialism in a Globalizing World, Christina Petterson

Unexpected Voices in Imperial Parliaments

Edited by
Josep M. Fradera, José María Portillo and Teresa Segura-Garcia

BLOOMSBURY ACADEMIC
LONDON • NEW YORK • OXFORD • NEW DELHI • SYDNEY

BLOOMSBURY ACADEMIC
Bloomsbury Publishing Plc
50 Bedford Square, London, WC1B 3DP, UK
1385 Broadway, New York, NY 10018, USA
29 Earlsfort Terrace, Dublin 2, Ireland

BLOOMSBURY, BLOOMSBURY ACADEMIC and the Diana logo
are trademarks of Bloomsbury Publishing Plc

First published in Great Britain 2021
Paperback edition published in 2022

Copyright © Josep M. Fradera, José María Portillo and Teresa Segura-Garcia, 2021
Josep M. Fradera, José María Portillo and Teresa Segura-Garcia
have asserted their right under the Copyright, Designs and Patents Act,
1988, to be identified as Author of this work.

Cover design: Tjaša Krivec
Cover Image © Blaise Diagne, first African deputy elected at the
French Parliament greeting its voters. Senegal (Africa), May 14, 1914.
Photo by Harlingue/Roger Viollet via Getty Images.

All rights reserved. No part of this publication may be reproduced or
transmitted in any form or by any means, electronic or mechanical,
including photocopying, recording, or any information storage or
retrieval system, without prior permission in writing from the publishers.

Bloomsbury Publishing Plc does not have any control over, or responsibility for,
any third-party websites referred to or in this book. All internet addresses given
in this book were correct at the time of going to press. The author and publisher
regret any inconvenience caused if addresses have changed or sites have
ceased to exist, but can accept no responsibility for any such changes.

Every effort has been made to trace copyright holders and to obtain their
permissions for the use of copyright material. The publisher apologizes for
any errors or omissions and would be grateful if notified of any corrections
that should be incorporated in future reprints or editions of this book.

A catalogue record for this book is available from the British Library.

Library of Congress Cataloging-in-Publication Data
Names: Fradera, Josep Maria, editor. | Portillo Valdés, José Ma. (José
María), editor. | Segura-Garcia, Teresa, editor.
Title: Unexpected voices in imperial parliaments / edited by Josep M.
Fradera, José María Portillo and Teresa Segura-Garcia.
Description: London ; New York : Bloomsbury Academic, 2021. | Includes
bibliographical references and index. |
Identifiers: LCCN 2021000349 (print) | LCCN 2021000350 (ebook) | ISBN
9781350193192 (hardback) | ISBN 9781350193208 (ebook) | ISBN
9781350193215 (epub)
Subjects: LCSH: Minority legislators–Biography. | Legislative
bodies–History. | Imperialism. | Europe–Colonies.
Classification: LCC JF511 .U548 2021 (print) | LCC JF511 (ebook) | DDC
328.092/24–dc23
LC record available at https://lccn.loc.gov/2021000349
LC ebook record available at https://lccn.loc.gov/2021000350

ISBN: HB: 978-1-3501-9319-2
         PB: 978-1-3501-9329-1
         ePDF: 978-1-3501-9320-8
         eBook: 978-1-3501-9321-5

Typeset by Integra Software Services Pvt. Ltd.

To find out more about our authors and books visit www.bloomsbury.com
and sign up for our newsletters.

Contents

Figures

Contributors

Dominique Chathuant is Associate Professor and Associate Researcher at the University of Reims Champagne-Ardenne's Centre d'études et de recherches en histoire culturelle (CERHIC), France. His work explores assimilationist political culture, black experiences in France and their connections abroad. He has published works on French black political elites and on Vichy in Guadeloupe. He recently contributed to *Combattants de l'empire: Les troupes coloniales dans la Grande Guerre* (2018) and *L'Encyclopédie de la colonisation française* (2017–18). He is the author of an English–French historical lexicon (2013).

Josep M. Fradera is Professor of Modern History at the Universitat Pompeu Fabra, Barcelona, Spain. He has published extensively on the economic, cultural and political history of nineteenth-century Catalonia, Spain and its empire, as summarized in *Colonias para después de un imperio* (2005). His comparative study of the empires of Britain, France, Spain and the United States from 1780 to 1914 was published in Spanish in 2015, in two volumes. Its abridged, English-language version is *The Imperial Nation: Citizens and subjects in the empires of Great Britain, France, Spain and the United States* (2018).

Eric Garcia-Moral holds a BA in History (Universitat de Barcelona, 2013) and a Master's in World History (Universitat Pompeu Fabra, 2014). He is pursuing a PhD in History at Universitat Pompeu Fabra, Barcelona, Spain, with a dissertation on colonial African history. He has undertaken fieldwork at Cheikh Anta Diop University in Dakar, Senegal. He is the author of *Breve Historia del África subsahariana* (2017).

David Geggus is Professor Emeritus at the University of Florida, Gainesville, USA where he taught courses on Caribbean history and slavery in the Atlantic world. His research, conducted in ten countries, has focused on Saint Domingue and the Haitian Revolution. He has published six books, including *Slavery, War, and Revolution* (1982), *Haitian Revolutionary Studies* (2002), and *The International Impact of the Haitian Revolution* (2014), as well as over a hundred academic articles. His most recent book, *The Haitian Revolution: A documentary history* (2014), was named a *Choice* Outstanding Academic Title.

Daniel Gutiérrez Ardila holds a PhD in History from University of Paris 1 Panthéon-Sorbonne, France. He is a professor at the Universidad Externado de Colombia's Centro de Estudios de Historia (CEHIS), Colombia. He is the author of *Un nuevo reino: Pactismo, geografía política y diplomacia durante el interregno en Nueva Granada, 1808–1816* (2010), *El reconocimiento de Colombia, diplomacia y propaganda en la coyuntura de las Restauraciones, 1819–1831* (2012) and *La Restauración en la Nueva Granada, 1816–1819* (2016).

Abel Alexis Louis is Associate Member of the research group Archéologie Industrielle Histoire Patrimoine/Géographie Développement Environnement (AIHP/GEODE), at the the University of the West Indies. He is also Associate Member of the Centre de recherches en histoire internationale atlantique (CRHIA), at the Universities of Nantes and La Rochelle, France. He has researched the lives of free people of colour in Martinique from 1660 to 1848, as well as the social elites of the French Antilles from the end of the eighteenth centiry to the 1860s. His most recent publications are *Le monde du négoce à Saint-Pierre sous la Monarchie de Juillet (1830–1848)* (2017) and *Le livre et ses lecteurs en Martinique de la fin du Directoire à la Monarchie de Juillet (1799—1848)* (2018).

Stephanie McCurry is the R. Gordon Hoxie Professor of American History at Columbia University, USA. Her research explores the history of the nineteenth-century United States, particularly on the history of the South and of women and gender, and the social history of politics. She is the author of *Masters of Small Worlds: Yeoman Households, Gender Relations, and the Political Culture of the South Carolina Low County* (1995), on the antebellum period and the politics of secession in South Carolina, and *Confederate Reckoning: Power and Politics in the Civil War South* (2010).

José María Portillo is a professor of History at the University of the Basque Country, Spain. He has also taught at Georgetown University (Prince of Asturias Professor) and Chicago University (Tinker Professor) in the United States, El Colegio de México and Instituto Mora in Mexico, and Universidad Externado in Colombia. His field of research is the history of political cultures during imperial crises in the Hispanic world. He is the author of *Crisis atlántica: Autonomía e independencia en la monarquía hispánica* (2006) and *Fuero Indio: Tlaxcala y la identidad territorial entre monarquía imperial y república nacional (1787–1824)* (2015).

Teresa Segura-Garcia holds a PhD in History from the University of Cambridge, UK (2016), with a dissertation on the global links of the Indian princely state of Baroda through the figure of Maharaja Sayaji Rao III (r. 1875–1939). After a postdoctoral fellowship from the International Centre of Advanced Studies: Metamorphoses of the Political (ICAS:MP) at the Centre for the Study of Developing Societies, Delhi, she joined Universitat Pompeu Fabra, Barcelona, as a postdoctoral fellow. Her publications include 'The Raj's uncanny other: Indirect rule and the princely states', in *The Routledge Handbook of the History of Colonialism in South Asia* (2020).

Adrian Shubert is Professor of History at York University, Toronto, Canada. He is the author of *A Social History of Modern Spain, 1800–1990* (1990) and *Death and Money in the Afternoon: A History of the Spanish Bullfight* (2001) and the co-editor, along with José Alvarez Junco, of *Spanish History since 1808* (2000). His awards include a John Simon Guggenheim Fellowship, a Killam Research Fellowship and being named a Commander of the Order of Civil Merit by King Juan Carlos I of Spain.

Tim Stapleton is a professor in the Department of History at the University of Calgary, Alberta, Canada where he teaches African and military history. His has published eleven sole-authored books, the most recent of which are *Africa: War and Conflict in the Twentieth Century* (2018) and *A History of Genocide in Africa* (2016). Previously, he taught at Rhodes University and the University of Fort Hare in South Africa and has held honorary positions at universities in Zimbabwe, Zambia, Botswana and Nigeria.

Introduction

Josep M. Fradera, José María Portillo and Teresa Segura-Garcia

It is not easy to judge the significance of political representation in parliaments, representative assemblies or Cortes (the use of these names aligned these institutions with well-established traditions) in the context of the political cycle that began with the Atlantic revolutions of 1776 and 1789, first in the Thirteen Colonies and then in metropolitan France. Needless to say, it constituted a fundamental part of 'formal' politics. But it is more difficult to explain, measure or weigh how it formed part of politics as a whole. In the end, formal politics and politics *tout court* were never entirely separate nor did they ever cease influencing one another. *Unexpected Voices in Imperial Parliaments* defines and clarifies the two great changes that defined contemporary societies and distinguished them from prior worlds – from the era we refer to as the Old Regime, without going into more detail. This book confronts these complex matters by studying the sudden appearance of political representatives from colonies and non-European possessions in parliaments and high chambers in some of the great imperial nations from the late eighteenth century. The first of these two changes was world integration – or global integration, if one wishes – which altered the meaning of modern politics. This book makes this evident: from Lima to Port-au-Prince to Bombay, and from Paris to London, people wished to debate essential issues in representative chambers which, by necessity, were situated in the great imperial centres – or in post-colonial contexts that had proclaimed their independence, such as in certain parts of Latin America and in the United States.

Secondly, if since the last decades of the eighteenth century those chambers were meeting points for certain aristocratic factions and members of rising social groups whose blatantly privileged status was protected by very transparent rules of exclusion, those same rules of exclusion, segregation and racial prejudice were bound to be discussed from the start by everyone who felt outside the rules of the game. Women and young people, non-white individuals and former slaves, people from the colonies or subjects from the far-away lands of imperial monarchies all fought to use the public voice granted by imperial and national parliaments. Political, social and sexual identities were never defined only from the bottom up; rather, exclusion from top to bottom, ensuring inherited hierarchies, defined them gradually and inevitably. The figures who appear in this selection of biographies paid careful attention to how they constructed their personal political identity against the context and symbolic elements of a world which they wished to represent. This book also shows how outside forces imposed upon them conditions of honour and loyalty to imperial institutions that went far beyond those imposed upon co-nationals.

Unexpected Voices in Imperial Parliaments describes in detail how some individuals broke down barriers and entered spaces of legislative debate and representation where they were not expected – spaces from which they had been excluded by republics or monarchies with both imperial and liberal vocations. In this regard, the book deals not only and not primarily with the activities of these 'exotic' parliamentarians but rather with how the extension of the electoral census and the obligatory inclusion of other groups broadened the range of political action as such. Public debates and the reading of commentaries on parliamentary sessions were simply one more part of the workings of politics. Other parts included the transformation of the newspaper business, the formation of parties beyond the old parliamentary lobbies, mass politics and the entrance on the scene of ever broader sectors of the population. In that sense, if we are quite familiar with the critical transformation of metropolitan centres, we are less familiar with how those transformations were transferred to vast territories of the expanding European empires. Above all – and this is the point of the book – there was a connection between these two aspects of the same reality.

The texts in this volume were first presented and discussed in June 2018 at a workshop hosted by the Research Group on Empires, Metropoles and Extra-European Societies (GRIMSE), at the Department of Humanities at Universitat Pompeu Fabra (UPF), Barcelona. The event was a gathering of historians from around the world, from different backgrounds and traditions – scholars of the Spanish and Latin American empires, Africa, the French colonial world and South Asia. The exchange of views among colleagues was fruitful and fulfilled our goal of moving the conversation beyond the metropolitan boundaries that generally confine us when we talk about political representation. Following the emblematic example of Jean-Baptiste Belley, we established a timeline extending from the French Revolution to 1945. Metropoles and colonies played on the same board, but with different rules. Our aim was to observe and explain these complexities, understanding that a subject that had hitherto been studied so insufficiently would have many unexplored facets and territories.

Finally, this book also studies the actions of those who managed to enter imperial parliaments that had not been prepared to welcome them and, when forced to do so, were not at all happy. Later on, under certain circumstances, they grew to understand the value of including these able politicians in their representative chambers. Conflict and co-optation were always two sides of the same coin. This book also reconsiders well-known mechanisms of exclusion that separated or limited entire groups from participating or defending themselves through legislation and debate due to their colonial status, because they were former slaves, or members of a particular race, gender or age group. These unwritten rules were never assumed to be eternal nor did they always tend toward more openness or integration in parliament. Some limits clearly worsened for decades at a time, as was the case in the French and Spanish worlds after the revolutionary cycle or in the United States after Reconstruction. This book explores these various realities with the aim of comparing them and having each shed light on the other.

Several institutions and individuals have contributed to this project, which Bloomsbury has so generously agreed to publish. In the case of institutional contributions, we would like to highlight the joint support of the Government of Spain's Ministry of Science, Innovation and Universities (MCIU) and State Research Agency (AEI), as well as the European Regional Development Fund (ERDF), through the research project PGC2018-096722-B100, the Catalan Institution for Research and Advanced Studies (ICREA) and the Department of Humanities at UPF. Among the people who have made the project possible, the contribution of Claudia Contente (UPF) in the preparation of the initial workshop and the careful reading of the subsequent texts has been absolutely indispensable. Equally, the quality of Penny Eades's translation work and of Ruth MacKay's translation and editing work should be recognized. We would also like to express our gratitude for the thoughtful reading and suggestions of the three anonymous readers chosen by Bloomsbury. Finally, we would like to highlight the generosity with which Adrian Shubert (York University) agreed to write the valuable conclusion that closes the volume.

One final note: when we gathered in Barcelona for the workshop that gave rise to this book, over two warm June days and facing the Mediterranean Sea, we were well aware that our efforts were pioneering. We were certain that we and many others needed to extend the examples and the cases studies. We have a long road ahead, and we sincerely hope this book inspires others to join us.

1

The value of political representation in modern empires

Josep M. Fradera

Already during the period of Old Regime monarchies in Europe, representative assemblies were venerable, inherited institutions. It is true that royal authoritarianism limited their reach, capacities and projection, with notable differences among countries. But growing financial and military demands arising from conflicts among monarchies both in Europe and in colonial dominions on various continents in the eighteenth century modified the perception of these ancient institutions' attributes and their representative foundations. Concepts such as liberty, democracy, universality and political equality took many years to acquire their shape in political debates that would end up defining their complete transformation during the nineteenth and twentieth centuries. Demands placed upon what we today refer to as the fiscal-military state triggered those political debates and the institutional transformations that defined the late-eighteenth-century revolutionary cycle. Patrician debates with classical trappings were suddenly interrupted with demands from consumers squeezed by new taxes, monopolies and by new forms of debt aimed at the disposable savings of the Creole elites in America and Asia, the scene of inter-imperial warfare. Taxes and representation, militia and civil status, personal freedom and servitude or slavery: these were the poles of modern politics starting from the last third of the eighteenth century.

One of the results of all this was that representative capacity and its value were no longer concepts belonging to aristocratic political culture. Rather, they became the very essence of the cause championed by the rising urban middle classes. Furthermore, discussions regarding the limits of worn-out aristocratic privileges and demands for greater political equality used the new language of mass politics – in the press, pamphlets, outdoor meetings and impassioned debates in beer halls and coffee houses – and they made evident the novel ability of these new groups to organize. The substance of these discussions, with their vital issues and new forms of propaganda, enabled the message to reach society at large, going beyond the limits of earlier eras in ways previously unseen (with the exception of the great religious and revolutionary upheavals). The margins of political participation broadened to an extraordinary degree, mixing social groups and classes: the Atlantic revolutions, with their enormous social reach, are a perfect example of this. If Paris in 1789 was the epitome of that transformation, it was due to its intensity and scope. In that revolutionary context, representative assemblies adapted to the new demands – they had no choice.

Parliaments, Cortes and other representative bodies, be they monarchical or republican, performed three crucial tasks in line with the complex and often opaque triad of power that Montesquieu delineated. The first was to ensure continuity of the legislative process, always with the initiative of the crown or the government in power. The second was to determine which factions represented in those bodies would gain the upper hand, either alone or with allies – in other words, who would win over the monarch or manage to form a new government. These two functions, described thus schematically, might give us an idea of the construction of the state and of liberal society were it not for the third factor, which was just as critical. Parliaments were the key location for the formation of public opinion, a rising force that overwhelmed readers of *Hansard* in England and similar publications elsewhere. The *Journal de Débats*, which not coincidentally appeared in 1789 Paris, would play a similar role, as would the official *Diario de Sesiones de Cortes* and the liberal publication of Manuel José Quintana, *Semanario Patriótico*, in liberal Spain in 1808. Publication of parliamentary debates was consolidated only in the last third of the eighteenth century and would become more stable through the 1820s. Before then it was not only difficult to read the debates, but in some places, such as in England until the 1770s, it was a risk. The combination of the printing revolution and an eager readership decimated the proverbial censorship ability of the modern Leviathan.[1] Not coincidentally, these summaries of parliamentary debates appeared both in the metropolis and in colonial cities. They formed part of the process we are attempting to describe, that is, the inescapable relationship between political life in metropolitan society and in non-European societies. The circulation of parliamentary debates was a key constitutive element of the legitimacy of parliaments and among public opinion, parties, politicians, the electoral process and the constitution of governments. The monarch could no longer simply call upon the head of one of the constitutive factions. In other words, he or she could no longer be ignorant of the opinions being formed ever more freely in civil society. Edmund Burke was well aware of this, and his eloquence helped encourage decisions that sometimes undermined established interests. So too was Georg Wilhelm Friedrich Hegel, the heart of whose early political theory was inspired, in the Scottish tradition, by the distinction between civil and political society. For Hegel, the state must be the keystone in a civil war to be fought according to new rules that still no one in the mid-nineteenth century was familiar with.

The sudden appearance in representative political bodies of people from colonial worlds was the outcome not just of the complexity of colonial relations and the impossibility of the metropolis exercising absolute control, an option viable only in social scientific models that exist far, far away from worlds in which people must fight for their welfare and dignity. It was also owed to the ability of certain individuals and social groups to make their presence known in given moments and circumstances. Clearly, joining an imperial representative body such as the French National Assembly, the Cortes of Cádiz in September 1810 or Westminster was not the same as joining assemblies of lesser rank or reduced territorial reach, be they in a Colombian province, the French Antilles or South Africa. In the former cases, the message of representation reached far and wide around the globe. In the latter, what was most important was close proximity to local or regional interests.

As we will see in the following pages, the appearance of figures such as Jean-Baptiste Belley and Inca Yupanqui in the French National Assembly and the Spanish Cortes of Cadiz, respectively, was linked to their and others' ability to negotiate the complexities of new political spaces opened up by the Atlantic revolutions. Finding themselves in spaces that bestowed upon them the utmost legitimacy, their worlds of origin suddenly became visible for the first time. It was one thing for religious figures, enlightened humanitarians or writers to criticize slavery or the condition of the Indians – it was quite another for the criticism to come from the mere presence of such capable and articulate personages. To make things more critical, many of those elected representatives had neither European origin nor white skin, a detail that made quite remarkable – to say the least – the role they suddenly embodied, immortalized by Belley's famous portrait. That presence, which was both unexpected and generally unwelcome, constituted a direct challenge to elaborately drawn hierarchical orders. The challenge was indeed so great that a major part of colonial and imperial politics in the nineteenth century consisted of an attempt to close off or deliberately distort constitutional possibilities that had opened up as a result of these men's disturbing arrival.[2] One way of doing this was to assign seats by ethnicity, thus building a sort of golden cage for minority representatives in parliament. This was the case with four Māori representatives in the New Zealand parliament from 1867, when the war over the North Island was still being fought. This model – derived from that of the Irish minority in Westminster – was hugely influential later on in other parts of the great liberal empire, from Fiji to Lord Curzon's British Raj. Minority representation based on ethnicity also existed in contemporary empires with very different parliamentary traditions.[3] Paradoxically, only in exceptional moments, such as in 1848 France or when European imperial territorial expansion was such that it had to pull back and co-opt groups – in India, in the French *vielles colonies* in the Antilles, in Senegal – do we find colonists becoming involved again in metropolitan politics. Their appearance was never incidental or episodic – on the contrary, it was a key part of colonial reforms and the rise of the Creoles and Pan-Africanism as European imperialism waned during the inter-war years of the twentieth century. Therefore, it is important to correctly identify and interpret the place of these unexpected voices in imperial and colonial history, their weight and importance in the larger arena of colonial and metropolitan relations.

I

The task of the historian is to understand the contexts in which historical change takes place without ever losing sight of the protagonists who actually make those changes happen, be they individuals or social groups common interests, ideas, religion or ethnicity. In 1993, the great American historian Eric Foner published *Freedom's Lawmakers: A Directory of Black Officeholders during Reconstruction*, a documented and exhaustive repertoire of biographies of public figures who, better than anyone else, symbolized the changes in the United States after the Civil War and passage of the Fourteenth and Fifteenth Amendments.[4] Each entry contains information about the individual's origin, if they had been a slave, their racial category in the hierarchy of the times, profession, place of residence and subsequent posts – no easy feat for the author given the enormous instability and mobility in the United States during those years. The figures in Foner's book were not the only ones who played a decisive role in their country's transformation, as alongside them stood the radical Republicans. But while the latter have always figured prominently in history books, the same cannot be said of Foner's parliamentarians and administrators. A few years after his book came out, another historian, the Frenchman Michel Winock, published *Les voix de la liberté*, a massive portrait of leading French political figures, a global narrative featuring the great protagonists of France's post-Revolutionary epic struggle for political liberty during both the republic and the monarchy.[5] Both are excellent books, and they are complementary in some ways. The difference in content and focus, however, is obvious. In the centre of Winock's analytical perspective stand the figures of classical liberalism along with those from other settings who challenged them, either from the right or from the left. This broad focus allowed him to create an ensemble with a common thread. He gathered the men who moulded French political culture, which had such great influence on the nineteenth-century world – men such as Benjamin Constant and Alexis de Tocqueville, but also others who spoke in different voices, such as the socialist François Proudhon and the German exile Karl Marx.

Both books are essentially group portraits during times of great change. Winock's wide view allowed him to also include leading figures in literature and culture, such as Jules Michelet, Charles Baudelaire and Victor Hugo, all of whom were also caught up in the endless political manoeuvrings between republicanism and Bonapartist or monarchical legitimism. But with the exception of those whom E. H. Carr called the 'romantic exiles', Winock's daguerreotype does not include anyone from outside France itself. There was no one from the faraway places that nonetheless flew the French flag. This absence becomes even more stark when the book is placed alongside Foner's. In the decade that followed the end of the Civil War, Reconstruction was marked by, among other things, a massive influx of African Americans into US administrative positions and, to a lesser degree, into legislative posts. This was the epitome of an obviously monumental transformation: the end of slavery and the rise of those whose lives changed with the Emancipation Proclamation of 1863 and the passage of the Thirteenth Amendment in 1865. Even before then, there were those who had managed to obtain marginal positions, but what occurred from 1865 had no historical equivalent anywhere.[6] However, ten years after the end of the Civil War, their progress in obtaining this modest political space was cut short and would undergo ceaseless regression in the face of the relentless political reaction of rising white supremacists.

What is the prima facie difference between the case studies chosen by Foner and Winock? The first and most obvious one is that the American republic since the War of Independence was a nation under construction, forged with the implicit inclusion of slavery so as to attain a geographic balance of power among the new states that would survive until the war broke out. France,

Britain, Holland, Portugal and Spain, on the other hand, all maintained empires that depended upon slavery – empires that obviously lay beyond their own metropolitan territory in Europe. The US Republic, by contrast, encouraged slavery within its own borders, which in theory were characterized by republican equality.[7]

That was of course not the only colonial situation within US borders: there were key Supreme Court rulings regarding the Cherokee and the other 'civilized' tribes, with the subsequent establishment of Indian Territory. The crisis between the North and the South almost inevitably, thus, turned into a civil war, an open national crisis. France, meanwhile, had colonial possessions both with and without slavery. Among the former, the Antilles, Senegal and Réunion were in 1848 sites of a great emancipatory experiment along the lines of Britain's in 1833, the latter being too close to ignore. The continuity of the old slave colonies after the republican catharsis brought about an experiment in assimilation and political representation made possible by the 'voices of liberty' in 1848, as well as by the republican restoration of 1870 and the establishment of a Third Republic that would prove lasting. The division of the French empire into two sorts of colonies, 'old' and 'new', explains the coexistence of places where it was impossible to undo the revolutionary legacies of 1793 and 1848 and places where that legacy was denied. That contrast, with all the necessary caveats for nuance, is one of the reasons why the French empire looms so large in this volume.

Many of the pages that follow address the complex events of an incipient democracy, institutions in the process of formation and social principles that appeared to announce neither expanded suffrage nor political representation for certain groups. And yet this is the history of the late eighteenth century that would continue through the following century and beyond. If the two republics par excellence marked such a contrast, other countries with colonies and an imperial vocation can perfectly enter into a larger-scale comparison. The chapters in *Unexpected Voices in Imperial Parliaments* add new elements to the historiography and debate surrounding empires and the struggle for political representation by colonial subjects. The case studies we present concern both the US model of internal colonialism and the more general case of countries with traditions of both colonialism abroad and liberalism at home, such as France, Spain and Great Britain. In all these cases, during the revolutionary era that began with the Declaration of Independence in the United States, and lasted through the Napoleonic Wars, the importance and weight of political representation underwent modifications. Old traditions and institutions were destroyed or reformed everywhere, though in some cases certain formulas and rhetoric would endure well into the nineteenth century. The period beginning with the Atlantic revolutions saw a notable expansion of subjects' civic life (for one is always a subject before becoming a citizen) in countries that had felt the flicker of the revolutionary and liberal flame. One of these modifications was the universalization of the very idea of representation and citizenship even for colonial subjects who were not intended to enjoy such benefits.

A clarification is due at this point: if European worlds were internally divided, so too were the colonies. Everywhere, extra-European societies were a complex superimposition of white colonists, Creoles and indigenous peoples, free and unfree, the outcome of the gigantic movement of Africans and the infinite variation in their offspring. Initially and emphatically, the possibility of representation was conceived as a way of coopting dominant groups in those faraway places. Predictably enough, amid the dynamics of the revolutionary era the ideas of extending citizenship, voting rights local representation, and access to imperial parliaments were interpreted as excessive concessions that were the result of circumstances. Such options could be eliminated by metropolitan fiat or by the more perverse option of *lois spéciales* – an invention of Napoleon that would be followed in spirit or in fact by other empires. What is beyond question is that that ambiguous political space opened up by the first generation of colonial parliamentarians was projected onto and sustained by societies that were intimately acquainted with slavery and forced labour. In the pages that follow, readers will find individuals who emerged out of those divided worlds, individuals who reached the apex of parliamentary representation through perilous circumstances, hard work and sophisticated skills – sometimes even including a reinvention of their own lineage and biography. Before continuing to speak of the larger context, let us now see how these people managed to stand out, and let us name them.

The chapter by David Geggus is about the near-mythical figure of Jean-Baptiste Belley, the first black parliamentarian ('black' to distinguish him from mulattos or *pardos*, the phenotypes obsessively used by contemporaries) to take a seat in a European chamber of deputies. The importance of this representative of Saint-Domingue has never been explored in all its breadth and ambiguity, though the famous oil portrait of him by Anne-Louis Girodet Trioson has immortalized him. He is less heroic and less consistent than previously thought (his mythology owes a great deal to C. L. R. James's *The Black Jacobins*, written in 1938). Geggus's chapter shows how free and enslaved blacks and mulattos in French colonies in the Caribbean and the Indian Ocean viewed the possibility of taking a seat in the National Convention in Paris as something both important and dangerous. Those who aspired to preserve slavery and keep things the way they were in the Sugar Islands, the key piece of French commercial prosperity, thought exactly the same. Geggus explores the complex relationship between colonies and metropolis during the revolutionary period, and the central significance of representation and law-making during the brutal transformation of slavery before its reestablishment by Napoleon Bonaparte in 1802 until Saint-Domingue's definitive emancipation in 1804.

Dionisio Inca Yupanqui, a Peruvian representative to the Cortes of Cadiz, is the subject of José María Portillo's essay, which describes colonists' need to fabricate ad hoc biographies in order to take their prestigious seats in imperial parliaments. Indeed, biographical anxiety was a distinctive feature of the Peruvian 'nobility' that traced its lineage back to sixteenth-century Inca royalty.[8] In Yupanqui's case, the aim was to create an identity to ease his way into the royal court; once political circumstances changed, the goal switched to the new institution, the Cortes, which was supposed to provide monarchical legitimacy during the French occupation. Dionisio's father also had traced his lineage to the Incas of Cuzco, which proved to be one of the keys to Dionisio eventually becoming a deputy in 1810. Such noble aspirations reached their height soon before the great 1780 uprising in the Andes. His election as an alternate deputy (owing to the lengthy travel time of those coming from America) relied upon the genealogy bequeathed to him by his ancestors. The most important of his three identities – Inca, Indian and American – was Inca, both in terms of gaining economic benefits for his family, which came first, and then for defending the political equality of Americans, to which end he spoke in the chamber only very rarely. The latter platform was a difficult message to sell to most peninsular Spaniards, given the doubts of leading parliamentarians such as Agustín de Argüelles who always insisted that overseas inhabitants must be subordinate.

Even with all the crises and disruptions during the Atlantic revolutionary cycle, European empires for the most part survived. Spain and Portugal, on the other hand, were succeeded by independent entities, and in the latter case with a home country that exported a dynastic branch. In the case of Spain's former possessions, many of the new republics perpetuated situations arising out of colonialism, in particular the limits imposed on social and political progress for certain sectors of the population who stood out either because of the colour of their skin or because they were not free. This was the case of the mulatto senator from Antioquia, Pedro José de Ibarra, before various parts of the old Viceroyalty of New Granada united to form the Republic of Colombia. In the fourth chapter of this book, the historian Daniel Gutiérrez Ardila explains how it was that a mulatto managed to gain access to the offlimits world of the patricians. Ibarra was born in 1763 to mixed-blood parents. He was considered a freeman of colour and received formal education in a province that had grown rich thanks to mining, a frequent route to upward social mobility. Ibarra solidified his position in the community by tutoring the children of the rich in Antioquia, a way of establishing important social relations. In addition, his savings granted him a certain economic position and independence, though always subject to the limits bequeathed to him by his ancestry. When the province of Antioquia approved its own constitution in the period between federalism and centralism, during the transition between empire and independence, Ibarra was elected as senator by the electoral college, a body in which the principal cities were represented. The provisional legislature had to address Indians' political status and possible emancipation of the slaves, which in fact arrived in 1814, obliging Ibarra to free his eleven slaves. Even after the old social order was re-established by Spanish counterrevolutionary troops, he respected the manumission. This did not help him later on, however, when in 1819–21 Spain definitively lost its power and the Republic of Colombia was proclaimed. Ibarra and other mulattos who had held important posts were removed and would not regain their positions. Ibarra never managed to get another representative or administrative position of importance. The colonial structures inherited by the first Republic of Colombia continued holding sway for people of his sort despite the political changes that came with independence.

The case of Cyrille Bissette, of Martinique, presented in Chapter 5 by Abel Alexis Louis, is an extraordinary example of post-revolutionary transformation in the French Antilles.[9] Through his maternal grandfather he was descended from Joseph-Gaspard Tascher, Empress Josephine's father, a rich and influential planter in Martinique. But Bissette also was the grandson of an African slave. As Louis points out, his ambiguous and interlaced biography is hardly ever mentioned in histories of French abolitionism, which began a decade before the Revolution and lasted until 1848, when the Second Republic definitively put an end to slavery. Bissette was the youngest child in his prominent family; his mother, in turn, was one of three daughters in one of his grandfather's two, parallel families. The mother, a mulatta, married a free mulatto of financial means. Louis describes what became known as the 'Bissette affair' in 1823, which well reflected the position of free people of colour, who easily could be co-opted by the plantation and military class after 1802, when Napoleon re-established slavery in the islands that France had managed to hold on to.[10] The affair began with the discovery in Fort-Royal and Saint-Pierre of pamphlets printed in France about the conditions of mixed-bloods. His subsequent imprisonment with others of his fellows, followed by a trial, was an outstanding event in Restoration Martinique. Bissette was given a life sentence and branded with the letters GAL, signifying galley oarsman (*galérien*). His sentence was later reduced to banishment from Martinique. Louis describes how he appealed and was acquitted, as well as his later activities in Paris. There he found protection from the Masons, thanks to which he became involved with colonial reform projects affecting freemen of colour. Only later on, and with great reticence, did he accept that slaves should be given their freedom. He and those who worked with him were enormously influenced by the example of British abolitionism, which was not only philanthropic but also recognized the unsustainable nature of the institution (as the 1831 revolt in Jamaica showed). His election in 1848 to represent Martinique marked the end point of his trajectory, first as a defender of freemen of colour and, later as a sincere abolitionist.

Robert Smalls had an extraordinary life. He was born a slave in Beaufort, South Carolina, the son of an enslaved woman and her owner, John McKee. Remarkably, he became a congressman in 1874. But the course of his life story, as told in this book by Stephanie McCurry, makes the exceptional nature of his life comprehensible. He first found fame and prestige in 1862 when he captured a steamboat, *The Planter*, in Charleston harbour and guided it to Union waters outside the port. Former slaves constituted the majority in Beaufort owing to their emancipation immediately followed by the flight of plantation owners. Smalls first gained a seat in the state legislature of South Carolina and later was elected to Congress toward the end of Reconstruction. During his time in office he built up a political base that ensured the continuity of his political career during arduous and violent times.

Gratien Candace, the grandson of slaves in Guadeloupe, was the second black legislative deputy to sit in the French legislature after the brief experience of Hépésippe Legitimus in 1898. Candace took his seat in 1912, an exceptional event for the times. There were other exceptional things worthy of note, for example the longevity of his service and his access to critically important political posts. It was indeed exceptional for a non-white person from the colonies to become a minister of the Republic, whether we are speaking of France or any other European country with consolidated representative institutions. The explanation lay in the Second Republic and the stabilization of the Third Republic after the interregnum ending in 1871, which led to the consolidation of a bloc of colonial representatives in the National Assembly. Its members included whites descended from Europeans (*bekés*) and mulattos; the exceptions to this rule are outlined in Dominique Chathuant's contribution to this volume. Before becoming a deputy, Candace had had a long career as a public servant, first in Guadaloupe and then in the town of Pau, in the French Pyrenees, where he participated in the regime's greatest accomplishment, the establishment of universal primary and secondary public education. From there he moved on to the socialist administration that took power after the 1906 elections. Thanks to his connections with the moderate socialists around Aristide Briand, he held various positions before winning election. Candace played a key role during the great civil unrest of the 1920s and 1930s, always in the name of Antilles colonists. This role, which continued for many years, allowed him to become an expert in a variety of fields affecting overseas politics such as naval and exchange matters. He also was able to set priorities in line with his own politics, for example his fierce defence of women's suffrage. He formed part of French delegations to international gatherings in Geneva, Berlin and Madrid in the 1930s. His moderate profile and deep knowledge of the intricacies of French politics ensured his relevance and longevity. His defence of racial equality, both assimilationist and patriotic – it was all of a piece with him – was consolidated during the 1940 crisis. His decided support for Petain and his interest in overseas Africans' military service (a matter that appears also in Chapter 10, dedicated to the Senegalese Blaise Diagne) can be understood only in the context of his long career as an intermediary between the metropolis and the overseas departments in the Antilles.

In September 1910, Mpilo Walter Benson Rubusana was elected to the provincial assembly of the Cape Colony, in British South Africa. He was the first African and the first black man to become a parliamentarian, though mulattos (called coloureds) had been elected in the 1890s. It is true that the Cape Colony was an exceptional case in British imperial Africa. It was a very Europeanized community, and Christian, as the Canadian historian Timothy Stapleton explains in his chapter. Rubusana was a classic example of the simultaneous decline of the Xhosa and the advance of missionary efforts encouraged by the metropolis ever since the colony passed from Dutch into British hands, which eventually led to the end of the slave trade in 1808 and the end of slavery itself in 1838.[11] The campaign for imperial consolidation emphasized education of young Africans, and Rubusana proved himself willing to learn. He attended Lovedale College, established by Scottish missionaries, and became a minister in the Congregationalist Church. After visiting London, he became a leading figure as an academic, preacher and translator, as well as a reformer, as the empire was expanding. When he entered local politics – closely allied with another key figure of the time, John T. Jabavu, editor-in-chief of the first Xhosa newspaper – the Cape Colony was an exceptional place, affected by metropolitan liberalism yet essentially and deeply colonial. He was well educated and had strong convictions. This was a period when the British authorities did everything they could to impede Africans' access to the vote. The Glen Grey Act of 1894, promoted by Cecil Rhodes, was designed precisely to reduce the number of Africans who could vote. The Cape Colony's broad suffrage marked a dangerous exception to white supremacist campaigns leading up to the establishment of the Union of South Africa in 1909 and the incorporation of former Boer territories. Rubusana and Jabavu fought both at home and in London against segregation. The former's election and the years that followed marked yet another episode of resistance, and they shed light on the importance of gaining a public voice in local assemblies.

If anyone had any doubts as to the importance of holding seats in the highest imperial legislatures, Teresa Segura-Garcia's chapter will lay them to rest. She explores the successful political career of Dadabhai Naoroji, a Parsi Indian who moved between Gujarat and Bombay. He was the first non-European member of the imperial Parliament par excellence, Westminster, serving from 1892 to 1895, a difficult and relevant accomplishment. Segura-Garcia begins with an explanation of the political strategy of the Parsis, the principal force of the powerful Bombay bourgeoisie. Naoroji's written and oral political and intellectual labours were aimed mostly at demonstrating the subcontinent's inhabitants' capacity to govern themselves. The chapter describes a little-known aspect of his activities: political decisions ever since he was young aimed at a careful strategy to occupy the hidden spaces within British imperial power. His trip to London, with sponsors from both sides of the imperial divide, formed part of this long-term strategy. By the time he won his seat in Westminster, Naoroji had spent a long time demanding that Indians be allowed to enter its hallowed halls. When he took his seat, he formed part of a collective effort that had begun in the subcontinent and reached the reformist circles in the capital of the metropolis. It is important to point out that he always counted on the support of the ruler of the princely state of Baroda (Gujarat), in whose administration he worked and who financed Naoroji's political career in Europe. Naoroji won a seat in the House of Commons on the second try thanks to that support and the backing of Liberal Party reformists.

Eric Garcia-Moral's essay is on Blaise Diagne, the most representative example of African assimilationism. He was born in one of the 'vielle' parish of Senegal, the only place where pro-assimilation opinions could be expressed and extend roots. Like Gratien Candace, Diagne's is an example of one of the longest and most successful political and administrative careers in twentieth-century France before the Second World War. He was a representative in the National Assembly from 1914 to 1934, being re-elected four times at the same time as he occupied important positions in various ministries. It is useful to compare the meaning and significance of his path with, for example, that of the Guadaloupian Candace. Such a comparison helps us understand the importance and limitations of the politics of assimilation, the pillar of overseas French politics from 1848 to the present. From 1892 to 1914, Diagne worked in French customs administration, which enabled him to become familiar with ground-level administrative practice where one could appreciate the importance of French economic interests in coastal West Africa. He used the fact that he became a Mason and married a white Frenchwoman to consolidate his position in the civil service despite harsh limits on colonists' movements and actions in the *code d'indigénat*, the rules emanating from Algeria throughout the entire French imperial complex.[12] His election in 1914 as deputy of Senegal indicated not only his pre-eminence in local politics but also Creoles' improved position. Garcia-Moral explores Diagne's search for support and his electoral programme, which at first was quite radically opposed to the commercial interests of Dakar, largely in the hands of representatives of Bordeaux. The extraordinary circumstances suffered by the metropolis during the First World War led to a shift in that early political program toward more military concerns such as the *tirailleurs sénégalais*, colonial troops sent to the front. It was in 1918, in fact, that Diagne consolidated his position as a broker for Senegalese interests in France and vice versa. Gradually he became an advocate of metropolitan interests, a controversial role he never gave up. His most important political actions probably took place during the interwar years, by which time his moderation and distance from radical Pan-Africanism were not going to change.

II

All these men, whose stories we have briefly synthesized here, lived between the late eighteenth century and the Second World War. Each reflects deep changes in the political, administrative and constitutional organization of empires and in the attitudes of colonized peoples. They also address different historical realities in the imperial worlds of France, Britain, the United States and Spain (and Spain's former colonies). Read and understood as a whole, these eloquent, personal trajectories of individuals and collectives offer us lessons. One of the most important of the many fundamental social, political and constitutional changes taking place during these men's lives was the transformation in forms of politics. Chambers of deputies and parliaments often traced their origins to the Middle Ages. It was in those spaces where monarchs, great lords, churchmen and representatives of important cities met to negotiate and reach agreements as well as to receive favours. In some cases, these institutions were exported, along with European colonists, across the Atlantic. This was the case of the Thirteen Colonies and of the British Antilles, whose limited powers and functions were similarly found in other Atlantic empires. These assemblies were transformed over time as concerned elections and legislative capacities – sometimes gaining powers, sometimes losing them to the monarchs. This serpentine and bifurcated road would continue under the aegis of liberalism, understood not as a compendium of the writings of Benjamin Constant or John Stuart Mill but as a political practice found at the heart of brutally unequal societies and their institutional systems.

There is no doubt that the revolutionary cycle of the last twenty-five years of the eighteenth century radically modified the role and forms of parliamentary representation, a process that this book aims to better understand through particular experiences in different countries. This movement of reinvention and construction was ceaseless from 1776 to the end of the nineteenth century, and it continued with decolonization in the twentieth century. In all cases, the forms of parliamentary representation with legislative capacity, be it great or small, and the balance of powers (or its appearance) that gave it meaning indicated the limits within which one could move in that most delicate space of political life. The breadth and restrictions of suffrage confirmed the centrality of that institution in contemporary politics.

If this was the case in the faraway possessions able to break the colonial nexus and ties with metropolitan sovereignty, it was not the only possible route. As new political realities were proclaimed during the Atlantic revolutionary cycle, the preamble to the general decolonization after 1947, a far more ambiguous and parallel reality was also being consolidated: eighteenth- and nineteenth-century metropoles had sufficient capacity, whether under monarchies or republics, to maintain, expand and universalize their colonial possessions during the next hundred years. If territorial colonialism during the eighteenth century was essentially Atlantic, British control over North India enabled Britain to acquire possessions across four continents. France followed – and it would never renounce its imperial vocation reopened in Algiers in 1830. Other European countries (and some non-European ones, such as Japan) with similar ambitions decided to compete, further inspired after Bismarck brought all reputable empires together to definitively slice up the world as if it were a cake. In that parallel process in which old metropoles and new nation-states found themselves on the same side of world colonization – some examples are the United States, Brazil and the former British dominions of New Zealand, Australia and Canada, all with solid colonial foundations – affirmation of imperial parliaments acquired new meanings, whether in London, Paris, Washington, Lisbon, Rio de Janeiro, Madrid, Ottawa or Melbourne. It was in those chambers, more or less majestic, more or less pure inventions of tradition, where legislation took place or was avoided out of fear of its repercussions. Those chambers were great instruments of co-optation, legitimacy and prestige for states and empires at the same time.

The formulas were designed for a political evolution that was neither simple nor achieved without a struggle (the failure of Irish home rule is a clear example – in fact, it brought down Gladstonian liberalism).[13] While the male population of European origin was relatively guaranteed the capacity of self-government and representation, other inhabitants, notably the native populations, were excluded. There is no representation without franchise. Therefore, whoever legislates also legislates that possibility, which is neither innocent nor arbitrary. Nevertheless, the magnitude of the great liberal empire was such that there were diverse means of evolution, not necessarily toward greater degrees of self-rule, as the Morant Bay crisis in Jamaica showed for the West Indies (with the exception of Barbados, which was entirely under the control of the plantation owners). As the chapter on Rubusana makes clear, the case of the Union of South Africa and the Boer Wars is not precisely one of uninterrupted progress toward greater political integration for the African majority. Of course, neither the Indian Raj nor Ireland, the first and oldest colony, could ever attain the parliamentary privileges enjoyed by Australians, New Zealanders and Canadians. Dramatic crises in the first two seriously damaged imperial stability – during the First World War in the case of Ireland and during the 1930s in the case of India. And far beyond the small details of local existence, the imperial Parliament, supreme arbiter of stability and continuity, majestically legislated. Dadabhai Naoroji's entrance into Westminster constituted a stark exception to the rule that for decades excluded the presence of native peoples in the representative assemblies of crown dominions. Obedience toward the imperial sovereignty of the White Settlements led directly (as in France) to military demands by the metropolis during the First World War, definitively undermining imperial prestige. As the 1918 Report on Indian Constitutional Reform made strangely explicit, one of the era's greatest empires considered that its mission had been accomplished, its resources exhausted by the war effort, unable to offer a viable response and compensations to the growing pre-eminence of its own colonial subjects.[14]

It is essential for us to think about the centrality of parliamentary representation, though there are many other areas worthy of reconsideration regarding the politics of empire and colonization, which often is reduced to a study of piecemeal and desperate responses by subaltern groups. As with all historical phenomena, we can understand the whole only by looking at the interaction among the different levels. In all the case studies presented in this book, parliamentary representation constituted an enormous challenge. The voices of parliamentarians and middlemen from around the world that appear in this book were never expected to be heard in those local or imperial chambers, nor were their owners expected to sit in those seats warmed by others more deserving than they.[15] Once these new arrivals were seated in institutions that had not expected to receive them, where they would always be a minority, their principal task was to help strengthen the prestige of an institution that was forced to accept them as historical freaks. In many cases – Spain from 1822; Jamaica in 1865; and the United States from 1876 – survival of interracial or colonial representatives became impossible, or at least highly improbable. In general, along with restrictions on their voices, the people who had elected them in the first place were also restricted. The elimination of free blacks and mulattos from electoral rolls in the Spanish Cortes in 1810–20, in France before the Second Republic and the Jim Crow laws in the US South – whose effects are still obvious today – show how precarious these political conquests were.

Given the enormous limitations imposed by colonial relations on land ownership, labour and political representation, the best way to appreciate the significance of each of the individual cases presented in this book is as a particular case study in a given context. Access to political representation, to a platform that was so critical for public discourse, illustrates the transformation of politics under the aegis of liberal culture. It was no longer the monopoly of magnates, lords and courtiers. Rather, it drew from society as a whole, as voters or as masses who mobilized around the ideological issues of the times. Once Pandora's box had been opened, the appearance of permanent organized factions, what we know today as political parties, spelled the end of the old monopoly. With that, the way was open for the particularities of contemporary politics which were the rule until only recently: electoral campaigns, political propaganda and programs, newspapers that offered more than news, demonstrations and rallies in the street (demanding first universal male suffrage and later the vote for women), increasingly sophisticated repressive and police tactics and greater public funding for citizen education. And with the increasing complexity of partisan debates and struggles, the rise of a new profession, that of politician, was inevitable. Starting in the mid-nineteenth century, there was an increasingly close relationship in the most powerful countries between street politics and the semi-private clubs of the privileged. In that context, having someone on one's side who had a seat in parliament, who had a voice, was clearly invaluable even if, realistically, one's ability to affect the legislative process was limited. And seats were even more valuable, for obvious reasons, in the colonies, in scattered places around the globe inhabited by peoples of diverse cultural and linguistic backgrounds. Long before it was a plausible reality, religious, cultural, social and racial equality and improved living conditions for workers and women were all the subject of debate in the streets, in civil society, in parliaments. There was no guarantee that these causes would triumph, but the debate gave meaning to the efforts of generations of people both in the metropolis and in the colonies.

This book explores the limits and possibilities of political representation and the politics of rights in imperial spaces over the period of around one century. Rather than coming to any firm conclusions, the editors wished to explore new interpretative approaches to politics and representation. We are restricting our analyses and conclusions to figures who were immersed in specific imperial complexes at particular times and places. Even so, it is clear that thinking about all these men together, as a whole, allows us to reflect on the importance of representation in the context of powerful imperial constructions that arose during the era of revolutions. Access to parliamentary representation reveals many of the mechanisms that both weakened and gave vitality to empires in the nineteenth and early twentieth centuries. Not even military force, legal codes devised to discriminate and exclude, a rising wave of proclaimed cultural superiority or technological and industrial gaps could slam the door against the excluded who wished to get in. Among those clamouring for entry, with all their individual ambiguities and nuances, are the people profiled in this book. When, after their efforts and suffering, they managed to enter the imperial Valhalla, it constituted an alteration of the accepted rules. They had broken the principle of exclusion of the country club, which imperial parliaments often resembled. Once the monopoly was broken, new expressions of discontent rose to the fore. In short, stability was a matter not just of imperial culture and discourse but also of the transformation of social and political relations in the broadest sense possible. It would be as absurd to attribute effective changes in those areas to actions taken from above by leaders as it would be to think that the changes were implemented solely in accordance with demands from below.[16] It is true, however, that co-optation occurred in more than one of the cases under examination. Nevertheless, it would be a grave error, one of condescension by posterity, to underestimate the combination of pressure from below with the efforts by reformers and intruders who wished to explore the fissures of the enormous imperial structure while seeking allies with whom to implement part of their ideological program.

The essays in this volume help us appreciate the ambiguous zones, the margins for negotiation, the emerging forms of new leadership groups in colonial societies and in the imperial structure. They also help us better understand the narrow spaces in which these men had to manoeuvre. Both aspects offer us a more comprehensive vision of decolonization and the end of the empires that were born, or reborn, during the revolutionary era.

Notes

1   Hannah Barker, *Newspapers, Politics, and English Society, 1695–1855* (London: Routledge, 2000); Robert Darnton and Daniel Roche, eds., *Revolution in Print: The Press in France, 1775–1800* (Berkeley, CA: University of California Press, 1989).

2   Josep M. Fradera, *The Imperial Nation: Citizens and Subjects in the British, French, Spanish, and American Empires* (Princeton, NJ: Princeton University Press, 2018).

3   Benno Gammerl, *Subjects, Citizens and Others: Administering Ethnic Heterogeneity in the British and Habsburg Empire, 1867–1918* (New York: Berghahn Books, 2018).

4   Eric Foner, *Freedom's Lawmakers: A Directory of Black Officeholders during Reconstruction* (New York: Oxford University Press, 1993).

5   Michel Winock, *Les voix de la liberté* (Paris: Éditions su Seuil, 2001) (published in Spanish as *Las voces de la libertad* (Barcelona: Editorial Edhasa, 2004)).

6   As a comparison, it is useful to consult Érick Noel, *Dictionnaire des gens de couleur das la France moderne* (Geneva: Droz, 2011).

7   Donald L. Robinson, *Slavery in the Structure of American Politics, 1765–1820* (New York: Harcourt Brace Janovich, 1970). See also the debate in the *New York Review of Books* that followed publication of Sean Wilentz, *No Property in Man: Slavery and Antislavery at the Nation's Founding* (Cambridge MA: Harvard University Press, 2018). Nicholas Guyatt's harsh review cited Calvin Schermerhorn's important *Unrequited Toil: A History of United States Slavery* (Cambridge: Cambridge University Press, 2018).

8   David T. Garrett, *Shadows of Empire: The Indian Nobility of Cusco, 1750–1825* (Cambridge: Cambridge University Press, 2005).

9 Louis is also the author of a three-volume work, covering the period 1635–1830: *Les libres de couleur en Martinique* (Paris: L'Harmattan, 2012).

10 For the general framework see Lawrence Jennings, *French Anti-Slavery: The Movement for the Abolition of Slavery in France, 1802–1848* (Cambridge: Cambridge University Press, 2000).

11 Nicole Ulrich, 'Abolition from Below: The 1808 Revolt in the Cape Colony', in Marcel van der Linden (ed.), *Humanitarian Intervention and Changing Labor Relations: The Long-Term Consequences of the Abolition of the Slave Trade* (Leiden: Brill, 2011), 193–222; Sampie Terreblanche, *A History of Inequality in South Africa, 1652–2002* (Scottsville, South Africa: University of KwaZulu-Natal Press, 2002), 188–91.

12 Olivier Le Cour Grandmaison, *De l'indigénat: Anatomie d'un monstre juridique: le droit coloniale en Algérie et dans l'Empire français* (Paris: Zones, 2010).

13 Eugenio F. Biagini, *British Democracy and Irish Nationalism, 1876–1906* (Cork, Mercier Press, 2014).

14 Richard Whiting, 'The Empire and British Politics' in Andrew S. Thompson (ed.), *Britain's Experience of Empire in the Twentieth Century* (Oxford: Oxford University Press, 2012), 163–64.

15 Albert O. Hirschman, *Exit, Voice, and Loyalty: Responses to Decline in Firms, Organizations, and States* (Cambridge, MA: Harvard University Press, 1970).

16 Priyamvada Gopal, *Insurgent Empire: Anticolonial Resistance and British Dissent* (London: Verso, 2019).

2

Jean-Baptiste Belley: France's
first black legislator

David Geggus

'Bellay [*sic*], the Negro, delivered a long and fiery oration, pledging the blacks to the cause of the revolution and asking the Convention to declare slavery abolished. It was fitting that a Negro and an ex-slave should make the speech which introduced one of the most important legislative acts ever passed by any political assembly.' This is how C. L. R. James, in a classic book about the impact of the French Revolution in the Antilles, described the parliamentary intervention of an emblematic deputy.[1]

Born in Africa, a former slave (and slave-owner), Jean-Baptiste Belley took his seat in the Convention Nationale on 3 February 1794, as the French Revolution was entering its most radical and violent phase. He remained in the legislature, after the Convention gave way to the Directory, until 1797 or 1798. Belley had lived most of his life in the wealthy Caribbean colony of Saint Domingue. He was a prime beneficiary of, and participant in, the revolution that progressively transformed the colony between 1789 and 1804, and ultimately created the independent black state of Haiti. He is best known because, the day after he took his place in the Convention, the assembly voted to abolish slavery in all France's colonies. It was the first major step in the century-long process that ended enslavement in the Americas. Belley's role in the event has sometimes been misrepresented (as in the quote cited above). Much has been learned about his life and career in recent years, and the striking portrait of him painted in Paris in 1797 is these days quite often encountered.[2] Yet he remains an obscure figure.

Saint Domingue and the Haitian Revolution

The French colony of Saint Domingue (modern Haiti) was eighteenth-century Europe's main source of tropical produce. A major producer of sugar, coffee and indigo, by the late 1780s its exports exceeded those of Mexico and the United States, and it rivalled Brazil as the principal destination of the Atlantic slave trade. The town of Cap Français, where Jean-Baptiste Belley lived, was one of the Caribbean's busiest ports.[3] The colony's slave population of nearly half a million was the third largest in the Americas. However, the most distinctive feature of Saint Domingue society was its middle sector, its free population of colour, which was larger and wealthier than most such groups. It contained many small and middling planters, as well as shopkeepers and artisans, and by 1789 it approached in size the white population's thirty thousand or so residents, who dominated the colony. Most free people of colour were of mixed Euro-African descent but about one-third were, like Belley, either emancipated or free-born *nègres libres*.

Coterminous with the revolution in France, the Haitian Revolution was essentially three, incompatible, revolutions in one. It began, in 1789, as a bid for self-government by wealthy white colonists that quickly succeeded. Their first success was to win the right to colonial representation in the national legislature. Freemen of colour soon challenged the whites but, only after much bloodshed, was France compelled to abolish racial discrimination in its colonies in April 1792. A massive slave rebellion put slavery on the revolution's agenda in August 1791 and led two years later to the first abolition of slavery in a major slave society. The emancipation proclamation, however, was issued by a local official without authorization from the French government. Belley's mission to Paris was to help win approval for it. For the rest of the 1790s, Saint Domingue was the scene of a radical social experiment that sought to combine a plantation economy with a racially egalitarian regime increasingly dominated by former slaves under the aegis of a militant and proselytizing French Republic. When Napoleon Bonaparte tried to restore the pre-revolutionary status quo in 1802, he precipitated a war of independence fought by the population of African descent that ended with the creation of the state of Haiti.

Colonial representation, racial equality, slave emancipation and colonial independence, the achievements of the Haitian Revolution were milestones in world history and, together with the economic significance of Saint Domingue, they give the revolution an importance that transcends its geographic and demographic limitations. Jean-Baptiste Belley owed his career to the first two of these achievements; he became a defender and symbol of the third and was an opponent of the fourth.

Belley's early life

Belley said he was born on Gorée island in present-day Senegal (probably in late 1746) and that he arrived in Saint Domingue on a slave ship at the age of two. He seems to have purchased his freedom – 'with my own sweat', he said – before he was twenty.[4] We know this only because of statements he made in France between 1794 and 1798. Later documents reveal that he had a half-brother, born in Cap Français around 1766, so we may assume that Belley arrived from Africa with his mother and that she was probably still a teenager.[5] Le Cap, where he grew up, was a small, bustling place – only sixteen thousand inhabitants in 1789, and far fewer when he first arrived. More than 60 per cent were slaves, of whom two-thirds were African-born and around one-tenth were tall Senegambians like himself.[6]

Specialized biographical dictionaries have provided little, often very inaccurate, information on Belley and almost nothing on his early years.[7] In 2010, however, French genealogists discovered a substantial number of references to him in Cap Français's parish registers which shed light on his life before the revolution.[8] They establish that, by 1777, he was a hairdresser (*perruquier*), a freedman and could sign his name. Known as the 'Paris of the Antilles', high-priced Le Cap provided good employment for men able to dress wigs, and Belley was not the only young African to achieve success in this field. Hundreds of urban slaves, moreover, were able to live fairly independent lives, hiring out their labour, paying their owners a monthly stipend and keeping whatever extra money they made.[9] Yet it was exceptional for a slave to buy his freedom at such a young age. Perhaps the economic downturn of the Seven Years' War had offered favourable conditions for such a transaction; perhaps his mother had helped. It was also unusual for an African freedman to be able to write. Only about two in five free black men in Saint Domingue could sign their name.[10]

The fact that Belley was already a free man by 1777 disproves the claims of several writers that he owed his liberty to military service in the American War of Independence. In 1779, more than five hundred men of colour participated in a French military expedition sent from Saint Domingue to attack British forces in Savannah, Georgia. Some were slaves whose service earned them tax-free emancipation, but most were, like Belley, freemen.[11] The expedition was a military disaster, and these Chasseurs Volontaires played a fairly limited role. Some helped dig ditches, but they enjoyed a moment of distinction when they beat back a sortie by British forces with a bayonet charge. They are important in Haiti's history because many of the men who became revolutionary leaders in the 1790s appear to have served in their ranks. Historians have long speculated how this military and political experience – either the self-confidence it brought, or the mistreatment many of them endured – shaped the careers of these future leaders.[12]

The experience probably earned Belley promotion in the colonial militia after his return to Saint Domingue. In 1781, when acting as godfather at a baptism, he was described as '*officier subalterne des nègres libres du Cap*'.[13] Militia service was compulsory for all free males. Militia companies were segregated (whites, blacks, *mulâtres*), and after the 1760s only whites could be officers in free coloured companies. Belley was presumably a sub-lieutenant or lieutenant (if the term 'officier subalterne' was correct), or a sergeant. Militia service in Saint Domingue did not confer the privileges that it did in Spanish colonies, but it must have enhanced his prestige within the city's free black community. Military activity apparently suited him, because in the mid-1780s he adopted the nickname 'Mars'. It replaced another, more mysterious nickname he had sometimes used, 'Tenbaz' (or Timbaze). Was this an African name, perhaps given him by his mother? Or was it merely an 'exotic' name, conferred as the law required, when he was manumitted? It is a reminder of how limited our knowledge of the man remains. 'Belley' was presumably the name of his former owner, though one cannot be sure. 'Jean-Baptiste' was easily the most popular baptismal name among Cap Français free blacks, albeit for unknown reasons. It is unclear if he was related to any of the few other Belleys in local records. A teenaged son who accompanied him to France is not mentioned in any earlier document. There is no record that he ever married.

Yet Jean-Baptiste appears many times in the parish records, because he was a frequent witness at burials and weddings and a godfather at baptisms. He was also named as guardian for a girl without a father.[14] Clearly he was a respected figure in the tightly knit community of black artisans and shopkeepers, although he was not wealthy. While free people of colour owned one-fifth of Le Cap's houses, and some of his friends in the militia owned small plantations, Belley always lived in rented accommodation and the only property he owned was slaves – 'thinking property', as he later stated in his Convention personnel file.[15] Free people of colour commonly owned slaves that they used in their businesses, or for speculative purposes, or that they hired out. Like all local slave-owners, Belley branded the Africans he purchased with a hot iron; 'Mars au Cap' was his mark.[16]

By the 1780s, the rapid growth and upward mobility of Saint Domingue's free population of colour was creating tensions with members of the white elite. They had pretensions above their station, some whites complained, and set a bad example to slaves. 'Even free blacks', were rude to whites who did not address them as 'Monsieur' or 'Mademoiselle'.[17] For his part, Belley branched out into commerce and opened a small 'grain shop' with two free black partners.[18] When unregistered gambling houses were targeted as sites of potential crime, Belley was arrested and fined for illicit gambling, but his conviction was quashed on appeal because of faulty police paperwork.[19] Although not wealthy, he was rich enough to afford a good lawyer.

Belley and the early Revolution

The first two years of the Haitian Revolution involved only the free population. Inspired by the weakening of the royal government and the libertarian ideology unleashed in 1789, white colonists quickly established a racially exclusive democracy but struggled among themselves as to how subordinate to France they should be. Simultaneously, they opposed the efforts of their free coloured counterparts to win equal rights with whites. While colonists in France manoeuvred to prevent any change in the regime of racial discrimination, free coloureds in Saint Domingue who advocated reform met with violent repression by both white vigilantes and the law courts. In October 1790, the mixed-race merchant Vincent Ogé led a brief rebellion of a few hundred freemen of colour in the mountains about ten miles south of Cap Français. It was brutally suppressed. Ogé's rebellion, like earlier petitions for reform, involved primarily the light-complexioned and landowning elite of the *gens de couleur libres*. Free coloured wage-earners who depended on whites for employment, and particularly free blacks, were said to oppose Ogé. Although Le Cap was Ogé's home, its free coloured residents declined his invitation to join him, and its militia participated in the repression of the rebellion.[20]

Nine months later, a far more formidable uprising began, of a quite different sort. In August 1791, tens of thousands of slaves took up arms and burned much of the Northern Plain around Cap Français. For two years the city was almost under siege, while its white and free coloured population, reinforced by troops from France, combined to fight an inconclusive guerrilla war against the slave insurgents in the surrounding plain and mountains. At the same time, elsewhere in Saint Domingue, whites and free coloureds fought each other in a bitter civil war over the issue of racial equality. Although several rural free blacks achieved prominence among the northern slave insurgents – notably Toussaint Louverture – and at least one from Le Cap joined their ranks, most of the town's free coloureds allied with the whites in combating this threat to their property. This fragile alliance was strengthened, and the civil war elsewhere was brought to an end, by the law of 4 April 1792, which finally instituted in the colonies the principle of racial equality. One of the landmark gains of the Haitian Revolution, it constituted recognition by the French government that it could not defeat the slave insurgents without the military assistance of the freemen of colour; it had to abandon white supremacy in order to preserve slavery.

To enforce the new law, the government sent out Commissaire Civil Sonthonax, a radical lawyer, who promoted freemen of colour while arresting and deporting large numbers of white colonists. In October 1792, a month after his arrival in Saint Domingue, he requested a position in one of the French regiments that accompanied him for a *nègre perruquier* from Le Cap, who very likely was Belley.[21] The hairdresser/militiaman must have impressed him. Integrating the armed forces, however, proved highly contentious, and it is not clear that Belley took up this position. More likely, he joined the new *compagnies franches* that Sonthonax created for free coloured men at the end of the year. This may explain his being described in June 1793 as '*commandant en second du 6me bataillon*'.[22] This is the first certain reference to him that we have during the revolutionary period.

Up to this point, Belley's political participation probably was more counter-revolutionary than progressive; in Le Cap's militia or the *compagnies franches*, he presumably had been deployed in suppressing the Ogé rebellion and in combating the slave insurrection.[23] The turning point came during one of the revolution's most dramatic episodes, the burning of Cap Français during late June 1793. In an intense outburst of urban warfare, freemen of colour gathered round Sonthonax to defend him against an attack launched by the white governor, Thomas Galbaud, leading hundreds of white colonists and sailors from warships in the harbour. Belley organized the defence of Government House and, at a critical moment, led a counterattack that drove the whites back through the streets. He supposedly was wounded six times by sniper fire from surrounding buildings.[24] Slaves pillaged the city; thousands of colonists fled to North America. Belley was made a captain in one of the French regiments in the colony, the 16th Infantry.[25]

In 1793, Sonthonax faced not only revolt by the white population and an undefeated slave uprising but invasion by Spanish and British forces as well, as the new French Republic fought for survival in Europe and the Caribbean. To combat these threats, the Commissioner took the desperate – and epoch-making – step at the end of August of declaring slavery abolished. He hoped to create an army of ex-slaves to preserve Saint Domingue for the Republic, but he needed to gain the French government's approval for his unauthorized actions. In September 1793, Sonthonax organized an election in the ruined city of Le Cap to choose deputies to represent Saint Domingue's North Province in the National Convention in Paris. After the mass exodus of colonists during the summer, most of the voters must have been of African descent. The result was a symbolically 'tricolour' deputation of two whites, two blacks and two men of mixed racial descent. The candidate who garnered the most votes, and still recovering from his wounds, was Jean-Baptiste Belley.

The official election report describes a two-stage election superficially conforming to legal norms; primary district assemblies (locations unspecified) met on 14 September and the electoral assembly (numbers unspecified) gathered in Le Cap, on 23–24 September in a meeting open to the public.[26] Sonthonax's critics, however, claimed that the results were publicly known in advance and that he had chosen the candidates.[27] The truth is uncertain, but it is astonishing that three years before, when Sonthonax was an anonymous journalist and precocious closet abolitionist, he had predicted in a Paris newspaper that 'the time is not far off when a frizzy-haired African, with no recommendation beyond his good sense and virtue, will come and participate as a legislator in the bosom of our national assemblies'.[28]

Belley and his fellow deputies set out to fulfill this prediction in late October 1793, leaving a colony rent by revolution and foreign invasion and on the brink of an unprecedented social experiment.[29] The journey to France proved perilous. In Philadelphia, vengeful refugee colonists from Saint Domingue seized the deputies' possessions and tried to prevent them continuing their voyage. Belley and the other black deputy, Joseph Boisson, were physically assaulted. Boisson was kidnapped, while Belley was threatened at knifepoint and had his tricolour cockade snatched from his chest. His money, watch and sword were stolen. When the colonists asked how he dared to command white people as a military officer, he responded that, having saved and protected white people (during the Cap Français fire), he could also command them, and that he had been serving France (in the militia) for twenty-five years.[30]

Officials at the French consulate helped the deputies escape this hostile milieu to New York. There an initially hostile consul came to admire the multi-racial group. He judged Belley self-confident but friendly, and the white deputy Louis-Pierre Dufaÿ, well educated and well mannered.[31] To lessen their chances of being captured at sea, it was decided they should split into two groups. Belley (and his teenaged son) would travel with Dufaÿ and his mistress, and the mixed-race deputy Jean-Baptiste Mills.[32] Before taking ship for France, they wrote a joint letter recounting their experiences to their constituents in Le Cap, to which Belley appended a brief, separate message 'To his brothers'. He urged them to stay loyal to Sonthonax and the Republic, to fight the foreign invaders, and 'to swear, all of you, to be victorious'. Printed a few months later in Paris, it counts as Belley's first publication.[33]

Arrival in Paris and the abolition of slavery

The deputies' problems were not over when they reached France in January 1794, for the colonial lobby in Paris, led by Pierre-François Page and Augustin Brulley, quickly had them arrested and jailed as dangerous envoys. Since the fall of the monarchy eighteen months earlier, Page and Brulley had astutely moved with the prevailing political currents and cultivated good relations with the Jacobin faction in power. During the previous year of maritime warfare, they had shaped the little news that arrived from Saint Domingue, and they had blackened the reputation of Sonthonax, who had been officially recalled. The Girondin leaders who had appointed him Commissaire Civil had been guillotined the previous autumn along with some of France's early abolitionists. With the Reign of Terror in full swing, it was hard to predict how the deputies would be received. Most white colonists felt the tricolour deputation represented, not them, but the subversion of their old way of life. Anti-slavery sentiment was much weaker in France than in England, and abolitionism was often perceived as an English plot. Only belatedly were some radicals showing an interest in it. Politicians wanted, above all, to know who to blame for the ruin of the country's colonial prosperity, which had been the French economy's strongest sector.[34]

Fortuitously, Belley was not jailed with his two colleagues, but his first week in Paris must have been a testing experience. The city was forty times the size of Cap Français with more inhabitants than the whole of Saint Domingue. It was his first northern winter. For several days, the deputies' fate – and that of 750,000 slaves – hung in the balance, as the influential network of exiled colonists mobilized to keep the deputation out of the Convention. From inside his unheated jail cell, Louis Dufaÿ fired off angry letters to government officials proclaiming the deputies' status as legally elected representatives of the Republic. Playing off the Committee of Public Safety against the Committee of General Security, he succeeded. Released on 2 February, he, Mills and Belley were formally admitted to the national legislature on 3 February.[35]

The National Convention, then sixteen months old, had some 750 deputies, among whom lawyers predominated. A law of 22 August 1792 had made provision for colonial representation in the assembly (including eighteen deputies for Saint Domingue) but revolution and war in the Caribbean had limited the colonial presence to a handful. All deputies were white men except for one, Janvier Littée, who was a 'quadroon' (with one black and three white grandparents). He was a merchant/planter from Martinique, who had been seated in September 1793.[36] The presence of Mills, and particularly Belley, therefore, must have really stood out when, as the parliamentary record states:

> The three deputies from Saint Domingue entered the chamber and took their seats on the Mountain, welcomed by bursts of sustained applause.
>
> Delacroix (d'Eure et Loire). For a long time, the assembly has been wanting to include among its members men of color who have been oppressed for so many years. Today it has two of them. I request that their admittance be marked by the fraternal embrace of the president.
>
> The two deputies stepped forward and, in the name of the assembly, the president embraced the deputation amidst lively expressions of joy.[37]

Behind the scenes, the colonial lobby protested that Belley was not French but 'de nation afriquaine-bambara'. In Jacobin circles, however, the tide was turning against the colonists.[38] The next day, 4 February (16 Pluviôse II), the public galleries of the Convention were packed with people of African descent and colonists, because the deputation was going to present its report on the situation in Saint Domingue. It was the culminating point of their mission. Two misconceptions regarding this momentous session long marked the historiography of the Haitian and French revolutions. One is that it was relatively brief; once the long report had been read out, the assembly passed spontaneously, it seemed, and without dissent to voting the abolition of slavery on a wave of emotion. This impression is sustained by the official parliamentary record, which is notoriously incomplete.[39] The historian Yves Bénot, by comparing many different newspaper accounts of the session, revealed several interventions, however, that sought to discreetly sabotage the discussion and, the next day, to remove the emancipation decree from the official minutes of the session.[40] Ideological opposition to slavery had certainly grown during the Revolution, and the treason of Caribbean colonists in wartime had lost them much support; the prospect of using slave emancipation as a weapon of war against the British also gave it patriotic appeal, but many otherwise radical politicians still feared the economic costs of abolition, only to be steamrollered by the upwelling of emotion in the Convention.

The other misconception concerning the session is that it was Belley who made the key speech, not Louis-Pierre Dufaÿ. This error is most associated with *The Black Jacobins* by Trinidadian Marxist C. L. R. James, which for sixty years after its publication in 1938 ranked as the most important and best-known work on the Haitian Revolution in English.

> Bellay [*sic*], the Negro, delivered a long and fiery oration, pledging the blacks to the cause of the revolution and asking the Convention to declare slavery abolished. It was fitting that a Negro and an ex-slave should make the speech which introduced one of the most important legislative acts ever passed by any political assembly. No one spoke after Bellay. ... The Assembly rose in acclamation. The two deputies of colour appeared on the tribune and embraced while the applause rolled round the hall from members and visitors. Lacroix led the Mulatto and the Negro to the President who gave them the presidential kiss, when the applause started again.[41]

Most of this description conforms to the account in the *Archives Parlementaires* except that the orator was not Belley but the white planter Dufaÿ.[42] While *The Black Jacobins* contains a fair number of factual errors, it is hard to understand how a historian of James's distinction could make such a major mistake, which he shares with very few others.[43] He does not cite a source for his statement. As the relevant volume of the *Archives Parlementaires* had not yet been published when he wrote, he seems, instead of consulting the manuscript *procès-verbaux* of the Convention's sessions, to have relied on the account in the more easily accessible *Moniteur Universel*.[44] However, that account identifies the speaker only as 'one of the deputies from Saint Domingue'. The sole historian who, prior to James, claimed it was Belley was, ironically, the white supremacist T. Lothrop Stoddard.[45] He considered slave emancipation a disaster and presumably was happy to blame the black deputy. Why James would follow Stoddard, whom he detested, rather than the French historian Saintoyant, who correctly identified Dufaÿ and whom James actually cites at this point in his book, appears explicable only as an act of wishful thinking and artistic license.[46] In a book that foregrounds black agency, the anti-colonial and Pan-African scholar must have found the false logic irresistible.

In truth, it would have been more than surprising if Belley, rather than Dufaÿ, had addressed the Convention. Dufaÿ was a well-educated, upper-middle-class

Parisian who had held high administrative office in Saint Domingue. Belley was of humble origin, a hairdresser by trade, who was surely more accustomed to speaking Creole than French. Dufaÿ had been preparing the report that he delivered for several months during the journey from Le Cap to Paris and, according to his biographer, he was the author of all the joint letters and publications issued in the deputation's name.[47] His denunciation of the colonists as counter-revolutionaries and his justification of Sonthonax's decisions had already changed opinions in New York and in the Committee of General Security in Paris before they were heard by the Convention. Over the next few years, moreover, Dufaÿ remained extremely active, speaking, publishing and lobbying, whereas Belley would play a relatively subdued role as a deputy in the legislature.[48]

Belley the deputy

Although Belley did not make the grandstand speech that ended slavery in the French Empire – and did not address the Convention at all that day[49] – he undoubtedly made an intangible contribution to the event simply by his physical presence. Dignified and impressive, it provided a visible, symbolic accompaniment to Dufaÿ's rhetoric. Born in Africa, a successful former slave, and now defender of the Republic, Belley embodied the outcome that emancipation was meant to achieve. In this way, his role resembled that of his contemporary Olaudah Equiano in the British anti-slavery movement, though he never became a best-selling writer and activist as Equiano did.[50] If Dufaÿ had arrived alone in the Convention, he would have found it more difficult to win over the assembly.

For the three years he was a deputy in the national legislature, Belley's importance would remain more symbolic than substantive. He would certainly prove more active than his companions Mills and Boisson (who arrived in June), but his importance resided more in the biography that he embodied rather than in any significant action that he took. In claiming him as 'an active spokesperson for the men of color in the Convention and then in the Council of Five Hundred down to 1797', Luce-Marie Albigès exaggerates somewhat, as his interventions seem to have been very few.[51]

His first intervention is easy to overlook, as it was brief and his name is misspelled in the parliamentary record. On 8 February 1794, a group of black citizens delivered an address at the bar of the Convention thanking the assembly for the emancipation decree, passed four days before, and warning that colonists should be prevented from returning to Saint Domingue until the new regime was organized. In response, Belley rose to speak.

> You will not expect brilliant eloquence from me. I will speak from my heart; the plain truth is all that my talents can manage. The colonists whose maneuvering you have just been told to fear have not ceased to mislead people in the colonies and to maintain links with the emigrés. The center of their silent plotting is in Paris; they meet there frequently and in secret. It is they who got us thrown in jail, my colleagues and me, when we first arrived. I demand that an arrest warrant be issued against these dangerous conspirators.[52]

The record perhaps paraphrases Belley's improvised words, for one newspaper thought he was referring to a 'colonial assembly', and another to colonists' clubs, whereas he was in fact targeting Page and Brulley, the two-man *commission de Saint-Domingue* that claimed to represent the colonists. The result was confusion and inaction, and it would require another month of active campaigning by Dufaÿ to finally get the Jacobins to break with their colonial supporters and imprison Page and Brulley. The *Journal de Paris*, nonetheless, chose to underline the symbolic significance of the black deputy's speech. 'The tribune of the Convention is now truly the tribune of Equality', it proclaimed, 'because a black citizen, a representative of Saint Domingue, has finally come and spoken there for the first time. He is Jean-Baptiste Belley'.[53]

Belley made another short speech three days later, this time when the Saint Domingue delegation was introduced at a meeting of the Paris Commune. This was a dangerous venue, at a time when the Jacobins were splitting into hostile factions and the dominant Robespierrists were about to send many erstwhile allies to the guillotine. The three deputies each said little. Belley opted for a biographical introduction.

> Citizens, I was a slave in my childhood. I became free 36 years ago through my hard work; I purchased myself. Since then, in the course of my life, I have felt worthy of being French. I served my country in the American campaign in the last war under General d'Estaing, and gained the respect of my commanders. During the [fighting in Cap Français] when the perfidious traitor Galbaud, at the head of counterrevolutionaries, tried to kill France's representatives, I took up arms with my brothers to defend them. I shed my blood for the French Republic, for the noble cause of freedom. I don't consider myself meritorious; I just did my duty ... I have only one word to say to you, and that is that the tricolor flag that summoned us to freedom, it is under that flag that we won our freedom ... As long as there remains a drop of blood in our veins, I swear to you in the name of my brothers, that this flag will always fly on our shores and in our mountains.[54]

Anaxagoras Chaumette, the radical *procureur* of the Commune who welcomed the Saint Domingue deputies, organized a large festival the following week in the secularized cathedral of Notre Dame to celebrate slavery's abolition. In early March, Page and Brulley were arrested and the Convention condemned all colonists who had been members of colonial assemblies. Belley and his companions could feel pleased with their achievements. However, they still faced, behind the scenes, opposition from the colonial lobby and in the Convention itself from the deputation of the Indian Ocean colony of Isle de France (Mauritius), where the plantation regime remained intact. Meanwhile, the hesitations about slave emancipation that had surfaced but had been overwhelmed in the Convention's abolition debate continued to trouble the all-powerful government committees now charged with the decree's implementation. Was it possible to maintain export agriculture and grant citizenship to the formerly enslaved? Would slave emancipation drive French planters into the arms of the British, as was already happening in Saint Domingue?

The future was therefore far from certain, and especially so as Paris politics traversed a period of extreme turbulence. Lethal rivalries and suspicions sent successive factions to the guillotine. Chaumette, long an anti-slavery activist, was executed in April; Danton, who hailed emancipation as a weapon of war, was guillotined shortly afterwards. With the elimination of the Robespierrists in July, the paroxysm subsided but, as the French Revolution began a slow descent from its most radical heights, the implications for slave emancipation remained unclear. Against this shifting background, the struggle to shape colonial policy continued.

In late June, the Saint Domingue delegation doubled in size with the arrival of Joseph Georges Boisson, Pierre Garnot and Etienne Laforest, whom Belley and Dufaÿ had left in New York. They were admitted to the Convention on 22 August. The same day, Belley delivered his first real speech to the Convention, which was then published as a short pamphlet. It came in response to a vote to free Page and Brulley. He began in the same self-deprecating manner he had used before, but this time with a nod toward the literary trope of the Noble Savage and a misleading hint that he himself was a beneficiary of the emancipation decree.

> I do not know how to speak with eloquence. I am one of those men of Nature whom the wisdom and principles of the French nation snatched from the yoke of despotism. I know nothing of intrigue; I scorn pretense; I am not so bold in speaking in your midst as I am in combat defending the interests of the Republic.[55]

Primarily an attack on Page and Brulley, the text ends, like Belley's maiden speech, with a call for their prosecution. This time he succeeded, at least in preventing their release from prison. The content is not original and reworks points that Dufaÿ had already made in his various writings: the *commissaires'* role in having the deputies jailed in January; their former royalist sympathies; the illegitimacy of their representative status, and their success in obscuring the truth about colonial events. The pamphlet employs both the boilerplate prose of the Year II and the standard tactic of the period of linking one's enemy with the British and the already disgraced opponents of the Revolution: the monarchy (Capet), the Robespierrists ('*la faction liberticide*'), and the regional *fédéralistes*, who were likened to the autonomist colonists alias '*l'hydre toujours renaissant des factieux Colonicides*'. Historian Jean-Charles Benzaken believes the pamphlet was essentially written by Dufaÿ.[56]

The claim that Belley's pamphlet was ghost-written was brandished in Page and Brulley's response, which came five days later in a pamphlet five times as long, *Reply ... to the slander Belley was made to sign*.[57] This divisive question of literacy and authorship has been receiving increasing attention in studies of the Haitian Revolution.[58] In Belley's case, it seems clear that his writing skills were very limited. Most of his surviving private letters were signed but not written in his hand – he used an intermediary – and the one he did write displays the crude syntax and quasi-phonetic spelling typical of his social milieu.[59] It is worlds removed from the literary ability displayed in his publications, as was presumably the writing of any hairdresser of the time. A collaborative authorship with Dufaÿ, therefore, seems beyond question. The two men enjoyed close relations during their time in Paris, and they probably had known each other for far longer, as Dufaÿ had served as a junior officer in the Chasseurs Volontaires that Belley had joined (and helped recruit) in 1779. Highly significant is what Dufaÿ wrote when recommending Belley for a job in 1795: 'I will point out that Belley ought not be appointed to a civil post; *he is really only suited for warfare.*'[60]

If Belley's first pamphlet did come from the prolific pen of Louis Dufaÿ, it is ironic how unfavourably it compares, in style and organization, with another published a few days later by Étienne Bussière Laforest, one of the new deputies who arrived with the second half of the tricolour deputation. The eldest of the deputation, Laforest was an extremely wealthy, mixed-race planter and shopkeeper, who had been educated in France. Furious that his right to sit in the Convention was challenged by Benoît Gouly, a covertly pro-slavery deputy from Isle de France, he delivered a blistering text, tightly argued and well documented, that excoriated the deputy.[61] Laforest remains an almost unknown figure, because he apparently never spoke again in the Convention. However, Gouly, the target of his ire, retains a certain notoriety, because Belley and Dufaÿ, too, each later published pamphlets attacking him.

Gouly was waging a one-man campaign in the Convention to subvert the decree of 16 Pluviôse and particularly to prevent it from disrupting the still-intact plantation regime in the Indian Ocean colonies, where he owned considerable property. In the ideological climate of the time, it was too early to advocate overturning the decree, but Gouly could count on the unspoken support of many who felt that the Convention had gone too far in February. At the end of November 1794, he published a long pamphlet that extolled the colonies' economic importance to France; denigrating the abilities of people of African descent, he argued for a cautious application of the 16 Pluviôse decree. The key provision was a restoration of the self-governing assemblies that most colonies had formed in the period 1790–2. As Gouly insisted that the former slaves were 'foreigners' and not French, this was a recipe for re-establishing white supremacy.[62]

Belley's response, in a high-flown, rhetorical style that certainly was not his own, was published as *Le Bout d'oreille des colons*. The title implies that the colonists had inadvertently revealed their true intentions.[63]

> Today, citizen colleagues, Gouly's profession of faith should give you the measure of the patriotism of colonial slaveowners. You will no doubt have felt how specious and treacherous his proposals are. The veil is now rent asunder: the *white aristocracy* of the West Indies is demanding the power to legislate, to reject the Convention's sovereignty, and the right to make more slaves and cause more unhappiness.[64]

Belley greatly exaggerated in stating that France's colonies had contained two million slaves 'snatched from their homelands' (rather than 750,000, of whom half had been born locally), but because of his personal experience, he was at his most effective in evoking their plight.

> Who cannot respond with anger and pity on reading the bizarre portrait that Gouly paints of blacks. Is it in fact a man that this colonist wanted to depict? Yes, citizens, it is a man, a man without vices … But, this man, brutalized by slavery, the whip raised permanently above his head, forced back to childhood by cruel and shameful punishments that degrade humanity and modesty, this man is not without feelings. His wounded soul, dead to hope, was for long discouraged by those cruel and lucky tyrants. Many was the time, with my back to the wall, I wiped away in secret a bitter tear of misfortune. The development of a lively mind by a slave led to certain death, if he dared to reveal it …

Citizen colleagues, do you believe that Nature is unjust, that it has created some men to be the slaves of others, as the colonists claim? Do you not see in this shameful assertion the true principles of these detestable ravagers of the human species? I myself was born in Africa. ... The executioners of the blacks impudently lie when they dare to claim that these oppressed men are brutes. If they lack the vices of Europeans, they have the virtues of Nature; they are sensitive and grateful beings. It is in their name, the name of all my brothers, who were invigorated on hearing the unexpected sound of happiness and freedom, that I urge you to maintain your beneficent laws. ... You have returned to life and happiness unfortunate men whom the colonists ... have for a long time classed among the animals and treated with great inhumanity.[65]

Besides defending the image of blacks at this general level, opposing a Rousseauist 'natural man' to the 'brute' of colonial propaganda, Belley also had to deal with unfavourable news arriving from Saint Domingue. The massacre in July of some seven hundred colonists at Fort Liberté by black insurgents allied to the Spanish invaders risked being seen in primarily racial terms. Belley recast it as an act of Spanish revenge against treasonous colonists, carried out by royalist blacks, whose rebellion in 1791 had been secretly organized by white conspirators.[66] Sonthonax and Dufaÿ had proclaimed that slave emancipation would create an army of defenders for Saint Domingue against foreign invasion. Yet, as Gouly observed, the Spanish and British had taken over several parts of the colony. Belley had to acknowledge that free coloured as well as white slave-owners had surrendered to the invaders, but he countered,

The reason the English have not succeeded in taking over all of Saint Domingue is because the blacks who have become free and French have made a rampart with their bodies to boldly defend the rights of the Republic against this invasion. There is no doubt that, if these brave patriots had arms and ammunition, the English and the traitorous colonists would water with their unworthy blood the land their presence has soiled for too long.[67]

Fortunately for Belley and his colleagues, the war in the colony was finally turning against the foreign invaders, thanks to another black freedman from Cap Français parish, Toussaint Louverture. Belley closed his speech with three demands: the dispatch of the emancipation decree to those places it had not yet been promulgated (notably Isle de France); an agricultural code based on free labour to be drawn up by the government; and the sending of help to the defenders of Saint Domingue.

Gouly replied swiftly, in the manner of Page and Brulley, claiming that Belley used insults rather than arguments, misrepresented Gouly's argument, and was not the real author of the text he 'distributed'.[68] Dufaÿ fired back a derisive, rather lightweight response, and Page and Brulley (now released from jail) turned to humour with a racist satire that exploited inconsistencies in Dufaÿ's writings, while depicting the non-white deputies as ignorant, Creole-speaking buffoons.[69] With the radical enthusiasm of the Year II fading, and the colonial lobby increasing the intensity of the pamphlet war, slave emancipation was facing a serious challenge. The campaign peaked in February 1795, when Dufaÿ obtained from the Convention the decree of 26 Pluviôse III. Proclaiming that France and its colonies were 'one and indivisible', it ensured that the citizenship granted to former slaves the year before could not be changed. The principle of legal unity between metropolitan and overseas France was then enshrined in the Constitution of the Year III passed in August.[70]

While Louis Pierre Dufaÿ remained front and centre in debating these momentous changes, Jean-Baptiste Belley disappears from view after his *Bout d'oreille* pamphlet around 1 December 1794. The only other trace of him in the parliamentary record is mention of a slightly idiosyncratic vote he took in November 1794. As the Thermidorian reaction against the Reign of Terror gathered speed, the Convention debated whether to indict the *terroriste* Jean-Baptiste Carrier for mass murder. Almost all the five hundred deputies who voted condemned him; just Belley and one other voted conditionally to indict, only if the charges against him proved to be accurate.[71] What this demonstrates, however, is not obvious.

When the Convention closed in October 1795, all the colonial deputies were carried over to the new legislature, now divided between the Conseil des Anciens and Conseil des 500. Belley held a seat in the latter until May 1797 (or March 1798 – historians disagree).[72] The first parliamentary dictionary published in France stated enigmatically that he 'maintained his republican principles' in the assembly, but this seems a discreet way of covering up a total absence of information regarding his activities at this time.[73] Like his colleagues Boisson, Mills and Garnot in the Convention, he appears to have abstained from speaking, and he seems to have held no office. During these years, Saint Domingue sent a dozen more deputies to the French legislature in successive elections. Several played important political roles. These included, not surprisingly, ex-commissioner Sonthonax and the former governor Laveaux, but also the young black deputy Étienne Mentor. The former slave Jean-Louis Annecy and the white engineer Martin Brothier both became secretaries of the Conseil des Anciens. The mixed-race planter François Boisrond published pamphlets, made speeches and carried out official enquiries. Pierre Thomany, a black deputy, gave speeches proposing the annulment of debts relating to slavery and making the anniversary of the 16 Pluviôse decree a holiday in the colonies.[74]

A possible explanation for Belley's low profile as a deputy during these years may be military service. It would seem that, in Paris, he was paid both his stipend as deputy and his salary as an officer in the 16th Infantry Regiment. In May 1794, he was promoted from captain to major (*chef de bataillon*), but what duties were required of him, if any, are not apparent; the regiment was then stationed in Flanders.[75] In August 1795, Dufaÿ wrote of him,

> It would be very appropriate and even very shrewd to send to Saint Domingue Belley, deputy to the Convention, who is a captain in the 16th Infantry Regiment, and even to promote him to a higher rank, so that he can command and organize his brothers in the name of the Republic. These are my reasons: Belley is very popular with and much respected by his brothers, and he deserves it because of his probity and extreme courage. His position of deputy, and his return from having been in France will inspire even more trust. Everyone will rally to the sound of his voice. He will cross the most difficult mountains from one end of the colony to the other without difficulty, and if need be, he will soon have 100,000 men. ... He will lead his brothers in combat against France's enemies ... You could make him a brigadier-general ... [; that] would enormously flatter his brothers.[76]

This glowing recommendation failed to earn Belley a place in the expedition that accompanied Sonthonax back to Saint Domingue in spring 1796, but it eventually bore fruit in early 1798, when Belley was attached to the expedition of General Hédouville. Before then, however, the black officer posed for a painting in his deputy's costume.

Belley's portrait

The portrait, by Anne-Louis Girodet-Trioson, a student of Jacques-Louis David, was first shown, in 1797, as *Portrait de Nègre*, and the following year as *Portrait du C[itoyen] Belley, ex-représentant des Colonies*. The first title seems to echo Belley's low individual profile and his primacy as a metaphor for slave emancipation. The portrait was controversial at the time – for reasons unknown – and it has remained controversial among art historians.[77] Arguments have centred on Belley's stance, the representation of his genitalia, and his pairing with the marble bust of abolitionist abbé Raynal. Those who see the picture as a

Figure 2.1 Jean-Baptiste Belley, deputy to the Convention for Saint Domingue, by Anne-Louis Girodet-Trioson (1797). Courtesy © Alamy.

straightforward celebration of slavery's abolition praise its realism and interpret it as simultaneously paying tribute to the Enlightenment as the intellectual foundation for Revolutionary emancipation.[78] Belley's unconventional pose, however, turning away from Raynal, might also be interpreted as expressing disdain for the Enlightenment's hesitant and ineffectual critique of slavery, or for Raynal himself, who recanted his anti-slavery views in old age.[79] For some, Belley's posture is openly erotic, and evokes both the Classical satyr and caricatures of contemporary dandies instead of the stern Neoclassical ideal then in vogue. In this view, the portrait is exoticizing, racist, even a covert justification of slavery. As to whether the dimensions of Belley's penis are exaggerated, scholars seem unable to agree.[80]

Belley's later career and death

Belley was promoted colonel (*chef de brigade*) in June 1797 and returned to Saint Domingue in March 1798, accompanied by two servants, as commander in chief of the colony's police. He formed part of the retinue of General Théodore Hédouville, whose mission was to reassert metropolitan control over the colony in the face of the increasing autonomy of its black governor, Toussaint Louverture. Belley became an early casualty of the contest of will between these two men. Refusing to grant him a personal interview, Louverture restricted his command to just the North Province of Saint Domingue, and Belley was never paid his salary, so he had to depend on local friends' hospitality. In a private letter to Boisson in Paris, Belley criticized Toussaint's dictatorial tendencies and his flouting of French policy. He claimed Toussaint was jealous of him, and he lamented the chaotic state of his administration. For his part, Louverture later claimed that Belley and Hédouville wanted to kill him.[81]

Both men were black freedmen from the Cap Français region, and they were of similar age. Each was a product of the revolution and associated with the idea of slave emancipation. They were equally suspicious of their mixed-race counterparts led by southerner André Rigaud. Yet their political paths had long since diverged. They represent the two contrary tendencies that free blacks tended to display during the revolution, allying with either whites or with slaves rather than with fellow free coloureds of mixed racial descent.[82] As Toussaint turned Saint Domingue into a de facto independent state, Belley sided with the French government. When Toussaint deported General Hédouville in October 1798, Jean-Baptiste returned to France with him. After Napoleon Bonaparte came to power the following year, Belley was among the many colonials who covertly called for the black governor's removal.[83]

Back in Paris, Belley occasionally attended meetings of the anti-slavery society, the Amis des Noirs. Otherwise, little is known of his activities until, three years later, he returned to Saint Domingue, once again as police commandant, in the major military expedition led by General Victoire Leclerc. Whereas Hédouville had merely attempted minor reforms in the colony, Bonaparte tasked Leclerc with breaking the power of the black colonial army and – though this was kept secret – with restoring slavery and racial inequality as soon as he could.[84] Although an opponent of Toussaint Louverture, Belley was apparently regarded as an unreliable collaborator in this mission, for he was sent back to France just two months after he had arrived. He thus saw little of the apocalyptic conflict that would end in December 1803 with Haiti's independence. For three years, he was held in detention on an island off the Breton coast but charged with no offence. He received a pension and had freedom of movement during the daytime, but could not leave. During this period, France restored slavery and racial discrimination in its colonies, prohibited immigration by non-whites, and ceased to be a republic.

Belley died in Belle-Isle military hospital on 6 August 1805. His death certificate ends his story with a curious enigma, because it gives his place of birth as Léogane, in Saint Domingue.[85] If this was not simply the result of some inconsequential misunderstanding, it raises the possibility that his African identity, so central to his image, was in fact a fiction that he (or Louis Dufaÿ) invented in France to strengthen the case for abolition. A similar controversy surrounds the activist Olaudah Equiano, who on occasion had claimed an American birthplace before becoming an abolitionist and testifying about Africa.[86] I am inclined to believe, however, that both men were indeed born in Africa but that, in certain situations (prison, baptism, naval recruitment), they may have chosen to invent a 'Western' identity.

The public career of Jean-Baptiste Belley traversed a period of extraordinary upheaval. He was the first black representative to sit in a European legislature, though not quite the first of African descent. Of the several non-whites who represented Saint Domingue during the French Revolution, only two, including Belley, were former slaves, and he was the only African. Although a slave-owner, who had fought against the slave insurrection of 1791–3, he became in France a symbol of that country's landmark abolition of slavery in 1794.

Some prominent historians have misrepresented his role in bringing about slave emancipation and somewhat exaggerated his activity as a deputy. Yet his contribution should not be underestimated. In Saint Domingue, where he was widely respected, he made a brief but important military contribution in June 1793 to defending the new regime of racial equality, without which the local abolition of slavery in August might not have occurred. His role in Paris was much less dramatic. Belley spoke and published little as a deputy, and he may not have been the author of his few publications, but there were other colonial deputies, white and black, who did much less. A dignified and imposing defender of the French Republic, his biography and physical presence embodied for a French audience the intended outcome of slave emancipation, and probably helped sway opinion on what remained a controversial issue even in revolutionary Paris. As emancipation was partly motivated by military calculation, it helped that he was an army officer and known as Mars. His ability to speak of his personal experience of enslavement, unique in the National Convention, may also have counted with politicians who weighed the human cost of slavery against the economic price of its abolition. His role as apt figurehead continues in the frequent reproduction of his 1797 portrait.

Notes

1   C. L. James, *The Black Jacobins: Toussaint L'Ouverture and the San Domingo Revolution*, 2nd edn. (New York: Vintage, 1963), 140.

2   For example, on the book covers of Robin Blackburn, *The Overthrow of Colonial Slavery* (London: Verso, 1988); Hugh Honour, *The Image of the Black in Western Art*, vol. 4, *From the American Revolution to World War I* (Cambridge, MA: Harvard University Press, 1989); Christopher Alan Bayly, *The Birth of the Modern World, 1780–1914* (Oxford: Blackwell, 2004); Paul Butel, *Histoire des Antilles françaises* (Paris: Perrin, 2007); Laurent Dubois and and Julius S. Scott, eds., *The Origins of the Black Atlantic* (New York: Routledge, 2010); Christine Levecq, *Black Cosmopolitans: Race, Religion, and Republicanism* (Charlottesville: University of Virginia Press: 2019).

3   David Geggus, 'The Haitian Revolution in Atlantic Perspective', in Nicholas Canny and and Philip Morgan (eds.), *The Atlantic World c.1450–c.1820* (New York: Oxford University Press, 2011), 533–49; Geggus, 'The Major Port Towns of Saint Domingue in the late 18th century', in Peggy Liss and Franklin Knight (eds.), *Atlantic Port Cities: Economy, Culture and Society* (Knoxville: University of Tennessee Press, 1991), 87–116.

4   He gave his age as forty-eight in September 1795, and as fifty-two in February 1798: Archives Nationales, Paris (hereafter AN), C352/1837, 'Déclaration d'age'; Boston

Public Library, Ms Haiti 70–14; Jean-Baptiste Belley, *Le Bout d'oreille des colons, ou le système de l'Hôtel de Massiac, mis au jour par Gouli; Belley, député noir de Saint-Domingue, à ses collègues* (Paris: Imp. Pain, n.d.), 5. He probably reached Le Cap early in 1749 on the Bordeaux slave ship *Levrette d'Argenton* (www.slavevoyages.org (accessed 16 May 2020)).

5   On his half-brother, see Jacques Petit, Pierre Bardin, Bernadette and Philippe Rossignol, 'Le décès de Jean-Baptiste Belley (ex-député de Saint Domingue à la Convention) et son demi-frère Joseph Domingue', *Généalogie et Histoire de la Caraïbe*, 241 (2010): 6506–11.

6   See David Geggus, 'The Slaves and Free People of Color of Cap Français', in *The Black Urban Atlantic in the Age of the Slave Trade*, ed. Jorge Cañizares-Esguerra, Matt Childs and James Sidbury (Philadelphia: University of Pennsylvania Press, 2013), 109–11.

7   Adolphe Robert, *Dictionnaire des parlementaires français* (Paris: Bourloton, 1889); Auguste Kuscinski, *Dictionnaire des Conventionnels* (Paris: Société de l'Histoire de la Révolution française, 1916); M. Prévost, *Dictionnaire de biographie française* (Paris: Letouzey, 1951); Michèle Oriol, *Histoire et dictionnaire de la revolution et de l'indépendance d'Haïti* (Port-au-Prince: Fondation pour la Recherche Iconographique, 2002); Claude Moïse, ed., *Dictionnaire historique de la Révolution haïtienne (1789-1804)* (Montreal: Cidhica, 2003).

8   Petit et al., 'Le décès de Jean-Baptiste Belley', which includes an appendix, 'Actes signés par JB Belley dans les registres conservés du Cap francais (1777–1788)'. Jean-Louis Donnadieu, 'Derrière le portrait, l'homme: Jean-Baptiste Belley, dit "Timbaze", dit "Mars" (1746?–1805)', *Bulletin de la Société d'Histoire de la Guadeloupe*, 170 (2015): 29–54, adds further documents.

9   Geggus, 'Slaves and Free People of Color of Cap Français', 113–15.

10 Personal database of 362 *gens de couleur libres* (1770–90). The revolutionary leader Toussaint Louverture, born just outside Le Cap, who was roughly Belley's age and freed not long after him, did not learn to sign his name until about 1790.

11 Belley mentioned his service in a speech he made in Paris fifteen years later: *Affiches de la Commune de Paris* 217 (23 Pluviôse II), 3. The absence of his name from Le Cap's parish registers and notarial archives during the period 1778–9 provides additional, indirect evidence of his departure overseas.

12 AN, Archives de la Marine, B4 142, ff. 170–200; John Garrigus, 'Catalyst or Catastrophe? Saint-Domingue's Free Men of Color and the Battle of Savannah, 1779–1782', *Revista/Review Interamericana*, 22, nos. 1–2 (1992): 109–25.

13 Archives Nationales d'Outre-mer, Aix-en-Provence (hereafter ANOM), Cap Français parish register, 16 August 1781.

14 ANOM, Notsdom 1522, 7 January 1786.

15 ANOM, G2, Cap Français cadastral surveys, 1776, 1787; AN, C/352/1838, 'Situation de fortune'.

16 ANOM, Notariat reg. 1012 [old classification], 19 January 1787; Notsdom 198, 19 June 1787; Notsdom 859, 23 October 1780. These are, respectively, contracts of manumission, sale and purchase for two young women and a girl,

17 Geggus, 'Slaves and Free People of Color of Cap Français', 105.

18 Jean-Charles Benzaken, *Louis Pierre Dufaÿ, conventionnel abolitionniste et colon de Saint-Domingue* (Paris: Éditions SPM, 2015), 649.

19 AN, 27AP/12, dossier 2.

20 AN, 505Mi85, Morange to Foäche, 30 and 31 October 1790; ANOM, 151APOM/4, dossier 1, Martin to Walsh, 12 November 1790.

21 Jean-Louis Donnadieu, 'Un officier français face à la Révolution outre-mer', *Revue Historique des Armées*, 265 (2011): 78.

22 *Relation détaillée des évènemens malheureux qui se sont passés au Cap* (Paris: Imp. Nat., 1794), 40–1.

23 However, one source claims that the *compagnies franches* remained 'spectators' in the major campaign against the slave insurgents in January 1793: [Jean-Baptiste Laplace,] *Histoire des désastres de Saint-Domingue* (Paris: Garnéry, 1795), 269.

24 See ibid.

25 Service Historique de la Défense, Armée de Terre, Vincennes, Yb 379, f. 172. Promotion, 18 August 1793.

26 AN, C 181/84; AN, Dxxv/64/654, f. 31.

27 Guillaume-François Mahy de Cormeré, *Histoire de la révolution de la partie française de St.-Domingue* (Baltimore, 1794), 1:10; [Laplace,] *Histoire des désastres de Saint-Domingue*, 363; Jean-Charles Benzaken, *Louis Pierre Dufaÿ*, 166–8.

28 Robert L. Stein, *Léger-Félicité Sonthonax: The Lost Sentinel of the Republic* (Rutherford: Fairleigh Dickinson University Press, 1985), 21.

29 'Unprecedented' because, although Massachusetts and other north-eastern states of the USA had abolished slavery in the 1780s, slaves there were very few in number, abolition was usually gradual, and it was not accompanied by racial equality.

30 *Lettre écrite de New-Yorck par les députés de Saint-Domingue à leurs commettans, imprimée par ordre de la Convention Nationale* (Paris: Imp. Nat., 1794), 7–9.

31 Jeremy Popkin, *You Are All Free: The Haitian Revolution and the Abolition of Slavery* (Cambridge: Cambridge University Press, 2010), 320–2.

32 Jean-Baptiste Mills (1749–1806), was the son of a white merchant and a black woman, who inherited substantial property and was a court bailiff. Louis-Pierre Dufaÿ (1752–1804) was one of the small circle of radical whites who had gravitated around Sonthonax. From a Parisian bourgeois background, talented but impecunious, he had been jailed for fraud in France but married into a planter family in Saint Domingue by pretending to be an aristocrat.

33 *Lettre de Belley, député à la Convention nationale, à ses frères,* 19–20 of *Lettre écrite de New-Yorck.*

34 On the colonial question in the French Revolution, see Blackburn, *Overthrow of Colonial Slavery,* 161–264; Yves Bénot, *La Révolution française et la fin des colonies* (Paris: La Découverte, 1988); Jean-Daniel Piquet, *L'Emancipation des Noirs dans la Révolution française (1789–1795)* (Paris: Karthala, 2002); Miranda Frances Spieler, 'The Legal Structure of Colonial Rule during the French Revolution', *William and Mary Quarterly,* 66 (2009): 365–408.

35 Benzaken, *Louis Pierre Dufaÿ,* 183–97.

36 Abel A. Louis, *Janvier Littée: Martiniquais, premier député de couleur membre d'une assemblée parlementaire française (1752–1820)* (Paris: Harmattan, 2013).

37 *Archives parlementaires de 1787 à 1860,* sér. 1, 84 (Paris: CNRS, 1962), 257. The Mountain referred to the high seats on the left side of the chamber. Delacroix's statement shows that Littée was generally regarded as white.

38 Yves Bénot, 'Comment la Convention a-t-elle voté l'abolition de l'esclavage en l'an II?', *Annales Historiques de la Révolution Française* (hereafter *AHRF*), 293 (1993): 353.

39 On the complicated publishing history of the revolutionary assemblies, see Françoise Brunel and Corinne Gomez-Le Chevanton, 'La Convention nationale au miroir des Archives Parlementaires', *AHRF,* 381 (2015): 11–29.

40 Bénot, 'Comment la Convention a-t-elle voté l'abolition', 353–60. Cf. Spieler, 'Legal structure', 393–5.

41 C. L. R. James, *The Black Jacobins: Toussaint L'Ouverture and the San Domingo Revolution* (2nd edn.; New York: Vintage, 1963), 140.

42 *Archives parlementaires,* 84: 276–85.

43 For example, Bayly, *Birth of the Modern World,* 375; Jacques Binoche, 'Les Deputés d'Outre mer pendant la Révolution française', *AHRF,* 231 (1978): 70.

44 AN, C/I/79; *Le Moniteur Universel* 137 and 138 (1794): 554–9; James, *Black Jacobins,* 380.

45 T. Lothrop Stoddard, *The French Revolution in San Domingo* (Boston: Houghton Mifflin, 1914), 242.

46 Jules Saintoyant, *La Colonisation française pendant la Révolution* (Paris: Renaissance du Livre, 1930), 1:328; James, *Black Jacobins,* 142. Note also that if either Stoddard or James had paid attention to the deputy's speech printed in *Le Moniteur,* they would have seen that it twice mentions 'my colleague, Belley' and hence could not have been written by him. The speech, moreover, was published under Dufaÿ's name: *Compte rendu sur la situation actuelle de Saint-Domingue, par Dufey, député de la partie du Nord. Le 16 pluviôse, l'an II. Imprimé par ordre de la Convention nationale* (Paris: Impr. nationale, n.d.).

47 Benzaken, *Louis Pierre Dufaÿ,* 30–1, 182, 228–39, 271.

48 Benzaken, *Louis Pierre Dufaÿ,* chs. 6–10.

49 The few sentences beginning, 'I was a slave during my childhood' and supposedly interjected into the debate by Belley, according to Laurent Dubois, *Avengers of the New World: the Story of the Haitian Revolution* (Cambridge, MA: Harvard University Press, 2004), 170, were in fact addressed to the Paris Commune several days later. See note 54.

50 See Vincent Carretta, *Equiano the African: Biography of a Self-Made Man* (Athens: University of Georgia Press, 2005).

51 Luce-Marie Albigès, 'Jean-Baptiste Belley, député de Saint-Domingue à la Convention', *Histoire par l'image*. Available online: www.histoire-image.org/etudes/jean-baptiste-belley-depute-saint-domingue-convention (accessed 8 March 2018).

52 *Archives parlementaires*, 84: 471.

53 Bénot, 'Comment la Convention a-t-elle voté l'abolition', 358; Benzaken, *Louis Pierre Dufaÿ*, 252–69.

54 *Affiches de la Commune de Paris* 217 (23 Pluviôse II), 2–3. The '36 years' must be a mistake. Later in the year, Belley claimed to have been free for thirty years (Belley, *Bout d'oreille*, 5). Dufaÿ said Belley had served thirty years (in the militia) (Benzaken, *Louis Pierre Dufaÿ*, 256).

55 Jean-Baptiste Belley, *Belley, de Saint-Domingue représentant du peuple, à ses collègues* (Paris: Imp. Pain, 1794), 1. Only a fragment appears in *Archives parlementaires* 95: 376.

56 Benzaken, *Louis Pierre Dufaÿ*, 308.

57 Augustin Brulley and and Pierre-François Page, *À la Convention nationale: Réponse de Page et Brulley … aux calomnies qu'on a fait signer au citoyen Belley* (Paris: Imp. de Laurens, 1794). Another colonist claimed Sonthonax and his colleague Polverel, recently returned to France, wrote the pamphlet: [Louis François] Verneuil, *Réponse des colons de Saint-Domingue à l'adresse de Polverel et Sonthonax, signée Belley* (Paris: Lefortier, 1794).

58 Philippe Girard, *The Memoir of General Toussaint Louverture* (New York: Oxford University Press, 2014); Deborah Jenson, *Beyond the Slave Narrative: Politics, Sex, and Manuscripts in the Haitian Revolution* (Liverpool: Liverpool University Press, 2011); David Geggus, 'Haiti's Declaration of Independence', *The Haitian Declaration of Independence: Creation, Context, and Legacy*, ed. Julia Gaffield (Charlottesville: University of Virginia Press, 2016), 27–9; Geggus, 'Print Culture and the Haitian Revolution: the Written and the Spoken Word', *Proceedings of the American Antiquarian Society*, 116 (2006): 297–314.

59 AN, T 988, four letters to Boisson; letter to Placide Louverture reproduced in Jean Price Mars, 'Les origines et le destin d'un nom: Jean-Baptiste Belley Mars, l'Ancêtre', *Revue de la Société Haïtienne d'Histoire et de Géographie*, 164 (1989): 128.

60 Benzaken, *Louis Pierre Dufaÿ*, 256, 271 (underlining in the original quotation). On Dufaÿ as Chasseur Volontaire, see ANOM, D2C/41.

61 Étienne Laforest, *Laforest, citoyen de couleur, député de Saint-Domingue, à son collègue Gouly, député de l'Isle de France* (Paris: Imp. l'Union, [1794]). The speech is dated '8 fructidor III' but the year must be a misprint. On his wealth, see Pierre Bardin, 'Règles d'élections à la Convention et patrimoine des députés des colonies', *Généalogie et Histoire de la Caraïbe* (2012): 4–5.

62 Benoît Gouly, *Vues générales sur l'importance du commerce des colonies* (Paris: Rubat, [1794]); Claude Wanquet, 'Un "Jacobin" esclavagiste, Benoît Gouly', *AHRF*, 293 (1993): 445–68; Dufaÿ to Rochambeau, 29 December 1794, online auction catalogue, www.rouillac.com (accessed June 2008).

63 See note 4. 'To reveal the tip of the ear' derives from a fable by La Fontaine in which a donkey tries to hide. 'The system of the Hôtel Massiac', in the subtitle, refers to the former club of Saint Domingue colonists in Paris, which had been closed for two years. Belley's pamphlet, misdated by several historians, must have appeared around the time Gouly's was disavowed by the Convention (29 November). It was apparently never delivered as a speech; there is no mention of it in the Convention's manuscript records or in *Le Moniteur Universel*.

64 Belley, *Le Bout d'oreille*, 3.

65 Ibid., 5–6.

66 Ibid., 7.

67 Ibid.

68 Benoît Gouly, *Réponse au libelle distribué par l'Affricain Belley*, (Paris: n.p., (1794)).

69 Louis Pierre Dufaÿ, *Encore une petite calomnie de Bazile Gouly* (Paris: Imp. Pain, [1795]); [Augustin Brulley and Pierre-François Page,] *Grand débat entre Duffay et consorts, Polverel et Sonthonax, les égorgeurs et les brûleurs de Saint-Domingue* (Paris: n.p., n.d.).

70 Nicolas Roche, 'La question coloniale en l'an III', *AHRF*, 302 (1995): 590–604.

71 *Archives parlementaires*, 102: 100–7.

72 For 1798, see Bernard Gainot, 'La députation de Saint-Domingue au corps législatif du Directoire' *Revue française d'histoire d'outre-mer* 84 (1997): 99, 105.

73 Robert, *Dictionnaire des parlementaires*.

74 Gainot, 'La députation de Saint-Domingue'.

75 Service Historique de la Défense, Armée de Terre, Vincennes, Yb 379, f. 172. This document also indicates promotion to lieutenant-colonel in May 1795. Belley's dossier in 2Ye 257 is missing.

76 Benzaken, *Louis Pierre Dufaÿ*, 271, 339, 342. Dufaÿ was presumably mistaken about his still being a captain.

77 Michèle Bocquillon, 'Le "Portrait parlant" de Jean-Baptiste Belley', *Nineteenth Century French Studies*, 33 (2004–5): 35–56; Helen Weston, 'Representing the Right to Represent: the Portrait of Citizen Belley, ex-representative of the Colonies', *Anthropology and Ethics*, 26 (1994): 83–99.

78 Honour, *Image*, 104–6; Stephen Eisenman, *Nineteenth Century Art: A Critical History* (London: Thames and Hudson, 2007), 43.

79 On which, see Louis Sala Molins, *Le Code noir ou le calvaire de Canaan* (Paris: PUF, 1987).

80 Bocquillon, 'Portrait parlant', 45–9; Sylvia Musto, 'Portraiture, Revolutionary Identity and Subjugation: Anne-Louis Girodet's Citizen Belley', *Racar*, 20 (1993): 60–7; Thomas Crow, *Emulation: Making Artists for Revolutionary France* (New Haven: Yale University Press, 1995), 228.

81 AN, T 988, Belley to Boisson, 30 Thermidor VI; Bibliothèque Nationale, Paris, Manuscrits, N.a.f. 14879, f. 36.

82 David Geggus, *Haitian Revolutionary Studies* (Bloomington: Indiana University Press, 2002), 117–18.

83 Philippe Girard, *The Slaves Who Defeated Napoleon* (Tuscaloosa: University of Alabama Press, 2011), 35–6.

84 David Geggus, *The Haitian Revolution: A Documentary History* (Indianapolis: Hackett, 2014), 173.

85 Auguste Nemours, *Histoire de la famille et de la descendance de Toussaint-Louverture* (Port-au-Prince: Imp. de l'Etat, 1941), 32–5.

86 See note 50.

3

Dionisio Inca Yupanqui: A 'lord' in Spain's Cortes de Cádiz

José María Portillo

Among [the deputies to the Cortes there was] an Inca of Peru, doubtless descended from the ancient sovereigns of that empire.

(Philos Hispaniae, preface to *The Political Constitution of the Spanish Monarchy*, London, 1813)

After Juan de Bustamante Carlos Inca sued to obtain the marquisate of Oropesa at the imperial court in 1747, Peru experienced renewed interest in the value of noble titles. Though he did not achieve his main goal, Bustamante managed to publicize his success.[1] He arrived in Madrid at just the right time, the year when Philip V died and the court of the new king, Ferdinand VI, was settling into place. There he found a position as a courtier at the king's table and a substantial salary of four thousand pesos, not bad for someone who had fled Cuzco to avoid paying his debts. Using his strategic position at court, he set up a system for facilitating requests by ambitious Americans to be admitted at court, and as a result met the father of Dionisio Inca Yupanqui, who also dreamt of obtaining noble titles in Madrid.[2]

When Domingo Ucho Inca, the father of our future deputy to the Cortes Dionisio Inca Yupanqui, undertook his journey from Lima to Madrid with his two children (as we shall see, it is not exactly clear who they were or if one of them was our main character), the Spanish monarchy was in the midst of making some critical decisions. His trip coincided almost exactly with that of the first Jesuits leaving the viceroyalty to go to Cadiz and then to Rome as a result of the expulsion of the Company of Jesus throughout the monarchy's territories in 1767. As is well known, that decision had been made by an extraordinary council led by the count of Aranda following a lengthy report by prosecutor Pedro Rodríguez de Campomanes. With this measure he wished to cut off any challenge whatsoever to royal sovereignty throughout the monarchy. Both the gravity of the decision and its implementation throughout Spain's immense geography constituted one of the moments when the Bourbon monarchy behaved most like a state.

Soon after Domingo Ucho Inca arrived with his children in Madrid another extraordinary council reached similarly momentous, though less effective, decisions. This council was also led by Aranda and it also considered a report by Campomanes, this time assisted by another prosecutor, José Moñino.[3] The reason for the council was outlined in letters from the Archbishop of Mexico, Francisco Antonio Lorenzana, delivered to Charles III by his confessor, Father Joaquín de Osma. The archbishop, a firm supporter of removing the Jesuits from Spanish territories, had arrived in Mexico soon before the expulsion order was announced. He published several letters in Mexico leaving no doubt as to the virtue of the monarch's critical decision in that regard. 'The Probabilists [i.e. the Jesuits] must accept', he wrote in his second pastoral letter of 12 October 1767, 'that the Church has condemned endless numbers of their propositions [and that] the uprisings and disturbances among the people in large part are suspected to have originated because of them'.[4] He followed that with a rejection of any arguments against monarchs' absolute sovereignty.

Along with the bishop of Puebla, Francisco Fabián y Fuero, Lorenzana conducted a significant campaign against probabilist doctrines and, especially, the Order of Jesus, causing the latter to react in such a manner that, in his opinion, New Spain was about to fall victim to an aristocratic plot. That was what he wrote about in his correspondence with the royal confessor, along with his inescapable suspicion that England was in on the anti-royal conspiracy. This was the situation that led to the summoning of an extraordinary council in March 1768.[5]

Though the Jesuit expulsion was met by considerable resistance in New Spain, the Crown's response was not exclusively repressive. Rather, prosecutors successfully proposed 'national' cohesion among the various parts of the monarchy. The fight against 'the spirit of independence and aristocracy' required an assumption by Spanish-Americans that they, too, enjoyed 'utility, honour, and grace'.[6] Prosecutors disputed the idea that there were different sorts of aristocracies in the monarchy, each assigned its own separate space; such a system could only lead to a spirit of independence.

Instead, they urged the adoption of concrete measures that might solidify the idea that there was just one Spanish aristocracy in the monarchy; or, put another way, they wished to generate among the various elites the idea of belonging to 'just one national body'. It is at this point that certain expressions made their first appearance, and would later be repeated during the 1808 monarchical crisis, though with far greater consequences: the notion that 'those countries' could not be considered 'as a pure colony' and that they formed 'an essential part of the monarchy'.[7]

The council's decisions were related to commerce, the promotion of industries such as fishing, and, above all, the aim of nationalizing the elites. To that end, the appropriate path was not to accept Creoles' demand for the right to petition, specifically for favourable treatment in the American juridical system, but rather the contrary.[8] The idea was to 'always send Spaniards to the Indies to hold the principal posts, bishoprics, and prebendaries, while putting Creoles in the equivalent posts in Spain'. This crossing among the elites, aimed at consolidating just one national body, was to be accompanied by a more ambitious communication programme among the elites aimed at 'drawing Americans to Spain to study' and to form specific military units on the peninsula.

Domingo Ucho Inca Yupanqui, Dionisio's father, was lucky enough to travel to Spain right between these two extraordinary council meetings: the one that decided to expel the Jesuits and the one that recognized the need to combat rebellion in America by nationalizing elites there. According to his letters to the Council of Indies, which he wrote once he arrived in Spain and began requesting royal favours, Domingo's last posting in Lima had been as an infantry lieutenant in El Callao. It is not clear if he moved to Spain upon his own initiative – he sometimes refers to 'licenses required for coming to Spain' – or if he was following orders by Viceroy Manuel de Amat y Junyent, as he suggests elsewhere.[9]

Starting in January 1768, Domingo began requesting royal favours by making clear to the council that he belonged to the Inca nobility. He was well aware that he had to prove both that his ancestors were related to the last Inca (or Tawantinsuyu) nobility and that they had intermarried with the Spaniards, so he was a Castilian *hidalgo*. His reconstruction of his lineage goes back to Don Gonzalo Ucho Gualpa Inca, who had overseen the settlement of Lambayeque. Along with his brother Felipe Tupac Inca, in 1545 he had been recognized by Charles V as belonging to the nobility, and they were granted a coat of arms and exempted from paying tribute.

Domingo's interest in having the imperial court recognize his nobility began in 1751, when he contacted Juan de Bustamante Carlos Inca, who at that time was enjoying the fruits of his success at court and working in Madrid to facilitate petitions by other members of the Peruvian nobility. Domingo's letters from Lima refer to Juan de Bustamante as a 'cousin' and, like many more of Bustamante's correspondents since he had established himself in Madrid, Domingo placed himself at his orders 'for anything you would like me to do'. Though he replied to none of the letters from Domingo, Bustamante used them to prove that in Peru he was widely recognized as Inca.[10]

When Domingo travelled from Lima in 1767 he took with him the documents that proved his Inca bloodline. The papers were examined in early 1768 by the royal accounts department, which concluded both that his lineage was proven and that he also belonged to the lineage of Captain Martín de Ampuero. This latter point is important because it illustrates the family type resulting from the blend of *conquistadores* and women of the local nobilities.[11] In both Mexico and in Peru, these new genealogies sought to re-establish relations of dominance by assimilating the Spanish notions and standards of nobility.[12]

With Domingo having proved 'his distinguished birth and quality', the council agreed to grant him the rank of colonel, made his son Manuel an infantry captain, and reimbursed them both for the cost of their long voyage. Domingo furthermore received an annual stipend of 18,000 reales, and Manuel was admitted to the Madrid Nobles Seminary, with the royal treasury picking up the cost.

When these favours were granted, the council specified that, 'for reasons of politics and prudence', neither of the two men should return to the Indies. This provision reflected the policy devised by the extraordinary council of March of that year, that is, to train the Peruvian nobility in Madrid for the royal service. The importance of coming to court in Madrid to solicit favours can be seen clearly with other examples. In 1794, Bartolomé de Mesa Túpac Yupanqui requested the royal favour of being promoted to army lieutenant colonel. His petition, like Domingo's, was based on his lineage. In his case he was related to Tito Atanchi, who had collaborated with Pizarro, and to the *conquistador* Alonso Mesa. He also mentioned his own merits, saying he had been chosen as 'commissioner of the Indian nation' to celebrate Charles IV's ascension to the throne. He also presented a document written by the viceroy, the duke of Peralta, in 1687 confirming his family's origins.

Such merits were, however, seen differently from the colonial perspective. The general under-inspector of the militia, Gabriel de Avilés, reported that 'among the well-known descendants of the old Incas there are many *caciques* in the City of Cuzco who have confirmed their loyalty in past revolutions, taking up arms against the rebels, and throughout the kingdom there are many others who, judging from our information, could similarly descend from such lineages'. Avilés knew what he was talking about, because he had personally participated

Figure 3.1 Dionisio Inca was never painted during his lifetime. This painting is a later, idealized portrait of Dionisio. Courtesy of Bar Association of Lima, Peru.

in putting down the revolutionary movement in Cuzco led by José Gabriel Condorcanqui, known as Túpac Amaru. He therefore knew how tricky a matter such as handing out honours among noble aspirants could be and that they would have to be closely watched from then on.[13]

In other words, there was a multiplication of direct descendants of noble Inca families in Peru as well as growth in the imperial family itself, making it necessary 'to give the same distinction to all the Indians who proved such nobility (an infinite number) or otherwise leave them all unhappy because of having satisfied the request by [Bartolomé] Mesa'.[14] Obtention of nobility, distinctions, favours and honours from the Crown can be documented from early on, adding to the accumulation of genealogical papers circulating widely throughout the Andes. They constituted the documentary basis of an Indian identity whose most outstanding feature was not localism but rather globalism.[15]

In the imperial court, however, as efforts were being made to impose a policy of nationalization of the American elites, the petition by Domingo Ucho fared better. But the larger constellation would have an impact in constructing the name and identity of the man who later on would become a deputy in the Cortes of Cadiz in 1810.

The strategy of a name

It is true that the father of the future deputy in the Cortes of Cadiz was skilful in handling all the papers and evidence in the briefcase he had brought with him from Peru. First, he was clever about the name he used, always referring to himself with surnames linking him to the Inca nobility (Ucho Inca Yupanqui), omitting Ampuero until he judged it expedient to use the surname of a Spanish *conquistador*.

In this respect it is of interest to compare the various birth certificates of Dionisio that we know of. One is in the episcopal archive in Lima; it reads that Dionisio was the son of 'Don Domingo Ampuero and Doña Isabel Bernal [illegible].'[16] So the child would have been named Dionisio Ampuero y Bernal, hardly an Inca name. Years later, a certified copy in Madrid, filed so that Dionisio could enter the navy guard in 1774, revealed that the father's name had been entirely changed. Here the priest certified: 'I exorcized and anointed with holy oil and chrism Deonicio [sic], who was born on 9 October of this same year [1760], legitimate son of Don Domingo Ucho Inca and Doña Isabel Bernal.'[17] We need to remember, as Samuel Villegas points out, that San Lázaro, where the baptism took place, was a marginal parish on the other side of the Rimac River traditionally linked to the leprosy hospital and to services for Spaniards and mulattos. The certified copy in Madrid specifically says that the event had been registered in the volume 'where certificates of baptism of Spaniards are performed in this Parish'.

Though we do not know the necessary details of this matter, it is very likely that Domingo was keen to use his Spanish surname in Lima when he baptized his son in the Spanish parish, while in Madrid, where he wanted to stress his noble Inca heritage, he used his Indian surnames. So in America he would Hispanize his family, and in Spain he 'Indianized' it. These strategies worked better in a culture of names that retained features typical of the colonial world such as the parallel use of masculine and feminine surnames or, less frequently and strictly controlled, variations in names over time.[18]

His children used neither their maternal surname, Bernal, nor the paternal Ampuero. Rather, they gradually slipped into the names they considered more appropriate to the Peruvian nobility. They began regularly using the first paternal surname, Ucho, which they later eliminated in favour of the other surnames that were more easily linked to their Inca past, especially to European ears. Thus, both Dionisio and Manuel Ucho Inca ended up with the surnames of Inca Yupanqui (with written variations: Inga, Yupangui and Pangui).[19]

Second, Domingo used his own genealogy in a very clever manner. As his petitions were floating from one royal office to the next in search of favours, a secretary noted that the petition was pending 'because I saw a note from someone involved who denies this Inca's qualifications'.[20] No further mention of this problem appears in the file, but it may well be that there was something to it. In the information that Domingo successfully presented to the Council in 1768 he said he was the grandson of Don Juan Ucho Quipe Topac, the *mitma* of Lambayeque, who had initiated the family's connection to Inca nobility by obtaining that recognition in 1655 from the viceroy, the marquis of Sonora. He had two children, Juan de la Rosa and Casilda Uchu Inca, who in 1701 received from Viceroy Monclova the *encomienda de indios* of Jaén de Bracamoros that Domingo refers to in his petition, saying it had been awarded to 'Casilda de la Rosa Ucho Inca, Domingo's aunt'.[21] In fact, it had been granted to her brother, Juan de la Rosa, who gave it to Casilda.[22]

If what Domingo said was true, he must have been the son of Juan de la Rosa, though in the documents I have examined he never refers to his father. We do know, however, that Juan de la Rosa had a daughter (*doncella*) and a son, Miguel Uchu Inca. It is remarkable that Domingo never mentions either Juan de la Rosa (allegedly his father) or Miguel (his brother), particularly given that Miguel in 1718 was sent to Spain to litigate his nobility before the imperial court. On 10 March of that year, the tribunal (*audiencia*) of Lima had examined the request by Juan de la Rosa for nobility for his son, Miguel, who immediately left for Spain to handle the case.[23] However, he never arrived; he got as far as New Spain, where he married María Teresa Dávila Gavidia. His daughter, Joaquina María Uchu Inca, would be the one to reinitiate the legal proceedings for nobility in 1787.[24]

The case files of both Domingo and Joaquina María should be examined together, as they both have Juan de la Rosa Ucho Inca as their connection to the family line going back to the leading Inca nobility. Looking at them simultaneously, we can see certain contradictions in Dionisio Inca's father's genealogical argument. Joaquina María's file says that Juan de la Rosa Ucho was born in 1668 and that Miguel, his son and Joaquina María's father, was born in 1697. These dates make it rather unlikely that Miguel and Domingo, who were brothers, never met.

It is also interesting to compare the two cases, one litigated by Domingo at court, the other by Joaquina María in Mexico. Given that Joaquina María should be Domingo's niece and Dionisio and Manuel's cousin, it is quite odd that there is no cross-referencing between the two applicants. Second, Joaquina María's genealogy included her father, Miguel, and her grandfather, Juan de la Rosa Ucho Quispe Tupa, whereas that of Domingo skipped the prior generation, naming only 'Casilda de la Rosa' as an aunt. Third, while Domingo quickly won recognition as a 'descendant of the emperors of Peru', Joaquina María, who had the clearer genealogy, received only some payments and financial awards for her younger brother and her children. She herself was not recognized as a member of the nobility.

The strategy of time

One of the tactics Domingo Ucho used at the imperial court in Madrid was very appropriate for the era: he submitted his requests one by one, over time. His first petition, in January 1768, in which he requested recognition as a descendant of the Inca imperial family and therefore a member of the 'American nobility', brought with it, as we have seen, the rank of colonel and a pension of 18,000 *reales* which, though not huge, allowed him to live well with his family in Madrid or in Denia, where he was stationed.[25] These allowances prompted him to try to improve his standing, referring to his 'necessary' trip to Spain upon the orders of the viceroy. His life in Peru had known 'no scarcity', he said, as he combined his military salary with what 'the Indians spontaneously gave him because they recognized he had ancient Inca blood'.[26]

Right from the start he focused his petitions on bettering his position, and he managed to find a post for his elder son, Manuel. In fact, the other son, Dionisio, literally disappeared. When Domingo arrived in Madrid, his first request to the Council stated that he had come with two children who, 'despite their young age, were already serving as cadets'. The minimum age for becoming a cadet in America if one was the son of an officer or of noble origin was ten years old, though it was more common for the boys to be between twelve and sixteen.[27] In that case, Dionisio was too young to have enrolled as a cadet in

Lima when Domingo began his trip to Spain, as he would have been just seven. In the subsequent requests in the years immediately following that, Dionisio disappears, and Domingo speaks only of Manuel.

He obtained a scholarship for Manuel from the king at the Royal Noble Seminary in Madrid and the boy was accepted into the royal infantry guards as a cadet. Manuel also received a pension and financial aid until he was promoted to be an officer, and later he got a salary. He studied at the prestigious seminary from 1767 to 1773.[28]

Given his success before the Council, Domingo continued along the same route. At this point, just before the 1780 Andean revolution, the stereotypical image of the Inca was at its height, both in Spain and in the rest of Europe.[29] Basing his requests on his proven Inca ancestry, in 1772 Domingo went so far as to request the marquisate of Oropesa, which had been vacant since 1741.

This was the same marquisate that, as we saw earlier, Juan de Bustamante Carlos Inca had requested; he was followed by Diego Felipe de Betancur, of Cuzco, and, starting in 1776, the revolutionary leader José Gabriel Tupac Amaru was also in competition. Domingo knew that the king had not given Bustamante the marquisate (the Council of Indies was consistently opposed), but Bustamante had received appointment as courtier to the king's table and a generous pension.[30]

This was the example used by Domingo, who insisted that the Crown's decision to reincorporate the marquisate had not taken account of his bloodline, 'which originated in the lords of Peru'. Until his arrival in Spain in 1767, the only member of his line who had made the same voyage was the first titleholder, Ana María de Loyola Coya. Yet he, who descended from the male line, was in a better position than Juan de Bustamante, who descended from the female line, a decisive distinction in a 'hereditary empire' such as Peru.[31]

Domingo most probably did not have the same goals as Betancur or Tupac Amaru when he requested the marquisate. Later on, he said he did not insist because he lacked the resources; indeed, the judicial road was enormously expensive, as both Betancur and the future revolutionary leader knew. Tupac Amaru wished to be recognized as a direct descendant of the Peruvian emperors, the 'last Inca', at a time of great unrest owing to colonial reforms initiated by Madrid and implemented by the *visitador* José Antonio de Areche. Domingo, meanwhile, sought recognition in a metropolitan setting in which recognition as Inca (which he won) was similar to that of *hidalguía*, a low-profile sort of nobility that fell short of a marquisate (and certainly fell short of the Oropesa title).[32]

But his insistence on the marquisate worked to get his older son admitted into the royal guards and to continue studying at the noble seminary. It was only when Manuel's military career and studies were well under way that Dionisio reappeared in Domingo Ucho's petitions. In 1774 for the first time he mentioned that one of his children had died shortly after arriving in Europe and that he thereupon decided to seek Dionisio's entry into the navy guards, considering 'the relevant circumstances of his birth, trusting that Your Royal justification would not fail to attend to [Domingo's children] with equal generosity'.

It is noteworthy that Domingo mentions no names other than Manuel and Dionisio, even in this same petition, where he remarks that in September 1768 (with nearly no time to send word to Peru of the death of his mysterious second son and supposedly prepare in a hurry Dionisio's voyage), 'the King granted to the petitioner and his sons, Don Manuel and Don Dionisio, cadets in the infantry regiment in the presidio of El Callao, the favour of membership in one of the military orders'.[33]

Regardless of whether or not this was a strategy, it allowed Domingo to establish a military career for his second son as well. It is unclear if Dionisio followed Manuel into the seminary.[34] When both brothers in 1784 requested more favours from the Crown, they mentioned only Manuel's presence at the seminary. However the archive at the Naval Museum has a file mentioning his entrance into the navy guards, 'considering he is a descendant of the royal branch of the Inca emperors', which would make him exempt from having to prove his nobility, given that it had already been 'recognized and approved by the Council of Indies'. He was sixteen years old at that point.[35]

Domingo died in 1782 (we do not know the date). In 1784 his pension was divided between the two sons: the elder son obtained 12,000 reales and Dionisio received 6,000. By then Manuel was a second lieutenant (*alferez*) and Dionisio was a frigate lieutenant. From January to August 1784 the two brothers, by now with the surname Ucho Inca Yupanqui, petitioned to be promoted to the rank of colonel, granted funds to pay off their father's debts and be awarded *encomiendas* 'to compensate for the high honour of presenting ourselves to Your Majesty and the royal throne from which we descend'.[36]

Both the financial and prosecutorial reports confirmed the assumptions regarding the Ucho Inca brothers' royal lineage. The financial official (*contador general*) Pedro Gallarreta referred to the fact that 'in their country' the brothers surely would have received what they had to beg for in Spain and, like the prosecutor, he favoured granting Manuel and Dionisio's requests. As a result, the brothers received two lifetime pensions and promotions in the military.

Evidence resulting from Manuel's court martial much later on, from 1809 to 1813, reveals that it was very likely that in 1784 he left the army and began an administrative career that would lead to his appointment as army and provincial intendant.[37] Dionisio, meanwhile, in 1787 switched military branches and became a lieutenant colonel of the Villaviciosa regiment, having failed in his request to join the Corps guard. A note in the file indicates there was no evidence of his having gone from the Navy to the Army.[38]

When Dionisio was elected as an alternate deputy from Peru to the Cortes of Cadiz he was fifty years old. The electoral minutes state that he was 'Dionisio Incayupangui lieutenant colonel *disperso* of the infantry'.[39] This means that he had held the same rank since 1787 and was on leave or retired, a common situation for those who were disabled.[40] Dionisio Inca referred to this retirement in 1819 and in 1824 when he asked that corrections be made in his pay in accordance with the Junta Central's decree of January 1810 establishing an extraordinary war contribution. According to this, along with what Joaquín Lorenzo Villanueva wrote in his diary, Dionisio was retired and earning a pension already before his election as deputy.[41]

The Inca in the Cortes

When Dionisio entered the Cortes of Cadiz as a deputy, he did so as Dionisio Incayupangui in the minutes and as Dionisio Inca Ypangui (or Yupanqui) in the Cortes registry. Both he and his brother had consolidated their surnames like this and, as we shall see, it provided the deputy with plenty of opportunities.

He was elected using a procedure to substitute for representatives who did not have sufficient time to be elected and then travel from America. These substitution elections consisted of a meeting of (in this case Peruvian) locals, who sometimes were grouped according to their towns of origin, chaired by a high-level magistrate. Their task was to choose electors to pick deputies, generally among themselves. A public announcement was made calling upon Americans residing in areas controlled by the French to present themselves. Orders were also sent to the authorities in these places to draw up lists to the same end, with differing results.

José Pablo Valiente, a magistrate of the Council of Indies, was put in charge of culling those lists according to jobs, class or race. The upshot was that 177 Americans were chosen to be electors; they, in turn, appointed the substitute deputies.[42] Dionisio was elected by a thirty-two-member electoral body of whom seven were chosen as electors, who in turn chose five Peruvian substitutes from among themselves.[43] Valiente, himself a deputy from Seville, was not at all enthusiastic about changes in the usual conceptualization of American races and social roles, which he made quite clear in his speeches to the Cortes. It can therefore be assumed that if Dionisio managed to be on all the lists it was because Valiente, who had first-hand knowledge of the American ethnic reality, correctly interpreted the manufactured identity of the deputy from Lima.[44] With all the privileges of his bloodline, the Inca at long last entered the heart of the Catholic monarchy's government through the Cortes. It made no difference if the alleged parentage was something invented over the course of two generations. The fact was that the son of Domingo Ampuero and Isabel Bernal could present himself in the General and Extraordinary Cortes of the Spanish Nation as an Inca, an Indian and an American. What Domingo had sought when he first travelled in 1768 from Lima to Madrid would be found by his son amid an unprecedented crisis of the Spanish monarchy.

When Dionisio addressed the Cortes in December 1810 with the aim of reviving America's goal of equal recognition with Europeans he did so as an Inca, an Indian and an American, and of these three identities he cultivated the first far above the rest. Following his father's tactics, Dionisio not only used the Inca identity to bolster and authorize his arguments but also to help him continue requesting favours. Having consolidated his surnames, with 'Inca' before the others, and having displayed his rhetoric to the Cortes, it was not difficult for him to convince his parliamentary colleagues that before them stood a direct descendant of the imperial house of Cuzco. Thus, in June 1811 he asked that the Cortes order the state treasury to continue granting him and his brother Manuel 'a pension given to them as compensation for the conquest of Peru'.[45]

Not long before that Manuel had had to call upon a complex series of identities to get out of a very complicated situation. In 1809 he was military intendant in Alto Aragón when the fortress at Jaca fell to the French, leading to his court martial. A decision handed down in April 1813 by the court indicates that this was a manoeuvre to blame someone else for the military missteps of Lt. Salvador Campos, who was temporarily replacing the ill governor.

Manuel Inca's best defence came from his wife, Ramona Irarzabal, who offered documentary proof that Manuel had turned down Napoleon's offers to join the French cause. This was one of the principal accusations against Dionisio's brother, who was thought likely to join with the invader; he posed a danger 'because he is a descendant of the Incas of Peru and might be sent to

America to revolutionize those countries'. Indeed, the viceroys were warned in advance of his possible arrival and ordered to intercept him.[46]

In her argument, Ramona refuted this accusation by once again taking advantage of her husband's complex identity: 'As my husband is fully justified, the only remaining charge is that of his birth, to which only Divine Providence can respond ... His origin was his crime, and that has expatriated him forever from Peru ... The government owed Inca the opportunity to cultivate his talent, and I challenge anyone to say that throughout his life he has ever been lacking in obedience to his monarchs'.[47] When the court in 1813 reviewed the case it accepted Ramona's arguments and concluded that, contrary to the crimes alleged, for which he had been sentenced to eight years' imprisonment in a castle, Inca had rejected 'the suggestions and appeals that the French might have made because of his last name and his relationship to the Incas of Peru, who could have so much influence in that part of America'.[48]

The Inca identity developed by the two brothers, starting with their manner of consolidating their names, was clearly proving beneficial. Dionisio was hardly a prolific or brilliant orator in the Cortes yet he is most definitely one of the best known and most frequently cited members of that Cortes, to the point that there is a street in Madrid named after him. There can be little doubt that had he stood before the sessions as Dionisio Ampuero y Bernal he would be forgotten. Historians have shown that he was revered and idealized in Peru, but it is also true that he became an idealized creation and that that is what lent value to his time as deputy in the imperial parliament of Cadiz.[49]

He was a member of parliamentary commissions on military affairs, probably because of his past service, though he had already retired.[50] The index of Cortes records (*Diario de Sesiones*) registers only seven occasions on which he spoke. We can learn a bit more from Joaquín Lorenzo Villanueva's diary and from Fernando Martínez's detailed study of everything related to the constitutional debates.[51] But the truth is that his presence in the Spanish Cortes was truly minuscule, despite being referred to so often on account of his ethnicity.

His fame was the result of the identity that was created starting with Domingo's journey from Lima precisely in order to gain recognition of that identity. Dionisio continued cultivating it, in the perfect setting, the imperial parliament of Cadiz. One common feature of all Inca Yupanqui's appearances in the Cortes was his eagerness to point to his ethnic identity and proclaim it as a virtue and also as something that authorized him to get involved in matters having to do with America, specifically with indigenous affairs.

He was one of the signatories of a proposal by the American deputies on 25 September 1810, the day after the session opened. The goal was to compensate for the elections' failure to concede sufficient importance to the January 1809 decree declaring the American dominions to be an essential and integral part of the monarchy. The debate, which has been thoroughly studied by historians, continued up through the writing of the Constitution, always focused on the meaning of equality for Americans and their representation in the Cortes.[52]

Inca, precisely in order to force the debate, presented a proposal on 16 December 1810 that Agustín de Argüelles, always vigilant when it came to the equality of the Americans, tried to halt. In his proposal, Inca – who had lived in Spain ever since he was a child – said the Cortes did not know America. 'Your Majesty [i.e. the Cortes in the monarch's absence] does not know [the Indies]. Most of the Deputies and the Nation have heard hardly anything of this vast continent.' Though one of the other American deputies remarked discreetly that this was precisely Dionisio's case, the latter managed to generally enjoy some sort of authority because of his identity. Using a didactic tone, he asked that viceroys be ordered to protect the Indians 'and ensure that they are neither bothered nor made to suffer in their persons or properties, nor hurt in any way concerning their personal freedom, privileges, etc.'.[53] Here one must remember that Dionisio's father had said he held an *encomienda* on which all the Indians had died, and that Dionisio himself and his brother in 1784 had asked the king for *encomiendas* allowing them to live according to their rank.

There were two basic arguments underlying the debate about Americans' equality in Spanish national representation. First, the Americans argued that equality could be found in the will of the Cortes itself, as the 15 October 1810 decree had proclaimed that 'Spanish dominions in both hemispheres form one and the same monarchy, one and the same nation and just one family', and that therefore there would be only one constitutional identity: that of Spaniards with identical rights.[54] The 'way to save the Americas' from imminent rupture with the metropolis, according to José Miguel Guridi, the deputy from Tlaxcala, was to immediately implement this equality of rights, starting with representation.

Several liberal Spanish deputies were opposed to the American initiative. They did not show their opposition directly or categorically but rather sought to move the question to the debate over the Constitution itself, where they could ensure that the discourse on equality was much more nuanced. The strongest stance in this regard was taken by Argüelles, one of the Constitution's chief authors, who had no hesitation in stating why European liberals were absolutely opposed to a decree providing equal representation: 'In that hemisphere, the population is larger than that of the mother country and it is difficult to classify.'[55]

Ethnic complexity, therefore, was the principal reason preventing European liberals from implementing the equality that had been proclaimed several times since January 1809. Their problem was not with the Spanish Americans who stood before them in the Congress of Cadiz in representation of the Americans but rather with the societies to which these representatives belonged. The complexity of these societies prevented them from accepting an argument put forth by Deputy Ramón Olaguer Feliú (a Peruvian born in Ceuta), drawing on the decree of October 1810, which suggested that equal representation for Americans could open the way to demands for emancipation. 'No one can be emancipated by an equal, only by someone under whose power he lies', he said, echoing the ideas published in José María Blanco-White's newspaper, *El Español*, published in London; despite what peninsular liberals believed, equality prevented rather than encouraged emancipation.[56] In the opinion of the American deputies, the emancipation movements in Caracas and Buenos Aires existed precisely because the Cortes were insisting upon preserving inequality, a situation that was closer to guardianship than to fraternity; that is, the subjection of a nation that previously had a paternal relationship to the king, rather than a new relationship between free and equal brothers.

The American deputies could see that the Cortes were encouraging the distance between rhetoric and political practice when it came to equality. José María Mejía Lequerica, a substitute deputy for Quito, saw perfectly that the Cortes were following the same tactics as other authorities in the past: 'No Sire, you will not decide. The cries from America are ignored or hindered. The provincial *juntas* referred them to the Junta Central, the Junta Central referred them to the regency, the regency came to Your Majesty, and Your Majesty will refer them to the Constitution.'[57]

Inca's defence of pre-Hispanic civilizations during this debate was aimed at arguing that it was impossible to continue with these delays. From the viewpoint of America, he said in the Cortes, after the October 15 decree anything short of immediate equal representation would appear as a continuation of the traditional politics of compassionate rhetoric and profoundly imperial practice: 'You are sadly mistaken if you believe Indians lack the ability and Americans the wisdom to carefully analyze the decree.'[58] By then, in fact, there were many manifestos circulating throughout America insisting on a literal reading of the various provisions that since January 1809 had proclaimed equality.

While Dionisio wished to be seen as an Inca in the Cortes, there was another member of the assembly who quite correctly pointed out that he was the only one there actually elected by an Indian province. This was José Miguel Guridi Alcocer, who represented Tlaxcala, in New Spain. The province, because of a special right it had been granted by the monarchy, had managed to obtain its own representation and send a deputy to the imperial Cortes in Cadiz.[59] Guridi developed an argument concerning indigenous anthropology more intelligently than Inca had as he recited the virtues of pre-Hispanic civilizations. According to Guridi, the question lay not in anthropological aspects such as language, customs or attire. If that were the case, he said, then the people of Biscay should not be admitted either, as most of them did not speak Castilian Spanish, nor should the Galicians, who dressed as peasants. Besides, he went on, some Indians dressed in Spanish clothing, spoke Castilian and had good manners. Equality was a matter to be resolved by law, regardless of the anthropological complexity of different societies. And, finally, Americans argued that equality consisted as well in a recognition of American elites' ability to govern their societies.[60]

On 7 February 1811 the Cortes voted in favour of equal representation for American and European Spaniards, at the same time voting against the immediate implementation of such equality.[61] So, as Mejía had predicted, they delayed, and the tactic only widened the gap between rhetoric and political practice, which would end up making the bi-hemispheric nation unviable. Inca, a *mestizo* with a doubtful identity, was a witness to these events, which themselves reflected the Spanish monarchy's complicated ethnic and political history.

Notes

1   Alcira Dueñas, *Indians and Mestizos in the 'Lettered City': Reshaping Justice, Social Hierarchy and Political Culture in Colonial Peru* (Boulder: University Press of Colorado, 2010), ch. 3.

2   Ari Zighelboim, 'Un Inca cuzqueño en la corte de Fernando VI: Estrategias personales y colectivas de las élites indias y mestizas hacia 1750', *Histórica*, 34, no.2 (2010): 7–62.

3   For the council's resolutions see Luis Navarro, 'El Consejo de Castilla y su crítica de la política indiana en 1768', in *Homenaje al Profesor Alfonso García Gallo* (Madrid: Universidad Computense, 1996), vol. 3, 187ff. Navarro points out that Campomanes's presence here was far greater than that of the man who would eventually remove him, the count of Floridablanca.

4   Francisco Antonio Lorenzana, *Cartas pastorales y edictos* (Mexico City: José Antonio de Horgal, 1770), 29.

5   On this very important series of developments, see the essential study by Gabriel Torres Puga, *Opinión pública y censura en Nueva España. Indicios de un silencio imposible, 1767–1794* (Mexico City: El Colegio de México, 2010), ch. 1. For an

excellent analysis of Lorenzana's ecclesiology, see Andoni Artola, *De Madrid a Roma. La fidelidad del episcopado en España (1760–1833)* (Gijón: Tea, 2013), ch. 5.

6   Cited in Luis Navarro, 'El Consejo', 204.

7   Ibid., 206. The same expression would be used somewhat later in a report by Francisco Saavedra, who in 1808 was charged with publicizing the Junta Central's decree officially declaring the American provinces to be an essential part of the monarchy: Francisco Morales Padrón, *Diario de Don Francisco de Saavedra* (Seville: Universidad de Sevilla-CSIC, 2004), 292.

8   For the development of this Creole discourse, see Carlos Garriga, 'La politización de la *América criolla (en torno a la Representación* mexicana de 1771)', in Pedro Yanzi Ferreira (ed.), *XVIII Congreso del Instituto Internacional de Historia del Derecho Indiano* (Córdoba: Universidad de Córdoba, 2016), 1423–53.

9   Domingo Ucho Inca's requests and file: Archivo General de Simancas [AGS] SGU 7092/57.

10   Archivo Histórico Nacional [AHN] Consejos 20161/51, 8–9. The letters are dated August and December 1751.

11   On the family politics that led to the development of this new nobility, see Jane E. Mangan, *Transatlantic Obligations: Creating the Bonds of Family in Conquest-Era Peru and Spain* (Oxford: Oxford University Press, 2016), ch. 1. In fact, Martín de Ampuero was the son of Inés Huayllas and a captain from La Rioja, Francisco de Ampuero. In the above-mentioned documents, however, the relationship is as I describe here.

12   Examples include Domingo Francisco Chimalpahin and Diego Muñoz Camargo, in Mexico, and the influential Inca Garcilaso in Pero; see José Antonio Mazzotti, 'Mestizo Dreams: Transculturation and Heterogeneity in Inca Garcilaso', in Robert Blair St. George (ed.), *Possible Pasts: Becoming Colonial in Early America* (Ithaca: Cornell University Press, 2000), 131–47.

13   Charles Walker, *The Tupac Amaru Rebellion* (Cambridge, MA: Harvard University Press, 2014).

14   AGS SGU 7104/27. The Mesa case, it turned out, involved a sales clerk who had pretended to be a merchant, making it difficult to bestow honours and distinctions upon 'a tired man standing behind a counter, taking down merchandise and displaying it according to the wishes of whichever Negro, Zambo, or Mulatto was there to buy from him'.

15   José Carlos de la Puente Luna, *Andean Cosmopolitans: Seeking Justice and Reward at the Spanish Royal Court* (Austin: University of Texas Press, 2018).

16   This document appears in Samuel Villegas, '¿Indio o criollo? Identidad étnica del diputado Dionisio Inca Yupanqui en las Cortes de Cádiz', *Nueva crónica*, 1 (2013): 1–10. The mother's second surname, which is illegible here, was Cañas, according to the information about the older brother, Manuel: Archivo del Museo Naval [AMN] 1517/32.

17 AMN 1517/32.

18 Ximena Medinaceli, *¿Nombres o apellidos? El sistema nominativo ayamara. Sacaca, siglo XVII* (La Paz: IEFA, 2003), 2nd part. Historians have published several cases showing the strategic use of names; for the well-known case of Felipe Guaman Poma (or Lázaro) see Rolena Adorno, 'Felipe Guaman Poma de Ayala: Native Writer and Litigant in Early Colonial Peru', in Kenneth J. Adrian (ed.), *The Human Tradition in Colonial Latin America* (Wilmington: SR Books, 2002), 140–163.

19 Dionisio is referred to as Ucho Bernal only on the occasion of his appointment to the navy guard in 1776; AMN 1517/32.

20 AGS SGU 7092/57; 20 March 1774.

21 AGS SGU 7092/57; 22 February 1768.

22 Laura Escobari, *Caciques, yanaconas y extravagantes: La sociedad colonial en Charcas, siglos XVI–XVIII* (Lima: IDEA, 2005), ch. 4.

23 Rubén Vargas, *Manuscritos peruanos del Archivo de Indias* (Lima: Universidad Católica del Perú, 1938), 366.

24 On this suit, see Rocío Quispe-Agnoli, 'Identidades fluidas: negociaciones de una mujer de la nobleza inca en los confines del imperio', in Catherine Poupeny et al. (eds.), *El Perú en su historia. Fracturas y persistencias* (Paris: Éditions le Manuscrit, 2016), 331–362.

25 The amount was around triple that of a guild artisan's salary: Earl J. Hamilton, *Guerra y precios en España, 1651–1800* (Madrid: Alianza, 1988), appendix.

26 AGS SGU 7092/57, 23 May 1768.

27 María de los Reyes Brisquet and Encarnación Fuentes, 'Las academias de artillería en América en el siglo XVIII', *Militaria. Revista de Cultura Militar*, 10 (1997): 265–77.

28 Scarlett O'Phelan, 'Linaje e Ilustración. Don Manuel Uchu Inca y el Real Seminario de Nobles de Madrid (1725–1808)', in Javier Flores and Rafael Varón (eds.), *El hombre y los Andes. Homenaje a Franklin Pease G.Y.* (Lima: IEFA, 2002), vol. 2, 316–30.

29 Fernanda Macchi, *Incas ilustrados. Reconstrucciones imperiales en la segunda mitad del siglo XVIII* (Madrid: Iberoamericana, 2009).

30 David Cahill, 'Becoming an Inca: Juan de Bustamante Carlos Inca and the Roots of the Gran Rebelion', *Colonial Latin American Review*, 22 (2013): 259–80; David Cahill, '*Primus inter pares*. La búsqueda del marquesado de Oropesa camino de la Gran Rebelión (1741–1780)', *Revista Andina*, 37 (2003): 9–51. An earlier study of the suit can be found in John H. Rowe, 'Genealogía y rebelión en el siglo XVIII: algunos antecedentes de la rebelión de José Gabriel Thupa Amaro', *Historica*, 6, no. 1 (1982): 65–85.

31 AGS SGU 7092/57, 20 August 1772.

32 On the importance of Tupac Amaru's suit in Lima, see Charles F. Walker, *Smoldering ashes: Cuzco and the transition from colony to Republic, 1780–1840* (Durham, NC: Duke University Press, 1999); and, by the same author, *The Tupac Amaru Rebellion.*

33 AGS SGU 7092/57. As remarked upon earlier, this narrative is implausible because it would signify that Dionisio had become a cadet when he was five or six years old. According to his birth certificate, a copy of which appears in his application to the navy guards, he was born on 9 October 1760. Domingo Ucho's trip must have commenced around his seventh birthday.

34 O'Phelan, 'Linaje e Ilustración. Don Manuel Uchu Inca y el Real Seminario de Nobles de Madrid (1725–1808)', says she found no documentation concerning Dionisio at the Archivo Histórico Nacional.

35 AMN 1517/32.

36 This file (AGI Lima, 906) was partially published by Daniel Valcárcel in 'Documentos sobre Manuel y Dionisio Inca Yupanqui', *Revista Universitaria*, 117 (1959): 73.

37 The prosecutor in the case said Manuel Inca's release 'would be very inadvisable because Inca, who is a descendant of the Peruvians, had always been suspicious of the previous Government and was a crafty, ambitious and arrogant sort': Archivo General Military (Segovia) (AGM Segovia), sec. 9, 5645.

38 AGS SGU 7092/57, 30 May 1787. The year before that, Dionisio had requested a transfer to the Corps guard.

39 Archivo del Congreso de los Diputados [ACD] 22/3 Lima.

40 '*Disperso*' referred to officers who 'after having served a certain number of years were granted leave or retirement'. They were separated from their unit and told where they could live, though they could opt not to live there for reasons of health and choose someplace else; José Fernández Mancheño, *Diccionario militar portátil* … (Madrid: Miguel de Burgos, 1822), entry for 'disperso'; Federico Moretti, *Diccionario militar español-francés* (Madrid: Imprenta Real, 1828), entry for 'inválido'.

41 AGM 1st sec. I-365; Joaquín Lorenzo Villanueva, *Mi viaje a las Cortes*, ed. Germán Ramírez Aledón (Valencia: Diputación de Valencia, 1998 [1860]), 237.

42 This procedure is described in detail in Marie-Laure Rieu-Millán, 'La suppléance de députes d'outre mer aux Cortes de Cadiz; una laborieuse préparation', *Mélanges de la Casa de Velázquez*, 17 (1981): 263–81 with a graphic on 281 showing the socio-professional background of those who participated in the elections.

43 See ACD 22/3; also in the Spanish Congress webpage, www.congreso.es/web/ guest/historico-diputados?p_p_id=historicodiputados&p_p_lifecycle=0&p_p_ state=normal&p_p_mode=view&_historicodiputados_mvcRenderComman dName=mostrarDetalle&_historicodiputados_texto=&_historicodiputados_

nombre=Dionisio%20Inca&_historicodiputados_genero=&_historicodiputados_
tituloNobiliario=&_historicodiputados_eleccionesDesde=&_historicodiputados_
eleccionesHasta=&_historicodiputados_division=&_historicodiputados_
circDistrito=&_historicodiputados_circunscripcion=&_historicodiputados_
distrito=&_historicodiputados_assu=&_historicodiputados_fraccion=&_
historicodiputados_fechaAltaDesde=&_historicodiputados_fechaAltaHasta=&_
historicodiputados_fechaBajaDesde=&_historicodiputados_fechaBajaHasta=&_
historicodiputados_orden=0&_historicodiputados_nume=1330 (accessed 4
February 2021).

44　For a royal official like Valiente, Dionisio accomplished the ideal of the American
noble by bringing together nobility and education. See Marissa Bazán, *La
participación política de los indígenas durante las Cortes de Cádiz: Lima en el ocaso
del régimen español (1808–1814)* (Lima: Universidad Nacional Mayor de San
Marcos, 2013), ch. 3.

45　Joaquín Lorenzo Villanueva, *Mi viaje a las Cortes*, 237, 7 June 1811.

46　AHN Estado 45A; on this case, see Marie-Laure Rieu-Millan, 'A propos de la
trahison de l'Inca Yupanqui, comissaire de guerre de la place de Jaca', *Caravelle:
Cahiers du Monde Hispanique et Luso-Brésilien*, 33 (1979): 49–75.

47　AGM sec. 9, 5645.

48　Ibid.

49　Scarlett O'Phelan has written in various places about Dionisio's knowledge of the
American reality; see 'Los diputados suplentes Dionisio Uchu Inca Yupanqui y
Vicente Morales Duárez; su visión del Perú', in Scarlett O'Phelan and Georges
Lomné (eds.), *Voces americanas en las Cortes de Cádiz: 1810–1814* (Lima: IFEA,
2014), 83–102.

50　Marta Ruiz Jiménez, *La Comisión de Guerra en las Cortes de Cádiz (1810–1813):
Repertorio documental* (Madrid: CSIC-Doce Calles, 2008).

51　Joaquín Lorenzo Villanueva, *Mi viaje a las Cortes*; Fernando Martínez Pérez,
Constitución en Cortes. El debate constituyente, 1811–1812 (Madrid: UAM, 2011).

52　Manuel Chust, *La cuestión americana en las Cortes de Cádiz* (Valencia: Centro
Francisco Tomás y Valiente, 1999).

53　*Diario de Sesiones* [DS] 91, 16 December 1811.

54　*Colección de los decretos y órdenes que han expedido las Cortes Generales y
Extraordinarias desde su instalación el 24 de septiembre de 1810 hasta igual
fecha de 1811* (Cádiz: Imprenta Real, 1811), 10. For a facsimile copy, see www.
cervantesvirtual.com/portales/constitucion_1812/obra-visor/coleccion-de-los-
decretos-y-ordenes-que-han-expedido-las-cortes-generales-y-extraordinarias-
desde-su-instalacion-en-24-de-septiembre-de-1810-hasta-igual-fecha-de-1811--0/
html/0027b5e4-82b2-11df-acc7-002185ce6064_28.html (accessed June 2019).

55　DS 105, 9 January 1811.

56 DS 107, 11 January 1811.

57 DS 114, 18 January 1811.

58 Ibid.

59 On Tlaxcala, see José M. Portillo, *Fuero Indio. La provincia india de Tlaxcala entre la monarquía imperial y la república nacional, 1787–1824* (Mexico City: El Colegio de México-Instituto Mora, 2014).

60 DS 121, 25 January 1811.

61 DS 134, 7 February 1811.

4

Pedro José de Ibarra: A mulatto senator in Colombia's Antioquia

Daniel Gutiérrez Ardila

In 1812 Pedro José de Ibarra, a mulatto, was chosen to be a member of the Senate of Antioquia, one of the little republics that emerged out of the territory of the viceroyalty of the New Kingdom of Granada after the crisis of the Spanish monarchy. This was a singular honour not only because the high chamber had five seats (in the lower chamber there were ten) but also because the rest of the deputies formed a homogeneous sociological group: they were the sons of old families with roots in the municipal governments of the province's four cities, understood to be white and frequently interrelated amongst themselves. So who was this man, and how can we explain his unexpected political pre-eminence? And, more important, is there something about his appointment that indicates that, indeed, free people of colour did gain from the revolution? Or, rather was this simply an exception to the rule, a red herring, an optical illusion?

The revolution, the New Kingdom

The story of Pedro José de Ibarra is part and parcel of the revolution that broke out in America as a result of three things: Napoleon's invasion of the Iberian Peninsula in spring 1808, the monarchical crisis that led to the abdications of Ferdinand VII and Charles IV in Bayonne, and the rising up of the Spanish people, who did not accept Joseph Bonaparte as their new sovereign.[1] In the New Kingdom of Granada (one of the four Spanish viceroyalties in the Indies) there was widespread sympathy for the peninsular resistance. But the imperial offensive in Andalusia brought about the dissolution of the Junta Central and isolated the representatives of free Spain in the city of Cadiz, a grim situation that convinced the towns of New Granada to secede. The creation of the Junta Suprema in Caracas quickly led to the removal of the governor of Cartagena as well as the *corregidores* of Pamplona, Socorro and Tunja. The viceregal capital, Santa Fe (present-day Bogotá) was the site of a junta which declared itself on 20 July to be 'supreme', though it was not recognized as such by most provinces, which preferred governing themselves. As a result, there were a multitude of juntas. After the collapse of the Congress of the Kingdom of New Granada, the aim of which had been to restore unity, and Santa Fe's decision to write its own constitution and become the State of Cundinamarca, each junta made its own rules for their independent entities, each with a president, courts and legislatures. Even so, the reconstruction of the Kingdom was not forgotten, and in fact was achieved little by little through federal mechanisms. In late 1811, diplomatic representatives of five provinces approved a treaty creating the United Provinces of New Granada, ratified later by other provinces, and in October 1812 a General Congress was opened. Cundinamarca refused to join until it was forced to do so at gunpoint in December 1814. The revolutionaries also had to overcome resistance by the royalist province of Santa Marta (not to mention the city of Pasto, the southern city of Popayán, the presidency in Quito and the Isthmus of Panama), but before they were able to do so Ferdinand VII had regained his freedom. He abolished the Cortes and declared their accomplishments null and void, and dispatched a military expedition that briefly passed through Venezuela, besieged Cartagena, and by July 1816 had destroyed the confederation of the United Provinces of New Granada.[2]

The restoration in New Granada had a promising start. However the frequent execution of revolutionaries (somewhere between 125 and 200 were killed); bad behaviour by soldiers; the requisitioning of cattle, tools and equipment; purges; imprisonment; and widespread corruption by royal agents all turned the viceroyalty's inhabitants against Ferdinand VII, the monarchy and the Spanish Empire. In August 1819, a battle near Santa Fe marked the end of the restoration regime and brought about the unification of the old Captaincy General of Venezuela and the New Kingdom to become the Republic of Colombia.[3]

The life of Pedro José de Ibarra, like that of all his contemporaries, was marked by these events. He was an inferior subject from the moment of his birth yet was called upon to occupy an eminent position in Antioquian society during revolutionary times. He had to request the king's clemency and in 1816 was included in a general pardon due to his involvement in political events. Later on, he became a citizen and held other public posts, which he could not have dreamt of before Napoleon's invasion of Spain.

Antioquia: Gold and *pardos*

His life story is thus unintelligible if seen apart from the independence movement or from the particular context of late-eighteenth-century Antioquia, a mining province similar to Chocó and Popayán but, unlike them, not dependent on large numbers of slaves to mine the gold. Rather, free labourers called *mazamorreros* were used; accompanied by fewer than five slaves or operators, they washed the sands of the rivers and the riverbanks in search of precious metals. This particular economic arrangement led to frequent manumission and social mobility for many mestizos and *pardos* (mixed blood) thanks not only to the gold but also to commercial activities difficult to monopolize because of the territorial breadth and inhospitableness of the province, with its dispersed population.[4] According to Governor Francisco Silvestre in 1797, many free people of colour were 'better off than many whites', so it seemed to him absurd to charge the former six castellanos (gold coins) for a burial when descendants of Europeans were charged fifteen.[5] Research by Beatriz Patiño has confirmed the 'improved living conditions of the poor' in the province after 1780 as a result of the mining bonanza, especially in the Valle de los Osos, where *pardo mazamorreros* were the majority.[6] So it is no surprise that by the end of the century many successful mulattos were referred to as *don*,[7] a courtesy title used in the province to distinguish 'whites from the lower ranks'.[8]

Pedro José de Ibarra's life story is an example of the impact of gold mining on a peripheral and mountainous province. Female slaves lived as concubines of well-off miners and merchants, which not only improved their living conditions and often led to manumission, it also generally led to the freedom and a certain economic independence for their children. Black slaves, meanwhile, became *libertos* by patiently accumulating the gold they managed to glean on their days off or by lending themselves out to their owners; they accumulated more earnings as muleteers, *mazamorreros* and retail intermediaries, investing their money in more or less prosperous businesses and took pains to provide their children with an education so they could rise as only the next generation can. Ibarra was born in 1763 to the mulattos Martín de Ibarra and Juana Zamarra and exemplifies a typical case of slow but steady social progress.[9] Martín on his paternal side came from a line of slaves owned by a church elder, Ignacio de Ibarra, and on his maternal side from the mulatto illegitimate son of a rich miner, Pedro Martín de Mora, who had organized the colonization of Valle de los Osos. In 1725, at his baptism in Antioquia, Martín's godfather was one of his uncles, Juan Mora Bolívar, a clergyman and a university graduate.[10] This was no doubt a gesture of respect toward the accomplishments of the family's cultured mulatto ancestors who had prospered thanks to the mines.

Martín became a captain in a mulatto unit in Antioquia and a well-to-do resident there in 1805 along with his wife and his three single children, two of whom (our Pedro José and José Ignacio) owned slaves (seven and six, respectively). This was a sign of privilege shared by other literate mulattos in the city to whom he was related, including the Sarrazola, Valenzuela and Yepes families.[11]

It is clear that Pedro José had an exceptional education for a child of his social group. At the end of the eighteenth century there was no 'primary school, grammar school or faculty' in the province of Antioquia, so his lessons fell to private teachers or educated relatives.[12] Possibly he was taught reading, writing and grammar alongside his first cousin Vicente de Ibarra Santana, who in 1776 was ordained as a curate in San Carlos, later getting posts in San Pedro, the Indian town of Sabanalarga and finally being named sacristan of the city of Antioquia.[13] The two cousins apparently were quite close: before Vicente died in the provincial capital in 1823, he named his cousin as his executor. He had few belongings; aside from a harp, a silver tack, two silver spoons, three pieces of gold jewellery, two holy images, four pigs, twenty-seven head of cattle and around fifty books (most of them on religion, though there were also some on medicine, the *Curia filípica*, and one issue of *Orinoco ilustrado*).[14] Despite what we do not know about Pedro José's early education, the fact is that on the eve of the revolution he was recognized in the provincial capital as a learned man and was hired as a post-mortem estate appraiser.[15]

Of the approximately 100,000 inhabitants of Antioquia in 1810, there were 13,000 slaves, 5,000 indigenous people and 61,000 *pardos*, who thus constituted the overwhelming majority. Their dominance was even greater in the capital city, where in 1790 there were 3,261 *pardos* of all ages (68 per cent) along with 1,161 slaves (24 per cent) and just 340 'whites' (7.1 per cent).[16] When the revolution broke out, at least two of the parishes of the provincial administration were led by mulatto priests (Sabanalarga, by Vicente de Ibarra, and Armaviejo) and on many occasions *pardo* subjects were district officials and even town council members.[17] For example, in 1790 in the town of Remedios eight *pardos* held government posts and all but one were referred to as *don*.[18] In the provincial capital, educated *pardos* had worked at least since 1780 as Latin grammar teachers; that, in fact, was the case of Pedro José de Ibarra. According to a 1797 notarial document, Dr José Pardo recalled how, before moving to Santa Fe to study law, he had studied Latin for three years alongside Carlos José Garro 'in a classroom with Pedro José de Ibarra, an instructor, from 1781 to 84'. Ibarra himself confirmed that when he recommended his former student for a job.[19] So Ibarra earned his living as a grammar teacher before he turned twenty, which permitted him to establish relations with the children of Antioquia's leading families. This undoubtedly was one of the reasons for his appointment as a senator in 1812. Another was that two channels of political involvement for black people had been cut off: the Jacobin route after Thermidor (which had allowed Jean-Baptiste Belley and other African-Americans to join the French Convention), and the route to the Cortes of Cadiz, which in Article 22 denied citizenship (other than exceptional cases) to 'those originating in Africa'.

There were other mulattos in Antioquia who worked as Latin teachers. Felipe Montes Herrón and José Sarrazola taught grammar and morals in around 1810.[20] When in 1800 the provincial capital created administrative positions (*procuradores de número*), the posts were given to two mulattos, José Vicente del Campillo and Lorenzo Yepes, the latter of whom six years later was a subscriber to *Redactor Americano*.[21] Ibarra held a good position within the mulatto population of the province of Antioquia, but it was not a particularly unusual one. Other *pardos*, including his own cousin, in the late eighteenth and early nineteenth centuries obtained positions that required education and a certain social standing.

Pedro José de Ibarra owed his rise not only to his education, however, but also to a series of profitable business deals. Thanks to his last will and testament, signed in Antioquia in 1814, we know that at that point he was in a position to give another mulatto, the merchant Mateo Molina, 2,500 patacones (equal to 1,250 gold pesos, a considerable amount) to buy goods of minor values in Jamaica.[22] This indicates a long and patient accumulation of capital and relationships with businessmen in Cartagena and Jamaica, hubs for the sort of merchandise mentioned in his will. He also got involved in the salt trade, a profitable business given salt's essential role in human diet, food preservation and cattle-raising. Salt was very expensive in the New Kingdom of Granada because crystallization was achieved using the pre-Hispanic method of boiling salt water in clay urns for several days. As the principal mines of the viceroyalty were near Santa Fe (Zipaquirá, Tausa and Nemocón), the price of salt increased as it was transported to more distant locations such as Tunja, Socorro, Neiva,

Mariquita and Popayán.[23] That was not the case in the coastal provinces or in the towns along the Cauca and Magdalena rivers, which used sea salt. Antioquia was self-sufficient, given the large number of natural salt-water springs in the area. Unlike the large deposits in the altiplano administered since 1788 by the crown, salt-water springs were run by officially certified private parties. There, crystallization took place not in clay but in copper pots, generally operated by free labourers who also provided tools, mules and wood in exchange for a percentage of the yield.[24] When there was discussion in 1777 about the possibility of the crown creating a salt monopoly (*estanco*), the people of Antioquia mobilized against the proposal; they argued that the profit margin was scant; that salt was priced low and anyway was not sold but bartered for candles, soap, eggs, bananas and tobacco; and that the coagulation process was imperfect and therefore warehousing would be impossible because the tiny grains had a limited life and would end up evaporating.[25] The business could not have been as unprofitable as the locals claimed in their efforts to avoid the *estanco* given that an investigation of salt flats in 1798–1802 showed that many well-off members of Antioquia society had a financial interest there, including judicial officials, city council members of Antioquia, Rionegro and Medellín, rich priests, successful lawyers and wealthy businessmen. One exception among the group was Vicente Ibarra Santana, who owned a salt flat along the Ituango riverbank in 1800. But the cast of characters was closer to the regional elites than to the well-off pardocracy.[26] Pedro José de Ibarra until 1816 owned a salt mine in the Indian town of Sopetrán with two shafts for water reservoirs and two stoves with four metal cauldrons, three of which were new.[27]

Pedro José de Ibarra continued rising steadily, helped by his father, a militia captain, and by other relatives who were landowners. His education allowed him to become a Latin teacher and a mentor to the sons of the capital city's most important families. Wise money management led him into business and the salt trade, which in turn allowed him to buy several slaves.

But despite all this, it is undeniable that beyond certain posts, social advancement was cut off for free people of colour on the eve of the revolution. One notable example of this is Vicente Vergara, who was appointed by Viceroy Amar as lieutenant governor of Valle de los Osos in 1805. Upon hearing the news, the residents of Santa Rosa protested the appointment, pointing to the nominee's African heritage and to the fact that his father had been prevented from joining the city council of Antioquia. The governor's office replied by saying that members of the Vergara family had occupied judicial posts in Sopetrán, including one who was *corregidor*. In the end, the court (*audiencia*) recognized that being a *pardo* did not mean one could not be appointed, but the nomination was withdrawn because of residents' opposition and 'for the sake of peace'.[28]

Pedro José de Ibarra himself experienced the limits to his people's social mobility when in 1794 he wished to marry a relative, Nicolasa Pérez, whose father was opposed and called the prospective groom 'black, the offspring of slaves'.[29] Ibarra's reply in defence of his matrimonial ambitions was very interesting as it showed that at the end of the eighteenth century there were *pardos* who, while still aware of their marginal position in society, had begun questioning the legitimacy of racial hierarchies and the 'discredit' of marriages between different sorts of people, even within the *castas pardas*. In response, the counterpart insisted on the distance separating mulattos from blacks, pointing to his appointment as district judge in Obregón as proof of his distinction. He also mentioned his father's Spanish origins and an aunt's marriage with a peninsular Spaniard, a former substitute treasurer, royal accounts official and judge in the city of Antioquia. In reply, Ibarra's opponent declared that marriage to his daughter would be the death knell (*afrentoso patíbulo*) for his family and would stain them with dishonour. The wedding would open the way for any 'impertinent black slave with mulattos of his own, tomorrow or the next day, if they wanted, to easily marry their own mistress and avenge themselves by reminding them of the oppression suffered during his enslavement'.[30] Pedro de Ibarra replied by defending his status as a mulatto and saying that his prospective father-in-law's attempts to denigrate him as 'black and a descendent of slaves' was ridiculous:

> By common agreement, one must assume that the mulatto race had its origin in blacks and whites, and that mestizos come from whites and Indians. In America at the start of its conquest there were no other sorts of people than the Spaniards themselves who came to conquer this land; the Indians, who possessed it; and the black slaves that they brought with them or who were later brought here, the ones said to be from Guinea. As a direct result, the Spaniards either had children by black women, who are the race of mulattos, or they had them with Indians, who are called mestizos. And if, on the contrary, Indians had children by black women, those are commonly called zambos.
>
> Therefore there is no other sort of person in these parts of the country.[31]

It is easy to see why Ibarra's blithe attitude concerning the flaws of his birth and his categorization of the racial colonial world into just three groups might have challenged one of the pillars of New Granada society. Instead of the traditional analysis of ancestry and blood more or less tainted by 'bad influences', the mulatto grammarian spoke of a vital present, stressing the importance of conducting oneself 'with honour' and 'without missteps'. His position was radically opposed to that of other respectable *pardos* who insisted, using the request for royal favour called *gracias al sacar*, that the crown should release them from their category and allow them to register as whites.[32] By casting doubt on the colour hierarchy, Ibarra was casting doubt on the very foundation of colonial society.[33] His argument was a precursor, in a narrow society, of a way of thinking that would later become the crucible of revolution. But the fact that when he wrote his last will and testament in 1814 he was still single ('*en el estado de celibato*') and had no heirs also shows that the sort of social mobility available to poor European immigrants or Creoles who worked in viceregal offices or married women of well-to-do families in the province was far beyond the reach of free people of colour such as himself, regardless of how much money or how much learning they had.[34] In fact, they could not even easily marry other leading *pardos* because the 'succession of disdain' on which the colonial order was predicated gave rise to ridiculous airs according to one's true or alleged shade of white.

Senator in the provincial chamber

Because of its demographic and economic importance, the revolution would succeed in Antioquia only if it benefited and was supported by freemen of all colours, who constituted the majority of the population. *Pardos* could benefit from such reforms as the elimination of the *mazamorrero* tax, the ability to vote and run for office, the creation of a militia system, equality before the law, the encouragement of colonization, new courts and parishes, and the opening and maintenance of roads. But beyond generalizations, particular personal itineraries are also of use in assessing the impact of the revolution on successful *pardos*' upward social mobility.[35] The example of Francisco González is quite representative in this sense. He was a rich merchant, a *pardo* and illegitimate; in Medellín he had established a foundry, of which he also was director. This success came well before the revolution, but he continued advancing afterwards as well. On 4 July 1812, he was legitimized by the Senate of the republic of Antioquia, and was appointed to be militia captain and treasurer of the board of abolitionist Friends of Humanity.[36] Both positions meant he lost his place at the foundry once royal troops arrived, but the provincial governor, trying to mitigate his actions, explained to the viceroy that González's flirtation with the rebels was because he was a *pardo* 'and thought he was better than Nature made him'.[37]

The cases of González and Ibarra show that before 1810 leading *pardos* in Antioquia were able to acquire a certain amount of education and wealth, though it was still more difficult than for whiter subjects. For the mulatto foundry director, the revolution offered the opportunity to erase unfavourable signs such as illegitimacy and acquire the honours and privilege inaccessible to his class under the old regime. Was this also the route taken by Pedro José de Ibarra? Did the political transformation confirm the social position of well-off *pardos*? The revolution reached Antioquia on 20 July 1810, when news arrived that a Supreme Junta was to be established in Santa Fe. Each of the four city councils in the province sent two representatives to the provincial capital, where they all met in sessions lasting from 30 August to 10 September. At the end, the assembly decided not to respect the supremacy of the Santa Fe junta and instead created their own, led by the governor and his aide, with one member from each city, who were replaced on 28 October by new members elected by heads of families. Three weeks later the junta acquired two new members: a secretary and a representative of 'peoples not subject to any *departamento capitular*', that is, people who lived in towns that had been abolished upon crown orders at the end of the eighteenth century. The second junta appointed two deputies for the Congress of the Kingdom and debated a Constitution for the province. Thus, a division of functions was created: members of the junta had legislative power; the executive consisted of a president of the state; the judiciary comprised a Superior Court with four members; and finance was addressed by an accounts tribunal, also with four members. The rivalry between Antioquia and Medellín threatened to divide the state when the latter demanded that a Constituent and Electoral College be summoned according to demographic representation, that is, leaving aside the municipal representation in place until then. Authorities in the capital agreed to the demand, in return for which new elections (28–30 October 1811) were held to choose new junta members. During this first stage of the revolution in Antioquia, there were four assemblies (one Provincial Congress and three juntas) with a total of twenty-nine seats. These were occupied by sixteen individuals (several served two or three times), none of whom were *pardos* or mulattos. The tribunals of justice and finance created by the Constitution had a total of eight seats, which were off-limits to distinguished free people of colour.[38]

The Constituent and Electoral College met for the first time on 29 December 1811. It had twenty-three members: eight represented Antioquia, five were from Medellín, six from Rionegro, two from Marinilla and two from the Northeast. Sociologically, the group was quite homogeneous; there were many connections among them (for example the Martínez family from the provincial capital was represented by two brothers, two nephews and one brother-in-law), many had held posts in prior revolutionary assemblies, and all were called *don*, characteristic of whites.[39]

On 21 March 1812, the convention ratified a Constitution to replace the one passed the previous year by the provincial junta. The legislature was made up of two chambers: a five-member Senate, representing each department, whose members had to be at least twenty-five years old, not a churchman and have at least four thousand pesos; and the House of Representatives, organized according to population, with one deputy per ten thousand inhabitants, with each one having at least two thousand pesos. There was a president with executive powers, and the legislature chose two advisers. Finally, the Superior Tribunal of Justice had five ministers and a prosecutor.[40]

Five senators and ten representatives in 1812 were designated by the Constituent and Electoral College before it dissolved. The assembly ordered them to carry out a precise list of tasks: draw up rules for formal exclusions for political post and tariffs; they were also required to draw up terms of imprisonment and to formulate an educational system and a law to regulate ecclesiastical rights. The legislature opened on 21 May in the provincial capital, though five deputies had resigned in the previous weeks; the honour was a dangerous one. The resignations of the senator and the representative appointed by the Northeast were approved by the legislature on 22 May, which also approved their replacements: Pedro José de Ibarra and José Antonio Benítez, respectively.[41] So, assuming the rules were being followed, the mulatto senator had at least four thousand pesos in 1812, which certainly made him a rich man in the provincial context.

Ibarra had to take his seat in the upper house that same day 'despite offering reasons for his own unsuitability'.[42] The next day he participated in elections for the prefect and vice-prefect of the body; on 25 May he agreed to the time schedule for the sessions; on the 26th he and his colleagues debated the consequences of making Indians into citizens (decree of the authorities of the State of Antioquia of 18 December 1811), exempted Cañasgordas from paying ecclesiastical taxes for ten years, rejected Sabanalarga's and Buriticá's requests to retain their previous status (as *indios de comunidad*) and ordering therefore that common lands (*resguardo*) be divided up. In June, July and August, Ibarra was involved in resolving many matters, including appointments, suspensions and salaries of employees; jurisdictional issues between the legislature and the judiciary; working out protocol for the Supreme Court; seeking information on provincial towns' management of their properties; the concession of the title of *villa* to some towns; organizing the militias; and taking extraordinary measures to ensure public order.[43] Ibarra's signature appears at the end of all the minutes (he missed only one meeting, for 'legitimate cause'), leading us to conclude that he was a conscientious legislator and committed to the revolution, which he believed protected his integrity and interests despite the alleged circumstances he had put forth when he was nominated. He did not fake illness or imitate Don Luis Lorenzana, who scoffed at his own nomination to the high chamber and simply refused to attend sessions for over a month until he was forced to declare that he had sworn an oath of loyalty to the king. With the argument that the king was not mentioned in the oath of office or in the entire Constitution, he refused to take his seat even when the Senate prefect said that the state of Antioquia had not withheld obedience to Ferdinand VII and indeed recognized him as its sovereign.[44]

As for legislative activities themselves, we know Ibarra participated in debates to regulate judicial norms, ecclesiastical rights and licenses for distilleries in the province along with taxes to make up for the abolition of the state monopoly.[45] He also participated in debates concerning primary education and the establishment of schools in each of the departments, and he was a speaker in the session devoted to the return of the tobacco monopoly, which the Constituent and Electoral College had imprudently abolished.[46]

Additionally, his colleagues chose him as their spokesman for court fees and public domain land reform measures presented in mid-1811 from Santa Fe by the provincial deputy to the Kingdom Congress, José Manuel Restrepo. In both cases he was given the task of speaking in favour of the measures and in opposition to objections posed by another senator chosen for that purpose. Regarding notarial duties, Ibarra was in favour of setting an average percentage to be owed to the assessor instead of a fixed amount per page because, as he said, there were

> matters of very few pages that are far more work than matters with many more pages. For example, there may be a case with fifty pages requiring an estate to be prorated among fifteen or twenty creditors though the amount is not enough for them all; in similar circumstances this means more work than a case with one hundred pages with no prorating. There might be another case in which there are many heirs and few pages, because the decedent confessed his debts and there was no opposition owing to the absence of heirs and the many debts ... this would not be paid well by the page, because there are few pages and a great deal of work.[47]

I include the above, lengthy quotation because senators' voices were rarely heard in the minutes of the assemblies, which did not have recorders. In that debate, Ibarra spoke as someone who knew how courts and litigation worked. In his words, one can imagine an administrative worker (*papelista*), someone continually called upon to assist in the legal claims of his neighbours. Thus, this educated mulatto was not in the assembly as a simple token or just for show; provincial revolutionaries saw an experienced man who knew a great deal, and that is why they chose him as a legislator.

Reform of crown lands entailed ambitious plans for encouraging land settlement, mining, and agriculture, as well as the redistribution of wealth through land donations to the poorest sectors, be they landless workers, unemployed, or thieves. According to Restrepo, this was the only way to prevent tyranny and ensure that freedom would last. The project involved simplifying the procedure for land grants and revoking widespread subsidies given in the past even though the land had not actually been worked. He also advocated ending the church entail and requested that settlers be exempt from all municipal and royal taxes and tithes (*diezmos*). This last measure was polemical because it assumed provincial control (*patronato*) at a time when the state of Antioquia had a confusing relationship with the metropolis. Independence would not be declared until August 1813.[48] The Senate accepted Restrepo's proposal on 5 June 1812 but only insofar as it concerned royal lands; that is, all discussion of *patronato* and permanent entail was excluded. With that limitation, ten days later Pedro José de Ibarra presented an amended proposal that eventually was the basis for successful legislation.[49]

The Constitution assigned members of both houses a three-year term but said the upper house must hold elections for one-third its membership each year. Thus, on 21 August the senators chose by lots the group that would have to leave, and Pedro José de Ibarra was among those chosen.[50] Ten days later the legislature wound up its sessions. During the revolution (1808–16) there were six legislative bodies in the state of Antioquia, but only the first and the start of the second complied with constitutional guidelines. Royal troops from Quito entered the city of Popayán on 1 July 1813. Seeing that the revolution was in danger, Antioquian legislators opted to appoint a dictator and reduce the size of the chamber to five members. Pedro José de Ibarra participated in the first session of those debates because he still had his seat while waiting for his replacement.[51] The single-house legislature with a reduced number of deputies would remain in place until 1816, when an army sent by Ferdinand VII, who had been restored to the throne, destroyed the federation of the United Provinces. Among the reduced group of legislators during the five-year period, Pedro José de Ibarra was the exception who proved the rule of political endogamy and purely illusory legislative renewal, as the replacements were often brothers, cousins or in-laws of families regarded as white.[52]

Legislature	Year	Structure	Members
First	1812	bicameral	15
Second	1813	bicameral/unicameral	11, then 5
Third	1814	unicameral	5
Fourth	1815 (1st semester)	unicameral	5
Fifth	1815 (2nd semester)	unicameral	4 (and a secretary)
Sixth	1816	unicameral	5 (and a secretary)

Revolutionary legislatures: The New Granada case (1811–16)[53]

Pedro José de Ibarra's departure from the Senate did not mark the end of his relations with the revolution, not even after 11 August 1813, when Antioquia declared independence. In accordance with the law of gradual emancipation passed by the legislature in 1814,[54] he manumitted his eleven slaves, according to a public document registered the following 10 February in which he was described as 'distinguished citizen of the Republic and friend of humanity'.[55] He also worked as a mediator on at least two occasions in accordance with Articles 9–10, sec. 3, tit. V of the 1812 Constitution regarding lawsuits and mediation. Both cases concerned estates of *pardo* families in the city of Antioquia, some of whose members belonged, like him, to educated circles.[56]

Restoration and purification

As mentioned above, an army sent from Spain by Ferdinand VII quickly defeated the United Provinces of New Granada. Royal troops entered the state of Antioquia in March 1816 and began demolishing the revolution's accomplishments, eliminating those who had participated in the political changes. The objective was that things go back to the way they were before the crisis of the monarchy, and therefore certain laws were declared invalid. That was the case with the manumission granted by Pedro José de Ibarra on 10 February of the previous year. As a result, the former senator had to return to the notary's office to confirm his slaves' freedom.[57] Unlike other slave-owners who took advantage of the new situation to get their slaves back, Ibarra confirmed his commitment to the abolitionist cause, one of the most radical components of the revolution.

The provincial governor, Vicente Sánchez de Lima, implemented a policy of light pacification, avoiding persecution and executions that were common in other parts of the New Kingdom. In fact, he asked the viceroy for a special pardon for his subjects, which was approved on 23 January 1817. In order to take advantage of the pardon, those who had sided with the revolution had to make a formal request indicating their degree of participation in the upheavals and presenting witnesses to vouch for their peaceful behaviour and describe them as fervent royalists. Pedro José de Ibarra undertook his purification measures in early April, admitting he had been a senator though he pointed to his initial resistance to taking the post. He also asked the city council of Antioquia to certify that the logbook containing vows of independence did not include his name. The councilmen not only did what he asked, they confirmed his 'spotless behaviour' during the revolution. Mayor Juan Manuel Lorenzana added that he had had many conversations with Ibarra during the turbulent times and had many times heard him criticize the actions of the 'insurgent government'. Antonio del Valle, the royal accounts official, and Cayetano Buelta Lorenzana, another official, said Ibarra was one of the most admired subjects in the province 'for his knowledge and fine behaviour, both moral and political', and they said he had taken the post as senator 'against his will'. Doctor José Pardo, who had stood out during the revolution, agreed with this last opinion, saying Ibarra previously had turned down the job of councilman and royal treasurer because his personality was 'entirely averse to any representational desire'. Tomás Arrubla confirmed his royalist leanings in private conversations in which he had spoken 'energetically in favour of the Peninsula', while Manuel María Bonis, less daring, simply stated that Ibarra had neither insulted nor harmed anyone. It took a month for the case to be put together, at the end of which an adviser to Governor Pantaleón Arango (who also had held posts during the revolution) recommended that Ibarra be included in the pardon. On 4 June, Ibarra went to the governor's office and promised to obey, respect and show loyalty to the monarch.[58]

Did the *pardos* see the restoration of the monarchy as a step backwards? I cannot definitively answer that question, but there are indications that indeed they did. In mid-1817 the attorney general blocked a mulatto, Felipe Montes, from temporarily occupying the post of city notary despite the fact that other mulattos had held the post in Mompox, Cartagena and Santa Fe.[59] Everything indicates that the end of the revolution in Antioquia also spelled the return of barriers that had separated categories of people before 1810 and which later had been significantly reduced. Montes defended his job, arguing that nobility could not be the only relevant factor for obtaining work and emphasizing how appropriate he was for the job:

Am I, then, someone who has crawled out of the mud, unqualified to mix with my equals? Am I, then, not fit for the duties of an honourable man? In other words, am I, perchance, a criminal? Convince me that I am, and I will be silent … Tell me if the notary has a vote on public matters. You will say that he has honour, but I will reply that honour is due to all men. I do not mean my sphere, which is not quite as low as the attorney general claims, but any sphere, as long as the person in question has the qualities of a man. Because nobility without the rest is like pearls in a trash heap. An honourable commoner has greater right to political representation than an immoral nobleman.[60]

Thus, the return of Ferdinand VII signified a terrible setback for *pardos* in Antioquia as concerned privilege and honour; their influence decreased and they encountered insurmountable obstacles to the realization of their dreams during the revolution. Montes Herrón, as we saw earlier, had been a grammar teacher before the revolution, following the path of Pedro José de Ibarra. During the political transformation he had been an honorary captain in the youth militia and therefore also had to request a royal pardon. Given that the notary's post that he coveted in 1817 was beyond his reach, he had to settle for the post of solicitor, a post also obtained by another *pardo*, José María de Aguirre Sarrazola.[61] Just like before the revolution, these were the only jobs available to educated *pardos*.

Influencing the Republic's legislation

The restoration lasted very briefly in the New Kingdom. In early August 1819, a pro-independence force crossed the Andes and defeated royalist forces in the province of Tunja. The viceroy and the judges left the capital, and a republican regime was quickly established to govern over a broad and populated territory. In December, the Congress of Venezuela created the Republic of Colombia, whose existence was confirmed in 1821 by a constituent congress in Cúcuta. What happened to Pedro José de Ibarra? And what about the rest of the *pardos* in Antioquia under the new regime? An incident in 1825 enables us to answer both questions. In late June the intendant of Cartagena warned the secretary of the interior about a publication in Santa Marta called *Aviso al público*, which he considered to be subversive.[62] Soon afterwards it was discovered that the pseudonym 'Amigo del buen orden', who signed the publication, was really a *pardo* businessman named Simeón Serna who lived in Jamaica. According to port authorities, the publication had entirely been distributed in the province of Antioquia, the author's homeland, so there was no reason to fear any unrest along the New Granada coast. Nevertheless, the secretary of the interior ordered Serna to return to the country and face charges. Why was this publication deemed so dangerous? Why was it said that its aim was to 'stir the waters' and irritate and divide society? First, because it denounced the fact that the principles underlying the new revolutionary regime were not being applied:

> We are still not knowledgeable about the liberal system we have embraced, and it is both difficult and painful to set aside the concerns that our negligible education has inspired in Colombians' sublime imagination. In one of the most educated provinces of the Republic, where stirring philosophical debates have been published about the great advantages of the form of government adopted by Colombia and where everyone everywhere praises patriotism, liberalism, equality, and union, still the aristocracy continues its despotic rule.[63]

Simeón Serna did not, however, limit himself to general observations. Rather, he railed against the unjust treatment meted out in Antioquia to worthy and virtuous men owing to absurd prejudices that were incompatible with the republic's guiding reason:

> Dividing up jobs among just a few men does not do justice to the many educated subjects in the capital against whom no objection can be made regarding their education or their behaviour. They are attacked solely for being *pardos*. It would seem that they believe that an essential requirement for obtaining a job is that a man be referred to as *Don*, though he may not deserve it. It is said that custom makes the law, but that custom was abolished ever since it was recognized that equality is one of man's basic rights. And today any Colombian would feel offended if *Don* were added before their name ... As a result of this error, a subject previously employed as an humble clerk was given the post of councilman; he continued in his old occupation until someone requested that he give up one of the two posts because they were incompatible.[64]

The problem was not just that the *pardos* of Antioquia were not being recognized for their merits but that posts were going to just about anyone accepted as white. So the publication was demanding that the revolution's promises be fulfilled and that any racial hierarchy be considered invalid in a country in which *mestizaje* was the rule. Stratification should be based only on education, and if that were the case then *pardos* would legitimately rise:

> Subjects who denigrate *pardos* because they are *pardos* never stop harassing them based on points of politics, jurisprudence, and other sciences, all of which the denigrated men know well and of which the rest are ignorant. A privileged man spends all day every day bothering someone called *maestro*

because a multitude of inhabitants owe their principles and their education to him. They go to him with their doubts, they hire him for their lawsuits, and he defends them earnestly and well, using the skills he has acquired over a long practice.[65]

The text clearly referred to the mulatto Pedro José de Ibarra who, as we have seen, was a professor of Latin grammar in the city of Antioquia for many years and who had been a provincial senator in 1812. After the bitter experience of the Restoration and once the Colombian project was under way, still the doors of the city council were closed to him, despite the fact that he had successfully performed important responsibilities. As far as I have been able to determine, Ibarra during the Colombian years received posts only as a member of the provincial commission that examined candidates for teaching posts in 1821, and a membership in the Sociedad de Amigos del País in 1823, created in the city of Antioquia upon the governor's order.[66] According to Gilberto Loaiza, these bodies, which carried out 'mediation functions between the general education plan and local realities', were not just the only expression of timid social civic life in the Republic of Colombia (aside from electoral assemblies and parish juntas of voters), they were also associations 'of the elites and for the elites' in that only local notables need apply.[67] Was Ibarra's presence in the Sociedad de Amigos del País in the city of Antioquia the exception that proved the exclusionary rule? In any case, the worst part, according to Simeón Serna's allegations, was that Ibarra may have been the most brilliant example but was not the only one:

There are other [*pardos*] who, though less well educated, are still better educated than those who have been given preference over them and who exercise a monopoly over authority. Our Constitution declares that the nation is not and cannot be the patrimony of any particular family, and from there one can infer that nor can a province be the patrimony of any particular family. They do not realize that in several places the Constitution confirms equal rights for equal merits; nor do they take into consideration that there are *pardos* in the Senate and in the House of Representatives. But please do not think that I am speaking of a barbarous province; keep in mind that some of our leading wise men were born in that same province.[68]

It is important to note here that the publication *El amigo del buen orden* was acquitted of sedition in early December 1825, which shows that despite what Marixa Lasso has said, 'elite repression … forced upon pardos the realization that public denunciation of racial grievances was dangerous, if not unpatriotic'.[69] But it is quite clear that republican consolidation did not satisfy *pardos'* aspirations in the province of Antioquia. An eloquent example of this are statements by the retired second lieutenant Ventura Correa to electors in Antioquia expressing his indignation because nearly a decade after the triumph of independence people still had not seen anyone in the town hall 'previously called *pardo*, despite the fact that there are *pardos* of virtue and fortune, that is, capable and deserving'. Their exclusion was all the more dramatic given the scarcity of whites in the area; their presence appears to have been a relic exclusive to the city. Correa backed up his statements with a complete list of *pardos* who had been not only deputies in Congress but also municipal judges or members of the city hall in Cartagena, Mompox, Panamá, Natá, Portobelo, Honda and Rionegro. In order to put an end to such discrimination, were not measures required to enable his people to enjoy the 'common rights of all citizens'?[70]

The life of the mulatto senator from the state of Antioquia is emblematic of that of an entire social group. Pedro José de Ibarra died in Antioquia on 5 February 1833. He was single and rich. He had managed to successfully survive two decades of revolution, leaving behind him not only a thatched house in the Santa Lucía neighbourhood worth seven hundred *pesos fuertes*, but also a cacao plantation near the city that was worth three thousand. His land bordered those of Simeón Serna, the mulatto businessman who was so indignant about his neighbour's unjust relegation in public affairs, and of Cayetano Buelta Lorenzana, who had intervened on his behalf during the Restoration to facilitate his political purgation. Two months before dying, Ibarra in his will declared that he also possessed certain images of saints and some books of theology, ethics and grammar, both in Latin and in Spanish, which must have dated back to his years as a teacher. He also mentioned the letters of manumission written years earlier for his slaves, saying that they had continued working for him given their inability to take care of themselves. This reminds us how difficult freedom was for former slaves and shows that we can understand the life of this former senator from the State of Antioquia only if we adopt an intergenerational perspective in the framework of the revolution. Equally significant is the fact that Ibarra named Manuel Sarrazola and his son Toribio as his executors.[71] Both were members of the mulatto provincial elite; the father was mayor of the city (a typical means for upward social mobility after the revolution) and the son was a presbyter (an older means of advancement). Ibarra's choices in this sense make clear he firmly believed he belonged to a marginal group that continued fighting to consolidate the social mobility that independence had both enabled and delimited.

Notes

1   José María Queipo del Llano (Count of Toreno), *Historia del levantamiento, guerra y revolución de España* (Pamplona: Urgoiti, 2008); Miguel Artola, *La España de Fernando VII* (Madrid: Espasa, 2008).

2   José Manuel Restrepo, *Historia de la revolución de la República de Colombia en la América Meridional* (Besanzón: José Jacquin, 1858), vols. 1–2; Rafael María and Ramón Díaz, *Resumen de la historia de Venezuela desde el año de 1797 hasta el de 1830* (Bruges and Paris, 1939), vol. 1; Daniel Gutiérrez Ardila, *Un Nuevo Reino. Geografía política, pactismo y diplomacia durante el interregno en Nueva Granada (1808–1816)* (Bogotá: Universidad Externado, 2010); Isidro Vanegas, *La revolución neogranadina* (Bogotá: Ediciones Plural, 2013).

3   Restrepo, *Historia*; José Manuel Greet, *Historia eclesiástica y civil de Nueva Granada, escrita sobre documentos auténticos* (Bogotá: Medardo Rivas, 1869), vol. 2; Antonio Rodríguez Villa, *El teniente general Don Pablo Morillo, primer conde de Cartagena, marqués de La Puerta (1778–1837)* (Madrid: Fortanet, 1910), vol. 1; Stephen K. Stoan, *Pablo Morillo and Venezuela, 1815–1820* (Columbus: Ohio State University Press, 1974); Juan Friede, *La otra verdad. La independencia americana vista por los españoles* (Bogotá: Carlos Valencia, 1979); Daniel Gutiérrez Ardila, *La Restauración en la Nueva Granada* (Bogotá: Universidad Externado, 2016).

4   Ann Twinam, *Mineros, comerciantes y labradores: las raíces del espíritu empresarial en Antioquia, 1763–1810* (Medellín: FAES, 1984). *Miners, Merchants and Farmers in Colonial Colombia* (Austin, Texas University Press, 1982), vol. 1.

5   Francisco Silvestre, *Relación de la provincia de Antioquia* (transcription, introduction and notes by David J. Robinson) (Medellín: Secretaría de Educación y Cultura de Antioquia, 1988), 228.

6   Beatriz Patiño, *Criminalidad, ley penal y estructura social en la provincia de Antioquia, 1750–1820* (Medellín: IDEA, 1994), 62 and 204–205.

7   Archivo General de la Nación [AGN] Minas de Antioquia, vol. 1, fol. 945.

8   Gabriel Ignacio Muñoz, quoted in his appeal to the Medellín lieutenant governor after being refused the title of *don* in 1786; Archivo Histórico de Antioquia [AHA] vol. 39, fol. 602.

9   'Testamento del ciudadano Pedro José de Ibarra' (7 May 1814), Notaría Única del Círculo de Santa Fe de Antioquia (NUCSFA), protocolo de instrumentos públicos otorgados ante el ciudadano Carlos Garro, escribano público del número y diezmos, 1814, fols. 193–8. I am grateful to César Lenis for pointing out this document to me.

10   I am grateful to Roberto Luis Jaramillo for helping me reconstruct Pedro José de Ibarra's genealogy.

11   AHA vol. 333 fols. 404 and 438, 'Padrón general de esta ciudad de Antioquia y su jurisdicción'.

12 AHA vol. 82, doc. 2777, Bishop of Popayán, Ángel Velarde, to Viceroy Mendinueta (Popayán, 27 November 1797).

13 Armando Martínez Garnia and Daniel Gutiérrez Ardila, eds., *¿Quién es quién en 1810? Guía de forasteros para el virreinato de Santa Fe* (Bogotá: Universidad del Rosario-UIS, 2010).

14 AHA vol. 58, doc. 1544; vol. 237, doc. 5359.

15 AHA vol. 230, fol. 9v, when he was hired in 1809 for the estate of presbyter Juan José Guzmán.

16 AGN Miscelánea de la colonia, vol. 99, fol. 163, 'Padrón de Antioquia y su jurisdicción' (1 December 1790).

17 Martínez and Gutiérrez, *¿Quién es quién en 1810?*

18 AGN Empleados Públicos de Antioquia [EPA], vol. 7, fol. 216. It is therefore incorrect to affirm that the castes lived in a world defined by 'exclusion of all privilege', nor is it true that their approach to free coloureds began as an 'immunological plan' driven by the politicization of the Antilles in the 1790s; see Clément Thibaud, *Libérer le nouveau monde. La fondation des premieres républiques hispaniques (Colombie et Venezuela, 1780–1820)* (Bécherel: Les Perséides, 2017), 80–1 and 138–9. The case of Antioquia shows, first, that somewhere between the rigid theory of segregation and actual practice there were doors offering access to certain sorts of status, including ecclesiastical and government posts; and, second, that blacks and mulattos began rising earlier in certain areas owing not to the Atlantic situation but to their inevitable economic progress.

19 AGN EPA vol. 12, fols. 656v and 687.

20 AHA vol. 83, doc. 2330 and vol. 621, fol. 243.

21 AHA vol. 648, doc. 10311, fols. 70–79; AGN EPA vol. 7, fols. 101–107.

22 'Testamento del ciudadano Pedro José de Ibarra'.

23 Marianne Cardale de Shrimpff, *Las salinas de Zipaquirá. Su explotación indígena* (Bogotá: Banco de la República, 1981); Ana María Groot, *Sal y poder en el Altiplano de Bogotá, 1557–1640* (Bogotá: Universidad Nacional de Colombia, 2008); Alexander von Humboldt, *Memoria racionada de las salinas de Zipaquirá* (Bogotá: Banco de la República, 1952); Joshua M. Rosenthal, *Salt and the Colombian State. Local Society and Regional Monopoly in Boyacá, 1821–1900* (Pittsburgh: University of Pittsburgh Press, 2012).

24 AGN Salinas vol. 4, fols. 367–424; AHA vol. 374, doc. 6973.

25 AHA vol. 374, doc. 6966.

26 AHA vol. 374, doc. 6985.

27 NUCSFA, protocolo de instrumentos públicos de 1816, fol. 226. I have been unable to specify when he bought the mine. I am grateful to César Lenis for pointing out this document to me.

28 AGN EPA vol. 7, fols. 286–315.

29 AHA vol. 68 doc. 1797.

30   Ibid.

31   Ibid.

32   The best-known case in Antioquia was that of the Valenzuela brothers, AHA vol. 647, doc. 10306; on *gracias al sacar* see Ann Twinam, *Public Lifes, Private Secrets. Gender, Honor, Sexuality, and Illegitimacy in Colonial Spanish America* (Redwood City, CA: Standford University Press, 1999).

33   Frédéric Régent, *Esclavage, métissage, liberté. La Révolution française en Guadeloupe, 1789–1802* (Paris: Grasset, 2004), 143–213.

34   'Testamento del ciudadano Pedro José de Ibarra', fols. 193–8.

35   On the benefits of studying personal cases for understanding coloured peoples' fight for liberty see Edgardo Pérez Morales, 'Itineraries of Freedom: Revolutionary Travels and Slave Emancipation in Colombia and the Greater Caribbean, 1789–1830', PhD diss., (University of Michigan, USA, 2013).

36   AHA vol. 823, fols. 72 and 352.

37   AGN Sec. Archivo Anexo, Purificaciones vol. 1 fol. 668, Vicente Sánchez de Lima to viceroy, Medellín, 25 October 1816.

38   Daniel Gutiérrez Ardila, 'Un estado al borde del precipio: El caso de la provincia de Antioquia (1810–1812)', in *Las asambleas constituyentes de la independencia. Actas de Cundinamarca y Antioquia (1811–1812)* (Bogotá: Universidad Externado-Corte Constitutional, 2010), 169–86.

39   Gutiérrez Ardila, 'Un Estado'.

40   'Constitución del Estado Soberano de Antioquia sancionada por los representantes de toda la provincia y aceptada por el pueblo el 3 de mayo del año de 1812', in *Constituciones de Colombia*, ed. Manuel Antonio Pombo and José Joaquín Guerra (Bogotá: Banco Popular, 1986), vol. 1, 471–531.

41   AHA vol. 824, fols. 86–8, 92–3, 106, and 391v–93.

42   AHA vol. 824, fols. 391v–92, Acta del Supremo Poder Legislativo (Antioquia, 22 May 1812).

43   Antioquia Senate minutes, AHA vol. 824, doc. 13019.

44   Antioquia Senate minutes, ibid, 26 June 1812, fols. 415v–417.

45   AHA vol. 824, docs. 13010 and 13012.

46   AHA vol. 824, docs. 1311 and 1313.

47   Antioquia Senate minutes, 9 July 1812, AHA vol. 824, fols. 437v–439.

48   AHA vol. 824, doc. 13014.

49   Ibid.

50   AHA vol. 824, fol. 512.

51   Antioquia Senate minutes, 8 June 1813, AHA vol. 826, fols. 65–66.

52   Daniel Gutiérrez Ardila, 'Legislaturas revolucionarias: El caso neogranadino (1811–1816)', *Estudios de Historia Moderna y Contemporánea de México*, 54 (July–December 2017): 44–61.

53   Ibid.

54 'Ley sobre la posteridad de los esclavos africanos y sobre los medios de redimir sucesivamente a sus padres', *Gaceta Ministerial de Antioquia*, October 1814.

55 NUCSFA, Registro de escrituras y demás documentos públicos otorgados por ante Don Nicolás de Lora, 1815, fol. 22v.

56 AHA vol. 235, doc 5328 and vol. 294 doc. 5891.

57 NUCSFA, protocolo de instrumentos públicos de 1816, fol. 367. I am grateful to Professor César Lenis for pointing out this document to me.

58 AHA vol. 849, fols. 300–9.

59 AHA vol. 859, fols. 5–26.

60 AHA vol. 859, fols. 25–6.

61 AGN Archivo Anexo, Fondo Gobierno, vol. 33, fols. 248–59.

62 AGN Miscelánea General de la República, vol. 2, fols. 59–66.

63 Ibid.

64 Ibid.

65 Ibid.

66 AHA vol. 924, doc. 14134, *El Eco de Antioquia* 34, 12 January 1823.

67 Gilberto Loaiza Cano, *Sociabilidad, religión y política en la definición de la nación* (Bogotá: Universidad Externado, 2011), 28–9, 37–8 and 55–9.

68 AGN Miscelánea General de la República, vol. 2, fols. 59–66.

69 Marixa Lasso, *Myths of Harmony. Race and Republicanism during the Age of Revolution: Colombia 1795–1831* (Pittsburgh: University of Pittsburgh Press, 2007), 150.

70 AGN Archivo Histórico Legislativo, Peticiones, vol. 40, fols. 448–52.

71 Last will and testament of Pedro José Ibarra and the sale of his house and estate (Antioquia, 1 November 1832; 19 February and 28 September 1833); in *Índice analítico del Protocolo de escribanos de la ciudad de Antioquia, 1821–1840*, ed. Roberto Luis Jaramillo and César A. Lenis, MS, 2015.

5

Cyrille Bissette: A singular voice in France

Abel Alexis Louis

Cyrille Charles Auguste Bissette was a man of colour whose life to this day remains unsettled.[1] While many republicans and abolitionists have managed to preserve their reputation in French history thanks to street names honouring them on both sides of the Atlantic – François-Auguste Perrinon, another Martiniquan of mixed race who distinguished himself by his later commitment to emancipation, has been elevated to the rank of the celebrated figures of the French Republic – Bissette has not received the same attention.[2]

Bissette was connected to one of the most important white Creole families in Martinique through his grandfather, Tascher, lord of La Pagerie, knight of Saint-Louis and dragoon captain, and father of the future Empress of the French – Marie Joseph Rose, Viscountess de Beauharnais, wife of Napoleon. Tascher was the owner of a sugar plantation and slaves in Trois-Ilets and maintained two families: on the one hand, his legitimate family and three daughters, born between 1763 and 1766; and on the other, an illegitimate family composed of three mixed-race daughters born between 1772 and 1784. Through his maternal grandmother, Marie Anne 'Adelaide' Albani (1748–1825), a freed mulatta, Bissette was a freeman from birth but with a close relative who had been a slave. Similar cases are common in notarial documents. Bissette's mother, Elisabeth Mélanie, known as Mémée Belaine (1772–1822), a free woman of mixed race, born in Fort-Royal, was one of Tascher de La Pagerie's three natural daughters. On 2 September 1794, she married Jean Charles Borromée Bissette (1756–1810), a native of Le Marin, a free mulatto, master mason and landlord in the administrative capital of the colony. He belonged to the world of skilled craftsmen, landlords and slaveholders who were free people of colour. He was one of its main representatives at the time. Moreover, 'the most important free people of colour in Fort-Royal served as witnesses' at his wedding: 'Pierre-Joseph Dumas, known as Dumas junior, master mason, and Louis Lot, master carpenter.'[3] Other close friends also signed the marriage certificate: Pierre Rusty, master cooper, Charles Alexandre, music teacher and Pierre Séverin, blacksmith, later master blacksmith and proprietor. Until the early 1820s, the Dumas, Lot and Séverin families figured among the social leaders of the free people of colour in the administrative capital as owners of houses and slaves. They were present to support Cyrille Bissette – born on 9 July 1795 in Fort-Royal – a mulatto[4] who had no formal profession when he signed his contract and marriage certificate on 6 and 20 February 1816 with Marie Rose Augustine Séverin, legitimate daughter of Pierre Séverin, aforementioned landlord, and Elizabeth Adelaide, known as Séverine, both free mulattos.[5] Louis Marie Esprit Lot, carpenter, then a proprietor without a profession, son of Louis Lot; Pierre Joseph Dumas, carpenter or building contractor, depending on the records; Pierre Athanase Angeron, 'without a profession' or merchant; and Jean Elie Fatime (later called Deproge), merchant, were their witnesses. Bissette's marriage contract refers to certain assets that were presumably inherited from his father. His fortune amounting to 10,600 colonial pounds included a slave, various items of furniture and other household effects.[6] His mother had become a merchant after the death on 8 October 1810 of her husband, Jean Charles Borromée Bissette, who left her a house on the main street (now Victor Hugo Street) and savings to open a small store. In 1818, Elisabeth Mélanie put an end to her trading activities and her eldest son, Cyrille, who was already in the business, took over the reins as a salesclerk and later as a merchant before his mother's death on 14 October 1822.

Before the case (December 1823–January 1824) that bore his name, Bissette had led a life in accordance with local decrees and ordinances. In January 1818, he was a member of the delegation of free coloured people from Fort-Royal who welcomed the new governor, François-Xavier Donzelot. In May 1823, Martinique became aware of the Spanish War. On that occasion, the free people of colour in Fort-Royal wrote a letter in which they offered their services to the governor. Bissette was present among the delegates of the free persons of colour who brought the document to General Donzelot.[7] Bissette thus appears to have been a zealous servant of the established order before December 1823 and of the slave system, especially since, according to the lawyer François-André Isambert, he possessed slaves and one or more houses through his wife.[8] Bissette participated with the Fort-Royal militia companies of colour in the repression of the revolt on 12–13 October 1822 of the Carbet slaves, who had killed two white landowners and wounded two landowners of colour.[9] Governor Donzelot had ordered the mobilization of the five Fort-Royal companies of colour on the morning of 13 October with other troops from the Second Battalion, composed of metropolitan soldiers.[10] However, Donzelot knew that by mobilizing the free Fort-Royal militia of colour and those of the parishes bordering the Carbet (particularly Saint-Pierre and Case-Pilote), he was teaming up with companies that were experts in hunting rebel slaves. Moreover, the free people of colour in these companies reacted as landlords and as a unified social group – which had not always been the case – since free landowners of colour had been wounded in the slaves' revolt.

Moreover, on the following 18 October, Donzelot published a list of congratulations to the troops involved:

> We also hasten to express our satisfaction to the dragoons and the five national guard companies of Fort-Royal who showed such enthusiasm and readiness to hasten to the scene where the crimes were committed to help in the prosecution and arrest of the rebels and murderers. All the companies of the two battalions vied with one another other in their zeal.[11]

Since the eighteenth century, the coloured militia – composed of freemen and slaves serving for their freedom – had been renowned for hunting blacks and dealing with slave insurrections. The historian Françoise Thésée wrote,

> the Carbet revolt marked progress in the awareness of slaves in relation to their liberation. They knew that only they would be the ones to make it happen. Freemen of colour did not have the same objectives as slaves since some of them owned one or more of the latter. They were only fighting for supplementary rights to those already acquired. They were fighting for the liberation of their bodies.[12]

This shows how distant the cause of slaves and their emancipation was from the egalitarian claims of free people of colour in Martinique, who played a significant role in maintaining and defending the slave system as militiamen but also as landlords and slave-owners. Free people of colour owned from 5 per cent to 10 per cent of the slaves on the island and a significant part of the houses in the colony's towns and villages at the beginning of the Restoration.[13]

The Bissette affair: A major political upheaval

The Bissette affair occurred at a time when tensions were beginning to appear among white landowners in Martinique. They had witnessed the rise in economic power of free people of colour since the beginning of the nineteenth century. The latter not only owned houses and slaves in the city but also subsistence farms and coffee plantations in the countryside. While they had really only competed with small white craftsmen in the eighteenth century, ever since the revolutionary period they had begun to play a significant role in fields such as goods and trade in Guadeloupe (Pointe-à-Pitre and Basse-Terre and in Martinique (in Saint-Pierre and in Fort-Royal)).[14] They were in possession of 35 per cent of 1,337 secondary private plantations (coffee, vegetables and cotton) in Guadeloupe, only a few of which were of medium size at the end of the eighteenth century.[15] In Martinique the situation was similar at the beginning of the nineteenth century. Whereas in 1816, there were 1,604 colonial enterprises, including 336 sugar plantations and 863 coffee plantations, free people of colour owned part of them, especially the coffee and subsistence plantations.[16] An estimate of the people exiled from Martinique recorded on 15 March 1824, after the Bissette affair, showed that of the 219 freemen of colour in twenty-four parishes on the island affected by judicial and extrajudicial measures there were five sugar plantation owners, forty-four coffee plantation owners, two coffee and subsistence plantation owners, nineteen subsistence plantation owners, one boiler house owner and one landlord without indication as to his occupation, for a total of seventy-two inhabitants.[17]

Free people of colour had therefore gradually entered all economic sectors, which sparked jealousy, fears and concerns among whites in Martinique, as indicated by the Commissioner of Justice de Lamardelle and by Moreau de Jonnès.[18] For the white population the most striking feature of their everyday life and their greatest cause for concern was the constant increase in the number of free people of colour, with the result that the balance of power between the two groups was reversed between 1789 and 1816: while in the earlier year whites had numbered 10,635 against 5,235 free people of colour, in 1816, the former numbered only 9,298 against 9,364 for the latter.[19] In 1822, the turnaround was more pronounced and definitive: 9,867 whites compared with 11,073 free people of colour.[20] In such conditions whites favoured strengthened segregation and the colour line between white and free people of colour, justified by the servile and shameful origin of the latter and the indelible stain written in their genes. Whites exalted the nobility of their skin to oppose incorporation of free people of colour or any rapprochement between the two.

The Bissette affair in Fort-Royal and the so-called 'conspiracy' discovered in Saint-Pierre in December 1823 resulted in prompt action by colonial judicial authorities, who took measures and made arrests. The aim of these two cases, linked by the distribution in Martinique of a brochure on the situation of free people of colour, was to attack elites in the colony's two cities and then also on the rest of the island. Some twenty years separated the end of the revolutionary period from the Bissette affair, which took place under the Restoration. Between these two periods, the political rights of free people of colour had not changed: they had none. Socially, they remained in an in-between state between whites and slaves. Legally free, their civil rights, despite the disappearance of certain trademarks of everyday segregation (such as prohibition of luxury clothing, wearing jewellery, taking the names of whites and wholesale trading), remained limited, as in Guadeloupe.[21] Civil and social inequalities persisted: free people of colour could not convene for weddings, feasts or dances without the permission of the royal prosecutor under penalty of a fine; they could not practise medicine or surgery, or prepare remedies or treat patients in towns or in the countryside, with a fine of five hundred pounds for a first offence and corporal punishment in the event of re-offending; and finally, they could not be used by notaries, bailiffs or registrars to prepare deeds and other legal documents.[22] On the other hand, the elites of this social sector, especially merchants, took advantage of their access to all types of trade to engage in enterprise and prosper, which generated new demands from free people of colour.

They addressed petitions to Donzelot and the Chamber of Deputies calling for removal of 'ordinances that oppress them' and reinstatement of Article 59 of the so-called Black Code, which had declared them equal to whites since 1685.[23] Faced with the increasingly assertive desire of free people of colour to enjoy the rights granted to them by the Edict of March 1685 'and to no longer be treated as second-class citizens', whites were determined 'to defeat any kind of innovation in colonial legislation, especially in the status of free people of colour'.[24] The story accelerated dramatically with the distribution on the island of a brochure entitled *On the situation of free people of colour in the French West Indies* and the resulting arrests during December 1823, firstly in Fort-Royal and Saint-Pierre. This brochure, legally printed in France in October 1823, had been given to the Marquis de Clermont-Tonnerre, Minister of the Navy and Colonies, as well as to the president of the Council and other political figures.[25] It had not been censored and did not result in any legal proceedings. One of the problems with this little red booklet was its authorship, which is unresolved. In Martinique, colonial authorities saw it as the work of free people of colour, including Bissette, one of the editors and spokesman for the people of Fort-Royal. Historians hesitate between Bissette and two of his close friends, Jean-Baptiste Volny and Louis Fabien, or metropolitans such as Félix Renouard, Marquis de Sainte-Croix or Lainé de Villevêque, the deputy for Loiret.[26]

Circulation of the booklet coincided with the return to the island in November 1823 of Joseph Eriché and Montlouis Joseph Thébia, two of the most prominent representatives of free people of colour in Saint-Pierre, both tailors and traders. The thirty-two-page manifesto on the situation of people of colour in the French West Indies detailed the plight and inequities suffered by them in Martinique and Guadeloupe. It called for the abolition of the special laws that governed free people of colour and demanded the same civil and political rights conferred on whites. It also sought to demonstrate that free people of colour were in compliance with the law and committed to respecting the laws of the metropolis, and it insisted on their desire to maintain the slave system.

The secrecy surrounding publication of this booklet has an explanation. The slightest action by free people of colour challenging the established order was likely to be considered the starting point for a plot or insurrection. In Saint-Pierre, and then in Fort-Royal, on 6 or 7 December 1823, the brochure began to be distributed covertly. A correspondent for Montlouis Thébia and Joseph Eriché and friend of Joseph Millet, confectioner and owner in the economic capital, Bissette circulated the brochure, two copies of which he had in his possession. The judicial machine was set in motion as soon as it was reported on 12 December by a Spaniard named Morando, a sworn interpreter for the government. Searches were quick to follow. On 16 December, Bissette was imprisoned in the civil and military prison of Fort-Royal. There were further arrests in the second half of the month. Bissette's friends, Fabien and Volny, both free mulattos and merchants, were charged with being accomplices and of having distributed the brochure. On 22 December, they were imprisoned.[27]

At the very same time, by a happy coincidence a 'conspiracy' was uncovered in Saint-Pierre. On 21 December 1823, a slave named Modeste informed the city's royal prosecutor, Champvallier, of its existence. The plot involved people in the slave workshops of all the dwellings around Saint-Pierre setting fire to the four corners of the city and the sugar cane plantations and gathering in Morne-Rouge, a neighbourhood bordering Saint-Pierre and its dependencies, which was to be the meeting-point with groups from the various parishes in the area: Basse-Pointe, Grande Anse, Marigot and Sainte-Marie.[28] The leaders of the plot were identified as Germain Dufond, merchant; Germain Saint-Aude, carpenter and coffee plantation owner; and Hilaire Laborde (recently returned from the Republic of Haiti), a former sailor and dentist, all of them freemen of colour. Faced with this situation, on 20 and 22 December Donzelot and the commissioners of three parishes (Macouba, Basse-Pointe and Grande Anse) sent out a circular and a formal notice to the people underscoring their desire for order and tranquillity and, above all, their opposition to any amendment to colonial legislation in favour of free people of colour. In such circumstances, the 'conspiracy' discovered in Saint-Pierre could only serve the cause of whites who were anxious to maintain their privileges and continue to strictly adhere to the slave system. The various offshoots discovered in different parts of the island led colonial authorities to take drastic and radical measures against free people of colour, particularly against the leaders, who were identified through direct and indirect corroborating evidence but who were also the scapegoats of rumour and mob justice. On the night of 22–23 December, Acting Attorney General Richard de Lucy ordered the arrest of fifteen free people of colour in Saint-Pierre, who offered no resistance whatsoever. These were some of the most important landlords and slaveholders representing the worlds of trade and commerce, including Eriché, Thébia and Millet, who alone possessed some nine hundred thousand colonial pounds.[29]

At the same time, the case against Bissette and his friends (Fabien, Volny, Eugène Delfille, Bellisle Duranto, Joseph Demile dit Zonzon and Joseph Frapart) was still being pursued. The judicial proceedings, carried out at full speed, resulted in two waves of measures and convictions, the former against the free people of colour of Saint-Pierre and the other towns on the island; the latter against Bissette and his companions at Fort-Royal. A special government council composed of Donzelot, Lucy, Military Commander Barré and Commissioner Ricard was set up to take extrajudicial measures in parallel with the normal procedure via the first-instance and royal courts against the defendants. It acknowledged that the perpetrators and protagonists of the plot in Saint-Pierre were intending to violently abolish the political legislation of the French West Indies. The council noted the lack of connection between this 'conspiracy' and the case decided at Fort-Royal, but also noted that 'these seditious manoeuvres were fomented by agents established at Fort-Royal'.[30] This special council issued six rulings between 27 December 1823 and 5 February 1824, in which 141 people were targeted, tried and deported for life and/or banished from Martinique in the record time of forty-two days.[31] Justice was swift and exemplary. Free people of colour from nineteen parishes and districts on the island were affected. For the most part they belonged to four sectors: construction (carpenters, masons, cabinet-makers), leather and clothing, landlords and commerce.[32]

At Fort-Royal, the judicial investigation against Bissette, Fabien, Volny and their four co-defendants, Delphile (or Delfille), Frapart, Demil and Bellisle-Duranto, issued its conclusions. On 2 January 1824, the royal prosecutor,

Deslandes, presented his report to the lower court. He requested that the brochure on the situation of free people of colour

> be ripped up and burned by the executioner under the gallows, that Bissette be sentenced to life as a galley slave, having first been branded with the letters GAL [indicating galley slave], that Fabien and Delphille be sent to the galleys for five years; that Volny be banished from the colony for life; and that Bellisle-Duranto, Demil, and Frappart be banished from the colony for three years.[33]

The presiding judge, Amboise Gouin, assisted by the deputy royal prosecutor, Bacquoy, the second deputy Genny and the lawyer Sarrau delivered the verdict on 5 January 1824 sentencing Bissette, who was 'strongly suspected of having contributed to the clandestine distribution of the libel', to banishment from French territory for life.[34] Fabien and Volny were banned from the colony for five years. Bellisle-Duranto, Frapart and Demil, known as Zonzon, were exonerated, while Delfille remained in prison for six months because of a request for 'further information' from the Court of First Instance.[35]

The royal prosecutor, Deslandes, appealed. A retrial began at the Royal Court on 7 January 1824, which re-examined the case in the space of five days. Composed of individuals all belonging to the landowning class, the court was presided over by the count of Grenonville, a white Creole from Le Vauclin, while Lucy, another white Creole from Saint-Pierre, was acting attorney general.[36] Sharing all 'the prejudices and principles associated with their mentality and social group', they rendered judgment on 12 January 1824.[37] Bissette, convicted of peddling, secretly distributing and reading to various people a libellous book entitled 'On the situation of free people of colour in the French West Indies', was sentenced to the galleys for life.[38] Fabien, 'convicted of having opened a letter addressed to the Public Prosecutor's Office last June ... of having made a copy of it, and of having tried to bribe two witnesses who were to testify in the trial', was also sentenced to life imprisonment. Volny, 'convicted for giving Bissette a document written in his hand ... composed with the aim of stirring up hatred and participating in Bissette's criminal projects', was the third person sentenced to the galleys for life.[39]

The other four defendants received varied sentences: Delfille was banished for life from the kingdom of France, while Duranto, Demille and Frapart were banned for life from the French colonies.[40] These free mulattos belonged essentially to the business world; Demille was described as a landlord, and Duranto as an entrepreneur. They all owned houses and slaves in the city. On 14 January 1824, Bissette, Volny and Fabien were branded with a red-hot iron with the letters 'GAL'. They were taken onboard the ship *Le Tarn* heading for Brest on 15 March 1824 along with forty-three other convicts sentenced under extrajudicial measures by the special council; some were destined for Senegal or Gorée, while Millet, Thébia, Eriché and Laborde were being deported to France.[41] According to colonial authorities, the urgency of the situation demanded a swift response. However, the real reason for all this haste, which meant that judicial proceedings were slapdash and marred by irregularities, was the imminent arrival of a new general prosecutor from France, Girard, who had no affiliation with the Creole whites nor was he in any way related to the principal landowners in Martinique. He could well have contravened the judges' views and disapproved of the evidence and other documents produced during the inquiry.

A new stage was about to begin for Bissette and his friends: deportation, detention in Brest and the fight for annulment of the verdict of 12 January 1824.[42] This was duly overturned by the Court of Appeal on 30 September 1826.[43] François-André Isambert and Chauveau-Lagarde, the deportees' lawyers, had won their first victory. Bissette, Volny and Fabien were retried, this time by the Royal Court of Guadeloupe, on 26–28 March 1827. Reasons similar to those invoked by the Royal Court of Martinique were again used to convict Bissette. However, his sentence was reduced to ten years of banishment from the French colonies. On the other hand, Fabien and Volny were exonerated and released.[44] Isambert lodged an appeal to the Supreme Court, which was rejected on 29 December 1827. This marked the end of the Bissette affair in judicial terms. By relocating to Paris with his two friends, he was to begin a new stage in his fight for civil and political equality for free people of colour. Under the July Monarchy (1830–48), he would undertake further struggle for the improvement of the condition of slaves and their emancipation.

In Martinique, the consequences of the Bissette affair and the so-called 'conspiracy' in Saint-Pierre were far-reaching. Free people of colour in the colony were deprived of some of their leaders. In addition to the 141 people convicted by the special council and the seven convicted by the Royal Court of Martinique, others were ordered to leave the colony and never return. In March 1824, the list of those targeted in this way by the colonial justice system numbered 219, almost all of them (213) men.[45] They belonged mainly to the world of slaveholders, landowners and coffee plantation owners.[46] As it turned out, a significant proportion of the free population of colour had to go into exile or was invited to leave Martinique. Behind each man affected, there was invariably a family that suffered the full force of exile. Between 700 and 1,500 people (5.9 per cent to 12.74

per cent of the free people in 1824) made their way to other destinations (Sainte-Lucie, Dominique, Saint-Thomas, Trinidad, Haiti and especially France).[47] The following data clearly illustrate that exodus: in 1824, 11,768 free people of colour were recorded; in 1826, only 10,786 remained, leaving a deficit of 982. This concurs with the figures mentioned above. Françoise Thésée has written of an 'ethnic cleansing practiced by the white community against free people of colour with the complicity of colonial magistrates'; we concur with the historian's view that it was impressive and unprecedented in Martinique.[48] Undoubtedly, the Bissette affair at Fort-Royal and the 'conspiracy' in Saint-Pierre caused the first deep crack between free people of colour and whites on the island. In France, the Bissette affair had a national impact by arousing public opinion thanks to a campaign conducted in the press and in the Chambers by Liberal leaders (Chateaubriand, Casimir Périer, Benjamin Constant and the Duke of Broglie, among others).[49] In political terms, though Bissette was retried in Guadeloupe, it took the Revolution of July 1830 and the arrival of Louis-Philippe on the throne of France for the fundamental question raised by this case to be resolved.

Bissette's reform proposals for the Colonial Charter

Once he set foot in France, Bissette soon found that his demands for free people of colour met with a favourable response. He also managed to interest the Freemasons in his cause by bringing together the Trinosophes lodge and his friend Louis Fabien in Paris on 4 July 1828.[50] The historian André Combes refers to their introduction as 'a great day ... in front of a crowd of visitors'.[51] The secretary of the lodge also stigmatized their persecutors. The Trinosophes embraced the Masonic triptych of freedom, equality and fraternity. During the men's stay in the lodge from 4 July 1828 to 15 November 1832 they were elevated to the rank of knights Kadosh (thirtieth degree).[52] Meanwhile, the two men continued the fight for racial equality in the colonies. A petition from the population of Martinique and Guadeloupe was addressed to the Chambers in February 1829, which Bissette and Fabien as well as several Martiniquan free people of colour residing in Paris also signed, demanded they be granted full and complete enjoyment of civil and political rights.[53] Among the other signatories, alongside former deportees of the Saint-Pierre 'conspiracy' such as Millet, were other free people of colour, owners and traders from Guadeloupe such as Corentin Belleroche, Auguste Girard and S. Zoel Agnès, the first two of whom had been initiated into the Trinosophes lodge in Paris.[54]

Figure 5.1 Cyrille Bissette in an 1828 lithography published in Paris. Courtesy © Alamy.

Bissette's struggle for the civil and political rights of free people of colour was to continue until the enactment in April 1833 of the Colonial Charter – composed of three complementary reform laws, the first on sugar, the second on civil and political rights and the last on the legislative regime of the French colonies. Bissette, as representative of the Martiniquan free people of colour, focused on three issues: organization of the colonies, civil and political rights and legislation. First, he proposed that the role and powers of the governor be revised.[55] According to the Royal Ordinance of 9 February 1827, the administration's role involved supervising the press, commissioning printers, authorizing newspapers and suspending them in the event of abuse. For Bissette, this was an open door to arbitrary decision-making since one individual was capable of preventing a work from being published. He therefore requested the cancellation or modification of the governor's discretionary power. He also supported the removal of the power by which the governor could, in serious cases, order the expulsion of non-white citizens from the colony. This possibility was to be left to ordinary courts after they had heard from both parties. He requested the right of any convicted person, free or enslaved, to appeal to the Supreme Court. This had to be enshrined in law in order to prevent others having to suffer what happened to him in 1824 when Governor Donzelot and Attorney General Lucy opposed his appeal. Bissette favoured restricting the governor's powers, especially since in February 1827 he had been assigned a Privy Council composed solely of leading white landowners, contrary to the spirit of reform of the first governments of the July Monarchy.

Bissette also advocated revision of Article 190 of the Royal Ordinance of February 1827, which established the method for appointment to the General Council created on that occasion. The council included twelve members chosen from among white Creole landowners and/or slaves. Bissette campaigned for members to be appointed by municipalities, which would allow broader representation of both whites and free people of colour. Consequently, any free person aged at least twenty-five, residing in the same municipality for two years – or owner of buildings in the same municipality – and paying a contribution could be a member of the Electoral College in charge of electing members of the General Council. The purpose of this proposal was to promote free people of colour who were homeowners in cities and rural towns. This General Council, which was purely consultative, would have included thirty-seven members – one per town, except for Fort-Royal, which had four, and Saint-Pierre, six – instead of the twelve members determined by the above-mentioned ordinance. Bissette was therefore seeking major changes to Martinique's administrative regime. He also called for reform in the way the colony's delegate was recruited. The representative, who advised the Minister of the Navy and Colonies on colonial matters, was chosen by the minister from a list of three names provided by the General Council with no particular conditions of eligibility, whereas on Bourbon Island, candidates for this position had to have resided in the colony for at least five years. Above all, Bissette lamented the fact that the delegate was merely a representative of the white Creole landlords who had appointed him. As such he did not represent the whole population, and certainly not the free people of colour. He also called into question the judicial regime in the colonies. He wished to end bigotry and the partisan approach of the white Creole members of the Royal Court, and he advocated their replacement by metropolitan judges not linked to the slave system.

What Bissette cared about most were the civil and political rights of free people of colour and, by extension, the legislative regime of the colonies. In his *Observations sur le projets de lois coloniales présentés à la Chambre de Députés*, published at the end of 1832, he revisited the draft law on civil and political rights presented by the Minister of the Navy and Colonies on 28 October in the Chamber of Peers.[56] He highlighted the ambiguity of the use of 'free person' in Article 1 of the said draft, which stated that any person born free in the French colonies, without distinction of colour, enjoyed civil and political rights under the conditions prescribed by law. Many 'free' people in the colonies had parents with non-regulatory freedom (obtained in foreign countries, or under patronage, or simply de facto).[57] In addition, Bissette objected to Section 2 of the same draft law, which granted civil rights to freed persons immediately after their release while initially denying them political rights, since they had to wait ten years to enjoy them and be able to read and write. Bissette, Fabien and Mondésir Richard (unofficial representative of the free people of colour of Guadeloupe) had to fight long and hard to see that all free people of colour – born free and emancipated – should be considered.

The granting of civil and political rights to free people of colour was linked to reform of the colonial legislative regime. Here we are interested only in the provisions of Articles 20 and 21 of the bill presented to the deputies on 16 December 1831, which determined electoral and eligibility taxes. It specified a payment of three hundred francs to be a qualified elector and six hundred francs to be eligible in Martinique and Guadeloupe, while in France the amounts were only two hundred and five hundred francs. These higher rates had to do with the large population of free people of colour in the two colonies and clearly were designed to limit representation of this group, which had a strong presence in urban areas. Furthermore, electoral tax revenue there amounted to the sizeable amount of thirty thousand and sixty thousand francs in terms of movable or fixed property. This favoured white slaveholders and landlords, who were more numerous and richer than free landowners of colour. There was therefore a discriminatory nature to this bill, which Bissette denounced, demanding absolute equality between whites and free people of colour.[58] He also proposed that Articles 20 and 21 be amended, reducing the electoral tax to 150 francs and the eligibility tax to three hundred francs.[59] The proposed amendments were not accepted by legislators.

Despite Bissette's objections, the Colonial Charter was passed by the Chamber of Deputies on 21 April 1833 and went into effect on April 24. The law on the exercise of civil and political rights in the colonies enshrined the idea that any person born free or having acquired freedom legally now enjoyed civil and political rights in the French colonies under the conditions prescribed by law, thus repealing all declarations, royal orders or other contravening laws, restrictions or exclusions against them.[60] Free people of colour were now to become full-fledged citizens. Would this mean that the assimilation of free citizens of colour had been achieved? Evidently not, since the law 'concerning the legislative regime of the colonies' (Martinique, Guadeloupe, French Guyana and Bourbon) considerably altered the scope of the law granting full citizenship to free people of colour. The legal historian Jean-François Niort noted that 'electoral and eligibility taxes were higher than in mainland France, and their basis, defined by land ownership, slaveholding and trading licenses, was particularly disadvantageous to free people of colour, who in this regard were poorly represented in the colony, without counting the division of electoral districts aimed at under-representing the urban electorate'.[61]

The immediate abolition of slavery

The historian Lawrence C. Jennings refers to the slow development during the Restoration and the July Monarchy of an 'anti-slavery culture' that achieved its goals as soon as the February 1848 Revolution overthrew the repressive Orléanist regime.[62] Making prudent and gradual progress during the 1830s, the French abolitionist movement moved towards a more immediate approach in the 1840s, when it turned out that the government would allow emancipation only in the very distant future. Bissette, Fabien and Volny, representatives of the Martinique free people of colour in Paris, from 1830 to 1834 were the first to rally behind the cause of the immediate emancipation of slaves.[63] Did this new commitment reflect a unanimous position of their social group in the colony given that in 1836 free people of colour owned half the island's coffee plantations, six out of ten subsistence plantations, one out of three slaves in urban areas and one out of six in rural areas?[64] This is obviously not the case, especially since Fabien still owned a quarter of a sugar plantation in Le François through his wife at the end of the 1830s.[65] Bissette and Fabien seemed to have gathered around them a thinking minority who were in favour of the idea of abolition but far too entangled in the slave system to actually get rid of it. In any case, with the support of Richard, representing freemen of colour of Guadeloupe, they pooled their efforts to start the process in the colonies and attract the attention of the central government.

Bissette was still speaking out of both sides of his mouth. In December 1830, in a text entitled *Lettres à un colon* (Letters to a colonist), he 'did not question metropolitan politics, including when it accepted trafficking. He affirmed the existence of two "classes" in colonial society: the "free" (whatever the colour of their skin) and the slaves'.[66] However, while discussions from 1830 to 1833 in the Ministry of the Navy and Colonies and both houses of parliament in favour of free people of colour had not yet resulted in the law of 24 April 1833, Bissette, Fabien and Richard had been looking into the plight of slaves.[67] The text that shows the evolution of their ideas dates from 22 October 1832 – it was published on 24 October – and was addressed to the editor of the *Journal des Débats*:

> Sir, the men of colour we represent will never be allied with any one party, whichever it may be, to repress another. Ready to make all the sacrifices that may be required of them, they will respectfully welcome the emancipation of slaves ... They only thought that the initiative for emancipation should be left to the government and the Chambers; far from rejecting it, they will hasten its enactment with their best wishes.[68]

This co-signed article is evidence of the beginning of a new phase, perhaps influenced by the English abolitionist movement, which used ideological considerations to demand the emancipation of slaves.[69] Nevertheless, they specified that the road to emancipation should be gradual, not rushed, because 'philanthropy blinded by zeal' could lead to massacres. In the meantime, they proposed certain improvements in the plight of slaves – judicial reviews in criminal matters, the abolition of the whip, no return to slavery for those who had enjoyed freedom on metropolitan territory and the possibility of inheriting from one's master and being repurchased. This stance met with the wrath of settlers who considered that free people of colour also took advantage of the slave system and were not sincere in their abolitionist principles.

In 1832, Bissette founded a *Société des Hommes de Couleur* in Paris, which first published its *Revue des Colonies* in July 1834. From the very first issue of the magazine, Bissette, who was its main editor, along with Fabien, Richard, Xavier

Tanc (a former magistrate), attorney Adolphe Gatine and a few others who lent their support, devoted themselves to this all-important issue: 'The great question of the abolition of slavery, the fundamental stone of freedom, will be addressed with the most conscientious care and the most ardent love for equality and the general good. Arbitrary and biased behaviour will be referred to the court of public opinion. The weak will find support and protection, the oppressor will find punishment.'[70] With each new issue of his magazine, Bissette introduced elements for reflection in support of abolition, with particular reference to the English emancipation law. In April 1835, he took a firm stance in an article entitled, 'On immediate emancipation'. This prompted Lawrence C. Jennings to state, 'Bissette called for the immediate and complete abolition of French colonial slaves, a gesture that established him as the first French abolitionist of the nineteenth century to focus on immediacy.'[71] In July 1835, Bissette submitted his abolition bill for the French colonies. He 'borrowed its main premise from the British precedent and part of its content from Haitian agrarian legislation'. Article 1 of the bill read, 'Slavery is abolished in all French overseas possessions. All inhabitants of the French colonies, without distinction of colour, are declared free and equal in rights.' That was followed by Article 2: 'They therefore enjoy all civil and political family rights on the same basis as other French citizens in accordance with the law.'[72]

Learning from the imperfections of the Slavery Abolition Act of 1833, Bissette advocated immediate abolition. He called for the development of a code of culture to regulate the working environment. In addition, the nature and proportion of growers' wages would be regulated by the French government. Recognizing the importance of education, from which slaves had hitherto been deprived, Bissette called for the creation of free schools in the communes of the French colonies for the civil and religious education of farmers, with compulsory education until the age of twenty-one. Finally, the bill abolished regulations and ordinances relating to slavery and therefore implicitly repealed the Black Code. There was nothing in the project about compensating owners. Bissette offered his opinion on the subject, stating that 'between master and slave there can be no question of compensation. If one absolutely wanted to establish such a system, it would be the master who would owe the slave compensation for the physical and moral violence he had exerted against him.'[73] Here again, Bissette differed from other French abolitionists – and from those of the *Société Française pour l'Abolition de l'Esclavage* (SFAE) created in 1834 – by taking a stand against the principle of compensation to masters. He was undeniably at the forefront of this movement.

'The position of King Louis-Philippe's ministers, even when they were briefly presided over by an abolitionist leader, was one of waiting and procrastination', Jennings wrote. And the SFAE, especially in its first twelve years, was so cautious that it was ready, on the whole, to accept such a policy.[74] A decade ahead of other French abolitionists, with the exception of Victor Schoelcher, who subsequently opted for the immediate abolition of slavery between 1838 and 1840, Bissette was a secondary figure in the abolitionist landscape of the time. With no substantial financial resources, he had to discontinue publication of the *Revue des Colonies* in June 1842. However, he did not stop his fight for immediate abolition despite a rift between Schoelcher and himself in the early 1840s.[75] This enmity put Bissette at the mercy of the abolitionist movement because Schoelcher, a *grand bourgeois* and by then a member of the SFAE, did not tolerate criticism by a mulatto living off the charity of his coloured brethren. In their confrontation, Schoelcher had the last word by excluding Bissette from the commission on the abolition of slavery created in March 1848, which included the moderate mulatto Auguste Perrin. During those difficult years of isolation in the early 1840s, Bissette withdrew from the front stage. Yet 'it was he, having returned after 1845, who played the greatest role in giving new impetus to French abolitionism before 1848'.[76] In fact, he suggested to a professor at the Protestant faculty of Montauban, Guillaume de Félice, that he would write an 'immediate' petition on 17 August 1846. It

> was widely reproduced and then distributed in Protestant circles ... By the beginning of 1847, some 10,737 signatures had been collected, mostly in Paris, but [also] in the provinces ... Even Schoelcher, despite his antipathy for Bissette, cooperated in this effort through his links with Félice. But it was Bissette who played the leading role, going from door to door in Paris and collecting more than half the signatures himself.[77]

He also launched another publication, the *Revue abolitionniste*, 'to enlighten French public opinion on the question of the colonies and the issue of slavery'.[78] He was the only contributor. Despite donations from English abolitionists, the three issues published in 1847 failed to rival their direct competitor, *L'Abolitionniste français*, the SFAE newspaper. Nonetheless, his efforts were not in vain. In 1847, the SFAE, reconsidering its position, finally opted in August–September for the 'immediacy' approach. Bissette's idea that a new petition campaign should be launched for 1848 was adopted by the SFAE, and on 30 August it issued its own petition – written by Schoelcher – for immediate emancipation. It would appear that the petitions reached a very wide audience, because by the end of 1847 some thirty thousand signatures had been collected.[79] In all, four petitions were circulated in the last months of 1847: one from the SFAE, one from Bissette and two of Protestant and Catholic origin. Bissette's participation in the abolitionist endeavour under the July Monarchy was significant. However, change of political regime was required before the immediate abolition of slavery was finally resolved by the Provisional Government of the Second Republic on 27 April 1848.

Legislative elections of 1849 and Bissette's agenda

Proclamation of the Second Republic on 25 February 1848 favoured the abolitionist movement. One of the first decisions of the Republican government was to choose Schoelcher as Under-Secretary of State for the Navy and the Colonies and have him act quickly for immediate abolition. The outcome is well documented and will not be dealt with here. French historiography has identified Schoelcher as one of the main architects of abolition.[80] Aware that freedom was on its way, slaves in Martinique played their part in 1848, leading to the declaration by Governor Rostoland on 23 May anticipating the decrees issued by the Commissioner General of the Republic, Auguste Perrinon, on June 3.

Bissette, having been sacrificed on the altar of passions, welcomed the fact that several of his compatriots were encouraging him to stand for election in August 1848.[81] He announced his candidacy and platform: he would endeavour to uphold the 'imprescriptible dogma' of the sovereignty of the people and would demand freedom of thought, the press and education. In July 1835, he had opposed compensating slave owners; in June 1848, however, he was in favour: 'Emancipation will impoverish former masters. I will seek … a wise transaction in the public interest.'[82] Aware of the situation in Martinique, Bissette knew that his compatriots, freed people of colour (about 38,729 in 1847, two-thirds of whom were freed after 1831), owned 12,878 slaves in 1848, or 18 per cent of the total.[83] Should it also be seen as a rapprochement initiated in 1847 in Paris with the 'conservative and clerical' colonial slave-owner class? The time for compromises and commitments seemed to have to taken root in the language of the man who would become 'Papa Bissette' in the eyes of the masses in the colony's urban and rural landscape.

The Constituent Assembly elections of 9–12 August 1848 in Martinique were favourable to abolitionists who had distinguished themselves in the decade preceding emancipation. Bissette, Pierre-Marie Pory-Papy and Schoelcher were elected by an overwhelming majority. Bissette's election was then invalidated 'because of personal ineligibility', a reference to his publishing company's declaration of bankruptcy. On 11 April 1849, the Commercial Court of the Seine declared null and void that judgment of March 1848, enabling him to present his candidacy to represent the people of Martinique in the elections in June 1849.[84] He made a triumphant return to Martinique at the end of March 1849 before a jubilant crowd in Saint-Pierre who welcomed him as a saviour. He proclaimed that he was ready to work towards forgetting the past and reconciling social groups: 'Let us therefore consent to letting bygones be bygones and cast aside our fateful divisions, our old prejudices of a time that is past, the old recriminations that never suited the parties and much less the country's happiness, which must dominate and silence all passions.'[85]

Bissette's discourse thus changed significantly after abolition. Yet as early as May 1835, he had advocated the 'fusion of races' and forgetting the past: 'By the power of persuasion, our cause will one day be victorious, and then those who are in prison today may well set a fine example by forgiving their implacable enemies and the juries ... who so viciously persecuted them. That day will come.'[86] Bissette was referring to the free militiamen of colour who had been convicted by the Creole white colonial judiciary on 30 June 1834 during the Grande Anse case (now the Lorrain commune) in Martinique and whose position he had supported at the time.[87] So in March 1849 Bissette was promoting ideas he had previously voiced: forgetting the past and bringing together whites and blacks. Now he was adding union and concord between the two. In this process of conciliation and union, he reconciled with his former persecutors who had mistreated and convicted him on 12 January 1824, and those whom he had opposed on the issue of abolition.

One of Bissette's first acts on arrival in Saint-Pierre was to reconcile with the lawyer, Cicéron, 'who had insulted his mother in the grossest fashion'.[88] Cicéron was the former colonial slave adviser under the July Monarchy with whom Bissette had fought a duel in Vincennes Forest outside Paris in October 1834. Gaston Souquet-Basiège, defender of the whites, described this interview in front of 'a large crowd':

> Mr. Bissette arrived accompanied ... by some other distinguished people from the city ... Bissette was the first to enter the great lawyer's living-room ... he stepped forward with a firm and dignified step in front of the former settler, holding out his hands; Mr. Cicéron opened his arms and pressed against his chest the good man who came to embrace in him an entire race, once his enemy, and from now on united through love and reconciliation.[89]

On 28 April 1849, Bissette went to the town of Sainte-Marie where, once again, he made peace with another prominent member of the white Creole class, Pierre Dessalles, owner of a sugar cane plantation and one of his judges in the December 1823–January 1824 case. As part of this rapprochement towards whites, Bissette met with the committee of owners formed in early 1849 in the city of Saint-Pierre to defend the colony's interests. He succeeded in obtaining their support in the National Legislative Assembly elections. He was joined by one of their own, François Augustin Pécoul, a major landowner and former adviser to the Royal Court, then in metropolitan France.

According to the committee, this was only a tactic to avoid a repeat of the August 1848 defeat. It was also necessary to thwart the influence of the republican Schoelcher's supporters in the colony, consisting of a whole segment of the population including his mulatto friends, Pory-Papy and Perrinon, as well as a section of the elite people of colour in Fort-Royal and Saint-Pierre, in particular those who became shareholders in *La Liberté*, a newspaper founded in April 1850.[90] This seemingly unnatural association was aimed at restoring control over colonial affairs and affording national visibility to large landowners who defended respect for order, property and labour, the latter obtained through binding measures. Bissette and his close circle of supporters – his family and loved ones at Fort-Royal – agreed with these three main principles. Bissette ardently defended work in his travels in Martinique, which brought him into contact with blacks, both farmers and workers.[91] Souquet-Basiège noted at the time: 'It was only the most prominent representatives of the mixed blood race who were missing from Mr. Bissette's circle of friends ... At the first mention of forgetting the past, of unity and a fusion of interests while waiting for the races to merge, the men of mixed blood simply viewed Mr. Bissette as a traitor.'[92] Hence Martiniquan society was divided between supporters of Bissette, or *bissettistes*, who favoured the ideas of this man of colour; and the followers of Schoelcher, or *schoelchéristes* (also qualified as 'red' by the administrators because of their – albeit more moderate – 'republicanism'), who did not necessarily agree with all Schoelcher's proposals on concessions to be granted to former slaves who were now black citizens.

In 1849, Bissette and François Augustin Pécoul created a mutual assistance society whose purpose was to teach and practice 'mutual union and assistance, respect for religion, laws, individuals, property, love, order, work, and fraternity, all of them conditions for prosperity in the colonies'.[93] Politics was prohibited from the organization, which existed until 1855. The real goals of this association were 'to stimulate the industry of farmers and to promote good understanding between the various races and classes of society'. The first objective seems to have been achieved, unlike the second.[94] In any case, thanks to this circumstantial alliance between whites and blacks, the tandem formed by Bissette and Pécoul was overwhelmingly elected on 3 June 1849 (16,327 votes and 13,482 votes), a resounding victory for supporters of union and order.[95] The elections did not put an end to the opposition between *bisettistes* and *schoelchéristes*, and evidence of this division was apparent until the early 1850s.

On 10 January 1850, Bissette sailed for France to carry out his work as a representative of the people. On his departure, he gave a farewell speech in Saint-Pierre in which he thanked his supporters and renewed his wishes for order, work and unity among the population: 'Union and conciliation, never forget, are the conditions for the best future … Friends, you are free and strong; be good and peaceful [*dociles*].'[96] Until the coup d'état of Louis-Napoléon Bonaparte on 2 December 1851, Bissette attended all meetings relating directly or indirectly to the colonies and participated in votes. He sat to the right of the Chamber, alongside the conservatives and reactionaries, and according to Pame he spoke out 'most of the time against the proposals of the republican government'.[97] In all his speeches, the representative of Martinique advocated order and collaboration in the colonies. In these parliamentary contests, Schoelcher and Perrinon, who sat on the left side of the Assembly along with other Republic supporters, were often among Bissette's opponents. In February 1851, Bissette's last notable intervention in the National Legislative Assembly came at a time when representatives Lopès-Dubec and Favreau were proposing to extend by ten years the time frame of Article 8 of the decree of 27 April 1848, which granted three years to French nationals living abroad to free their slaves.[98] The entire bill was passed despite Bissette's speech, in which he pleaded: 'Do not let this shame of owning slaves continue any longer in the hands of our countrymen … Do something moral.'[99] He always showed his radical opposition to slavery, the only issue on which he had not deviated since the early 1830s. Throughout the legislature, Bissette constantly recalled the principles to which he remained faithful: 'Sent by you to the Legislative Assembly and imbued with the importance of this mandate, my flag will always be unfurled and its slogan will always be: order and work! Justice and conciliation!'[100] In this respect, the politician had undeniably sided with the conservatives who, as early as November 1849, with the arrival of Rear-Admiral Bruat, the new governor of Martinique, had decimated the social and political improvements that accompanied the abolition of slavery.

Conclusion

In the early part of his life, Cyrille Bissette represented a classic example of a man fully integrated into colonial slave society because of his family background, his friends and his social and professional origins. He defended its essential principles by owning slaves and, as a militiaman, by repressing a revolt against the established order. A change seems to have occurred in 1823–4 due to the case that bore his name, the Bissette affair, which brought to light the egalitarian claims of free people of colour. Throughout the second part of his adult life and his participation in elections to represent the people (1824–51), Bissette was guided by his fight for equality and the assimilation of these second-class citizens into white society, the improvement of the condition of slaves and the immediate abolition of slavery under the July Monarchy. The coup d'état of 2 December 1851 put him in the shadows, since from then onwards the colonies had no representatives. The year 1852 marked the beginning of his political retirement. Bissette received the cross of the Legion of Honour in March 1851, which was welcomed by conservative newspapers in Martinique supporting the *bissettiste* party (*Le Courrier de la Martinique* and *Les Antilles*), and he was recognized by the French government for his actions in favour of blacks in the colonies and his post-abolition endeavours to make them respect the rigour of metropolitan laws. Nevertheless, Bissette had to embark on a long and lonely pilgrimage in the anonymity of French colonial history resulting from his marked opposition to Victor Schoelcher, the fact that elite Martiniquans of colour disowned him because of his perceived betrayal, and presumably because of a desire to downplay his role after abolition when he promoted reconciliation and rapprochement between whites and blacks. Bissette, like others of his social group – for example Janvier Littée and Jean-Pierre Eugène Clavier – had a definite career path and attitude and he made occasionally ambiguous choices in Martinique and France.[101] Yet, unlike these others, his commitment to the immediate abolition of slavery was both documented and clear.

He died in Paris on 22 January 1858. The government gave him an 'honourable funeral'.[102] While many former free people of colour distinguished themselves in the colonies after 1848 as mayors, members of municipal councils, councillors at the Court of Appeal or General Council, or even as representatives of the people (the Didier brothers and Clavier brothers in Fort-de-France, in particular), after the conservative turnaround in France of June 1848 and the following November in Martinique, none requested that the remains of the man who had claimed civil and political rights for free people of colour and the immediate abolition of slavery be returned to his birthplace. Although not exemplary in all his activities, as shown by his personal choices, should not Martiniquan and national history consider the actors and protagonists in all their complex facets by placing them in context? He probably was excluded from the national abolitionist pantheon because of his relentless opposition to Schoelcher. As Christophe Cassiau-Haurie points out, Schoelcher's 'redemptive figure' satisfied

> all parties: the long-time assimilationist local intellectual bourgeoisie … [and] the national political power that cultivates the idea that the abolition of slavery was granted by the Republic through the work of one of its great defenders, Schoelcher. In the national imagination, the end of slavery was not the result of a struggle but an act of fraternity and national reconciliation.[103]

The omission of Cyrille Bissette from national and local history is also the omission of many events that are insufficiently emphasized or taught in official French educational programmes.

Notes

1   It is worth mentioning a remarkable biography by Stella Pame, *Cyrille Bissette: Un martyr de la liberté* (Fort-de-France: Éditions Désormeaux, 1999). Also, Jacques Adélaïde-Merlande, 'Bissette', *L'Historial Antillais* (Fort-de-France, Société Dajani, 1980), vol. IV, 457.

2   Concerning the renowned '*affaire Bissette*', it is worth consulting: *Revue de la Martinique*, 3 (1928): 19–27; Lawrence C. Jennings, 'Cyrille Bissette, radical black French abolitionist', *French History*, 9 (1) (1995): 48–66; Eric Mesnard, 'Les mouvements de résistance dans les colonies françaises: l'affaire Bissette (1823–1827)', in *Les Abolitions de l'esclavage de L. F. Sonthonax à V. Schoelcher, 1793, 1794, 1848*, ed. Marcel Dorigny (Vincennes, Paris: Presses Universitaires de Vincennes et Éditions Unesco, 1995), repr. 1998, 293–7; Françoise Thésée, *Le Général Donzelot à la Martinique. Vers la fin de l'Ancien Régime colonial (1818–1826)* (Paris: Karthala, 1997), 147–89; Nelly Schmidt, *Abolitionnistes de l'esclavage et Réformateurs des colonies 1820–1851. Analyse et documents* (Paris: Karthala, 2000), 254–63; Abel Alexis Louis, *Marchands et Négociants de couleur à Saint-Pierre (1777–1830). Milieux socioprofessionnels, fortune et mode de vie* (Paris: L'Harmattan, 2015), vol. I, 222–44.

3   Emile Hayot, 'Les Gens de couleur libres du Fort-Royal 1679–1823', *Revue Française d'Histoire d'Outre-Mer*, 56 (202) (1969): 5–98.

4   Cyrille Bissette was described as *mulâtre* (a child born of two mulattos or a white man and a black woman) or a half-breed (a child born of two half-breeds or a white man and a half-breed).

5   Archives of Martinique (ADM), series E, civil status and notary, study of the notary Baylies-Dupuis (Fort-Royal), microfilm 1 Mi 583, 'Contrat de mariage de Cyrille Bissette et de Marie Rose Augustine Séverin le 6 février 1816'; and Pame, *Cyrille Bissette*, 239–40.

6   Abel Alexis Louis, *Les Libres de couleur en Martinique. De septembre 1802 aux débuts de la Restauration* (Paris: L'Harmattan, 2012), vol. 3, 195.

7   Pame, *Cyrille Bissette*, 10

8   François-André Isambert, *Affaire des déportés de la Martinique* (Paris: Constantin, 1824), 107; Hayot, 'Les Gens de couleur libres du Fort-Royal 1679–1823', 107.

9   Pame, *Cyrille Bissette*, 10; Thésée, *Le Général Donzelot à la Martinique*, 120–34.

10   Thésée, *Le Général Donzelot à la Martinique*, 124.

11   Cited by ibid., 127.

12   Ibid., 142.

13   Alexis Louis, *Les Libres de couleur en Martinique*, vol. 3, 173.

14   See Anne Pérotin-Dumon, *La Ville aux îles, la Ville dans l'île. Basse-Terre et Pointe-à-Pitre, Guadeloupe, 1650–1820* (Paris: Éditions Karthala, 2000), 508–15 and 828–44; and notably Frédéric Régent, *Esclavage, Métissage, Liberté. La Révolution française en Guadeloupe 1789–1802* (Paris: Bernard Grasset, 2004), 301–17; Abel Alexis Louis, *Les Libres de couleur en Martinique. Des origines à la veille de la Révolution française 1635–1788* (Paris: L'Harmattan, 2012), vol. 1, 189–227; and by the same author, *Les Libres de couleur en Martinique*, vol. 3, 110–69.

15   Régent, *Esclavage, Métissage, Liberté* 320–3.

16   Archives Nationales Outre-Mer (ANOM), Fonds Ministériels 39, Série Géographique Martinique (1), carton 3, dossier 13, '*Mémoire du roi, pour servir d'instructions au sieur lieutenant général baron Donzelot, gouverneur et administrateur de la Martinique*' (Paris, 4 September 1817), 28; Alexis Louis, *Les Libres de couleur en Martinique*, vol. 3, 173.

17   Alexis Louis, *Les Libres de couleur en Martinique …*, vol. 3, 174 and 196–9.

18   See Pame, *Cyrille Bissette*, 39.

19   Bernard David, 'Les Origines de la population martiniquaise au fil des ans (1635–1902)', *Annales des Antilles*, 3 (1973): 87 and 92.

20   Ibid.

21   Josette Fallope, *Esclaves et Citoyens. Les Noirs à la Guadeloupe au XIXe siècle dans le processus de résistance et d'intégration (1802–1910)* (Basse-Terre: Société d'Histoire de la Guadeloupe, 1992), 135–6.

22   ADM, Registre manuscrit du Conseil souverain, B[25] (1809–December 1813), 'Règlement concernant la police générale de la colonie, Fort-Royal le 1er novembre 1809 (29 November 1809)', fol. 32.

23   Thésée, *Le Général Donzelot à la Martinique*, 149.

24   Pame, *Cyrille Bissette*, 44.

25 ANOM, F. M. 39, S. G. Martinique (1), carton 51, dossier 420; and François-André Isambert, *Mémoire justificatif des hommes de couleur de la Martinique condamnés par arrêt de la cour royale de cette colonie, contenant l'histoire des hommes de couleur dans les colonies françaises* (Paris: Imprimerie de E. Duverger, 1826), 2nd part, 74–91; Pame, *Cyrille Bissette*, 49.

26 Liliane Chauleau, *La Martinique et la Guadeloupe du XVIIe siècle à la fin du XIXe siècle* (Pointe-à-Pitre: Émile Désormeaux, 1973), 261; Pame, *Cyrille Bissette*, 49; Thésée, *Le Général Donzelot à la Martinique* 151.

27 Isambert, *Mémoire justificatif des hommes de couleur de la Martinique condamnés par arrêt de la cour royale de cette colonie*, 1st part, 159–60.

28 Pame, *Cyrille Bissette*, 55.

29 Isambert, *Mémoire justificatif des hommes de couleur de la Martinique condamnés par arrêt de la cour royale de cette colonie*, 166–7.

30 Quoted by Thésée, *Le Général Donzelot à la Martinique*, 168–9.

31 ANOM, F. M. 39, S. G. Martinique (1), carton 51, dossier 409.

32 Alexis Louis, *Marchands et Négociants de couleur à Saint-Pierre (1777–1830)*, vol. I, 236–7.

33 Thésée, *Le Général Donzelot à la Martinique*, 174–5.

34 Pame, *Cyrille Bissette*, 61.

35 Thésée, *Le Général Donzelot à la Martinique*, 175.

36 Pame, *Cyrille Bissette*, 63–4.

37 Ibid., 64.

38 ANOM, F. M. 39, S. G. Martinique (1), carton 51, dossier 409, '*État nominatif des hommes de couleur libres qui ont été condamnés par arrêt de la cour royale en date du 12 janvier 1824*' (At Fort-Royal, 25 January 1824, the lieutenant general and king's administrator, signed Donzelot).

39 Ibid.

40 Ibid.

41 Thésée, *Le Général Donzelot à la Martinique*, 179–80.

42 We refer to the studies of Françoise Thésée and Stella Pame to explore this question further. See Thésée, *Le Général Donzelot à la Martinique*, 179–84; Pame, *Cyrille Bissette*, 70–98.

43 Isambert, *Mémoire justificatif des hommes de couleur de la Martinique condamnés par arrêt de la Cour royale*, 1st part, 309–15.

44 Pame, *Cyrille Bissette*, 91; Thésée, *Le Général Donzelot à la Martinique*, 184.

45 'Affaire Bissette', in *Revue de la Martinique*, 3 (1928): 19–27; Alexis Louis, *Marchands et Négociants de couleur à Saint-Pierre (1777–1830)*, vol. I, 241–3.

46 Alexis Louis, *Marchands et Négociants de couleur à Saint-Pierre (1777–1830)*, vol. I, 241–2.

47 Eric Mesnard refers to more than seven hundred people driven out of the colony while Françoise Thésée refers to the figure of 1,500 people. See Eric Mesnard, 'Les

mouvements de résistance dans les colonies françaises', 295; Thésée, *Le Général Donzelot à la Martinique*, 179; Alexis Louis, *Marchands et Négociants de couleur à Saint-Pierre (1777–1830)*, vol. I, 244–59.

48 Thésée, *Le Général Donzelot à la Martinique*, 179.

49 Eric Mesnard, 'Les mouvements de résistance dans les colonies françaises: l'affaire Bissette', 295.

50 André Combes, *Histoire de la Franc-maçonnerie au XIXe siècle* (Paris: Éditions du Rocher, 1998), vol. I, 117–18.

51 Ibid.

52 Bibliothèque Nationale de France (BNF), DM (Département des Manuscrits), Fonds Maçonniques (FM)² 121, dossier 2, Chapitre et Conseil des *Trinosophes*.

53 *Pétition des hommes de couleur de la Martinique et de la Guadeloupe* (Paris: E. Duverger, February 1829).

54 BNF, DM, FM² 120bis (Paris), dossier 2, loge des *Trinosophes*, and FM² 121, dossier 2.

55 Cyrille Bissette, *Mémoire au ministre de la marine et des colonies et à la commission de législation coloniale sur les améliorations législatives et organiques à apporter au régime des colonies françaises* (Paris: Mie, 1831).

56 Cyrille Bissette, *Observations sur les projets de lois coloniales présentés à la Chambre des Députés* (Paris: Mie, 1832).

57 Patronage: a slave working for a boss, be he white or a free person of colour, who was not his master.

58 Cited by Pame, *Cyrille Bissette*, 139.

59 Pame, *Cyrille Bissette*, 140.

60 ADM, 3 K 2/6, *Bulletin des lois des Actes Administratifs de la Martinique*, no. 6, June 1833, no. 72, 'Loi concernant l'exercice des droits civils et des droits politiques dans les colonies' (Paris, 24 April 1833), 81–2.

61 Jean-François Niort, 'La condition des libres de couleur aux îles du Vent (XVIIe– XIXe siècles): ressources et limites d'un système ségrégationniste', 2002, 18. Available online: http://calamar.univ-ag.fr/cagi/NiortConditionlibrecouleur.pdf; see also ADM, 3 K 2/6, *Bulletin des lois des Actes Administratifs de la Martinique*, no. 6, June 1833, no. 74, 'Loi concernant le régime législatif des colonies' (Paris, 24 April 1833), title 1, articles 2 to 10; and title III, articles 20 and 21, 85–8.

62 Lawrence C. Jennings, 'Le second mouvement pour l'abolition de l'esclavage colonial français', *Outre-Mers*, 89 (2002): 177–91, 180.

63 According to Léo Elisabeth, the representatives of the free people of colour had an article published in the *Journal des Débats* in 1830, which was 'a very clear statement in favour of general emancipation'. Lawrence C. Jennings noted that Bissette would have explicitly made abolition his main objective in 1834. See Léo Elisabeth, 'L'abolition de l'esclavage à la Martinique', *Annales des Antilles*, 1983, 5, 6; and Jennings, 'Cyrille Bissette, radical black french abolitionist', 58.

64 Vincent Cousseau, *Prendre nom aux Antilles. Individu et Appartenances (XVIIe-XIXe siècle)* (Paris: CTHS, 2012), 120.

65 Abel Alexis Louis, *Jean-Pierre Eugène Clavier: premier homme de couleur membre du Conseil colonial et de la Cour d'appel de la Martinique (1810–1863)* (Paris: L'Harmattan, 2016), 112.

66 Cited by Mesnard, 'Les mouvements de résistance dans les colonies françaises', 297.

67 Cyrille Bissette, Louis Fabien and Adolphe Gatine, *Pétition à la Chambre des députés relative au droit dénié aux esclaves de se pourvoir en cassation* (Paris: Mie, 1831), 12; and Cyrille Bissette, Louis Fabien and Mondésir Richard, *Pétition à la Chambre des députés relative à l'amélioration du sort des esclaves aux colonies* (Paris: Dupont et Laguionie, 1832).

68 Quoted by Schmidt, *Abolitionnistes de l'esclavage et Réformateurs des colonies*, 680–1.

69 Marie-Jeanne Rossignol, 'L'Atlantique de l'esclavage, 1775–1860', *Transatlantica*, 1 (2002): 4. Available online: http://journals.openedition.org/transatlantica/418 (accessed 5 February 2021).

70 *Revue des Colonies*, July 1834, 1; quoted by Schmidt, *Abolitionnistes de l'esclavage et Réformateurs des colonies*, 665–6.

71 Jennings, 'Le second mouvement pour l'abolition de l'esclavage colonial français', 183.

72 Quoted by Schmidt, *Abolitionnistes de l'esclavage et Réformateurs des colonies*, 256.

73 Ibid.

74 Jennings, 'Le second mouvement pour l'abolition de l'esclavage colonial français', 183.

75 On this subject, among others, see Victor Schoelcher, *Des colonies françaises. Abolition immédiate de l'esclavage* (Paris: Pagnerre, 1842), 190–1, 192–4, 201–3; Cyrille Bissette, *Réfutation du livre de M. Victor Schoelcher, intitulé 'Des colonies françaises'* (Paris: Breton, 1843), 17, 61, 72–84.

76 Jennings, 'Le second mouvement pour l'abolition de l'esclavage colonial français', 188.

77 Ibid.

78 Schmidt, *Abolitionnistes de l'esclavage et Réformateurs des colonies*, 261.

79 Jennings, 'Le second mouvement pour l'abolition de l'esclavage colonial français', 189.

80 Schmidt, *Victor Schoelcher et l'Abolition de l'esclavage* (Paris: Fayard, 1994), 440; Anne Girollet, *Victor Schoelcher, Abolitionniste et Républicain. Approche juridique et politique de l'œuvre d'un fondateur de la République* (Paris: Karthala, 2000).

81 Cyrille Bissette, *Lettres politiques sur la question de l'esclavage dans les colonies* (À mes compatriotes de la Martinique, 10 juin 1848) (n.l.: n.p, n.d.), 35–8.

82 Ibid., 38.

83 Elisabeth, 'L'abolition de l'esclavage à la Martinique', 5.

84 Pame, *Cyrille Bissette*, 206.

85 Cited in ibid., 209.

86 *Revue des Colonies,* May 1835, 5; quoted by ibid., 208.

87 The Grand Anse case began on 24 December 1833 in the commune of Lorrain. The rebels were black and mixed-blood freemen, citizens with full rights according to the law of 24 April 1833. They mostly belonged to the colonial militia, whose members were whites, freemen of colour and slaves who served in exchange for their freedom; members had to be from fifteen to fifty-five years old, and they provided support to French professional troops. The militiamen of colour from Gran Anse, small and medium landowners, rose up because their civil and political equality under the law of April 24 was not being recognized. The uprising led to arrests and the dissolution of the Martinique colonial militia in 1834. Participants were subject to expedited justice by white Creoles and sentenced to death, though some of the sentences were later reduced. Bissette defended the accused in a pamphlet printed in Paris.Cf. Abel Alexis Louis, 'L'affaire de la Grande Anse en décembre 1833 à la Martinique', *Résistances et révoltes contre les pouvoirs établis de l'Antiquité à nos jours* (n.l.: Ibis Rouge éditions, 2004), 263–81.

88 Pame, *Cyrille Bissette*, 210.

89 G. Souquet-Basiège, *Le Préjugé de Race aux Antilles françaises. Étude historique,* 1883 edn. (Fort-de-France: Emile Désormeaux, 1979), 92–3.

90 Of the number of these individuals who were shareholders in the newspaper *La Liberté* we should mention: Alcide Dufail, Elisée jeune, Alcide Raymond, Antoine Montfleury, Auguste Riffard, Alexandre Berne, Rémy-Néris, Gustave Lacourne, Charles Larcher, Barthelemy Larcher, Pierre Henry Larcher, Louis and Illide Deproge, Alphonse Didier and Gaëtan Quiqueron. They were for the main part owners, businessmen, lawyers and doctors. See Alexis Louis, *Jean-Pierre Eugène Clavier: premier homme membre du Conseil colonial,* 157–60.

91 Souquet-Basiège, *Le Préjugé de Race aux Antilles françaises,* 94–5.

92 Ibid., 95.

93 Quoted by Pame, *Cyrille Bissette*, 213.

94 Ibid.

95 Alexis Louis, *Jean-Pierre Eugène Clavier: Premier homme de couleur membre du Conseil colonial,* 165.

96 Quoted by Pame, *Cyrille Bissette*, 217–18.

97 Pame, *Cyrille Bissette*, 218.

98 Ibid., 220.

99 Quoted by ibid.

100 Cyrille Bissette, *À mes compatriotes* (Paris: Poussièlgue, 1850), 3.

101 Abel Alexis Louis, *Janvier Littée. Martiniquais Premier député de couleur membre d'une Assemblée parlementaire française (1752–1820). L'homme, son milieu social, son action politique* (Paris: L'Harmattan, 2013), and by the same author, *Jean-Pierre Eugène Clavier: premier homme de couleur membre du Conseil colonial et de la Cour d'appel de la Martinique*, 130–9.

102 Souquet-Basiège, *Le Préjugé de Race aux Antilles françaises*, 100.

103 Christophe Cassiau-Haurie, 'Cyrille Bissette, héros de l'abolition de l'esclavage'. Available online: http://afribd.africultures.com/article.php?no=12202 (accessed 5 February 2021).

6

Robert Smalls: In majority and in minority in Washington

Stephanie McCurry

Robert Smalls rose to power as part of a revolutionary wave in American political life, what the great African American historian W. E. B. Du Bois aptly called the 'black reconstruction *of democracy* in America'.[1] In the history of the United States, the term 'Reconstruction' refers to a period and a process that unfolded between 1865 and 1877. It involved a highly contingent series of developments that came in the immediate aftermath of the American Civil War which had delivered the total and uncompensated emancipation of four million enslaved people of African descent. It was a radical break in history opened up by the military defeat and unconditional surrender of American slaveholders in their war for independence (1861–5), and by the squandering of the opportunity subsequently provided to white southerners to reconstruct their affairs themselves. When they failed, the United States Congress put the defeated South back under military rule and men like Robert Smalls seized their opening in political life.

Starting in 1867, in the most singular development of Reconstruction, African American men gained the right to vote and to hold office. Some, like Robert Smalls, won election to the US Congress and went on to represent their constituents in seats formerly held by the country's largest slave-owners. Du Bois wrote searingly of this 'great human experiment' as a test of labour and democracy itself world-wide. It remained at the very centre of his historical sensibility. 'Reconstruction', he said, 'was an economic revolution on a mighty scale and with world-wide reverberations'. Robert Smalls was part of a revolution in the political order unmatched by any other post-emancipation society in the western hemisphere.[2]

Robert Smalls was born a slave in the rich plantation district of low country South Carolina. It was a place with a very particular history that it is key to understanding his political career. Smalls was one of more than two thousand African American men who held public office in the US during Reconstruction. Only a few – seventeen – represented their states in the US Congress as he did.[3] When Robert Smalls served in the United States Congress, he was always in minority. But he won that seat and derived his power from a political base in a place where African Americans were always in majority. It takes both things to understand Robert Smalls's career. For more than forty years after the Civil War, Smalls was the preeminent politician in Beaufort County, South Carolina, a place that had been majority black since the late seventeenth century. Throughout Reconstruction Beaufort had the largest black majority in any place in South Carolina and perhaps in the United States.[4]

It was there that Robert Smalls built a formidable political machine. Unlike many other minority representatives in national legislative assemblies in the nineteenth and early twentieth centuries, Robert Smalls was a real politician with a real political career – a constituency that elected and remained devoted to him, and which he served faithfully, spoke for in state and national councils and to whom he delivered a share of government largesse. Because of it he lasted longer in office and in Congress than almost any other African American politician in the nineteenth-century United States.[5] Robert Smalls's most significant legislative career was in the South Carolina state house. He entered the US Congress when Reconstruction was in decline. But that meant he was at the centre of the action in Congress at the key moment in 1877 when the deal was struck that sold out African Americans and the southern wing of the Republican party. Indeed, Smalls's own congressional seat was at the heart of the final struggle. Smalls fought the abandonment of African Americans' civil and political rights all the way and after. In the end, even his formidable political machine was not enough to withstand the white supremacist tide, and Smalls – and with him American democracy – was overthrown by violence. The lessons of Robert Smalls's political life weigh heavily in our own dangerous times.

The person

Robert Smalls was born in the town of Beaufort, South Carolina, in April 1839, in the slave quarters behind the house on Prince Street owned by his mother's master John McKee. It is likely that McKee was Smalls's father as well as his owner. In 1864 Smalls bought McKee's house in a tax sale.[6] It is now a nationally registered Historic Landmark, and Smalls himself a key part of the history of a place – Beaufort – recently and officially recognized as of national significance. In January 2017, with only a week left in his administration, President Barack Obama designated a cluster of sites in Beaufort as a national monument – The Reconstruction Era National Monument – in recognition of its role as 'the birthplace of Reconstruction'. In his proclamation officially establishing the monument, President Obama spoke extensively about Robert Smalls, lauding his long career from Civil War hero to national politician.[7] As he recognized, it is impossible to talk about Reconstruction without talking about Robert Smalls.

Smalls sprung from obscurity to instant national celebrity in May 1862, one year into the American Civil War, when he seized a Confederate steamship, the *Planter*, on which he had been conscripted to work. Smalls was an accomplished pilot, a skill acquired in many years of hiring out his time on the Charleston docks. Steaming out of Charleston harbour in the dark of night, Smalls piloted the ship to another wharf where he picked up his wife, children and other family members, all of whom were enslaved, then, giving the requisite whistle signals to Confederate patrols, Smalls piloted the *Planter* out of Charleston harbour and delivered it as a prize of war to the US fleet blockading the port. Smalls's heroic exploits were widely publicized and documented, including in official United States War Department reports and in the many Congressional pension bills subsequently filed on his behalf. Confederate records likewise recognize the damage Smalls dealt both to the Confederate military and to the morale of the proslavery nation. US Flag Officer S. F. DuPont personally reported the matter to the Secretary of the Navy. Robert Smalls was hailed as a war hero. An article in the widely read *Harper's Weekly* magazine published soon after the event described his escape as 'one of the most daring and heroic adventures since the war commenced'. The article was illustrated by an engraving of both the ship (the *Planter*) and Robert Smalls, dressed in a three-piece suit looking solemnly at the artist.[8] Robert Smalls built his political career on that war record.

By the time the Civil War ended Robert Smalls was a freeman with a national reputation and a number of powerful patrons. He was also, by that point, a man of some property and wealth. During a stint in Philadelphia working for the navy he had hired a tutor and acquired a basic literacy.[9] He had also been drawn into national political life. During the war he made public appearances in New York City in support of emancipation and the recruitment of black soldiers. As early as 1864 Smalls was elected as a representative from Beaufort, South Carolina to the Republican Party Convention. He was among the first black men ever sent to a national convention. Smalls did not attend (probably because his military duties prevented it) and the delegation was not allowed to vote, but he was already a man of interest to the nascent Republican Party in the South and a participant in an emergent free black political life. In Beaufort, he worked with the Gideonites, a group of missionaries organizing relief and education for refugee and resident freed people. He was also well connected to Union officers and missionaries working in and around Port Royal, South Carolina, including General Rufus Saxton who would become the head of the Freedmen's Bureau, the chief federal agency charged with overseeing the transition to freedom of former slaves in the state. Smalls was a guest of honour in April 1865, symbolically piloting the *Planter* (with the black political leader Martin Delaney onboard) to a ceremony honouring the end of the war. Smalls was described by one participant as 'a prince among them'. His very presence at the event speaks to his local stature and national connections. By the time the Civil War ended, Robert Smalls was already recognized as 'the natural leader of the freedmen's community', in Beaufort, South Carolina. '[H]e did not shrink from the task'.[10]

The place

Beaufort, South Carolina, was the most promising place in the re-United States of America for black political power and self-representation. It was, as President Obama's proclamation indicated, the '*birthplace* of Reconstruction'. It was also a key testing ground of the 'massive experiment in interracial democracy', that Reconstruction represented.[11] There was no place quite like it, owing both to its long-term history and the contingencies of war. In November 1861, when the Union navy and army captured Port Royal harbour, just six months into the Civil War, resident slaveholders fled the surrounding islands for the mainland, leaving their slaves behind. Local people would remember that crucial event as the day of 'the big Gun Shoot'.[12] With a large population of enslaved African Americans now under the authority of the US government and army, the Lincoln administration began to experiment with modes of governance, aided by an array of philanthropists and capitalists committed to the free labour project.

This first 'rehearsal for reconstruction', as the historian Willie Lee Rose dubbed it, has drawn the interest of scholars for generations.[13] Coastal Beaufort would become a 'black paradise' in large measure because of the flight and subsequent dispossession of the planter class. In that part of the old plantation South, planters were permanently dispossessed, not just of their property in slaves (by virtue of the Emancipation Proclamation and the Thirteenth Amendment) but of their lands as well, by virtue of the Direct Tax Act of 1862. By that law, the US government awarded itself the right to foreclose and auction off the property of absentee proprietors delinquent on their taxes, as most Confederate planters were. Coastal Beaufort country – Robert Smalls's home turf – was the only place in South Carolina and in all of the defeated Confederacy where that law was fully applied, an accident of early occupation. In other parts of the South in 1865–6 planters succeeded in having their lands restored by the government of President Andrew Johnson, which had adopted a (too) generous plan of amnesty and reconstruction. But in the areas of Beaufort closest to the Atlantic coast where Robert Smalls was from, their dispossession and war-time exile was permanent.[14] To local whites after the Civil War Beaufort was 'another Hayti'. A local planter, Joseph Daniel Pope, claimed that the 'abolition of slavery has worked the most gigantic practical confiscating of property that has ever been enforced in the history of the world'.[15] In a singular experience, freed people in coastal Beaufort mostly escaped the devastating terms of Johnson's property restoration policy. With the old planters gone, political power was transferred to freedmen.

Among the men who rose to political power with emancipation Robert Smalls was preeminent. He was uniquely positioned to represent the freed people of low country South Carolina. Beaufort had been a plantation society since the late seventeenth century, a black majority place with a class of large, seasonally absentee slave-owners. In 1860 the district was 90 per cent black and enslaved. It was also a place where black culture thrived, a separate culture with its own distinctive language – Gullah – and Afro-Christian religion, both particular to the enslaved.[16] Robert Smalls was the only Gullah speaker, native son and former slave among the black men who rose to high political office from Beaufort during Reconstruction.[17]

Over more than forty-five years Robert Smalls was the man local African Americans trusted to represent them. The South Carolina low country and Beaufort remained a mostly rural place, with a population of impoverished, newly freed people negotiating the new terms of labour on rice and sea island cotton plantations. The terms of that labour remained a matter of open conflict throughout the entire period of Reconstruction. In the early years as struggles over land restoration continued, workers held out, refusing to return to contract labour on plantations, and threatening planters who returned. Empowered by the Johnson administration, planters tried to dictate. Using their retained political and police power they wrote a series of Black Codes, imposing a system of passes and permits and compulsory annual labour contracts, designed to restrict black mobility, civil rights and to shut down alternative forms of independent black social organization and force African Americans back to plantation labour.[18] As late as 1876 the region was hit by a wave of strikes by rice workers at harvest time. When the region spiralled into violence Robert Smalls stepped in to mediate.[19] As in the rest of the conquered South, issues of land, labour and politics were inextricably connected. In this world Robert Smalls was the 'indispensable man', uniquely trusted to represent the black electorate of what his rivals called the 'Black Republic of Beaufort'.[20]

Beginnings of a political career

Robert Smalls's political career spans the entire epic history of the black reconstruction of democracy in America: the radical transformation of political life in the United States that began with war and played out under the highly contingent conditions of military occupation. For two years after the Confederacy surrendered, reconstruction was in the hands of President Andrew Johnson and proceeded under the terms of what historians call Presidential Reconstruction. Johnson was a former Democrat and vice-president who came to office upon the assassination of President Abraham Lincoln in April 1865. He had never been elected president. The terms of reconstruction he offered were extremely generous to the defeated slaveholding class and restored them to political power within the southern states. This first effort at 'self-reconstruction' was a total disaster.[21] Restored southern legislatures immediately wrote a series of laws – collectively referred to as Black Codes – designed to undercut the legal emancipation of former slaves and development of a free labour economy in violation of basic norms of civil rights of free people. In addition, in the first set of elections held in the fall of 1865, white southerners returned an unrepentant set of Confederates to office. Georgia sent the Confederate Vice-President Alexander Stephens to represent it in the US Senate. For eight months Johnson had affairs exclusively in his hands. But when Congress finally reconvened in December 1865, a struggle opened up between a Republican-dominated Congress and President Johnson over the terms of Reconstruction which ended in the impeachment of the President.[22] As Congressional Republicans seized control of the reconstruction process in 1867, they turned US – and African American – history in a radical new direction. Combining to override a set of presidential vetoes, a temporary coalition of radical and moderate Republicans pushed through a series of progressive laws and constitutional amendments designed to secure freed people's civil and political rights and personal safety.[23]

This was the revolutionary conjuncture W. E. B. Du Bois found so promising. And indeed, in March 1867 national politics took a very unpredictable turn. Outraged at the continued violence against African Americans and determined to defeat the planter class politically, the Republican Party-dominated Congress put the southern states back under military occupation. They passed three laws (together called the Military Reconstruction Acts), which divided the Confederate South into five military districts, put them under military governance and law and, most striking of all, authorized the army to organize elections in which 'all male citizens' could vote and run for office.[24] It was the first time in American history that large numbers of African American men could vote. 'Here, at the stroke of the pen, more than one million Negroes were given the right of vote', Du Bois wrote, 'of whom probably three-fourths could not read or write'. 'It was the greatest test of democracy that the nation had known' – and a far greater measure of democratization, he added pointedly, than any accomplished by England and its vaunted reform bills of 1832 and 1867.[25] This radical experiment in inter-racial democracy preceded the passage of the 15th Amendment and was done under military rule. In the spring of 1867, the US army fanned out across the southern countryside to register African American men to vote. It was a world turned upside down. The US experiment in racial democracy was of consequence far beyond the United States. As Great Britain struggled to put down the Morant Bay rebellion in Jamaica and manage a reform of its own limited electorate, the British Foreign Secretary, Lord Stanley, looked on in horrified fascination at 'the singular scene which American politics present'. 'The American Revolution', he called it, 'for the practical change in their government amounts to nothing less'. 'The world', he reported to the minister at Washington, 'has nothing like it'. As Du Bois insisted, black reconstruction reverberated world-wide.[26]

Nowhere was the fate of black reconstruction tested more directly than in Beaufort, South Carolina. In this radical break in history Robert Smalls was ready. By the time African American men got the right to vote and hold office he was the acknowledged leader of Beaufort Republicans. Smalls got in on the ground floor of black political life in the post-Civil War South. He not only led the party but was the key institutional player in building it. As in the rest of the South, black public political organization had started immediately with the end of the war. In early 1866, even before passage of the Reconstruction Acts, Smalls was a member of the Union League which provided the original infrastructure of the Republican party in the South. He was a founding member of the local board of education and purchased land in town for a school. Education would remain his signature issue throughout his career. In March 1867, he called the first meeting of the Beaufort Republican Club; then he and thirty-six other black and three white Republicans went on to form the state-wide Republican Party in South Carolina. He was a strategist and organizer of local elections from the start. In the 'registration summer' of 1867 the army appointed him a registrar of voters. It was a dangerous job. He gave speeches at a host of meetings across the rural district and signed up voters. By mid-November, an astounding 90 per cent of South Carolina's eligible black electorate had registered to vote in the referendum on the constitutional convention.[27] It was a moment of mass political mobilization of African American people and Robert Smalls was at the centre of it. Between 1,500 and 2,000 people attended an 1867 Republican rally in the town of Beaufort. In those heady days, political meetings were community events, which drew male voters, but also women and children, with women oftentimes guarding the meetings with muskets.[28] In preparation for the first election, Smalls organized the political caucuses which nominated delegates to county conventions, and chaired the Beaufort Republican Party convention 'with dignity and credit', according to one white observer. It was no surprise that he was selected to attend both the county and then state convention charged with nominating delegates for election and writing the Republican Party platform.[29]

Robert Smalls first stood for election in November 1867 to represent his district in the upcoming, federally mandated, state constitutional convention. It was the first election in which black men could vote. He won by a landslide, with 496 votes out of 518 cast in the town of Beaufort. It took no small courage to register to vote in the South in 1867, and even more to run for office. Smalls was adept and courageous. He knew how to fight and was not afraid to use his fists. The elections were rowdy and voter intimidation was a constant issue. Smalls made sure Republicans had a strong military presence at the polls. In that first election, many black men arrived en masse, in military formation, and dressed in their old Union army uniforms. Local newspapers identified Robert Smalls as the architect of the election day strategy. One claimed he urged followers to 'shoot knock the brains out or kill any man who attempted to vote any ticket other than the so called red [Republican] ticket'.[30] Paramilitary violence had been part of political life in the American South for generations. By 1867 white vigilantes self-designated as 'Regulators', were already waging a campaign of terror against African Americans. The violence would get exponentially worse when Republicans came to power in the state. Robert Smalls knew what it took to defend black men's right to vote. Starting in 1867 he built a formidable political machine in Beaufort, South Carolina; he also built the most effective militia unit in the state. As Smalls's political career advanced he rose through the military hierarchy as well, reaching the rank of Major General commanding the Second Division of the National Guard.[31] Together the political machine and the militia kept him in office almost continuously for forty years. As Smalls knew, in the American South, you had no rights if you couldn't defend them.

The key experiment in labour and bi-racial democracy came in South Carolina, which explains the inordinate focus on that state in histories of the period, including the one written by Du Bois. His history of Black Reconstruction begins with 'The Black Proletariat in South Carolina'. And indeed, when Robert Smalls took his seat in the state Constitutional Convention in January 1868 he was part of a black majority body and the constitutional text they wrote was part of a revolution in government in the United States. Between 1860 and 1870 the electorate doubled, enfranchising an entirely new class of people – former slaves, three-quarters of them illiterate, almost all property-less labourers. In many deep South states whites now faced a majority (or almost majority) black electorate. It was revolution in representation and office-holding. Reconstruction in the United States involved some highly symbolic moments – such as when Hiram Revels, a black Senator from Mississippi, was sworn into the seat previously occupied by Jefferson Davis, the former President of the Confederacy. But if that was the dramatic summit, the revolution in government was far more significant at the level of the states and localities. Smalls was one of 76 black delegates out of a total 124 representatives at the Constitutional Convention; 57 of the African American delegates were, like him, former slaves. At least 267 black men served in such conventions across the South.[32] Du Bois called this reconstruction effort 'the greatest test of democracy that the nation had ever known' – and, as he pointedly noted, it involved far more democracy and new voters than Britain's lauded reform bill of the same year.[33]

The state constitution Smalls and his colleagues wrote reflected a radical new vision of government and of the public it served.[34] They instituted 'universal' male suffrage, eliminated all tax and property qualifications to vote; introduced popular election to most state offices; and wrote a new bill of rights that prohibited discrimination, including in public facilities. They also tried to limit the domination of property, forcing a more equal sharing of the tax burden (which planters had always prevented) and more equal benefit of state funds. Among these initiatives the most important was publicly funded education and it was here that Robert Smalls made his most significant contribution. Like many ex-slaves at the convention, he mostly kept a low profile, leaving the floor to white delegates and free-born (often northern) black delegates with more formal education. But Smalls had an abiding commitment to public education, and at the convention he offered a resolution for a system of common schools free and open to all children, and compulsory for those aged seven to fourteen. His plan was modified but it was, one historian confirmed, 'the constitutional foundation of the public-school system of South Carolina'.[35] The Constitution Smalls and his colleagues wrote was so far superior to any the state had ever adopted that most of it survived the best efforts of white supremacist Democrats to wipe out its principles in the late nineteenth century. That constitution, Du Bois wrote, was as good as any out there and conservative whites were 'content to live under it for eighteen years after they recovered control of the state government'.[36]

In terms of impact, the most important part of Robert Smalls political career was the years he spent in the state legislature. He served for seven of the nine years of Reconstruction. In 1868, he was elected to represent Beaufort in the house and two years later he was elected to the Senate. There he was part of a Beaufort delegation that was majority black for the entire period – Beaufort sent thirty African Americans and only five whites to represent it between 1867 and 1890 – in a legislature that was also majority black until 1876, when democracy in the state was overthrown by violence. Smalls controlled the local Republican party machine, rose up in the hierarchy of the militia, fought to enforce the civil rights of his constituents and to direct state resources to his district. His political supremacy was unchallenged, and he reliably delivered the black enclave of Beaufort for the Republican Party at every election. Smalls was a loyal party man and that put him in the eye of the storm. Black democracy and Republican government was under violent attack in South Carolina, as in the rest of the South, for the entire period of Reconstruction. The backlash against what whites dubbed 'Negro rule' was ferocious and aimed from the start at the restoration of white supremacy. In the deep South black majority states, Republican governments could not be removed by electoral means and white Democrats turned to intimidation and punishment of voters. By 1868 their election strategy seamlessly integrated legal public party organizations and violent para-military organizations collectively known as the Ku Klux Klan. The KKK formed in 1866, but its reign of terror peaked around the elections of 1868 and 1870. The leading historian of the Klan called it the single most significant 'domestic terrorist movement' in US history. The Klan, he said, was 'a terrorist arm of the Democratic Party'.[37] In 1868 the violence was already so great that the first elections were conducted under military supervision with the US army deployed at the polls to protect black voters.

South Carolina did not escape the violence. On the contrary, the upcountry counties of the state were among the worst in the South. To vote or stand for office was to take your life in your hands. In 1868 in Abbeville County, which Smalls would later represent in Congress, one Democratic leader and planter, David Wyatt Aiken, publicly urged the murder of the district's newly elected black state Senator, Benjamin F. Randolph. He was gunned down on a railroad platform soon thereafter in broad daylight. It took only a few such examples to broadcast the message that Democrats murderous threats were not empty ones. Randolph was in fact one of nineteen black Republicans murdered during the 1868 election campaign in that district. No less than 156 black public officials were victims of violence associated with the Klan or other paramilitary arm of the Democratic Party during Reconstruction; thirty-four office holders were murdered. Democrats who had lost most counties in elections in April 1868 won two Congressional districts in November. In Abbeville less than 20 per cent of black voters managed to cast ballots in that election.[38] What Democrats made clear in 1868 was that as a tool of voter suppression violence worked. The burst of violence that accompanied the first wave of Democratic 'redemption' was documented in a congressional investigation.[39] In 1871, after another election bloodbath, the federal government finally took action to suppress the Klan and restore law and order. South Carolina was the key case in the government's strategy. President Grant suspended habeas corpus in the worst areas of the state, and sent in troops and a team of federal lawyers. They executed a strategy of mass arrests and select high profile trials of ringleaders that successfully broke the back of the Klan in South Carolina. But by the time the federal government acted the Klan had already successfully reversed the will of the majority in at least two southern states and black reconstruction was overthrown by violence.[40]

Robert Smalls had to stare down this kind of violence throughout his entire political career. Eric Foner, who has studied all of the black politicians who held office during Reconstruction, notes that 'the roster of black officials victimized by violence offers a striking insight into the personal courage required to take a position of prominence in Reconstruction politics'.[41] But with a black majority and a serious black militia Beaufort was not Klan country. The first KKK chapter was not formed in the county until 1921.[42] The region – and Robert Smalls – could not escape the violence that defined southern political life. But for a decade of reconstruction, even as the rest of the state and the South fell under the tide of white supremacist violence, Beaufort – and Robert Smalls – survived. Robert Smalls did get snared, however, in one major line of Democratic attack during his time as a state legislator. He was charged with corruption associated with funds disbursed by the printing committee on which he served. The general charge was that Senators (like Smalls) would approve huge appropriations to cover the cost of printing public documents and arrange kickbacks from the printing company to which they awarded the state contract. Smalls was tried on charges of corruption in 1875 and acquitted. But after white supremacist Democrats retook control of the South Carolina legislature in 1876 he was convicted and sentenced to prison. Smalls escaped the penalty in a political deal that secured his pardon. He long denied the charges of corruption which were, as he claimed, a political tool of the Democratic Party in its multi-pronged assault on the legitimacy of black Reconstruction governments. Those charges of corruption were the first line of attack against reconstruction governments – and, as both Du Bois and Foner have documented, became the basis of a racist white historiography that prevailed in scholarly and popular opinion until the Civil Rights era. Du Bois went to great lengths to push back against the charge of corruption against Republican regimes which, as he saw it, were really a tactic to 're-establish the dominance of property in southern politics'.[43] Smalls escaped the prison term, but the charge of corruption followed him into Congress and surfaced in every subsequent campaign for office.

Congressman

Robert Smalls entered national politics as Reconstruction was ending. Indeed, his election to Congress, and especially his re-election in 1876, was the key Congressional race on which the fate of Reconstruction hinged. Smalls was elected to Congress in 1874 from the newly created Fifth District of South Carolina. Nominated and carried by his 'finely-honed' machine Smalls defeated his conservative opponent easily. Smalls served five terms; his last in 1887.[44] By the time he entered Congress, Reconstruction was effectively over, not just in retreat but about to be defeated both in the southern states and in national politics. In the US Congress, the House of Representatives was in the hands of Democrats for the first time in eighteen years. The vast majority of southern delegates (80/107) were white Democrats and hardened veterans of the Confederate army. All told, seventeen black Americans served in Congress during Reconstruction; six of those seventeen were from South Carolina. In 1875 when Smalls arrived he was one of seven black members in Congress. By the time he left he was one of two. Black political power came earlier and lasted longer in South Carolina than anywhere else. At one point five of six South

Figure 6.1 Robert Smalls, Beaufort, South Carolina, United States of America, b. 1839 d. 1915. Elected Offices held: South Carolina Constitutional Convention, 1868; South Carolina House of Representatives, 1868–70; South Carolina Senate, 1870–5; US House of Representatives, 1875–9, 1881–7; South Carolina Constitutional Convention, 1895. Photo. *c.* 1870–80. Courtesy of Brady-Handy Collection, Manuscript Division, Library of Congress.

Carolina representatives were black.[45] Robert Smalls outlasted them all, in no small measure because he represented the black republic of Beaufort.

As those numbers make abundantly clear, even in the heyday of black democracy in the United States in the period of Reconstruction, African Americans were always in minority in the national representative assembly. The official history calls Smalls and his peers 'the symbolic generation of black Americans in Congress, 1870–1887'.[46] And indeed, in minority as they were they lacked any real power to enact legislation. There were many reasons. Washington DC was a segregated city and African American Congressmen faced ongoing discrimination that impeded their work; few served at any one time and so were isolated, unable to form a critical mass on key issues; they had no seniority in Congress so received few important committee assignments, although Smalls did get a seat on the prestigious agriculture committee; they were blocked by leadership even in their own party; and they were harassed by Democratic congressmen especially in the house of representatives, where Smalls served. All of this meant that even when African American men made it to Congress, they did not have power to set a legislative agenda.[47]

This was the highly constrained setting in which Robert Smalls had to work in the US Congress. Nonetheless like other black Congressmen he used his seat to represent his race – not just his constituents in South Carolina's Fifth, but in the United States. Indeed, Smalls seems to have seen himself as a 'surrogate representative for millions of newly free African Americans'. His compatriot Richard Cain once referred to 'the five million people for whom I speak'. All of the black congressmen supported the Ku Klux Klan bills allowing the use of federal troops to suppress Klan activity (1869–73). In 1875, they rose as a group, Smalls now among them, to defend the Civil Rights Bill – a highpoint of their visibility in Congress, when there were seven black congressmen. There is no indication Robert Smalls spoke in that debate.[48] But by the end of his first term, as the nation headed toward a final brutal reckoning over reconstruction, Robert Smalls became the voice of southern blacks and the conscience of the federal government as it allowed the violent disfranchisement of African Americans and the overthrow of reconstruction government in its last stronghold – South Carolina. In 1884, he and the one other African American left in the house attempted unsuccessfully to revive portions of the bill prohibiting discrimination in railroad cars. As the official historians note 'by that point they served in a minority and were speaking in a different era'.[49]

When Robert Smalls entered Congress as representative of South Carolina's Fifth District in 1875, he found himself in the very eye of the state and national storm. As a state legislator and senator, he had represented a small coastal, black majority constituency. But as a congressman, he ran for election in a newly drawn district that included Edgefield County, or 'bloody 96' as it became known. Edgefield was Klan country.[50] By 1875, white supremacists led by men such as Mathew Butler, (General) Martin Gary and the brothers George and Benjamin Tillman had regrouped in the district and forged the 'Edgefield Plan', the model for white Democrats' 'redemption' of the state from (black) Republicans. As one historian recently confirmed, it was in Edgefield that white Democrats spearheaded the tactics by which they 'succeeded in overthrowing the elected Republican government of South Carolina'. The Edgefield plan was a simple one: to use violence to suppress the black Republican vote. In the SC Fifth District 'cold-blooded murder [was] a campaign tactic' and the basic philosophy of men like Butler and the Tillmans was that you couldn't vote if you are dead.[51] To that end, Edgefield Democrats built a network of rifle clubs, which picked up where Klan had left off. But this time the violence was not hooded or conducted in the dark of night. Instead, rifle club members operated in the open. They provoked confrontations with the state militia and its black members, formed paramilitary escorts to Democratic candidates at campaign events and descended mounted, armed and en masse on Republican events where they openly threatened candidates and rushed the stage to speak. In the run-up to the election of 1876 they took to wearing their trademark red shirts which signalled the unified purpose of ostensibly disparate 'clubs', while evading the reach of the federal KKK Acts. The Rifle Clubs operated with impunity. In one episode in the summer of 1876, planned by 'the leading men of Edgefield', one thousand Red Shirts descended on the town of Hamburg where they gunned down a group of black militia members who had been summoned to attend court. After the Hamburg Massacre there was no question about the tactics Edgefield Democrats intended to use to eliminate the Republican majority.[52] A month before that, the Republican governor, Daniel H. Chamberlain, finally called on President Grant to use the army to restore order and ensure a fair election. Grant outlawed all rifle clubs in South Carolina and agreed to post troops at some polling places. Even then the rifle clubs did not disband but simply reorganized under innocuous names; the Columbia Flying Artillery became the Columbia Music Club which claimed the use of four '12 pounder flutes'. By the time of the election in November there were three hundred rifle clubs in the state and dozens in Edgefield alone.[53]

In 1876 Robert Smalls waded through a sea of blood to re-election from the Fifth Congressional District. In that second run for Congress he was challenged by George Tillman, one of the leading architects of the Edgefield Plan, brother of the notorious 'Pitchfork' Ben Tillman who would later preside over the state as Governor at the height of Jim Crow and segregation. By all accounts Smalls was fearless, standing down direct threats on his life at numerous campaign events in Edgefield District, accompanying the Republican Governor, Daniel Chamberlain, to events mobbed by Red Shirt thugs. Smalls even provided personal protection to the white supremacist gubernatorial candidate, General Wade Hampton, during a campaign stop in Beaufort, hostile territory for Democrats, when he was confronted by thousands of armed black national guardsmen. It was at this moment that Smalls emerged in Congress into the role he would thereafter hold as an impassioned defender of his race and party and indeed of democracy itself. He still was in Congress during the final battle over Reconstruction. Starting in the summer of 1876 he began to use his position in the US House of Representatives to broadcast the political crime unfolding in South Carolina and to try to hold the Grant administration and the federal government to its obligation to protect the civil and political rights of black Americans. In July 1876, he rose on the floor of Congress and gave an impassioned speech against the removal of federal troops from South Carolina to the Texas–Mexico border, warning that 'private Red Shirt militias' would make war on the government and freedmen if left unrestrained. He proposed an amendment that no troops could be withdrawn 'as long as the militia of that state are … massacred in cold blood by lawless bands of men'. He also read into the *Congressional Record* an eyewitness account of 'the massacre at Hamburg', and publicly named Mathew Butler and other red shirt leaders as masterminds of the attack. When Democratic congressmen rose on the floor to defend the honour and reputation of 'General Butler' and the Edgefield men against any imputation that that they were 'Ku-Klux', Smalls and Rainey insisted on the veracity of their account.[54] This was to be Smalls's role. He paid a price for this at home for his principled stand in Congress and refusal to cede the election in Edgefield to Tillman and the Red Shirts. In the fall of 1876, he survived numerous attempts on his life. At one Republican rally Smalls attended in Edgefield with Governor Chamberlain in October 1876, Matthew Butler and six hundred of his followers overran the meeting and threatened Smalls's life. Demanding time to speak, Butler denounced Smalls for identifying him as the head of the KKK – which, of course, he had – and, daring Smalls to name him again that day, publicly instructed his followers to 'kill the damn son of a bitch'. A Red Shirt posse followed Smalls and Chamberlain to the train station and boarded the train. *The New York Times* covered these rallies and Red Shirt tactics. Smalls described his opponent, George Tillman, as 'the personification of red-shirt Democracy [and] the arch enemy of my race'.[55] He was not intimidated.

In the SC Fifth congressional district in November 1876, Robert Smalls managed a narrow win over Tillman in even as the rest of the state fell to the Democrats in a deluge of violence. Tillman, predictably, contested the election. When he did, Smalls arrived in Washington with a mountain of evidence about Democratic tactics which he used to defend his claim to the seat. The vote in Edgefield County – which Tillman had won – should not be counted at all Smalls insisted, as it was 'carried by fraud, violence, intimidation, and repeat [voting] by partisans' of Tillman. He took that occasion to keep the memory of the Hamburg Massacre alive as Exhibit A of Red Shirt democracy. Replete with details about the number of armed white men crowding the polls, the 689-page document Congress produced as a result of its investigation into the contested election offered a remarkable record of the gauntlet black men had to run to put a ballot in a box for a Republican candidate.[56] Smalls held his seat.

In that critical presidential election year of 1876–7 Robert Smalls's political fate intersected directly with that of the nation. For in resisting Tillman's challenge, Smalls fought not just for his own seat but for the national Republican party and the future of Reconstruction. Contested elections were a signal feature of Reconstruction politics – there were more elections contested during the Reconstruction years than any other moment in Congressional history.[57] But Smalls's contested election was part of a much bigger political battle being waged in 1876–7 for control of the presidency. That election (like the famous one in 2000) produced results so close no winner could be declared. The contest between the Republican presidential candidate, Rutherford B. Hayes, and the Democrat, Samuel Tilden, turned on a recount from four states, three of which were in the South in elections tarnished by obvious violence and fraud. In resolving the stand-off, South Carolina was the key state and Edgefield one of the two key disputed county, which directly linked the outcome of Smalls's election with that of the presidency. If Hayes held South Carolina, Florida and Louisiana he would win the electoral college by one vote.[58]

The black representative stayed in Congress during the protracted struggle over the disputed presidential election which was not resolved until March 1877. He had already testified to the conditions in his district in the investigation of Tillman v. Smalls in November 1876. In February 1877, as Rutherford B. Hayes's advisors negotiated secretly with Democrat leaders in South Carolina to earn their support (in a deal that involved significant concessions to the party in the state), Smalls rose again on the floor of the House and gave the most powerful speech of his career. He introduced a mountain of evidence about the scale of electoral violence and fraud in his state, all of which, he insisted, made election day in South Carolina 'a carnival of bloodshed and violence'. He documented the 'reign of terror' Red Shirts had unleashed against black voters in the state: openly calling for the murder of political opponents from the stage of public meetings; shooting into crowds on election day; blocking access to the polls with mobs of mounted, armed men. He cited sworn depositions from various county officials listing the number of men murdered — ten in Laurens County, fourteen in Barnwell, twenty-three or twenty-four in Aiken, going district by district. He proved voter suppression by violence and intimidation. But also by fraud. Tactics included the enclosure of duplicate tickets in Democratic ballots; repeat voting by Democrats who 'rushed from poll to poll voting 2 or 3 times'; the distribution of fraudulent tickets to confuse illiterate black voters; polls blocked and ballot boxes destroyed. By such tactics, he insisted, the number of Democratic votes had increased implausibly since the previous election. There were only 74,000 white men of voting age in South Carolina, he pointed out, but in 1876 the Democratic candidate for governor got 92,210 votes, 6000 more than had ever been polled for his party. The intimidation reached its most extreme limit, predictably, in Edgefield. At polls on election day 'men were beaten in the very presence of the officers of the army', a claim he backed up with the sworn testimony of one stationed there, a Major Kellogg. He had only four men to control the crowd which he estimated at about three hundred armed white men, Red Shirts, black men trying to get to the ballot box had to pass within 3 or 4 feet of drawn pistols and shots of 'shoot, God damit, shoot!'. No coloured men were armed. Thus did Democrats secure 'by fraud and murder what could not be obtained by honorable means'.[59] Everything Robert Smalls claimed in that defiant speech has been subsequently corroborated by historians from archival materials.[60]

When Robert Smalls gave this impassioned speech he still had faith that a fair investigation would sustain the claims of Republicans in South Carolina and the nation, confirming both Chamberlain, the Republican candidate for governor, and Hayes, the candidate for president. He was half right. On 4 March, Rutherford B. Hayes was inaugurated as president. A few days later he summoned Robert Smalls and a larger delegation of black Republicans from South Carolina to a meeting and informed them in no uncertain terms that his administration would no longer permit the use of the US army in civil affairs in their state. Historians remain uncertain about the terms of the bargain cut between Hayes and leading Democrats in South Carolina. But the result was clear. In early April Hayes ordered the withdrawal of all federal troops from the state capital where they had been protecting the Republican governor in office, and the white supremacist Democrat, Wade Hampton, took office as chief executive of the state. Democrats had thrown their support to Hayes for president on the condition that federal troops would be withdrawn from the state. Notwithstanding their courage in resisting Red Shirt violence at the cost of their own lives, black Republicans in South Carolina – and in the South as a whole – had been sacrificed by the national Republican party. As the governor Daniel Chamberlain put it in a letter to his supporters written the day he was forced out of office, 'the Government of the United States abandons you, deliberately withdraws from you its support, with full knowledge that the lawful Government of the State will be speedily overthrown'. As he acknowledged, that decision officially ended Reconstruction in the state and handed the southern states over to home rule run by white supremacist Democrats. As Robert Smalls had warned, once federal troops removed there was nothing left to protect African Americans against the murderous violence of southern whites. The 'Bargain of 1877' was a deadly one with immediate consequences for all African Americans, the Republican party and black democracy in the state, the region and the nation.[61]

Robert Smalls won three more terms in Congress where he served as the only African American in a delegation of Red Shirt Democrats. He was literally the last man standing after black Reconstruction was overthrown by violence. As Democrats redrew electoral districts Robert Smalls's enclave of Beaufort remained the last safe district for Republicans in South Carolina. But eventually even the black republic of Beaufort and its congressional district fell to Democratic control through the now patented combination of violence, voter intimidation and ballot box fraud. Once African Americans were disfranchised by violence the Tillmanites wrote laws making it all legal – the American way. Republicans retained control of the local government in the town of Beaufort and in 1895 they sent Robert Smalls to the constitutional convention where Democrats aimed to undo the radical constitution of 1868 that Smalls had helped to write when he was twenty-nine years old. Robert Smalls did not lie down even then but protested the disfranchisement of his people to the bitter end.[62]

Conclusion

There are many lessons to be taken from the political career of Robert Smalls and the history of Reconstruction in the United States, none, perhaps, more influential than the one drawn by Woodrow Wilson and deployed at Versailles. Wilson, who had grown up in Georgia and South Carolina during that era of black democracy, warned against the kind of harsh peace the United States had imposed on the conquered South. Reconstruction was a 'perfect work of fear, demoralization, disgust, and social revolution', Wilson insisted. That upending of the 'natural political and racial order' had failed because African American people were 'unfit to exercise their new liberty'.[63] But that was itself a product of a white supremacist history first enacted on the ground in places like Robert Smalls's congressional district and only then written into the history books. Arguably the better – or larger – lesson of Reconstruction is about how well violence worked to repress democracy, and about what happens to it under conditions of domestic terrorism such as those African Americans confronted for most of the nineteenth, twentieth and twenty-first centuries.

Robert Smalls's political career covers that entire history and marks its high points and its low ones. His most important political impact was at the local level. By building a political machine which controlled local political appointments and a militia to defend African Americans hard-earned civil and political rights, he managed to protect the black population of that one place from the tidal wave of violence and racist law that swept the rest of the US South with the defeat of Reconstruction. In Congress, his impact was much less significant, although like other black politicians of that era, he used his extraordinary and lonely position to speak for his race and to stand against the capitulation of democracy to white supremacy.

Notes

1   The original title of his book. See W. E. B. Du Bois, *Black Reconstruction in America: An Essay Toward a History of the Part Which Black Folk Played in the Attempt to Reconstruct Democracy in America, 1860–1880* (1935; repr., New York: The Free Press, 1992), ix.

2   Du Bois, *Black Reconstruction in America*, 383, 346; Steven Hahn, 'Class and State in Post-Emancipation Societies: Southern Planters in Comparative Perspective', *American Historical Review*, 95, no. 1 (February 1990): 75–98.

3   For the numbers, see Foner, *Freedom's Lawmakers: A Directory of Black Officeholders During Reconstruction* (Baton Rouge: LSU Press, 1993), xi, and *Black Americans in Congress, 1870–2007*, ed. The Committee on House Administration of the US House of Representatives, by the Office of History and Preservation,

Office of the Clerk, US House of Representatives (Washington, DC: US GPO, 2008), 22–3.

4 Peter Wood, *Black Majority: Negroes in Colonial South Carolina From 1670 Through the Stono Rebellion* (New York: W.W. Norton and Co., 1974). In 1870 Beaufort was 85 per cent black. On the history of Beaufort in Reconstruction and on Smalls's outsize role, see *Rebellion, Reconstruction, and Redemption, 1861–1893: The History of Beaufort, South Carolina*, vol. 2, Stephen R, Wise and Lawrence S. Rowland (eds.) (Columbia: SC, University of South Carolina Press, 2015); numbers at 477.

5 Foner, *Black Americans in Congress*, table on 50.

6 On purchase, see Wise and Rowland, *Rebellion, Reconstruction, and Redemption*, 267. Smalls's title to the property was challenged amidst a decade of lawsuits brought by white families; Smalls fought the case all the way to the Supreme Court and won. His was the key case settling title issues pursuant to wartime tax sales. See 460.

7 Establishment of the Reconstruction Era National Monument, Proclamation No. 9567, 82 FR 6167 (12 January 2017). Available online: www.federalregister.gov/documents/2017/01/19/2017-01363/establishment-of-the-reconstruction-era-national-monument (accessed 5 February 2021). Jennifer Schuessler, 'President Obama Designates First National Monument Dedicated to Reconstruction', *The New York Times*, 12 January 2017. On Smalls's parentage, see Edward A. Miller, Jr, *Gullah Statesman: Robert Smalls from Slavery to Congress, 1839–1915* (Columbia: University of South Carolina Press, 1995). Millers's biography is useful but flawed.

8 For the pension bills, see Robert Smalls, Committee on Invalid Pensions, House of Representatives, Report No. 1546, 30 April 1896, and Senate, Committee on Pensions, Report No. 1134, 8 June 1896, 54th Congress, 1st Session. 1st Reports include contemporaneous official War Department dispatches; 'The Steamer Planter and Her Captor', *Harper's Weekly*, 14 June 1862, 372–2. The Planter episode is also recounted in the handful of biographies of Smalls. See most recently Miller, *Gullah Statesman*.

9 Reports indicate that he remained semi-literate throughout his life, a great orator but not writer. His daughter served as his clerk in his time in Congress. He made sure his children were well educated. Smalls's wealth came from prize money for the *Planter* and from wages of about $1,500 per year paid by the Army and Navy. See Miller, *Gullah Statesman*, 41 (on wealth), and Wise and Rowland, *Rebellion, Reconstruction, and Redemption*, 460, 483 (on wealth and literacy).

10 Quotes in Wise and Rowland, *Rebellion, Reconstruction, and Redemption*, 424, 483. Smalls's Civil War career is detailed in Miller, *Gullah Statesman*, 1–34.

11 See Foner, *Reconstruction: America's Unfinished Revolution* (New York: Harper and Row, 1988), quotation on xxv.

12 Stephanie McCurry, *Confederate Reckoning: Power and Politics in the Civil War South* (Cambridge, MA, and London: Harvard University Press, 2010), 235.

13 Willie Lee Rose, *Rehearsal for Reconstruction: The Port Royal Experiment* (New York: Oxford University Press, 1964).

14 The law applied to all captured property equally, but Beaufort was the place it was first and most fully enforced. Wise and Rowland, *Rebellion, Reconstruction, and Redemption*, 270–2, 457–63. Andrew Johnson, 'Amnesty Proclamation' (May 29) in *The Papers of Andrew Johnson*, vol. 8, ed. Leroy P. Graf and Ralph W. Haskins (Knoxville: University of Tennessee Press, 1989), 128–31.

15 Quotations in Wise and Rowland, *Rebellion, Reconstruction, and Redemption*, 270–2, 462. For more on Pope see the excellent article, 'The Terrain of Freedom: The Struggle Over the Meaning of Free Labor in the US South', in Ira Berlin et al. (eds.), *History Workshop*, no. 22 (Autumn 1986): 108–30.

16 Margaret Washington Creel, *A Peculiar People: Slave Religion and Community-Culture Among the Gullahs* (New York: New York University Press, 1988); Erskine Clark, *Dwelling Place: A Plantation Epic* (New Haven: Yale University Press, 2005).

17 Of the four leading African American politicians in Beaufort during Reconstruction, only one (Smalls) was a local man and a former slave; one (Miller) was a free-born local man; and the other two (Gleaves and Whipper) were northern-born free black men. See Wise and Rowland, *Rebellion, Reconstruction, and Redemption*, 483.

18 On the black codes, see Theodore Wilson, *The Black Codes of the South* (Tuscaloosa: University of Alabama Press, 1965), but also James L. Roark, *Masters without Slaves: Southern Planters in the Civil War and Reconstruction* (New York: Norton, 1977); Michael Perman, *Reunion Without Compromise: The South and Reconstruction, 1865–1868* (Cambridge: Cambridge University Press, 1973); Foner, *Reconstruction*.

19 The rice strikes are a famous episode in southern labour history. See Scott Strickland, in Hahn and Prude (eds), *The Countryside in an Age of Capitalist Transformation*; Julie Saville, *The Work of Reconstruction: From Slave to Wage Laborer in South Carolina, 1860–1870* (New York: Cambridge University Press, 1994); Brian Kelly, 'Black Laborers, the Republican Party, and the Crisis of Reconstruction in Lowcountry South Carolina', *International Review of Social History*, 52 (2006): 375–414.

20 Wise and Rowland, *Rebellion, Reconstruction, and Redemption*, 483–4. Starting around 1873 and for twenty years thereafter, Beaufort became one of the leading mining, timbering and maritime centres in South Carolina. It was home to a US naval station and shipyard, federal contracts which Smalls was instrumental in delivering to his district. See ibid., 492–540.

21 On the failure of self-reconstruction, see Dan T. Carter, *When the War was Over: The Failure of Self Reconstruction in the South, 1865–1867* (Baton Rouge: Louisiana University Press, 1985).

22 Johnson came one vote short of conviction. For the most recent treatment, see Brenda Wineapple, *The Impeachers: The Trial of Andrew Johnson and the Dream of a Just Nation* (New York: Random House, 2019).

23 The key legislation was the Freedmen's Bureau Bill (March 1866), the Civil Rights Act (April 1866) and the 14th Amendment (passed in Congress June 1866).

24 Passed three Reconstruction Acts starting March 1867, together often referred to as the Military Reconstruction Acts. For the context, see Foner, *Reconstruction*.

25 Du Bois, *Black Reconstruction*, 370.

26 British Foreign Secretary, cited in Brooks T. Swett, 'Reconstruction Refracted: British Statesmen and American Democratic Politics, 1865–1868', unpublished paper in author's possession.

27 Saville, *Work of Reconstruction*, 167; Miller, *Gullah Statesman*, ch. 2.

28 On the Beaufort meeting, see 'The Political Meeting at Beaufort, S.C', *The Christian Recorder*, 4 May 1867 and Saville, *Work of Reconstruction*, 169, and more generally the outstanding article on black political culture by Elsa Barkley-Brown, 'Negotiating and Transforming the Public Sphere: African American Political Life in the Transition from Slavery to Freedom', *Public Culture*, 7 (1) (1994): 107–46.

29 Wise and Rowland, *Rebellion, Reconstruction, Redemption*, 478.

30 Ibid., 479.

31 Miller, *Gullah Statesman*, 67.

32 On the US South as a whole, see Foner, *Freedom's Lawmakers*; two states had black majority electorates (South Carolina and Mississippi) and four others black voters constituted 45–50 per cent (Georgia, Alabama, Florida, Louisiana). On South Carolina, see Miller, *Gullah Statesman*, 47; Beaufort's delegation to the Constitutional Convention of 1868 was comprised of five black men (including Smalls) and two whites.

33 Du Bois, *Black Reconstruction*, 370.

34 The best history of these new state constitutions is still Du Bois, *Black Reconstruction*.

35 Quotation from Wise and Rowland, *Rebellion, Reconstruction, Redemption*, 480; Miller, *Gullah Statesman*, 50.

36 Du Bois, *Black Reconstruction*, 400.

37 The best comprehensive history of the first, nineteenth-century Klan remains Allen Trelease, *White Terror: The Ku Klux Klan Conspiracy and Southern Reconstruction* (New York: Harper and Row, 1971), quotation on xlvii. On South Carolina, see also Richard Zuckek, *State of Rebellion: Reconstruction in South Carolina* (Columbia: University of South Carolina Press, 1996), 88–117.

38 Trelease, *White Terror*, 116–17; Stephen Kantrowitz, *Ben Tillman and the Reconstruction of White Supremacy* (Chapel Hill and London: The University of North Carolina Press, 2000), 54.

39 For the twelve volumes of testimony gathered in the Congressional Investigation see US Congress, Joint Select Committee to Inquire into the Conditions of Affairs in the Late Insurrectionary States, *Testimony Taken by the Joint Select committee to Inquire into the Conditions of Affairs in the Late Insurrectionary States (The Ku-Klux Conspiracy)* (Washington, DC: Government Printing Office, 1872).

40 Trelease, *White Terror* and Robert J. Kaczorowski, *The Politics of Judicial Interpretation: The Federal Courts, Department of Justice, and Civil Rights, 1866–1876* (New York: Fordham University Pres, 2005). The two states were Georgia and Alabama.

41 Foner, *Freedom's Lawmakers*, xxvii–xxix.

42 Wise and Rowland, *Rebellion, Reconstruction, and Redemption*, 548.

43 For the details on Smalls, see Miller, *Gullah Statesman*, 70–3; Du Bois, *Black Reconstruction*, 421–9 and 'The Propaganda of History', 711–29; Foner, *Reconstruction*, xix–xxvii, 385–9.

44 1875–7, 1877–9, 1881–3, 1883–5, 1885–7. Miller, *Gullah Statesman*, 78–9; Wise and Rowland, *Rebellion, Reconstruction, and Redemption*, 484

45 According to the official history of African Americans in Congress, 'South Carolina was arguably the crucible of the black congressional experience in the Reconstruction South'. For the quote and all the numbers, see the excellent report, *Black Americans in Congress*, 28 and throughout.

46 *Black Americans in Congress*, 19. About half had been former slaves; many were mixed-race people (thirteen), and a handful (four) like Smalls were the offspring of their masters (see 22–3). Six of the seventeen to serve in Congress were from South Carolina (see 28). Miller, *Gullah Statesman*, quotation on 93.

47 When Democrat John Harris asked if there was no one on floor of house who can honestly say that a 'black man is created his equal', Congressman Alonzo Ranzier, SC quietly replied 'I can' (*Black Americans in Congress*, 32.) Eric Foner has emphasized that one of the failures of the Republican Party in Reconstruction was the unwillingness of white Republicans to share power and office with black members (Foner, *Reconstruction*).

48 Foner, *Black Americans in Congress*, 28, 36, 42.

49 Ibid.

50 On the history of Edgefield, see Orville Vernon Burton, *In My Father's House Are Many Mansions: Family and Community in Edgefield, South Carolina* (Chapel Hill: University of North Carolina Press, 1985).

51 Kantrowitz, *Ben Tillman*, quotations on 3, 41, 75.

52 Wise and Rowland, *Rebellion, Reconstruction, and Redemption*, 557–8; Miller, *Gullah Statesman*, 99–107; Kantrowitz, *Ben Tillman*, 70. On the changing patterns

of white supremacist violence, see Kidada E. Williams, *They Left Great Marks on Me: African American Testimonies of Racial Violence from Emancipation to World War I* (New York and London: New York University Press, 2012).

53 Wise and Rowland, *Rebellion, Reconstruction, and Redemption*, 557–8.

54 4 Congr. Rec. 4641, 1876; Foner, *Black Americans in Congress*, 140. I would like to thank Judah Kraushaar for sharing his research on Smalls, and particularly for the copies of Smalls's key political speeches.

55 Miller, *Gullah Stateman*, 103; 5 Congr. Rec. 123, 1877, Speech of Hon. Robert Smalls of South Carolina, 24 February 1877, 123.

56 Tillman vs. Smalls, 45th Congress, 1st Session, House of Representatives, Misc Doc No. 11, 6, 588.

57 See the table in Foner, *Black Americans in Congress*, 50.

58 Zuczek, *State of Rebellion,* 192–201; Foner, *Reconstruction*, 574–5. The other county was Laurens County.

59 5 Congr. Rec. 123, 1877, Speech of Hon. Robert Smalls of South Carolina, 24 February 1877, 123, 127, 132–3. On the violence of the election in 1876, see Zuczek, *State of Rebellion*; Stephen Kantrowitz, *Ben Tillman and the Reconstruction of White Supremacy.*

60 Zuczek, *State of Rebellion*, 188–201.

61 These events can be followed in Zuczek, *State of Rebellion*, 188–201, quotation on 201 and Foner, *Reconstruction*, 575–87.

62 *Journal of the Constitutional Convention of the State of South Carolina* (Columbia, SC, 1895), Speech of Hon. Robert Smalls, 473–5.

63 For the quotations, see the excellent essay by Samuel L. Schaffer, 'A Bitter Memory Upon Which Terms of Peace Would Rest', in *Remembering Reconstruction: Struggles Over the Meaning of America's Most Turbulent Era*, Carole Emberton and Bruce Baker (eds.) (Baton Rouge: LSU Press, 2017), 203–24.

7

Dadabhai Naoroji: Indian Member of Parliament in Westminster, 1892–5

Teresa Segura-Garcia

'[T]he Mother of Parliaments', wrote Mohandas Karamchand Gandhi in 1909, in reference to the Britain's imperial parliament of Westminster, 'is like a sterile woman and a prostitute'. These terms, he conceded, were harsh, but they were also fair. Gandhi went on to explain the simile: 'That Parliament has not yet, of its own accord, done a single good thing. Hence I have compared it to a sterile woman … It is like a prostitute because it is under the control of ministers who change from time to time.'[1] In presenting the Westminster not as a 'mother' but as a 'sterile woman and a prostitute', Gandhi rejected the idea that India could achieve *swaraj* (self-rule) through the state processes and structures of the British Empire. As he wrote these words on a voyage from London, where he had trained as a barrister years before, to South Africa, where he had established his legal practice to defend the rights of the local Indian community, he was not alone in taking an extra-legal approach to *swaraj*. While he advocated non-violent civil disobedience, in 1909 proponents of anti-colonial violence assassinated British officials in British India and London.[2] A small but influential part of the Indian anti-colonial movement had come to see the institutions of the British Empire, and above all the 'Mother of Parliaments', as ineffective arenas in which to advance towards *swaraj*.

This chapter examines an earlier period, one in which Indian nationalists saw Britain's imperial parliament, as well as other state institutions, as spaces to challenge and redress colonial inequalities.[3] This was the main strategy of the Indian National Congress (INC) – the political movement established in 1885 that would not only eventually lead India to independence in 1947, but also rule it for most of its independent twentieth-century existence.[4] A particular group of men played an important role in shaping the INC's early approach: the wealthy,

Bombay-based Parsi men who populated the organization at the time. As Mitra Sharafi has established, their insistence of these Parsi individuals on working through existing state institutions was an extension of the law-focused, state-focused strategy that had helped their small, diasporic community thrive for the preceding half-century.[5] This constitutional approach – by no means unique to Parsi *Congresswallahs* – was not fully abandoned until the interwar period, when the nationalist movement became a mass movement under Gandhi.[6]

A central figure in the earlier, constitutional phase of Indian nationalism was Dadabhai Naoroji. Born in Bombay's Parsi community in 1825, Naoroji was active in the fields of religious, social and political reform from his mid-twenties until his death in 1917, at the age of ninety-one. In the political domain, he was one of the protagonists of the dominant strand of Indian political ideology of the nineteenth and twentieth centuries: liberal, secular, republican progressivism. He was also an heir to early-nineteenth-century socio-religious reformers such as Rammohan Roy, taking up a liberal tradition later represented by Jawaharlal Nehru, the first prime minister of independent India.[7] Naoroji was among the founders of the INC, which he presided in 1886, 1893 and 1906.[8] As many of his INC contemporaries, he was a Parsi who firmly believed in working through existing imperial institutions.[9] He put this idea into practice with more zeal than any of them: in the British general election of 1892 he was elected Member of Parliament (MP) for the Liberal Party in Central Finsbury, North London, becoming the first Indian MP in Westminster. He used his position to press for political change in India, as well as to gain a wider audience for his long-standing critique of colonialism. He served as MP for three years, losing his seat – along with many other Liberal MPs in constituencies across the country – in the general election of 1895, which saw a major Conservative victory.

Naoroji's term at Westminster was one stage in a protracted trajectory that turned him into India's foremost intellectual celebrity – he was known as 'the Grand Old Man of India'. He spent his life moving between India and Britain, playing an active political role in both countries. Across his itinerant career Naoroji was, to borrow Mitra Sharafi's expression, a 'constitutional agitator'.[10] He was tireless in writing to the press to correct a wrong impression about Indian politics and society, air a grievance or criticize a high-handed decision from the Government of India. He was also an industrious letter-writer and orator. His main tactic across all his writings was, as C. A. Bayly felicitously termed it, 'counter-preaching'. This was a tactic designed to subvert the self-confidence of colonial elites by emphasizing their moral failure as colonial rulers.[11] For instance, he frequently used official government statistics to disarm the

Government of India, highlighting that its policies in India were doing little to improve social conditions in the country. His most notable example of counter-preaching was, however, *Poverty and un-British rule in India* (1901). This was the book that brought attention to the idea that India's wealth was being drained to Britain.[12] Naoroji's pointed economic critique of British colonialism was followed by Indian economists, journalists and politicians. To this day, it remains powerful in informing popular understandings of the legacy of British rule in India.[13]

Just as Dadabhai Naoroji's intellectual and political legacy is present in contemporary India, research on his political thought and endeavours constitutes a rich, ongoing area of inquiry within the historiography of Modern South Asian. While there is no recent biography to replace the hagiographic accounts of his life that were published in the early twentieth century, his letters, speeches and other writings have been extensively published.[14] Over the past decade, academic articles and book chapters have made use of these sources to explore diverse facets of Naoroji's political activity, from the multiple audiences he addressed through his writing to his contribution to shaping partisan ideologies in Britain.[15] Two recent, as yet unpublished doctoral dissertations by Dinyar Patel and Vikram Visana have explored his political thought.[16] While Antoinette Burton and Sumita Mukherjee have analysed the racialized reactions of British journalists and politicians to his presence in Westminster, no text has explored the long path to his seat for Central Finsbury and the factors that made it possible.[17] This gap in the scholarship would certainly come as a surprise to Mahmudal Huq, a Bengali Muslim resident in London in 1892. At a meeting of Indians held at the National Liberal Club to congratulate Naoroji on his victory, Huq augured that the election of Britain's first Indian MP would 'not fail to arrest the attention of the historian'.[18]

The chapter fills this scholarly gap by exploring Naoroji's electoral campaigns, his election and his tenure as MP. Neither his long years of campaigning nor his three years in office are a rosy tale of the inclusivity and tolerance of the British Empire, but one of many defeats and racial prejudices. Naoroji ran for Parliament on four occasions across a period of twenty years – in 1886, 1892, 1895 and 1906 – obtaining one sole electoral victory, in 1892. As an MP, he was disheartened by the glacial pace of change in British policies towards India, as well as by the racism he faced from some sections of British society, both metropolitan and colonial. It is these darker areas that the chapter underscores, examining the conditions that made it possible for Naoroji to reach Westminster despite considerable obstacles.

In the first place, the chapter explores the following question: what made Naoroji's parliamentary participation possible? The most immediate prerequisite is easy to identify: due to the absence of a clearly defined policy on citizenship, it was possible for a British colonial subject to stand for a seat in a British constituency. As an Indian resident in Britain during his four campaigns, Naoroji additionally benefited from liberal attitudes to enrolment of resident Indians in the British electorate after 1884.[19] This is not enough, however, to explain his one electoral success, or indeed why so few British colonial subjects had run for Parliament before him. In examining Naoroji's path to Westminster, the chapter unfolds chronologically, pinpointing the factors that propelled him along: a long history of Parsi interaction with the colonial state; Naoroji's extensive personal connections with progressive 'old India hands' – retired British officials who had worked in India; an alliance with a wide array of often overlapping British progressive movements, from freethinkers to feminists; financial support from the rulers of India's princely states; and racial, gendered British metropolitan perceptions of his physical appearance, comportment and speech, which he was sometimes able to use in his favour. The conclusion addresses a wider double question that permeates the entire chapter: why was parliamentary participation useful for this solitary Indian MP, in the context of his work towards *swaraj*? And, on the other hand, where did Naoroji discover the limits and constraints of such participation? In highlighting Dadabhai Naoroji's parliamentary experience, the chapter sheds light on the complex interplay between imperial institutions, liberal critiques of empire and political participation in the British Empire and India.

Bombay, 1825

Dadabhai Naoroji was born into India's small but influential Parsi community. An ethnoreligious minority, Parsis gradually left their Persian homeland from the tenth century, coinciding with the rise of Islam in the region. They took their Zoroastrian religion with them as they settled in Gujarat, on the northern shore of western India.[20] With the arrival of colonialism, this diasporic minority thrived. From the sixteenth century, Parsi merchants occupied powerful intermediary positions as commercial brokers for Portuguese interests in the thriving port of Surat, as well as in other coastal enclaves of western India.[21] With the waning of Portuguese trade and the rise of the East India Company, Parsis deployed their commercial acumen as mercantile middlemen between the Company and Indian traders.[22] As Surat decayed and Bombay morphed from a fishing village into the subcontinent's commercial and financial capital, they migrated south from Gujarat to the new city.[23] Parsis were, in fact, part and parcel of Bombay's transformation, as leading dynasties such as the Wadias and the Jejeebhoys became enormously wealthy building ships and trading opium with China. From the late nineteenth century, these *seths* (wealthy merchants) intensified their links with the colonial state, investing in the building of infrastructure through joint ventures with the British.[24] It was in no small measure due to the might of these Parsi families that Indians maintained more political power in Bombay than in other parts of India.[25]

If Bombay's maritime, diasporic character as a nexus of Asian trade allowed Parsis to become deeply embedded in the colonial state, it also turned the city into a particularly fertile place for early discussions on the nature and extent of British overseas sovereignty. On top of that, Parsi community life – centred around the *panchayat* (community council) – gave added force to early debates on the nature of representation, as leading Parsi men debated issues of representation and authority within the community.[26] From the late eighteenth century, they overwhelmingly turned to colonial law as litigants, legislators and lobbyists.[27] Whether it was time to build a school through philanthropy or to engage in legislative lobbying, Parsi elites invariably sought to influence colonial life in the same way: by becoming deeply involved with the colonial state.[28] This liberal world of maritime western India, shaped by a diasporic community used to working from within and through the empire, rather than from outside or against, was the background in which Dadabhai Naoroji, liberal thinker and Liberal MP in Westminster, emerged.

In the early 1820s, Manekbai and Naoroji Palanji Dordi, a married but childless Parsi couple, left their village in southern Gujarat. Naoroji's ancestors, the Dordis, hailed from Navsari, a Gujarati stronghold of Parsi priesthood in the territory of the Maharaja of Baroda.[29] Despite Naoroji's exalted priestly lineage, the couple's financial position turned precarious as the local textile economy collapsed. Following the footsteps of other Parsis they travelled south, hoping to earn a living in the emerging port city of Bombay. Manekbai and Naoroji settled in Khadak, a nearby fishing village. On 4 September 1825, Manekbai gave birth to Dadabhai, who was to be the couple's only son. His father, whose first name Dadabhai later adopted as his surname, died when he was only four years old. Manekbai voluntarily remained a widow and threw herself into raising Dadabhai, with occasional support from her brother.[30]

Manekbai dotted on her son. She was particularly proud of two of the boy's physical features: his fair skin and his 'pretty little limbs'.[31] She put Dadabhai on display at weddings and community gatherings, dressing him up – sometimes in the uniform of an English general or admiral, sometimes in English court dress – and parading him in front of admiring relatives.[32] If the sight of a tiny child in the clothes of an adult authority figure was intended to have a comic effect, the choice of European clothes was meant to draw attention to the boy's pale skin. Significantly, as the chapter later establishes, both the colour of Naoroji's skin and the slightness of his frame played a substantial role in his reception by metropolitan British audiences during his election campaigns.

Above all, as the sole parent of a Parsi boy from a priestly lineage, Manekbai fulfilled two important obligations. In the first place, she enrolled Dadabhai into a school established by the Native Education Society, which provided free English-language education – the only education she could afford, given her strained circumstances as a widow. Here was yet another source of pride, as her son proved to be a bright student. In the second place, when Dadabhai was eleven years old, Manekbai arranged his marriage to a suitable Parsi girl. His bride was seven-year-old Gulbai Shroff. It would be decades before the couple had any children: their first, Ardeshir, was born in 1859, when Gulbai was around thirty. The boy was followed by two girls: Shirin (b. unknown) and Manekbai (b. 1868).

After finishing his secondary education, Dadabhai was awarded a scholarship to study at the British-administered Elphinstone College, where he continued to distinguish himself as a student. In 1845, at the age of twenty, he became one of the institution's first Indian graduates.[33] His academic ability caught the attention of Sir Thomas Erskine Perry – Chief Justice of Bombay, President of the Board of Education, and former MP for the Liberal Party. Perry proposed to send Naoroji to London to train as a barrister.[34] In doing so, Perry was acting *in loco parentis*: Parsi fathers had been some of the first Indians to send their sons to London to study for the Bar. Perry offered to contribute half of the expenses himself, expecting the young man's own community to provide the other half – it was common for Parsi *seths* to make charitable donations to fellow Parsis in need of financial aid. Perry approached Jamsetjee Jejeebhoy, opium and cotton trader, as well as other leading Parsi philanthropist merchants.[35] They turned down the Chief Justice of Bombay's proposal, as community elders feared that Dadabhai might convert to Christianity in Britain. Indeed, two or three conversions of Parsis in Britain had taken place earlier. Dadabhai's priestly status may have also played a role in the *seths*'s refusal, as the ritual purity expected of priests made their travel abroad particularly unsettling in the eyes of Orthodox Parsis.[36]

Forced to stay in India, Naoroji secured the post of Native Head Assistant at Elphinstone College. In 1854, at the age of twenty-nine, he became the first

Indian to be appointed professor in a British-administered college. It was in this period that he began to slowly build his reputation as an intellectual celebrity – not in the field of imperial politics, but of social reform within the Parsi community. As the Orthodox Parsis who had blocked Naoroji's training in London advocated adherence to strict, elaborate versions of Zoroastrian ritual, young reformists such as Naoroji argued for a more flexible, less ritual-bound Zoroastrianism.[37] Naoroji published his views on Parsi socio-religious reform in the *Rast Goftar* (Herald of the Truth), a Gujarati weekly he co-founded and edited for two years.[38] It was also in this period that he began to play an active role in Bombay's rich association life. He helped to establish the Bombay Association (1852), which paved the way for the INC, and the Widow Marriage Association (1861), which aimed to improve the social status of widowed women by eroding social prejudice against remarriage. He also emerged as one of the pioneers of female education in Bombay, even as he struggled to educate Gulbai, his own wife, who remained illiterate. Years later, Naoroji's authorized biographer lamented that Gulbai had 'not the least aptitude for study' and was 'far from being prepossessing, and awkward in speech and manners'.[39] As his son's public profile rose, Manekbai regretted having arranged the marriage and tried to convince him to take a second wife – bigamy was possible, if rare, for Parsi men. Naoroji refused, with the argument that should he have the 'disabilities' his wife had, he would not be happy if she were to take a second husband.[40]

London, 1855

In 1855, Naoroji resigned from his professorship at Elphinstone College to go into business. Along with two Parsi associates, he set up Cama & Co., which was to be the first Indian firm established in Britain, with branches in London and Liverpool. The venture gave him the opportunity to move to Britain, where he would live for the next two decades. During his first decade in the country he quit Cama & Co. on ethical grounds, as the company's trade in – among other goods – opium and alcohol clashed with his temperance views. He set up his own cotton trading company, Naoroji & Co. He also served as professor of Gujarati at University College London (1856–65). After a decade in Britain, however, he became increasingly concerned with one idea: India's increasing impoverishment under foreign rule. His sight was set on redressing this colonial inequality though political agitation at the heart of empire, where imperial policy was formulated.[41]

In 1861, Naoroji wrote 'England's duties to India', his first major work on his well-known drain of wealth theory.[42] Employing the statistical evidence of British officials to refute colonial analyses, Naoroji declared that British rule had turned India into 'the poorest country in the world'.[43] In this way, he dismantled British claims of benevolent imperial rule. He also created new spaces of colonial debate in the metropole: he helped to establish the London Indian Society (1865) and the East India Association (1866), two organizations where 'old India hands' and Britons with an interest in Indian affairs came together to discuss contemporary Indian affairs and influence government policy.[44] Naoroji's efforts in shaping opinion on British policy in India were not centred exclusively on London: he travelled across England to address meetings and read papers before learned societies. He also wrote to newspapers and periodicals with wide readerships. His relentless lobbying made him particularly well known among Britons connected with the Indian Civil Service (ICS) and the Government of India, including those in the highest-ranking positions, such as provincial governors and viceroys.

From the 1860s Naoroji argued for Indian representation in legislation and administration in India so that, when the British left India, Indians would be in place to replace them.[45] To this end, he was particularly concerned with the employment of Indians in the ICS. In 1865, the old system of nominations to the ICS was abolished, and one of recruitment by open competition was adopted. Among the candidates in the first open competition was an Indian candidate, R. H. Wadia, a scion of the distinguished Parsi shipbuilding family. When ICS commissioners objected to admitting Wadia on a technical ground, Naoroji took up his cause. While he did not succeed in helping Wadia to join the ICS, the affair led him to tackle the issue of the holding simultaneous ICS examinations in Britain and India. In the 1860s, examinations were held exclusively in Britain, which put Indian candidates at a disadvantage. Naoroji did not stop agitating for simultaneous examinations in Britain and India until 1893: when he was an MP, the House of Commons declared itself in favour of the policy. Naoroji's long-standing interest in the employment of Indians in an institution that was central to the colonial state is a prime example of his constitutional, through-the-state strategy to political change – a strategy he favoured long before his tenure in Westminster.

By 1874, after nearly two decades in Britain, Naoroji had earned a reputation as a liberal thinker and reformer, both in Britain and in India. This resulted in an invitation to move to southern Gujarat, the land of his ancestors: Maharaja Malhar Rao of Baroda, ruler of the leading princely state of western India, wished to appoint him *diwan* (prime minister) of Baroda.[46] In response to growing British demands for administrative reforms in his state, Malhar Rao hoped Naoroji's political skills and good standing among British administrators and Indian nationalists alike would help him secure his precarious hold on power in Baroda. Naoroji took up this high-ranking, well-paid position – a diwanship in a princely state was one of the few posts where an able Indian administrator could exercise real political power, as similar positions in India's British-administered provinces were closed to Indians.[47] Naoroji spent two years in Baroda, reforming the state's administration and attempting to put an end to corruption. His efforts were in vain, as the British deposed Malhar Rao in 1875 and exiled him to Madras. After resigning from his office as *diwan* of Baroda, Naoroji moved to Bombay and stayed there for some years, serving as a member of the city's Municipal Corporation.

In 1886, Naoroji left India for the second time, hoping to resume his constitutional agitation in London. This time he sailed from Bombay with a clear, ambitious goal: to be elected by a British constituency to sit in the House of Commons. The 'Mother of all Parliaments', to use M. K. Gandhi's phrase, was the highest-ranking institution that an Indian constitutional agitator bent on forcing change from within could reach. Naoroji was not the first Indian to attempt to gain a seat in Westminster: the general election of 1885 had seen the first Indian candidate for the House of Commons. This was Lalmohan Ghose, a London-based, London-trained Bengali barrister who would, just as Naoroji, later preside the INC.[48] Ghose, who had run on funds raised from his supporters in Bengal, had been defeated on the Liberal Party ticket at Deptford, a dockyard area to the south-east of London.[49] Ghose was reviled in the British press as a 'baboo' (a pejorative term for a Western-educated Indian), an 'Asiatic foreigner' and a 'stranger to English civilisation and Christianity'.[50] Undeterred by Ghose's failed attempt and by the frenzied racial prejudice it engendered, Naoroji hoped to put pressure on the imperial system from Westminster – if he could first find a constituency that would accept him as a candidate.

Holborn, 1886

Naoroji's arrival to London in April 1886 marked the start of seven years of forging alliances, lobbying and campaigning to find a constituency and win a general election. A sympathetic commentator later described this period as

Naoroji's 'Seven Years' War'.[51] The would-be MP's struggle, however, had begun before even leaving Bombay.

Before his departure, Naoroji wrote to friends in Britain asking for help in finding a constituency, to no avail. In his first few weeks in London, he filled his schedule with meetings with old acquaintances from his first stint in the city – friends, journalists, politicians and colonial administrators – to find support and a constituency. He received advice and help from the Marquess of Ripon, Liberal politician and Viceroy of India from 1880 to 1884; John Bright, Radical, Quaker and MP from 1843 to 1889; Henry Hyndman, a prominent socialist; Josephine Butler, feminist and social reformer; and William Digby, Liberal journalist and humanitarian. All were liberals who were committed, in differing degrees, to political reform that would provide India with greater self-government. Some saw Naoroji's prospective run as MP as an opportunity to test Britain's commitment to liberalism. The pacifist Hodgson Pratt, for instance, pointed out to Naoroji that France had humiliated Britain in the domain of political representation: in allowing men from its dominions to serve as representatives, the French Empire had displayed 'more liberalism' than the British Empire. Despite the common political ground that united Naoroji and his British contacts, he did not always find the support he sought. During a meeting with General Orfeur Cavenagh, a former Governor of the Straits Settlement who chaired the Council of the East India Association, Cavenagh subjected Naoroji to a long tirade about his dislike for Bengalis and his admiration for the far superior 'manly people' of the Punjab. 'About my object to get into Parliament', Naoroji reported laconically, 'he mentioned the various difficulties and seemed to like that I should succeed'.[52]

The assistance of Naoroji's supporters in finding a constituency willing to accept him was finally successful. On 18 June 1886, the Executive Committee of the Holborn Liberal Association unanimously resolved to commend him to the electors of Holborn as a 'fit and proper person to represent the Liberals and Radicals of the borough' in Parliament.[53] The electors of this London borough, as the electors of all other constituencies, were exclusively male and certainly not poor. In 1884, the Representation of the People Act had given the vote to all men paying an annual rent of £10 or more, as well as men holding land valued at £10 or more. This left all women and 40 per cent of adult males across Britain without the vote. When it came to Holborn, its voters were strongly Conservative. Both the Holborn Liberal Association and Naoroji knew there was no hope for anyone contesting the borough as a Liberal candidate – especially one in favour of Home Rule for Ireland, as Naoroji was.[54] His Conservative rival – Colonel Duncan, a wealthy and influential candidate – was guaranteed to win.

At the election, Duncan polled 3,651 votes against Naoroji's 1,950. Despite the defeat, Naoroji's campaign in Holborn attracted a great deal of attention in the press, both in Britain and in India. It gave him the opportunity to become well known beyond the small circle of India sympathizers and liberal 'old India hands' he had cultivated for years. His Holborn experience earnt him support from socialists, labour leaders, members of the women's suffrage movement and Irish nationalists — progressive groups who by and large lent their support to India's political aspirations.[55] He did not waste the momentum: immediately after news of his defeat came out he wrote to some of his key supporters, including Josephine Butler and Henry Hyndman, indicating his wish to find a more favourable constituency for the next election.[56] Of all the options suggested to him, he considered one to be especially promising. In March 1887, he excitedly wrote to Behramji Malabari, a noted Parsi social reformer: 'This week I had pretty good work in canvassing the executive of a particular constituency – Central Finsbury. This is private!'[57] His second attempt to sit at the House of Commons, which would occupy him for the six following years, had begun.

Finsbury, 1892

Central Finsbury, in London's Clerkenwell district, was a marginal seat with a predominantly working-class electorate. The path to Naoroji's candidacy in the borough was not smooth, as there were other Liberal candidates and the Party split in supporting him. Eventually, Naoroji was left the sole Liberal and Radical contender for Central Finsbury. In his manifesto and campaign addresses, he followed the Liberal Party's Newcastle Programme of 1891, including its most salient point – Irish Home Rule. He campaigned on reforms that responded to working-class demands, such as the provision of free education under public control; the establishment of the Free Breakfast Table – the abolition of duties on basic foodstuffs such as tea, coffee and sugar; the setting up of affordable industrial courts; and the creation of the legal eight-hour work day or the forty-eight-hour work week.[58] He also spoke in favour of allowing women to run for seats in the London County Council, the main local government body for the county of London. India remained absent from his campaign addresses until the very end, when he brought up the topic that had brought him to Central Finsbury in the first place: 'Indian reforms'.[59] In strategically placing India at the end of a long list of reforms – reforms concerning Ireland, the British working-class and British women – Naoroji hoped to demonstrate to his constituents that his priorities lay closer to home than to Britain's fractious, faraway colony.

Naoroji's Conservative rival, Captain Frederick Penton, was well known in Central Finsbury as a large landlord and a generous supporter of charities. He was also well connected with Britain's political elite.[60] Naoroji, however, had gained endorsements from leading Liberal politicians, from William Gladstone to William Harcourt. Some of these influential Liberals had firsthand experience of India: the Marquess of Ripon was a former Viceroy, while Lord Reay had served as Governor of Bombay from 1885 to 1890.[61] Among Naoroji's closest supporters during this period were also Keir Hardie, a prominent labour organizer and founder of the Independent Labour Party (1893); John Burns, a trade unionist and Liberal politician; and James Rowlands, who had been Liberal MP for Finsbury East since 1886. Support for the Central Finsbury candidate also came from western India – in particular, from the princely state of Baroda, which furthered Dadabhai's political career once again. In 1875, with the deposition and exile of Maharaja Malhar Rao – whom Naoroji had served as *diwan* – a distant relative of the ousted king became the new Maharaja of Baroda. With an interest in social, religious and political reform, Maharaja Sayaji Rao III quickly emerged as one of India's most progressive rulers. Eager to burnish his liberal reputation, in 1892 he donated £1,000 to Naoroji's campaign.[62] The Maharaja also offered his assistance on the day of the election, which he spent in London as part of one of his annual international tours. If the Marquess of Salisbury and other British aristocrats sent several carriages to Captain Penton so that the Conservative candidate could bring voters to the polling station, the Maharaja of Baroda placed twenty coaches at Naoroji's disposal for the same purpose.[63]

It was women, however, who played an unusually important role in Naoroji's path to Westminster, both as campaigners on the ground in Central Finsbury and as endorsers of the candidate to a wider British audience. Some British commentators remarked upon the support he received from these women with some surprise, noting that Naoroji's 'friends' included 'a goodly number of their fair sex'.[64] The candidate's defence of progressive reforms, including women's suffrage, drew him to female activists who moved in overlapping London circles – radicals, freethinkers, atheists, peace activists and women's suffrage activists.

Several women worked directly for Naoroji's campaign in Central Finsbury. At least two of them started their advocacy for the candidate well before 1892. This was the case of Emily Magnus and Ernestine Evans Bell, a mother–daughter duo of women's suffrage activists. A radical and a freethinker, Emily Magnus was the widow of Thomas Evans Bell, an Indian army officer who had been highly critical of British rule in India.[65] For three years – starting in 1889 – mother and daughter canvassed the borough in preparation for Naoroji's run.[66] In the run-up to the election they intensified their efforts, going from house to house and from shop to shop to win votes.[67] The two other women who worked directly for Naoroji during the campaign were Hypatia Bradlaugh Bonner, a freethinker, atheist and peace activist, and Harriette Colenso. While Colenso had no previous links with India, she did have a colonial connection – a white British missionary raised in Natal, she had been active in expanding the work of the Church of England in the region.[68] She had also emerged as an advocate for a particular group of colonized subjects, as she had defended the rights of disaffected Zulu royals to the Crown.[69] During the campaign, Florence Nightingale and Josephine Butler publicly endorsed Naoroji's candidacy.[70] Butler, who had already endorsed him in Holborn in 1886, hailed him as 'one of the most uncompromising friends of womanhood' for his support of women's suffrage.[71] Women also featured prominently in the final campaign meeting, which saw four women speak in support of the Liberal candidate: Hypatia Bradlaugh Bonner; Harriette Colenso; Emily Keary, an Irish countess; and Leonora Philipps, co-founder of the feminist Pioneer Club, a club for professional and working women.[72]

The links of personal affinity and political activism that united Naoroji with these literate, articulate, politically active women stand in stark contrast with his wife's absence from his career – Gulbai remained in Bombay throughout her husband's time in Britain and never learnt to read and write. In the late nineteenth and the early twentieth centuries, western India's foremost male social and political reformers worked in tandem with their spouses, who were noted activists in their own right – Mahadev Govind and Ramabai Ranade, Jyotirao and Savitribai Phule, Mohandas Karamchand and Kasturba Gandhi. The relationship between Naoroji and the women he worked with in a joint struggle for political reform was very different from these partnerships, as he nurtured connections with a network of some of the like-minded, middle- and upper-class white women who animated London's feminist, progressive spaces. The role these women played in Naoroji's campaign signals towards the importance of friendship in transnational, anti-imperialist collaboration – an important point that has been persuasively argued by Leela Gandhi and Jennifer Regan-Lefebvre in their studies of anti-imperial politics in Britain's fin-de-siècle empire.[73]

The campaign efforts of Naoroji and his supporters paid off. On 7 July 1892, the day of the election, Naoroji won the Central Finsbury seat by five votes – a margin that soon earned him the derisive nickname 'Narrow-majority'.[74] Captain

Penton was probably undone by Naoroji's campaigning, as well as by his refusal to endorse the eight-hour working day in a largely working-class constituency. Despite Naoroji's small margin, the announcement that Westminster was to have its first Indian MP was received with enthusiasm by the crowd assembled near the Houses of Parliament, outside the National Liberal Club, which had provided facilities for Liberal campaigners: 'The cheering … might have been heard at St Paul's on one side and Chelsea Hospital on the other.'[75] The celebrations were more far-reaching in India, where schools closed down, shopkeepers shut their stores and rows of coloured lights were put up in houses and streets.[76] In Bombay, Madras and other large cities, meeting halls were packed for public meetings to congratulate the new MP for Central Finsbury.[77] In Bombay, a speaker proclaimed 7 July to be 'the proudest day in the political history of India as well as the Parliamentary history of England'.[78] Even in villages and hamlets, meetings were held to congratulate Naoroji and thank his Central Finsbury electors.[79] Indians across the subcontinent rejoiced that Naoroji would communicate 'Indian wants and Indian aspirations' to Great Britain.[80] The newly elected MP was well aware of the far-ranging, imperial dimension of his victory: when he addressed his constituents, he thanked them for having helped India 'obtain a voice in the Imperial Parliament'.[81]

Before the chapter examines how and to what extent Naoroji used this 'voice in the Imperial Parliament' during his tenure as MP from 1892 to 1895, the following section pauses the chapter's chronological exploration of Naoroji's path to Westminster. It does so to examine the racial and gendered lenses through which metropolitan audiences saw Naoroji from the 1880s to 1892, underscoring how these understandings influenced British perceptions of his suitability to sit at the House of Commons.

Race and gender in the election of Dadabhai Naoroji

While Dadabhai Naoroji was the first Indian MP in Westminster, he was not the first MP with colonial origins. It is highly likely that John Stewart, elected as MP for Lymington in 1832, was from a mixed ethnic background, as the illegitimate son of a British man who owned sugar plantations in the West Indies and a woman who was possibly black or of mixed race.[82] While Stewart's ethnicity was not mentioned during his tenure as MP, he was later described as 'a man of colour' and the first 'coloured' MP.[83] Almost a decade later, in 1841, the election of David Ochterlony Dyce Sombre as a Radical-Liberal to the seat of Sudbury, in Suffolk, provides a second example of a mixed-race MP. The descendent of a German mercenary active in India and an Indian woman, Dyce Sombre inherited a large fortune from his stepmother – Begum Samru, the formidable ruler of the principality of Sardhana – and moved to England.[84] Dyce Sombre, however, lost his seat just a few months after becoming MP: in 1842 Parliament overturned his victory, citing 'gross, systematic, and extensive bribery' during his campaign.[85]

In 1832, John Stewart's mixed-race, colonial origin was silenced. In 1841, David Ochterlony Dyce Sombre's was glossed over, perhaps because of the candidate's fortune and aristocratic stepmother – although neither wealth nor rank prevented him from losing his seat the following year. Dadabhai Naoroji, for his part, became MP five decades later, when Britain's 'high noon of imperialism' built on the racial categories of the earlier nineteenth century to turn them more rigid.[86] As a Parsi, Naoroji was in a privileged position to navigate the empire's hardened racial boundaries. With their enduring commercial, financial and legal links with the British colonial enterprise in western India, with their English-language education and their early adoption of Western-inspired clothes, upper-class Parsi men were seemingly the sort of Indians that T. B. Macaulay aspired to create in his 1835 *Minute on Indian education*: Indian 'in blood and colour', English 'in taste, in opinions, in morals and intellect'.[87]

While Naoroji's membership to the Parsi community eased his acceptance by metropolitan society, during his campaigns and tenure as MP some conservative commentators were eager to present him as a racialized 'other'. The *St Stephen's Review* decried the election of a 'Bengali Baboo' and a 'fire-worshipper from Bombay'. Naoroji was neither Bengali nor a fire-worshipper: these two characterizations were meant to arouse long-standing British suspicions about Indian men. Bengalis were commonly derided as effeminate, disloyal and capable of acquiring only a veneer of Western education – this was especially true of the 'baboo', the British stereotype of the English-speaking Bengali clerk.[88] Accusations of fire-worshipping, on the other hand, were a common European trope against Parsis and their Zoroastrian practice. In response to this long-standing prejudice, in one of his early works on Zoroastrianism Naoroji had seen it necessary to establish that European critics were wrong in claiming that Parsis worshiped fire.[89]

In the face of metropolitan suspicions around his racialized otherness, Naoroji's supporters were particularly anxious to stress his 'Englishness'. During the Holborn election the journalist William Digby, a close friend of Naoroji, argued that the candidate was 'to all intents and purposes an Englishman as well

Figure 7.1 Dadabhai Naoroji around the time of his tenure as a Member of Parliament in Westminster. Courtesy © Getty Images.

as an English subject'. As proof, he offered three observations. In the first place, Naoroji's 'long residence' in the country. Secondly, his 'mastery of the English language'.[90] Indeed, *The Manchester Guardian* assured its readers that Naoroji's speech was entirely free from 'foreign accent or phraseology'.[91] Finally, Digby drew attention to Naoroji's 'English appearance'.[92] This English appearance was the result of a long process of sartorial transformation amongst the Parsi men of Bombay. In Britain, Naoroji dressed in slim and tailored European-style suits, similar to the garments that upper-class Parsi men had worn for decades in Bombay. These men had been some of the first Indians to adopt European trousers and shoes, which they wore with the *phenta*, the distinctive conical hat of the Parsis.[93] While Naoroji initially wore a *phenta* in London, he abandoned it in favour of a European hat in 1886. This sartorial change was linked to his first attempt to reach Westminster: William Digby advised him to ditch the Parsi hat before the start of the Holborn campaign. Naoroji's appearance had the effect Digby sought: during his campaign debut, a commentator described the candidate as having 'the appearance and the manner of a cultivated English gentleman'.[94] Naoroji, however, did not completely follow Digby's advice: while he rarely appears with a *phenta* in images dated after 1886, he was never captured with a European hat, opting on every occasion to appear with an uncovered head. In doing so, he rejected the colonial binary of the rulers versus the ruled, positioning himself as a new, emerging imperial subject that transcended both categories.

From Naoroji's Holborn campaign, metropolitan commentators mentioned two aspects of the candidate's physical appearance with startling frequency: his skin colour and his frame. Naoroji described his adult self as 'fair of skin and small of frame' – the two features that had earned him the admiration of relatives, family friends and acquaintances as a child in Bombay. In fin de siècle London, his pale and slight adult body revealed entrenched colonial anxieties around the connection between race, masculinity, skin colour and physical strength.

While Naoroji's identification as a Parsi granted him the status of 'honorary white', it did not stop him from receiving racist attacks that fixated on his skin colour. In 1888, in reference to Naoroji's Holborn defeat, Conservative Prime Minister Lord Salisbury remarked that an English constituency was not ready to elect a 'blackman'.[95] As Antoinette Burton has shown, Naoroji adeptly used Salisbury's racism to expose the contradictions of Britain's imperial democracy.[96] After this incident, supporters and sympathetic commentators were much more likely to stress the fairness of Naoroji's skin. For these individuals, the standard against which to judge Naoroji's skin colour was not the 'blackman' at all, but the white Briton. In this way, a commentator argued that Naoroji was 'not darker than many a travelled Englishman'.[97] An eyewitness of his Holborn campaign agreed: the candidate's face was 'a shade or two off-colour, perhaps, but certainly not darker than many an Australian, tanned from long exposure to tropical suns'.[98] Naoroji emerged once again as an imperial subject who was able to straddle the world of the colonizers and the colonized – an Indian who looked just as an Englishman who had perhaps spent too much time in a white settler colony.

British commentators were as likely to mention Naoroji's skin colour as his slight frame. The 'pretty little limbs' of his childhood, which captivated the Parsi community in Bombay, turned him into a non-threatening adult Indian male in Britain – a counterbalance to the commanding masculinity and unrestrained sexuality of India's martial races.[99] Here was a 'short, slight man', 'a little harmless-looking person' – an acceptable Indian man at the heart of empire.[100] Naoroji's mild, gentlemanly masculinity may explain the absence of British criticism against his cooperation with white British women – an alliance that unfolded in a period in which, as a wide body of research has established, social contact between Indian men and white British women was regarded with great suspicion.[101]

Westminster, 1892

When Naoroji was sworn in as MP he refused to take the oath on the Bible, using instead his copy of the *Khordeh Avesta*, a sacred Zoroastrian text.[102] The ceremony marked the beginning of months of hard work for Westminster's first Indian MP. In the early days of his tenure Naoroji reached the Houses of Parliament at noon and did not return home until one or two in the morning, working to understand how to vote on every question. Having invested a great deal of his own funds in the campaign, he found that he could not afford the private secretary he sorely needed as an MP.[103] He turned to the rulers of India's princely states for financial help. After supporting his campaign, Maharaja Sayaji Rao III of Baroda proved once again to be 'very free and kind', sending in a £1,000 cheque as the first instalment in a series of payments.[104] Two other progressive rulers from Gujarat, the Maharaja of Bhavnagar and the Maharaja of Gondal, also contributed to Naoroji's expenses. These princely contributions allowed him to face his tenure as MP without too much financial anxiety.[105]

On 28 February 1893, Naoroji gave his maiden speech in the House of Commons. He began the evening by sitting discreetly on the back benches, only moving down to the second row just before he was due to speak. He characterized his presence in Westminster as the inevitable outcome of the British instincts of 'justice and generosity'. As Britain had decided to rule India with these two principles, it had introduced Western civilization, education and political institutions to the subcontinent. By further granting Indians freedom of speech,

Britain had enabled them to voice their grievances. Therefore, as a result of Britain's original 'justice and generosity', Naoroji could speak 'openly and freely' at the House of Commons.[106] By appealing to Britain's justice and generosity, Naoroji hoped to convince the House of Commons that political reform that gave India greater autonomy was necessary, as the organic continuation of Britain's long-established civilizing mission in the subcontinent. When he returned to his seat, MPs flocked around him to congratulate him on his maiden speech.[107]

Naoroji began his term in office by forging alliances with other members of parliament who had an interest in India. These connections were to take an institutional form: with MPs William Wedderburn and William Sproston Caine he formed the Indian Parliamentary Committee, a pressure group on behalf of India in Westminster.[108] Wedderburn, a former ICS officer, was a veteran of Indian self-government, as he had helped to found the INC in 1885. Caine had no previous links with India, but he was a prominent member of the temperance movement – a cause that Naoroji supported.[109] The Indian Parliamentary Committee, which began with twenty members, grew to include over 150 Liberal and Labour MPs. The committee existed until 1915 and was, in Rozina Visram's words, 'the Indian Opposition' in Westminster.[110]

Naoroji's demands for Indian reform, however, garnered little support beyond the Indian Parliamentary Committee. The most substantial result of Naoroji's parliamentary career did not come until 1895, when his campaign against Britain's financial drain of India led to the creation of the Royal Commission on Indian Expenditure. Also known as the Welby Commission, it included Naoroji, Wedderburn and Caine as the representatives of Indian interests. The statistical evidence Naoroji submitted to the commission was incorporated into its report, which highlighted cases where the Government of India had made excessive payments to British companies using Indian revenues. The text called on the House of Commons to ensure that financial arrangements between Britain and India did not lead to the colony's drain of wealth, thus adopting the theory popularized by Naoroji. The report, however, was not published until 1900.

Finding that his demands for his Indian constituency fell on deaf ears, Naoroji concentrated on working for his British constituency while engaging with activists from other corners of the British Empire. On the first front, he backed the Liberal programme, attending all parliamentary debates and voting for the Irish Home Rule Bill in 1893. He also supported the provision of pensions for the elderly and the abolition of the House of Lords. He became involved with progressive local organizations, from charity and temperance societies in Finsbury to trade unions and working men's clubs across London. He also continued his engagement with feminist and women's suffrage organizations, such as the Women's Liberal Federation, the National Union of Women's Suffrage Societies and the Women's Franchise League. On the second front, Naoroji became an important presence in London's Pan-African movement. In 1893, he joined the Society for the Recognition of the Brotherhood of Man, as an elected member to the institution's governing council.[111] From 1897 he was one of the most notable supporters of the African Association, a London-based society co-founded that same year by Henry Sylvester Williams, a Trinidadian lawyer. The Association's aims were strongly connected with Naoroji's political career and strategy, as it hoped to instruct MPs that 'the better treatment of Native Races' should command greater attention in Parliament.[112] Here was another project of colonial activism that, just as Naoroji's, turned to Britain's highest representative institution to redress colonial wrongs. In 1900 Naoroji continued his association with Pan-Africanism through the first Pan-African Conference, convened by Henry Sylvester Williams in London. Naoroji not only attended the event, but also financially contributed to it.[113] The conference attracted thirty-two official delegates from Africa, the West Indies, Britain and North America, including W. E. B. DuBois.[114] In continuing to nurture the Irish, working-class and feminist links that were partially responsible for bringing him to Westminster, while seeking new alliances with parliamentary-minded Pan-African circles, Naoroji signalled his intention to continue to participate in British parliamentary politics.

On 14 March 1895, with the dissolution of Parliament, Naoroji was accepted as Central Finsbury's Liberal and Radical candidate for the upcoming general election.[115] Naoroji's opponent was the Conservative William Massey-Mainwaring, a well-known Irish art collector. Massey-Mainwaring won the seat by a majority of 805 votes – 3,588 against Naoroji's 2,783. Naoroji's defeat was part of a wider Conservative victory against Gladstone and Irish Home Rule. While the Conservative upswing removed Britain's first Indian MP, it brought in its second: Mancherjee Bhownaggree was elected Conservative MP for Bethnal Green, in north-east London.[116] Also a Bombay-born Parsi, Bhownaggree's staunch support for an unreformed British Empire – for an empire that need not rethink its relationship with India – earned him the mistrust of the INC.[117] Naoroji himself regarded Bhownaggree with unease: 'I tried my utmost to keep him straight about India', he lamented, '[b]ut, I am afraid, in vain. I cannot help thinking, I may be wrong, that he has sold his soul to his masters.'[118] As for his own electoral defeat, Naoroji was undeterred. At the age of seventy, he declared he meant 'to try to get into the House of Commons again, as it is there that the battles of the grievances and necessary reforms of India, and the stability of the British Empire have to be fought'.[119] His commitment to imperial reform from within one of the central institutions of the British Empire was unfaltering, despite the modest advances of his first stint in Westminster.

Naoroji after Parliament

After losing his Central Finsbury seat in 1895, Naoroji remained in London. Bad health prevented him from running in the 1900 election. He returned to the drain of wealth theory, launching a renewed economic critique of colonialism in his influential book *Poverty and un-British Rule in India* (1901).[120] He argued that British rule in India was destructive and despotic to India, but also un-British and suicidal to Britain. He maintained that the only way to stop the devastating drain of wealth that crippled India was a rapid movement towards *swaraj* within the empire, with the establishment of a full adult franchise.[121] In 1905, in an address to the INC, he reiterated that India's much-needed self-government could only be achieved by exerting pressure on one imperial institution: Westminster. It was in in Parliament 'that the fight is to be fought, and the last word to be said'. Naoroji called for '[a] few competent and truly patriotic and enthusiastic Indian members in Parliament', who would 'largely accelerate work there'. 'Persevere', he concluded, 'until the victory of self-government is won'.[122]

Naoroji's plea to the INC to stick to the constitutional path was a pointed reminder of the changing landscape of anti-colonial politics in early-twentieth-century India. Liberal nationalists such as Naoroji, who had dominated the INC since its inception in 1885, were being superseded by proponents of anti-colonial violence – a radical shift reinforced by Viceroy Curzon's partition of Bengal in 1905, which prompted protests across the subcontinent. In the face of this shift within the Indian anti-colonial movement, Naoroji stuck to his brand of agitation, which abstained from violence and was strictly constitutional in character. In 1906, at the age of eighty-one, he stood as MP for the fourth and last time. He ran for a different seat – Lambeth North, in south London – and was once again unsuccessful. A year later he retired from politics and moved to Bombay, where he received a pension from Maharaja Sayaji Rao III of Baroda.[123] With the arrival of the Great War, he emerged from his retirement to entreat Indians to join the British Empire's war effort – hoping, along with Gandhi and many other nationalists, that this would advance Indian demands for self-government. He did not live to see the outcome of India's crucial wartime support for the British Empire: he died in Bombay in 1917, at the age of ninety-one. A few weeks after his death, Edwin Montagu, secretary of state for India, made an unprecedented declaration in Naoroji's former political home, the House of Commons. Montagu announced that the British government's policy towards India was to move towards the 'gradual development' of self-governing institutions, aiming for the 'progressive realization of responsible government in India as an integral part of the British Empire'.[124] While the ensuing Montagu–Chelmsford Reforms responded to Naoroji's constitutional demands of just a few years before, they were too little, too late. By the early 1920s, the INC was a mass movement under the Parliament-averse Gandhi, and the path towards Indian independence in 1947 was to unfold with Naoroji's liberal values held in political limbo.

Conclusion

In 1892, after Naoroji's election, *The Manchester Guardian* argued that Westminster's 'Imperial Parliament' was 'the grand court of review for all that happens in India, for any calamities that need to be lightened, for any grievances that need to be redressed'.[125] To what extent was Naoroji successful in using Westminster to further his campaign of constitutional agitation? Did his parliamentary experience do anything to redress the colonial system's power imbalances? Naoroji's lifelong liberal, constitutional project helped to bring about slow changes in British rule in India, while his 'counter-preaching' created doubt and discomfort among British politicians, colonial administrators and Indian subjects.

The success and limitations of Naoroji's constitutional approach cannot be evaluated solely through his three years as MP: his four electoral campaigns were equally important in raising metropolitan awareness about Indian affairs, as they allowed him to forge alliances with overlapping progressive circles in London. While some of the men and women who supported him had extensive experience of Indian affairs, many had no previous connections with India before their paths crossed with that of Naoroji. Liberals, Radicals, socialists, Irish nationalists, feminists, temperance activists and other reform-minded individuals left their encounters with him with a deeper understanding of the inequalities of imperialism. In this sense, Dadabhai Naoroji was instrumental in popularizing Indian *swaraj* beyond India's borders, through imperial critique in his writings and direct engagement in parliamentary politics. While his constitutional means became secondary in Gandhi's era of mass politics, they came back to the fore during and after Independence – particularly through the Constituent Assembly (1946–50), the institution that was tasked with producing the Indian Constitution of 1949.[126]

Dadabhai Naoroji paved the way for Britain's next two MPs from the colonies, as well as for other men of colonial origin who occupied posts in a variety of metropolitan institutions. Mancherjee Bhownaggree, elected MP in 1895, was elected again in 1900. Shapurji Saklatvala – another Bombay-born Parsi – moved to Britain in 1905 to work for his uncle, the industrialist J. N. Tata. Becoming active as a trade unionist, Saklatvala campaigned against both capitalism and colonialism to improve the condition of workers in Britain and India during the Great Depression. He was elected in 1922 as Labour MP for the working-class constituency of North Battersea, claiming to be a 'member for India' in Westminster.[127] He was re-elected on a Communist ticket in 1924, but lost his seat in 1929. Naoroji's affinity with the Pan-African movement led him to encourage the notable Pan-African activists Henry Sylvester Williams and John Archer to make use of the British Empire's political institutions to reform the empire from within. He introduced Williams to the National Liberal Club, unsuccessfully attempted to find a constituency he could run for in the 1906 election, and then steered him to serve an apprenticeship in local government. John Archer, who was also mentored by Naoroji, was elected Mayor of Battersea in 1913, becoming the first black mayor in London. The interwar period also witnessed the electoral success of Indians in British local politics, particularly in London.[128] However, after Saklatvala's election in 1924, Britons would not elect another colonial or non-white MPs for sixty-three years. In 1987, the general election resulted in the first ever black MPs – Diane Abbott, Paul Boateng and Bernie Grant – and one MP of Goan descent, the Aden-born Keith Vaz. It was not until 2010 that the first women of South Asian descent served as MPs.[129]

Notes

1   M. K. Gandhi, *Hind Swaraj and Other Writings*, ed. Anthony J. Parel (Cambridge: Cambridge University Press, 2009), 30.

2   V. N. Datta, *Madan Lal Dhingra and the Revolutionary Movement* (New Delhi: Vikas Publishing House, 1978); Harald Fischer-Tiné, *Sanskrit, Sociology and Anti-imperial Struggle: The life of Shyamji Krishnavarma, 1857–1930* (New Delhi: Routledge India, 2014); and Harindra Srivastava, *Five Stormy Years: Savarkar in London (June 1906–June 1911)* (New Delhi: Allied Publishers, 1983).

3   *Dadabhai Naoroji: Selected private papers*, ed. S. R. Mehrotra and Dinyar Patel (New Delhi: Oxford University Press, 2016), xi–xlix; and Nawaz B. Mody, *Pherozeshah Mehta: Maker of modern India* (Bombay: Allied Publishers, 1997).

4   Ramachandra Guha, *India After Gandhi: The history of the world's largest democracy* (New Delhi: Picador India, 2017).

5   Mitra Sharafi, *Law and Identity in Colonial South Asia: Parsi legal culture, 1772– 1947* (New York: Cambridge University Press, 2014).

6   Sugata Bose and Ayesha Jalal, *Modern South Asia: History, culture, political economy* (London: Routledge, 1998), ch. 13, 'Gandhian nationalism and mass politics in the 1920s', 135–45.

7   Cristopher A. Bayly, 'Rammohan Roy and the advent of constitutional liberalism in India, 1800–30', *Modern Intellectual History*, 4 (2007): 25–41, 40.

8   Rustom Pestonji Masani, *Dadabhai Naoroji: The Grand Old Man of India* (London: Allen & Unwin, 1939).

9   Sharafi, *Law and Identity in Colonial South Asia.*

10   Ibid.; and Jonathan Schneer, *London 1900: The imperial metropolis* (New Haven Yale University Press, 1999), 187.

11   Cristopher A. Bayly, *Recovering Liberties: Indian thought in the age of liberalism and empire* (Cambridge: Cambridge University Press, 2011), 105.

12   Dadabhai Naoroji, *Poverty and un-British rule in India* (London: Swan Sonnenschein & Co., 1901).

13   Bayly, *Recovering Liberties.*

14   The standard biography remains Rustom Pestonji Masani's 1939 *Dadabhai Naoroji: The Grand Old Man of India*. For published primary sources, see *Dadabhai Naoroji: Selected private papers*, ed. S. R. Mehrotra and Dinyar Patel; *Dadabhai Naoroji correspondence*, ed. R. P. Patwardhan (Bombay: Allied Publishers, 1977); and *Essays, speeches, addresses and writings on Indian politics of the hon'ble Dadabhai Naoroji*, ed. Chunilal Lallubhai Parekh (Bombay: Caxton, 1886).

15   Julie F. Codell, 'Decentring and doubling imperial cosmopolitan discourse in the British press', *Media History*, 15 (2009): 371–84; and Matthew Stubbings, 'The partisan nature of race and imperialism: Dadabhai Naoroji, M. M. Bhownaggree and the late nineteenth-century British politics of Indian nationalism', *The Journal of Imperial and Commonwealth History*, 44, no. 1 (2015): 48–69.

16   Dinyar Patel, 'The Grand Old Man: Dadabhai Naoroji and the evolution of the demand for Indian self-government', unpublished doctoral diss. (Harvard University, USA, 2015); and Vikram Visana, 'Liberalism, imperial citizenship, and Indian self-government in the political thought of Dadabhai Naoroji, 1840–1917', unpublished doctoral diss. (University of Cambridge, UK, 2015).

17   Antoinette Burton, 'Tongues untied: Lord Salisbury's "Black Man" and the boundaries of imperial democracy', *Comparative Study of Society and History*, 42,

no. 3 (2000): 632–61; and Sumita Mukherjee, '"Narrow-majority" and "Bow-and-agree": Public attitudes towards the elections of the first Asian MPs in Britain, Dadabhai Naoroji and Mancherjee Merwanjee Bhownaggree, 1885–1906', *Journal of the Oxford University History Society*, 2 (2004): 1–20.

18 *The first Indian member of the imperial parliament, being a collection of the main incidents relating to the election of Mr Dadabhai Naoroji to Parliament* (Madras: Addison & Co., 1892), 69.

19 S. R. Bakshi, *Dadabhai Naoroji: The Grand Old Man* (New Delhi: South Asia Books, 1991), 124.

20 Jenny Rose, *Zoroastrianism: An introduction* (London: I.B. Tauris, 2011), 192; Patricia Crone, *The nativist prophets of early Islamic Iran: Rural revolt and local Zoroastrianism* (Cambridge: Cambridge University Press, 2012); and *Parsis in India and the diaspora*, ed. John R. Hinnells and Alan Williams (London: Routledge, 2008).

21 Bayly, *Recovering Liberties*, 117.

22 For their precolonial history, see Jenny Rose, *Zoroastrianism: A guide for the perplexed* (London: Bloomsbury, 2011); and Delphine Menant, 'Zoroastrianism and the Parsis', *The North American Review*, 530 (1901): 132–47 (134–5).

23 Nile Green, *Bombay Islam: The religious economy of the western Indian Ocean, 1840–1915* (Cambridge: Cambridge University Press, 2011).

24 Jehangir Barjorji Sanjana, *Ancient Persia and the Parsis: A comprehensive history of the Parsis and their religion from primeval times to present age* (H. T. Anklesaria: Bombay, 1935), 588–9.

25 Bayly, *Recovering Liberties*, 117.

26 Eckehard Kulke, *The Parsees in India: A minority as agent of social change* (Delhi: Vikas, 1975), 34–46.

27 Sharafi, *Law and Identity in Colonial South Asia*.

28 Jesse S. Palsetia, 'Partner in empire: Jamsetjee Jejeebhoy and the public culture of nineteenth-century Bombay', in *Parsis in India and the diaspora*, ed. Hinnells and Williams, 81–99.

29 Masani, *Dadabhai Naoroji: The Grand Old Man of India*, 20. For his family tree, see *A farman of Emperor Jehangir given to Dr Dadabhai Naoroji's ancestors three centuries ago, and a short history of his Dordi family of Navsari, with poems on Dadabhai Naoroji by Rustam Barjorji Paymaster*, ed. Jehangir Behramji Dordi (Bombay: n.p., 1925).

30 Dadabhai Naoroji, 'The days of my youth', *M. A. P. (Mainly About People)*, 1904.

31 Ibid.

32 Masani, *Dadabhai Naoroji: The Grand Old Man of India*, 27–8.

33 Codell, 'Decentring and doubling imperial cosmopolitan discourse in the British press', 373.

34 'Perry, Thomas Erskine (PRY823TE)', in *ACAD: A Cambridge Alumni Database* (Cambridge: Cambridge University Library), http://venn.lib.cam.ac.uk/cgi-bin/ search-2018.pl?sur=&suro=w&fir=&firo=c&cit=&cito=c&c=all&z=all&tex=PRY82 3TE&sye=&eye=&col=all&maxcount=50 (accessed 30 March 2018).

35 *The first Indian member of the imperial parliament*, 1; and Sharafi, *Law and Identity in Colonial South Asia*, 22.

36 Sharafi, *Law and Identity in Colonial South Asia*, 8, 21.

37 Monica M. Ringer, *Pious Citizens: Reforming Zoroastrianism in India and Iran* (Syracuse: Syracuse University Press, 2011).

38 Uma Das Gupta, 'The Indian press, 1870–1880: A small world of journalism', *Modern Asian Studies*, 11 (1977): 213–35; and R. P. Karkaria, 'The revival of the native press of western India: *The Rast Goftar*', *Calcutta Review*, 107 (October 1898): 238–43.

39 Masani, *Dadabhai Naoroji: The Grand Old Man of India*, 85.

40 Ibid.

41 *The first Indian member of the imperial parliament*, 5.

42 J. V. Naik, 'Forerunners of Dadabhai Naoroji's drain theory', *Economic and Political Weekly*, 36, no. 46–47 (2001): 4428–32.

43 'Famine in India: Address by Mr Dadabhai Naoroji', *India*, 1 March 1901, 103; and Bayly, *Recovering Liberties*, 174.

44 'The Jubilee of the East India Association, founded 1866', *Asiatic Review*, 29 (January 1917): 1–14.

45 Dadabhai Naoroji, 'On the commerce of India', *Journal of the Society of Arts*, 19 (18 November 1870–10 November 1871): 239–45 (242).

46 Masani, *Dadabhai Naoroji: The Grand Old Man of India*, 134.

47 For Naoroji's critique on this issue, see *Poverty and un-British Rule in India*.

48 *British Parliamentary Election Results 1885–1918*, ed. Frederick Walter Scott Craig (London: Macmillan, 1974); and Sri Ram Mehrotra, *The Emergence of the Indian National Congress* (New York: Barnes and Noble, 1971).

49 Romesh Chunder Dutt, *Three Years in London, 1868 to 1871* (Calcutta: S. K. Lahiri & Co., 1896); and *The first Indian member of the imperial parliament*, 25.

50 Rozina Visram, *Asians in Britain: 400 years of history* (London: Pluto Press, 2002), 130.

51 P. M. Mehta, cited in *The first Indian member of the imperial parliament*, 26.

52 Masani, *Dadabhai Naoroji: The Grand Old Man of India*, 233.

53 *The first Indian member of the imperial parliament*, 10.

54 Masani, *Dadabhai Naoroji: The Grand Old Man of India*, 240.

55 For Naoroji's Irish connections in London, see Jennifer Regan-Lefebvre, 'Imperial politics and the London Irish', in *Ireland in an Imperial World: Citizenship, opportunism, and subversion*, ed. Timothy G. McMahon, Michael de Nie and Paul Townend (London: Palgrave Macmillan, 2017), 111–30 (120–7); and *Cosmopolitan*

Nationalism in the Victorian Empire: Ireland, India and the politics of Alfred Webb (London: Palgrave Macmillan, 2009).

56 Masani, *Dadabhai Naoroji: The Grand Old Man of India*, 248.

57 Ibid., 257.

58 For the free breakfast table, see Frank Trentmann, *Free Trade Nation: Commerce, consumption, and civil society in modern Britain* (Oxford: Oxford University Press, 2008).

59 *The first Indian member of the imperial parliament*, 12.

60 *Bombay Gazette*, cited in ibid., 116.

61 *The first Indian member of the imperial parliament*, 13; and Masani, *Dadabhai Naoroji: The Grand Old Man of India*, 273.

62 BL-APAC, IOR/MSS Eur D 510/2, Curzon to Hamilton, 'Memorandum of conversation with the Gaekwar of Baroda', 12 July 1899.

63 *The first Indian member of the imperial parliament*, 15, 108; and Masani, *Dadabhai Naoroji: The Grand Old Man of India*, 276.

64 *Bombay Gazette*, cited in *The first Indian member of the imperial parliament*, 116.

65 Irene Cockroft, 'Sylvia Pankhurst in the context of her radical family background' (Sylvia Pankhurst Memorial Lecture, Wortley Hall, Sheffield, 13 August 2010).

66 Elizabeth Crawford, *The Women's Suffrage Movement in Britain and Ireland: A regional survey* (New York: Routledge, 2006), 201; and Masani, *Dadabhai Naoroji: The Grand Old Man of India*, 277.

67 *The first Indian member of the imperial parliament*, 49.

68 Jeff Guy, *The View Across the River: Harriette Colenso and the Zulu struggle against imperialism* (Charlottesville: University of Virgina Press, 2001), 342.

69 *The first Indian member of the imperial parliament*, 15.

70 Ibid., 13.

71 Masani, *Dadabhai Naoroji: The Grand Old Man of India*, 276.

72 *The first Indian member of the imperial parliament*, 100–2.

73 Leela Gandhi, *Affective Communities: Anticolonial thought, fin-de-siècle radicalism and the politics of friendship* (Durham, NC: Duke University Press, 2006); and Jennifer Regan-Lefebvre, *Cosmopolitan Nationalism in the Victorian Empire*.

74 Mukherjee, '"Narrow-majority" and "Bow-and-agree"'.

75 Local report cited in Masani, *Dadabhai Naoroji: The Grand Old Man of India*, 279.

76 *The first Indian member of the imperial parliament*, 54.

77 Ibid., 69, 71; and Anthony Lejeune, *The Gentlemen's Clubs of London* (London: Parkgate, 1997).

78 *The first Indian member of the imperial parliament*, 29.

79 Ibid., 54n.

80 Ibid., iv.

81 Ibid., 16.

82 'John Stewart', in 'Legacies of British slave-ownership', www.ucl.ac.uk/lbs/person/view/8816 (accessed 30 March 2018).

83 *The History of Parliament: The House of Commons, 1790–1820*, ed. R. G. Thorne (London: Haynes Publishing, 1986), vol. 5.

84 Michael H. Fisher, *The inordinately strange life of Dyce Sombre, Victorian Anglo-Indian MP and Chancery 'lunatic'* (London: Hurst and Company, 2010).

85 *Hansard's parliamentary debates: Third series, commencing with the accession of William IV*, Vol. LXXI (London: Thomas Curson Hansard, 1843), 92.

86 Kenneth Ballhatchet, *Race, Sex and Class Under the Raj: Imperial attitudes and policies and their critics, 1793–1905* (London: Weidenfeld and Nicolson, 1980).

87 Thomas Babington Macaulay, *Speeches by Lord Macaulay, with his Minute on Indian education*, ed. George Malcolm Young (London: Oxford University Press, 1935), 345–61.

88 Mrinalini Sinha, *Colonial Masculinity: The 'manly Englishman' and the 'effeminate Bengali' in the late nineteenth century* (Manchester: Manchester University Press, 1995).

89 Dadabhai Naoroji, *The Parsee Religion* (England?: [n.p.], 1861?), 25.

90 Digby, 16 February 1888, to the Liberal Association of Holborn, cited in Masani, *Dadabhai Naoroji: The Grand Old Man of India*, 264–5.

91 Cited in *The first Indian member of the imperial parliament*, 122.

92 Digby, 16 February 1888, to the Liberal Association of Holborn, cited in Masani, *Dadabhai Naoroji: The Grand Old Man of India*, 264–5.

93 Emma Tarlo, *Clothing Matters: Dress and identity in India* (London: Hurst, 1996), 48; and Masani, *Dadabhai Naoroji: The Grand Old Man of India*, 234.

94 Masani, *Dadabhai Naoroji: The Grand Old Man of India*, 243.

95 Robert Gascoyne-Cecil, third Marquis of Salisbury, cited in 'Lord Salisbury in Edinburgh', *The Times*, 1 December 1888.

96 Antoinette Burton, 'Tongues untied', 633; and *At the heart of Empire: Indians and the colonial encounter in late-Victorian Britain* (Berkeley: University of California Press, 1998), 67–8.

97 *Gajarati Weekly*, cited in *The Review of Reviews*, 160–1.

98 Masani, *Dadabhai Naoroji: The Grand Old Man of India*, 243.

99 Sinha, *Colonial Masculinity*; and Heather Streets, *Martial Races: The military, race, and masculinity in British imperial culture, 1857–1914* (Manchester University Press, 2004).

100 *The Evening News*, cited in *The first Indian member of the imperial parliament*, 117; and *The Western Daily Press of Bristol*, cited in *The first Indian member of the imperial parliament*, 112.

101 Ballhatchet, *Race, Sex and Class Under the Raj*; and Ronald Hyam, *Empire and Sexuality: The British experience* (Manchester: Manchester University Press, 1990).

102 Codell, 'Decentring and doubling imperial cosmopolitan discourse in the British press', 373.

103 Masani, *Dadabhai Naoroji: The Grand Old Man of India*, 325.

104 Ibid., 324.

105 Ibid., 325.

106 *The first Indian member of the imperial parliament*, 98.

107 Ibid., 120.

108 Masani, *Dadabhai Naoroji: The Grand Old Man of India*, 337.

109 John Newton, *W. S. Caine, MP: A biography* (London: Nisbet, 1907).

110 Visram, *Ayahs, Lascars and Princes*, 89.

111 Schneer, *London 1900*, 201.

112 Hakim Adi, *Pan-Africanism: A history* (London: Bloomsbury, 2018). For a biography of Williams, see Marika Sherwood, *Origins of Pan-Africanism: Henry Sylvester Williams, Africa, and the African diaspora* (London: Routledge, 2011).

113 Schneer, *London 1900*, 177, 180–2.

114 Laura Tabili, 'Race and ethnicity', in *The fin-de-siècle World*, ed. Michael Saler (London: Routledge, 2015), 528.

115 Masani, *Dadabhai Naoroji: The Grand Old Man of India*, 368.

116 John McLeod, 'Mourning, philanthropy, and M. M. Bhownaggree's road to Parliament', in *Parsis in India and the diaspora*, ed. John R. Hinnells and Alan Williams (London: Routledge, 2007), 136–55.

117 Schneer, *London 1900*, 241.

118 BL-APAC, IOR/POS 11707, Naoroji to Wacha, 8 October 1896.

119 Cited in *Dadabhai Naoroji: A sketch of his life and life-work* (Madras: G. A. Natesan & Co., 1920), 28.

120 Naoroji, *Poverty and un-British rule in India*.

121 Naoroji, *Speeches and Writings*, 81.

122 Cited in *The Indian Nation Builders, Part II* (Madras: Ganesh & Co., 1904), 38.

123 John R. McLane, *Indian Nationalism and the Early Congress* (Princeton: Princeton University Press, 1977), 142–3.

124 *House of Commons Debates*, vol. 97, c. 1695–97 (20 August 1917); and Richard Danzig, 'The announcement of August 20th, 1917', *The Journal of Asian Studies*, 28, no. 1 (1968): 19–37.

125 *The Guardian*, 26 July 1892.

126 Bayly, *Recovering Liberties*, 3.

127 The British Library, Mss Eur D 1173/6.

128 Sunil K. Choudhary, 'From sojourners to settlers: The changing role of the Indian diaspora in British politics', *Diaspora Studies*, 5, no. 2 (2012): 170–196, 177.

129 Nazat Khan, 'Six Asian women MPs elected in UK', https://www.desiblitz.com/content/six-asian-women-mps-elected-in-uk (accessed 30 March 2018).

8

Mpilo Walter Benson Rubusana: South Africa's first black parliamentarian

Timothy Stapleton

Elected in September 1910, Mpilo Walter Benson Rubusana was a unique and isolated member of the Cape Provincial Council in the newly created Union of South Africa. He was South Africa's first black parliamentarian. Rubusana was the first and only black South African elected to the Cape legislature and the only black South African elected to one of South Africa's governing bodies until the advent of democracy in 1994.[1] Some South Africans of mixed racial heritage, locally known as 'Coloured' and positioned slightly higher than blacks on the colonial/apartheid racial hierarchy, were elected to South African legislatures before the early 1990s. The first of these was Dr Abdullah Abdurahman, leader of the African Political Organization (APO) which sought to mobilize mixed-race people against racial segregation, who was elected to the Cape Town city council in 1904 and the Cape Provincial Council in 1914. As discussed below, Rubusana and Abdurahman became allies and would collaborate on political issues during the early twentieth century. This chapter will discuss Rubusana's atypical and short-lived career as an elected representative in colonial South Africa within the context of the rise and fall of the ambiguous Cape Liberal Tradition and the emergence of a mission-educated black Westernized elite that pioneered a Western-style black political movement in pursuit of civil rights.

Rubusana was a prominent leader within the embryonic Westernized and Christianized African community of the late-nineteenth- and early-twentieth-century Cape Colony. Although he was evidently proud of his African heritage and strongly opposed racial discrimination, Rubusana worked energetically to spread Christianity and what he understood as 'civilization' among his Xhosa people. Typical of his mission-educated group, he accepted colonial laws and government, and worked within their limits. Born in 1858 near Somerset East in the eastern part of the British ruled Cape Colony, Mpilo Rubusana grew up as part of a traditionalist and non-literate Xhosa family. During the early and mid-nineteenth century the Eastern Cape had been the scene of a series of horrific wars between the expanding Cape settler society and indigenous Xhosa communities that gradually lost their land and came under colonial rule. At the time of Rubusana's birth, Xhosa society had just been shattered by a millenarian movement that encouraged people to slaughter their cattle and refrain from planting crops the result of which was mass starvation, the collapse of some traditional Xhosa polities and the absorption of many displaced Xhosa into the colonial economy as cheap labour.[2]

Another important process happening in the nineteenth-century Eastern Cape was the expansion of European missionary propagated Protestant Christianity among the Xhosa people who were becoming divided between traditionalists and a small but growing faction of Westernized Christian converts. Central to the missionary project was the creation of a written form of IsiXhosa (the Xhosa language), the publication of an IsiXhosa Bible and the training of Xhosa clergy such as Tiyo Soga who studied in Scotland and became the first ordained Xhosa minister in 1856.[3] In the early 1870s the missionary Richard Birt noticed a bright Xhosa teenager working in the stables of the London Missionary Society (LMS) institution at Peelton near King William's Town in the Eastern Cape. The stable hand was Rubusana. In 1874 Birt arranged for him to begin attending the Peelton Boys' School. One year later, the seventeen-year-old Rubusana converted to Christianity and was baptized Walter Benson. Successful in his studies, Rubusana taught at Peelton from 1879 to 1892 and during the early 1880s he completed teaching and theological courses at Lovedale College which was a foundational missionary institution in the Eastern Cape and a centre of the early development of Xhosa literature. In 1885 he was ordained as a Congregationalist minister. At Peelton, Rubusana married fellow teacher Nomhaya Deena Nzanzana who had attended Dollar Academy in Scotland. Although Rubusana was the obvious successor to Birt as head of the Peelton Mission when the later passed away, the growing racism in mission circles and elsewhere in the late nineteenth century meant that the position was given to a new white missionary and Rubusana was transferred out. From 1892 to 1910, Rubusana served as a clergyman and school superintendent in the nearby port of East London where he established a network of new African churches and schools despite obstacles posed by denominationalism, financial restrictions and racist government regulations. As a leading African educationalist, he testified before the 1908 Cape government committee on 'Native Education' where he advocated compulsory schooling and mother-tongue education for black children and better salaries for black teachers. He also pressed for the establishment of a 'native college' that would reduce the new trend of aspirant black students going to African American colleges in the United States where they were not learning much given their short stays and allegedly acquiring anti-white sentiments.[4]

Rubusana also became a central figure in the growth of African literature. In 1886 he was appointed to the inter-denominational board that was revising the translation of the Bible into IsiXhosa. He was the first African on the board since the 1871 death of Tiyo Soga. Over the course of his career he also translated other works of religious literature such as the Seventh Day Adventist 'Steps to Christ' and wrote hymn books. In 1905 Rubusana spent seven months in Britain supervising the printing of the new edition of the Xhosa Bible and during this remarkable trip he spoke at many church events, visited Paris and studied shorthand. While in Britain working on the Bible translation, Rubusana also compiled and published the 570-page *Zemk'iinkomo Magwalandini* (The Cattle are Running Away, You Cowards) which represented the first major book published in IsiXhosa (besides the Bible) and contained a mixture of traditional poetry, history and folklore with the overall aim of motivating the Xhosa people to preserve their culture though within a Christian context. The anthology included pieces by William Gqoba, who had died in the 1890s, and S. E. K. Mqhayi: both would become known as great Xhosa authors. In recognition for the publication of *Zemk'iinkomo*, which Rubusana seems to have referred to in English as 'A History of South Africa from the Native Standpoint', he was awarded an honorary doctorate by an African American university in the United States.

Rubusana had collected many of the pieces contained in *Zemk'iinkomo* through his involvement with African journalism. In the 1880s and 1890s he wrote pieces for the pioneering IsiXhosa newspapers *Isigidimi SamaXosa* (the Xhosa Messenger) which was a missionary publication and *Imvo Zabantsundu* (Black Opinion) which was operated by J. T. Jabavu in King William's Town and was the first independent African newspaper in South Africa though it depended on financial support from white liberals. In 1897 Rubusana opened his own East London-based newspaper called *Izwi Labantu* (Voice of the People) which was meant as a political foil to Jabavu's *Imvo* and received some funding from Cecil Rhodes's Progressive Party in an effort to attract black voters. However, *Izwi* folded in 1909 given financial problems.

The development of an African press in the Cape was related to the rise of African political organizations and emerging political divisions within the

Westernized African elite. The first Western-style African political organization in South Africa was the Cape-based Native Educational Association (NEA) which was formed in 1879 and advocated improved educational opportunities for blacks within a context of broader social improvement. Rubusana and Jabavu were both involved in the NEA. In 1882 Jabavu formed Imbumba Yama Nyama (Unity is Strength) which was the first overtly political African organization and pursued African advancement using the *Imvo* newspaper as a platform. However, this body did not meet regularly as Jabavu, who maintained a personalist regime over it, wanted to avoid antagonizing white liberals with whom he vainly hoped to form a non-racial movement. In 1898, the slightly more radical Rubusana and the like-minded group involved in *Izwi* launched the South African Native Congress (SANC) which tried to become a regularly established and proactive association. The almost life-long rivalry between Jabavu and Rubusana was fuelled by more than politics and newspapers. The two represented different and competing Christian denominations as Jabavu was a Wesleyan Methodist and Rubusana a Congregationalist, and this also put them at odds over education as Cape government rules stipulated that only one denomination could establish a school in a single area. Indeed, Rubusana and Jabavu eventually championed opposing schemes to create an African university with the latter succeeding given white missionary funding, and this led to the creation of the South African Native College (later called the University of Fort Hare) in the Eastern Cape in 1916. Although both Jabavu and Rubusana spoke IsiXhosa as a first language, they adhered to different ethnic identities as Jabavu was from the Mfengu community which had a long history of alliance with colonialism and missionaries, and Rubusana came from the larger Xhosa population.[5]

Rubusana's 1910 election to the Cape Provincial Council was made possible by the existence of the Cape Liberal Tradition. Founded by the Dutch in 1652, the Cape Colony developed a colonial slave economy and racially hierarchical society but its strategic location prompted a takeover by abolitionist Britain at the start of the nineteenth century. While the British eliminated slavery in the Cape and elsewhere in the 1830s, they also imported more settlers and supported the colonial side during the violent dispossession of the Xhosa kingdoms. By the mid-nineteenth century British missionaries, humanitarians and abolitionists in the Cape had developed a social and political convention that promoted non-racial access to civil rights based on a common membership in the Christian colonial society and economy. For Africans, this was essentially an assimilationist system which promised respect and consultation to those who adopted Western ways of life. At the same time, Cape Liberalism was opposed by an element of white settler society, particularly in the Eastern Cape with its recent history of vicious colonial wars, which advocated complete white supremacy and black subjugation. As Britain devolved political responsibility to the Cape Colony during the middle and late nineteenth century, the Cape Liberal Tradition became enshrined in the territory's constitution. In 1853 the Cape Colony was granted representative government with a legislature consisting of members elected by a qualified non-racial franchise. Any male citizen who earned £50 a year or owned £25 worth of property could vote and stand for election. Although traditional communal African land holding could be used to qualify to vote, the existing socio-economic reality of the Cape Colony and its informal though pervasive racial hierarchy meant that mixed-race and black voters remained in the minority and none stood for election. The non-racial franchise continued when the Cape Colony obtained responsible government, a form of internal self-rule, in 1872. However, as more mixed-race and black men began to qualify to vote and exercised this right, many white politicians including liberals became nervous about losing their privilege and they began working to undermine the non-racial franchise. More broadly, attacks on the Cape's non-racial franchise were informed by late-nineteenth-century trends such as rising white racism seemingly vindicated by the pseudo-science of Social Darwinism, mineral discoveries in the Southern Africa region which saw the development of a racially ordered migrant labour system and the relatively rapid European colonial conquest of most of Africa. In 1887 the all-white Cape parliament, under the leadership of Prime Minister Gordon Sprigg, passed a law that extended voting to the newly incorporated Transkei Territory in the east, where there were many potential black voters, but prevented land held under African communal tenure from satisfying the property qualification of the franchise which dramatically reduced the number of black voters, particularly in the Eastern Cape. The controversial legislation provoked resistance from liberal members of parliament who claimed it was unconstitutional and resentment among emerging black political leaders like Rubusana who saw their rights being gradually eroded. In 1892 the Cape government of Prime Minister Cecil Rhodes, a mining magnate and ardent British imperialist, passed another franchise law that increased the property qualification to £75 and introduced a literacy requirement. A large number of poor whites and very many 'Coloureds' and blacks were disenfranchised. Rhodes's Glen Grey Act of 1894 also restricted black voting as it stipulated that land held on individual tenure in certain racially defined areas could not be used to qualify for the Cape franchise. By the start of the twentieth century, mixed-race and black people comprised the vast majority of the Cape population but constituted only about 15 per cent of voters. These attacks on the non-racial franchise in the Cape during the late nineteenth century prompted the formation of African political organizations and newspapers, such as Jabavu's Imbumba and *Imvo* and Rubusana's SANC and *Izwi*, to mobilize black voters in defence of their rights. Late-nineteenth-century restrictions on black civil rights in the Cape were not limited to voting but also included disarmament laws that made it illegal for them to own guns. With the conquest of the last independent African states such as the Gcaleka Xhosa in the Eastern Cape and the Zulu further up the coast in the late 1870s, black colonial military allies were no longer needed and whites increasingly saw armed blacks as a threat.[6]

By the end of the nineteenth century, the Cape Colony's non-racial franchise had become an oddity among the region's newer and expanding colonial states. Located on the Indian Ocean coast and founded in the 1840s, the British colony of Natal developed a racially segregationist administrative system. When Natal gained representative government in 1856, it adopted a non-racial franchise similar to the Cape though the qualification was set higher, at £50 worth of individual property, to reduce the number of blacks who would qualify. However, during the 1860s the all-white legislature effectively disenfranchised blacks before any could qualify to vote. In Natal, Africans would be administered and represented by their traditional leaders applying codified customary law and supervised by a powerful colonial official. In 1893 Natal gained responsible government and the next year the settler legislature took the vote away from the colony's sizable Indian population despite legal protest by M. K. Gandhi, a lawyer who would go on to lead India's independence movement.[7] Founded by Dutch-speaking settlers who had left the Cape in the mid-nineteenth century and moved into the interior, the Boer republics of the Transvaal (South African Republic) and Orange Free State were governed by entirely white legislatures elected by the white minority. In the republics blacks were conquered subjects with no political representation. During the late 1870s, Britain, given diamond discoveries in the region, had tried to coerce the Boer republics into participating in a settler governed regional confederation under British supervision but the plan was spoiled by the 1881 Transvaal Rebellion. The South African War (1899–1902), fought between imperial Britain and the Boer republics against the backdrop of an evolving gold mining industry in the Transvaal, was seen by white missionaries and black elites like Rubusana as an opportunity for the expansion of black political rights throughout the region. After his SANC met in May 1900 and officially declared loyalty to Britain, Rubusana pushed for the establishment of a British Royal Commission that would investigate the conditions of Africans in South Africa so as to counter ignorance in Britain and thwart locally based colonial officials who were engaged in a 'deliberate conspiracy ... to hamper the Natives by harassing and unjust legislation'.[8] Rubusana and other Westernized African elites were disappointed when, after the British conquest of the Boer republics, the Cape Liberal Tradition was not extended north. A clause of the 1902 Treaty of Vereeniging, in which the Boers surrendered their independence in return for a series of concessions, stipulated that black political rights would not be introduced to the former republics turned British territories. London had sacrificed black aspirations to acquire the co-operation of Boer leaders in the creation and administration of a new larger regional union under the British flag. In 1907 Britain granted responsible government to the former republics, now called Transvaal Colony and Orange River Colony, which continued their previous white-only voting system.

In 1909 the British government considered legislation to create the Union of South Africa which would bring together the Cape Colony, Natal, Transvaal and Orange River Colony as provinces within a single self-governing British territory similar to Canada and Australia. At the start of that year an all-white convention in South Africa had drafted a constitution for the proposed union. While the Cape Province would retain its historic non-racial franchise with reference to local representative bodies such as its provincial council, the Union government would consist entirely of whites elected by the country's white minority. Furthermore, the Union government would have the authority to change the Cape's voting system which represented an obvious threat to its continued existence. In response, African Westernized elites from across the region met in Bloemfontein in March 1909 and formed the South African Native Convention, with Rubusana as president, to support the principle of a South African union but to object to the racist elements of its proposed constitution. In July and August 1909 Rubusana joined a delegation, led by the white liberal and former Cape Prime Minister W. P. Schreiner and which also included Jabavu and Abdurahman, that visited London to lobby British parliamentarians against the racial voting restrictions of the proposed Union. Rubusana stated publicly that 'we are not going to England as agitators, but as humble citizens of His Majesty's Colony to plead ... for the deletion of those colour clauses in the Act which should never have been allowed in the Draft Constitution'.[9] Given limited funds, the number of African delegates was less than originally planned which caused some tensions among those left out. As such, A. K. Soga accused Rubusana, president of the South African Native Convention and coordinator of black participation in the delegation, of being a self-appointed delegate. Once in

London, Schreiner's group coordinated with an Indian-South African delegation which included Gandhi and which shared similar objections over the proposed Union. Like other delegates, Rubusana delivered speeches to various sympathetic organizations in Britain and spoke to British journalists, one of whom quoted him as saying that the future South Africa should raise its standards to that of the Cape rather than lowering them to match the Northern provinces. Although the Schreiner group gained some compassion from British humanitarians and the Labour Party and may have been influential in keeping the neighbouring High Commission territories out of the Union, the racial limitations on voting remained in the Act of Union that was passed by the British parliament. At the second meeting of the South African Native Convention, held in March 1910 in Bloemfontein, Rubusana was re-elected as president but there was little to be done to stop the creation of the new regime. As such, the Union of South Africa came into existence at the end of May 1910 and with the all-white national election of September, Louis Botha, who had been a Transvaal Boer general during the South African War, became its first prime minister.[10]

Figure 8.1 In 1909, Walter Rubusana (*seated, second from the right*) participated in a delegation that travelled to London to object to the white supremacist constitution of the Union of South Africa. In 1910, the year the union was founded, Rubusana was elected to the Cape Provincial Council becoming the only black South African parliamentarian until 1994. Courtesy of National Library of South Africa.

It is likely that the London delegation of 1909 and protest over the Union constitution inspired Rubusana to challenge the unofficial racial restriction in the Cape that blacks, while they could qualify to vote, did not run for political office. Legal opinion on the matter was acquired from W. P. Schreiner and his brother. Although there had been some rumours in the local press, Rubusana's candidacy for the Thembuland constituency of the Cape Provincial Council was announced at the last minute. It is worth noting that Rubusana had good contacts in Thembuland[11] as, for example, he was an advisor to the traditional king of the area's Thembu people. At the official nomination meeting in Umtata in mid-August 1910 two African participants, Rev. R. Funani and E. S. Mbembe, nominated Rubusana, who was in attendance along with the two white candidates who had already declared their interest in running. The local returning officer tried to resolve the contest on the spot by asking for a show of hands that overwhelming favoured one of the white candidates but Rubusana demanded a formal election. At the meeting, Rubusana declared that the constitution gave black people the right to run for office in the Cape and that he was seeking election in order to represent black people in the Cape legislature given that many South African whites held racist attitudes and did not understand the situation of blacks. In addition, he explained his independent political status as stemming from the fact that the Union parliament contained many racist whites who were members of established parties. Furthermore, Rubusana requested that Jabavu run for election in the Fort Beaufort constituency of the Eastern Cape and that Abdurahman run in Cape Town but both men declined.

Reactions to Rubusana's 1910 candidacy to represent Thembuland within the Cape Provincial Council were polarized. Not surprisingly, his two white opponents were very critical. J. T. Houghton-Grey, a Grahamstown advocate who was running as a member of the Unionist Party which would form the official opposition in the Union parliament, warned voters that the white representatives in the Cape Council would not tolerate a black colleague and therefore Thembuland would lack a voice if Rubusana were elected. W. J. Clark, a trader from Engcobo, was more explicitly racist and wrote to newspapers that it would be 'deplorable' if an African were elected to the council. Clark's supporters claimed that Rubusana's candidacy was a stratagem by the Unionists to undermine their man's support among black voters. Some prominent white liberal Cape politicians, who had promoted themselves as 'friends of the native', warned that it was premature for a black candidate to run for office and that it might cause a backlash among white voters who would then more vigorously support efforts to reduce and eventually remove the African franchise. These ideas were repeated by the Cape white liberal press, usually sympathetic to black aspirations, which became hostile to Rubusana's electoral campaign. Similarly, Jabavu, through his newspaper *Imvo*, criticized Rubusana for announcing his candidacy at the last minute and for not seeking the approval of other black leaders before entering the race. Jabavu advised black voters in Thembuland against supporting Rubusana who he characterized as an independent operative of the Unionist Party and a 'crusted old Progressive' which was a dig at his newspaper's past association with Rhodes. Jabavu's own decision not to run for election was based on his opinion that a black representative would become ineffective in an otherwise all-white council and that black voters would be better off backing sympathetic white candidates. In the pages of *Imvo*, Rubusana was accused of being a self-serving opportunist and of seeing himself as superior to other blacks. Publishing reports of confusion among black voters in Thembuland, *Imvo* predicted that Rubusana's election bid would fail. On the other hand, the Cape Town mixed-race leader Abdurahman and his APO, which had six branches in Thembuland and published its own newspaper, wholeheartedly endorsed Rubusana as a candidate.[12]

During the campaign Rubusana, like other candidates, used newspaper advertisements and public appearances to mobilize support. He appealed to white voters to discard racial bias and to black voters to remember his previous struggles in pursuit of their common cause. When questioned about his independent political status, Rubusana explained that it would make him a better representative of Africans as he were free from party policies on race. His election platform put forth a number of practical proposals that reflected his educationist background and were oriented toward African advancement and consultation within the colonial context. He advocated compulsory education for black children, free education for black students whose families could not afford school fees, the creation of boards to oversee black schools and mother-tongue education in the lower grades. He had previously promoted some of these views on education. With reference to health, Rubusana campaigned for the formation of community boards to manage hospitals and for the employment of African nurses who would care for African patients. At the same time, he did not believe in a one-person-one-vote system and proposed increasing the educational qualification for the Cape franchise so that voters would be intellectually competent.

With the white vote split, Rubusana narrowly won the election in Thembuland. Located in the predominantly black Transkei region of the Eastern Cape, Thembuland had slightly more black than white voters; 1,597 to 1,447, respectively. While 741 voters opted for Houghton-Grey and 235 for Clark, Rubusana gained 766 votes giving him a narrow majority of 25. Not all ballots, however, were cast along racial lines. It appears that Rubusana gained slightly more white votes than black ones and that Houghton-Grey obtained more black than white votes. As the only candidate present at the official announcement of results in Umtata, Rubusana delivered a speech in which he thanked the voters for their support and criticized the white newspapers that had attacked his candidacy. Subsequently, he wrote a letter of thanks to the mixed-race APO newspaper in which he pledged to represent the interests of all the people of Thembuland regardless of race. While Jabavu used his *Imvo* newspaper to acknowledge the significance of Rubusana's electoral victory, he warned that an independent black council member would be between 'The Devil and the Deep Blue Sea' as the established white parties would be hostile to him. While one letter to *Imvo* criticized Rubusana for abandoning his religious duties as a Congregationalist minister for a selfish political career, another portrayed him as a hero. A. K. Soga, a former ally of Rubusana who had fallen out with him over the 1909 London delegation, accused the newly elected Thembuland representative of putting personal ambition ahead of the interests of the SANC and Africans in general. Disparaging the Jabuvu-Rubusana feud and maintaining that Africans should rise above white party politics, Soga thought that Rubusana risked disgracing Africans if he had lost the vote and predicted that whites would conspire to deprive him of his seat in the next election. Abdurahman and the APO felt vindicated in its support for Rubusana. The APO newspaper pointed out that Rubusana was intellectually, educationally and socially superior to many of the white members of the Cape Provincial Council. For the APO, African voters in Thembuland had shown their political maturity by electing one of their own to a representative body. Simultaneously, Abdurahman and his newspaper took revenge on the moderate Jabavu by claiming that the election had shown that he had lost influence among African people. In Natal, where no blacks could vote, John L. Dube's African newspaper *Ilanga LaseNatal* (The Natal Sun) published a profile of Rubusana and celebrated his election as sign of progress in South Africa. Just after the election Rubusana visited Natal where he attended a large meeting held in his honour and talked about the African pursuit of equality of opportunity in politics, education and the economy.[13] Assessing the broader impact of the election, historian Andre Odendaal noted that 'Rubusana's win in the Tembuland constituency came as a powerful psychological boost for the Africans'.[14] The prominent Indian lawyer Gandhi congratulated Rubusana in a Natal-based Indian newspaper and maintained 'That Dr. Rubusana can sit in the

Provincial Council but not in the Union Parliament is a glaring anomaly which must disappear if South Africans are to become a real nation.'[15]

The new Union of South Africa was a unitary state in which provincial administrations had little real authority. As a member of a provincial council, Rubusana was limited to engaging in mostly mundane local matters only a few of which directly related to wider African interests. In 1911 he was involved with council issues such as telegraph services in Thembuland, the construction of a bridge over the Mbhashe River, measures to counter the spread of East Coast fever, ox transport in Umtata and teachers' pay and racial discrimination in teachers' examinations. The last two issues must have obviously interested him a great deal. Nevertheless, Rubusana's new position came with a first class rail pass and council salary which must have been a useful given the financial problems that often constrained black political groups and newspapers. The prestige of council membership also opened doors with journalists, international activists and higher levels of the South African and British governments that he used in pursuit of a larger black oriented agenda.[16]

In July 1911 Rubusana and Jabavu attended the Universal Races Congress in London which had been organized by 'the transatlantic pacifist humanitarian and ethical movement as a project to promote interracial harmony'.[17] The event was attended by about two thousand delegates and observers including African American intellectual and pioneering Pan-Africanist W. E. B. Du Bois and civil rights activist Mary White Ovington, both of whom were founders of the National Association for the Advancement of Coloured People (NAACP) in the United States. Both Jabavu and Rubusana gave presentations during a session on 'the Negro and the American Indian' that was opened by Du Bois. Jabavu gave a bland presentation on the history of different races in South Africa which highlighted the need to raise funds for an African college that would train teachers to uplift the black masses. The typically more radical Rubusana, who was introduced as a member of the Cape Provincial Council, informed the gathering that 'South Africa would never be a white country; the native was going to remain there' and that black South Africans 'required no favours, only equal opportunity and an open door'. He maintained that the idea of a 'black peril' in South Africa was a fearmongering myth and that if it existed then there must also be a corresponding 'white peril'.[18] After the session, Rubusana expanded on these statements in an interview with a British journalist that was reprinted in newspapers across the empire. In the interview, Rubusana pointed out that while the actions of a few black criminals in South Africa were used as an excuse to indict an entire race, crimes committed by whites did not result in the same stereotype but he viewed them as less forgivable given the long history of white civilization. Moreover, Rubusana thought that a black person standing trial for a crime in South Africa should do so before an all-black jury of his peers as in other parts of Southern Africa such as Rhodesia the conviction of black defendants by all-white juries was a 'foregone conclusion'.[19] While Jabavu's moderate fundraising presentation was published as a chapter in the scholarly book that came out of the congress in which Rubusana was not mentioned, the British press ignored Jabavu and focused on the more dramatic Rubusana with his formal government title.[20]

In early January 1912, Rubusana attended the inaugural meeting of the South African Native National Congress (SANNC) in Bloemfontein. To some extent, the new organization stemmed from the meetings of the South African Native Convention that had opposed the racially discriminatory Union constitution. Later renamed African National Congress (ANC), the SANNC was South Africa's first nationwide African political organization and was the first such group to bring together African traditional leaders and prominent members of the Westernized African elite. Supporting the motion by Pixley Isaka Seme, the first black South African university graduate, to formally establish the organization, Rubusana gave a 'powerful speech which was loudly cheered'. Rubusana's political status was recognized by his appointment to the SANNC's Upper House in which he was the only non-royal among twenty-three honorary presidents. Additionally, Rubusana became one of several vice presidents on the SANNC executive and chaired an important committee which drafted a set of detailed resolutions that were forwarded to the Union government. These included the withdrawal of a squatters bill which would hinder African economic independence, the appointment of a commission to investigate spurious rumours of potential black uprisings, an expression of concern over the replacement of black railway workers with whites, a call for better compensation for families of miners killed on the job and for improved safety conditions in the mines, and yet another request for an African college of higher education. In addition, the resolutions asked for the removal of rules impacting African women such as the requirement that they carry passes (like male workers) which restricted their movements and that female domestic servants undergo humiliating medical inspections. There has been some speculation over why Rubusana, the most senior African politician at the meeting, was not elected as the founding SANNC president. Theories include that newspaper editor John L. Dube became president as a sign of sympathy toward his home province of Natal where the 1906 Zulu rebellion had been brutally suppressed; that the new organization sought to promote African unity by avoiding the infamous Jabavu–Rubusana rivalry which was evident as the former was not in attendance in Bloemfontein; that there was a desire to engage leaders from provinces other than the historically prominent Cape; and that Rubusana was simply not available given his many commitments including as a member of the Cape Provincial Council.[21]

While Rubusana worked on local affairs in the Cape Council, his attention was drawn to a central piece of national legislation. In 1913 the all-white Union government passed the Natives Land Act which restricted the purchase of agricultural land by black South Africans. The aim of the law, which became a cornerstone of white supremacy in South Africa, was to reinforce and expand white economic dominance by undermining the growth of African commercial agriculture thereby forcing more blacks into low-paid migrant labour. Rubusana opposed the land act as a member of the Cape Provincial Council and continued his objections after he left that position. In June 1914 Rubusana, who had recently lost his seat in the Cape Council (see discusson later), was part of a five-man delegation of SANNC leaders that travelled to Britain to request that the imperial government overturn South Africa's Natives Land Act and institute an inquiry into the treatment of blacks in South Africa. At the time it was possible for the British government to veto legislation in dominions like South Africa and Canada. Before boarding a ship in Cape Town for his third trip to Britain, Rubusana along with John L. Dube visited Prime Minister Botha to explain their mission and to inform him that they would postpone their voyage if the Union government set aside the new law. Rubusana warned that there was considerable anxiety within African communities in the Eastern Cape about the 'oppressive policy' of the Union government and he described how Africans were being evicted from their land and prevented from buying new land. An annoyed Botha interrupted him several times to point out that much of what had been said had nothing to do with the land act, that the new law had not yet been applied in the Cape and that it was the duty of educated Africans like him to discourage dangerous talk among their people.[22] The mission continued though it would prove Rubusana's most disappointing visit to Britain. In London the delegation, including Rubusana, received some press attention but British politicians were generally unsympathetic, and the visit was quickly overshadowed by events in Europe that would lead to the outbreak of the First World War. Quarrelling among themselves and running out of money, the delegation's members returned home separately. Without his council pay, Rubusana supported himself by getting a loan from a friend in Britain.[23]

During the First World War (1914–18) Rubusana and other members of the SANNC formally suspended their protest against the land act as a display of patriotic solidarity with South Africa and Britain. South Africa's mixed-race and black political leaders thought that their loyalty and support might represent an investment in future civil rights but they were ultimately disappointed. Of course, patriotic demonstrations by black leaders also could represent an indirect method of protest. Rubusana's enthusiastic offer to personally recruit and lead a five-thousand-strong armed black contingent during South Africa's invasion of neighbouring German South West Africa (now Namibia) was informed by a desire to demonstrate the patriotism of black South Africans despite their disenfranchisement. Of course, Rubusana was also certainly aware that his proposal, which was rejected by Pretoria, challenged the legally mandated all-white composition of the new Union Defense Forces (UDF). Rubusana understood the link between armed military service and battlefield sacrifice, and citizenship rights.[24] After the war, African protest against the land act continued as black wartime loyalty and patriotism had failed to impress the white authorities. In 1922 Rubusana wrote an editorial in the African newspaper *Umteteli wa Bantu* (Mouthpiece of the People) stating that:

> In 1913 the Native Land Act gave definite form to the anti-Native trend in European thought. It was a sop to the Negrophobe tendency of the day; and to those Europeans who had rid themselves of the unreasoning prejudice which characterised the majority it was promised that the more objectionable features would shortly be weeded out, and that amendments then under consideration would rob the measure of its admitted harshness. The Act stands today in its original form, and for nine long years Natives have waited to be relieved of the suffering which it has inflicted.[25]

As A. K. Soga had predicted, Rubusana lost his Thembuland council seat in the March 1914 Cape provincial elections. He had won the seat given the splitting of the white vote in the previous election but now it was the black vote that was divided. Rubusana was opposed by Jabavu, who had departed from most African political leaders by supporting the Natives Land Act, and a single white candidate called A. B. Payne. There were rumours that white politicians had encouraged Jabavu to enter the race as a way of ensuring that Rubusana did not return to the Cape Provincial Council. Although Jabavu secured only 294 votes compared to 852 for Rubusana, it was enough to secure victory for Payne who received 1,004 votes. As a result, Jabavu was permanently discredited among black South Africans and never returned to political prominence. Rubusana attempted but failed to regain his council seat in the 1917 Cape election and in this effort he was now supported by a repentant Jabavu who had renounced the land act and was desperately trying to regain his lost standing.[26]

After the First World War Rubusana, now in his sixties, continued his educational and church work in East London but his relevance as an African political leader slowly waned. The Eastern Cape-based SANC, for which Rubusana had been the main spokesman, suffered after the closure of the *Izwi* newspaper and seems to have disappeared during the war. While Rubusana had once appeared to be a dynamic and radical leader, he now appeared more elitist and conservative in comparison to the emerging black trade union movement which had a much wider appeal to the growing and impoverished black urban community. In 1918 Rubusana, serving as an intermediary between the white East London Chamber of Commerce and black workers who were struggling with rising prices, convinced the latter to moderate their demands for increased wages though this proved temporary. In October 1920, at a meeting of the Industrial and Commercial Workers' Union (ICU) in Port Elizabeth, Rubusana was physically attacked for speaking out against an anticipated strike. The assault gave police an excuse to arrest union leader Samuel Masabalala for allegedly assaulting Rubusana (whom he had actually tried to protect) and this led to a violent altercation between armed white police and white vigilantes and black protestors in which twenty-four people were killed and forty-five injured.[27] Around the same time, Rubusana shifted his political allegiance from the SANNC, which had ousted the cautious Dube as president in 1917 and was more prominent in the Transvaal, to the new but slightly more conservative Bantu Union which was an Eastern Cape organization led by black businessman Meshach Pellem. The Bantu Union tried to bring together members of the old Imbumba and SANC movements, and focused on trying to defend and expand black voting rights in the Cape. Rubusana was also active in groups like the Cape Native Voters' Convention which was founded in 1924 in King William's Town and advocated the extension of the franchise to blacks in South Africa's other provinces and criticized racial discrimination such as found in the pass laws, labour practices and criminal courts.[28]

With the rise to political power of the more strictly segregationist and Afrikaner oriented Nationalist Party of J. B. M. Hertzog in Union coalition governments, the Cape's non-racial franchise was gradually phased out during the 1920s and 1930s. In a programme meant to break down the continued growth of a broad black identity and national political movement, Africans across the country would be administered and represented by non-democratic and hereditary traditional leaders administering customary law within a network of ethnically defined homelands. The Natal system of 'Native Administration' was expanded across South Africa.[29] In 1927 Rubusana, representing the Cape Native Voters' Convention along with Professor D. D. T. Jabavu who was the first black university faculty member in South Africa and the son of the now late J. T. Jabavu, spoke before a Union government committee on proposed legislation that would restrict black voting. Rubusana criticized the supposed reasons for the new policy such as that voting rights had not economically benefited blacks which he thought was a ridiculous excuse as it had also failed to benefit many whites, and that black voters would eventually swamp white voters which he contended would be prevented by enforcing educational qualifications for the franchise. During the session Rubusana, outspoken as always, contradicted Bantu Union leader Pellem who had testified that his organization was in support of separate representation for black South Africans. Rubusana warned that 'the passage of these bills into law will create hatred between the black and white people of this country'.[30] At the start of the 1930s, the Cape educational and property qualifications were removed for white voters but not for mixed-race or black ones and the franchise was extended to white women. This further decreased the percentage of non-white voters within the Cape electorate. In 1936, the year a 78-year-old Rubusana passed away, black voters were removed from the Cape common voters' roll with the few who qualified to vote having to cast their ballots for three white representatives and these positions were later abolished. The apartheid government, elected in 1948, imposed a similar process on mixed-race voters in the early 1950s.[31]

Conclusion

Rubusana's 1910 election to the Cape Provincial Council arguably represented the climax of the Cape Liberal Tradition. The Cape's assimilationist and non-racial political system had allowed a black man to be elected to a hitherto all-white colonial representative institution. Since he was a highly successful and respected clergyman and educator, Rubusana's electoral victory seemed to confirm the inherent promise and potential of the Cape system that Africans who fully incorporated into colonial society and worked hard would eventually gain equality and civil rights. It must be remembered that Rubusana was not elected to represent Africans only but that he was the elected representative of all the inhabitants of his constituency as were other council members. However, the formation of the Union of South Africa in 1910 meant that the Cape's non-racial and qualified franchise became a provincial anachronism and was eventually phased out in favour of the blatant and institutionalized racial segregation and oppression of the country's other provinces. As such, there would be no more black parliamentarians in South Africa until the advent of democracy eighty-four years after Rubusana's election and fifty-eight years after his death. Although Rubusana served only one term in the Cape council and his work there focused on local concerns, the status that membership conferred – which continued for the rest of his life – created opportunities to pursue larger objectives toward black empowerment within South Africa. At the time of his election Rubusana was a very well-known black political leader within South Africa but the prestige of his council position, and his novelty as the only black council member, clearly enhanced his ability to work on a national level where he was prominent in the formation of the African National Congress and occasionally on an international level where he publicized the plight of black South Africans and interacted with activists from Britain, North America, Asia and other parts of Africa. Rubusana's council position also demonstrated the inherent weakness and ambiguity of the Cape Liberal Tradition. Reactions to his candidacy revealed the hypocrisy of the Cape white liberal politicians who portrayed themselves as sympathetic to black aspirations but, in practice, did not want a black man to become their equal. By the time of Rubusana's election, black voting in the Cape had been threatened and reduced for years and it was becoming obvious that the inherent promises of Cape Liberalism were false. Suspicions of this kind of insincerity would continue to cripple white liberal objections to racism in South Africa for decades to come. It eventually contributed to the emergence of the Black Consciousness movement in the late 1960s and 1970s in which black anti-apartheid activists like Steven Biko, also a Xhosa-speaking resident of the Eastern Cape like the earlier Rubusana, refused to accept the permanent tutelage of their sympathetic but paternalistic white colleagues. Rubusana's 1910 election also highlighted the internal problems of South Africa's early black political movement. The Western political context which the African mission-educated elite had adopted emphasized individual merit and success but this periodically clashed with African cultural values emphasizing communalism, consultation and consensus. As a result, in running for elected office, Rubusana was sometimes accused by other black South Africans of pursing selfish desire over the interests of his people. These tensions overlapped with the personal rivalries and jealousies that existed within the emerging black political leadership and this ultimately led to Rubusana's electoral defeat. In retrospect, the case of Rubusana's council seat shows that while Westernized black South Africans of the early twentieth century attempted to improve their situation and that of their people by working within the limits of colonial governmental institutions, this was ultimately futile as the white minority controlled system was rigged against them. During the second half of the twentieth century black South Africans would have to employ extraconstitutional means to gain long sought after civil rights within a non-racial democracy. As a solitary black voice in the Cape Provincial Council of the early twentieth century, Rubusana was not a token representative of a subject majority but an inconvenient reminder of the disappointment of Cape Liberalism, and of continuing and increasing demands for black civil rights. Rubusana was the first and for a long time held the status of the only black South African parliamentarian but eventually, after a long struggle, South Africa would have many more black legislators, cabinet ministers and presidents.

Notes

1   During the late twentieth century some black South Africans were elected to the legislatures of self-governing and ethnically defined homelands (often called Bantustans) that were granted independence by South Africa's apartheid state in the 1970s and 1980s but not recognized by any other country. Since the Bantustans were defined as separate states and meant to deprive black South Africans of citizenship in their own country, members of these legislatures should not be considered to have been elected to a governing body of South Africa.

2   For some works on the Cape-Xhosa Wars (1789–1878) see J. B. Peires, *The House of Phalo: A History of the Xhosa People in the Days of their Independence* (Johannesburg: Ravan Press, 1981); John Milton, *The Edges of War: A History of Frontier Wars* (Cape Town: Juta, 1983); J. B. Peires, *The Dead Will Arise: Nongqawuse and the Great Xhosa Cattle-Killing Movement of 1856–57* (Johannesburg: Ravan Press, 1989); Noel Mostert, *Frontiers: The Epic of South Africa's Creation and the Tragedy of the Xhosa People* (New York: Alfred A. Knopf, 1992); Timothy J. Stapleton, *Maqoma: The Legend of a Great Xhosa Warrior* (Claremont, South Africa: Amava Heritage Publishing, 2016).

3   There is a large literature on missionary Christianity in South Africa. For a few examples, see Richard Elphick and Rodney Davenport, eds., *Christianity in South Africa: A Political, Social and Cultural History* (Claremont, South Africa: David Philip, 1997); Elizabeth Elbourne, *Blood Ground: Colonialism, Missions and the Contest for Christianity in the Cape Colony and Britain, 1799–1853* (Montreal: McGill-Queens Press, 2002); Richard Price, *Making Empire: Colonial Encounters*

and the Creation of Imperial Rule in the Nineteenth Century (Cambridge: Cambridge University Press, 2008); Tolly Bradford, *Prophetic Identities: Indigenous Missionaries on British Colonial Frontiers, 1850–1875* (Vancouver: University of British Columbia Press, 2012).

4   Report of the Select Committee on Native Education, Cape Town, August 1908, 209–63.

5   It is a shame that there is no complete full-length published biography of Rubusana. For shorter biographical works, see 'Rev. Dr. Walter B. Rubusana', *The African Yearly Register, Who's Who*, 1930, 251, T. D. Mweli Skota Papers, 1930–74, Wits Historical Papers, A1618. Available online: www.historicalpapers.wits.ac.za/inventories/inv_pdfo/A1618/A1618-C4-2-011-jpeg.pdf (accessed 5 February 2021); Songezo Joel Ngqongo, 'Mpilo Walter Benson Rubusana', in Mcebisi Ndletyana (ed.), *African Intellectuals in the 19th and Early 20th Century: South Africa* (Pretoria: HSRC Press, 2008), 45–54; Songezo Joel Ngqongo, 'Mpilo Walter Benson Rubusana, 1859–1910: The Making of the New African Elite in the Eastern Cape', MA thesis, University of Fort Hare, 1997; Pallo Jordan, 'Zemk' iinkomo Magwalandini! – The Life and Times of W.B. Rubusana', *Sechaba*, 1984, 4–13; Fransie Rossouw, 'W.B. Rubusana's History of South Africa from the Native Standpoint – Does it Exist?', *Quarterly Bulletin of the South African Library*, 51, no. 2 (December 1996): 62–7; Rubusana is mentioned repeatedly by many historians of African politics and journalism in South Africa, see Peter Walshe, *The Rise of African Nationalism in South Africa* (Berkeley: University of California Press, 1971); Andre Odendaal, *Black Protest Politics in South Africa to 1912* (Totowa: Barnes and Noble Books, 1984); Les Switzer, 'The Beginnings of African Protest Journalism at the Cape', in Les Switzer (ed.), *South Africa's Alternative Press: Voices of Protest and Resistance, 1880–1960* (Cambridge: Cambridge University Press, 1997), 57–78.

6   Julie Evans, Patricia Grimshaw, David Philips and Shurlee Swain, *Equal Subjects and Unequal Rights: Indigenous Peoples in British Settler Colonies, 1830–1910* (Manchester: Manchester University Press, 2002), 162–6; Robert Ross, *Status and Respectability in the Cape Colony, 1750–1870; A Tragedy of Manners* (Cambridge: Cambridge University Press, 2004), 174; Mohamed Adhikari, *Not White Enough, Not Black Enough: Racial Identity in the South African Coloured Community* (Athens: Ohio University Press, 2005), 3; William K. Storey, *Guns, Race and Power in Colonial South Africa* (Cambridge: Cambridge University Press, 2008).

7   Stanley Trapido, 'Natal's Non-Racial Franchise, 1856', *African Studies*, 22, no. 1 (1963): 22–32; Nigel Worden, *The Making of Modern South Africa; Conquest, Apartheid and Democracy* (Chichester: Wiley-Blackwell, 2012), 80; Peter Baxter, *Gandhi, Smuts and Race in the British Empire: Of Passive and Violent Resistance* (Barnsley: Pen and Sword, 2017), 85; Jeff Guy, *Theophilus Shepstone and the Forging of Natal: African Autonomy and Settler Colonialism in the Making of Traditional Authority* (Pietermaritzburg: University of Kwa-Zulu/Natal Press, 2013).

8   Greg Cuthbertson, 'Missionary Imperialism and Colonial Welfare: London Missionary Attitudes to the South African War, 1899–1902', *South African Historical Journal*, 19 (1987): 107.

9   Odendaal, *Black Protest Politics*, 207.

10 Ibid., 197–227; Les Switzer, *Power and Resistance in an African Society: The Ciskei Xhosa and the Making of South Africa* (Pietermaritzburg: University of Natal Press, 1993), 173–5.

11 Thembuland was also the birthplace of later ANC leader and South African president Nelson Mandela (1918–2013).

12 Ngqongqo, 'Rubusana: New African Elite', 177–97; D. T. T. Jabavu, *The Life of John Tengo Jabavu: Editor of Imvo Zabantsundu, 1884–1921* (Alice, South Africa: Lovedale Press, 1922), 18.

13 Ngqongqo, 'Rubusana: New African Elite', 197–209.

14 Odendaal, *Black Protest Politics*, 251.

15 Anil Nauriya, 'Freedom, Race and Francophonie: Gandhi and the Construction of Peoplehood', *Identite, Culture et Politique (CODESRIA)*, 10, no. 2 (2009): 83.

16 Odendaal, *Black Protest Politics*, 251 and 257.

17 Ian Christopher Fletcher, 'Introduction: New Historical Perspectives on the First Universal Races Congress of 1911', *Radical History Review*, 92 (Spring 2005): 99; Paul Rich, 'The Baptism of a New Era: The 1911 Universal Races Congress and the Liberal Ideology of Race', *Ethnic and Racial Studies*, 7, no. 4 (1984): 534–50.

18 *Record of the Proceedings of the First Universal Races Congress Held at the University of London, July 26–29, 1911, published for the Executive* (London: P.S. King and Son, 1911), 61–2; 'Universal Races Congress', *The Times*, 29 July 1911, 4.

19 'The Negro Problem: Views of a Native', *The Telegraph*, 11 August 1911, 3. Available online: https://trove.nla.gov.au/newspaper/article/175833979?searchTerm=Rubusan a&searchLimits (accessed 5 February 2021).

20 John Tengo Jabavu, 'Native Races of South Africa', in Gustav Spiller (ed.), *Papers in Inter-Racial Problems: A Record of the Proceedings of the First Universal Races Congress Held at the University of London, July 26–29, 1911* (London: P.S. King and Son, 1911), 336–41; 'Universal Races Congress', *The Times*, 29 July 1911, 4, this report focuses on the presentations by Du Bois and Rubusana and does not mention Jabavu.

21 Odendaal, *Black Protest Politics*, 270–7.

22 'South Africa's Problem: Interview with General Botha', *The Evening News*, 11 July 1914, 3. Available online: https://trove.nla.gov.au/newspaper/article/115812491? searchTerm=Rubusana&searchLimits (accessed 5 February 2021).

23 Heather Hughes, *First President: A Life of John Dube Founding President of the ANC* (Auckland Park, South Africa; Jacana Media, 2011), 188.

24 Bill Nasson, *Springboks on the Somme: South Africa in the Great War, 1914–18* (Johannesburg: Penguin Books, 2007), 19.

25 Harvey M. Feinberg, 'Protest in South Africa: Prominent Black Leaders' Commentary on the Natives Land Act, 1913–36', *Historia*, 52, no. 2 (November 2006): 127.

26 Catherine Higgs, *The Ghost of Equality: The Public Lives of D.D.T. Jabavu of South Africa, 1885–1959* (Athens: Ohio University Press, 1997), 93; Jordan, 'W.B. Rubusana', 11–12.

27 P. L. Wickens, 'The Industrial and Commercial Workers' Union of Africa', thesis, University of Cape Town, 1973, 135–6, 155–69; P. L. Wickens, 'The One Big Union Movement among Black Workers in South Africa', *International Journal of African Historical Studies*, 7, no. 3 (1974): 391–416.

28 Switzer, *Power and Resistance*, 251–4.

29 For more on this, see Mahmood Mamdani, *Citizen and Subject: Contemporary Africa and the Legacy of Late Colonialism* (Princeton: Princeton University Press, 1996).

30 Minutes of Evidence, Selection Committee on Subject of Native Bills, 30 May 1927. Available online: www.sahistory.org.za/archive/testimony-professor-d-d-t-jabavu-walter-rubusana-and-rev-abner-mtimkulu-cape-native-voters (accessed 5 February 2021).

31 Switzer, *Power and Resistance*, 223; Paul B. Rich, *White Power and the Liberal Conscience: Racial Segregation and South African Liberalism, 1921–1961* (Manchester: Manchester University Press, 1984); Saul Debow, *Racial Segregation and the Origins of Apartheid in South Africa, 1919–36* (New York: Palgrave MacMillan, 1989); Ian Loveland, *By Due Process of Law? Racial Discrimination and the Right to Vote in South Africa, 1855–1960* (Oxford: Hart Publishing, 1999).

9

Gratien Candace: In the name of the French Empire

Dominique Chathuant

In 1928, a tall black man speaking on behalf of France addressed the forty-three delegations attending the conference of the Inter-Parliamentary Union in Berlin with a plea for co-operation among 'advanced nations' in helping 'backward races'.[1] Five years later, at the meeting of the same organization in Madrid, Gratien Candace, already 'a former minister', espoused the practice of forced labour in France. By 1940, he was one of those who could speak to the President of the Republic, Albert Lebrun, or to Marshal Pétain directly. The parliamentarian claimed to speak 'in the name of the empire'. Born in Guadeloupe and the grandson of a slave, Candace was not the first black politician, but he was the first to hold a long-term seat in the French parliament. After Blaise Diagne (1931), whom he preceded in the Chamber of Deputies, he was the second black minister to be appointed in France (1932–3). By comparison, the first appointment of a black minister to the British cabinet was not until 2002. The definition of 'black' here is based above all on perceptions of the time, differentiating it from that of the United States, where the notion of African-American included men who were classified as 'coloured' but who would have gone almost unnoticed in France. Based on this criterion there were French precedents to Candace in the French parliament in 1794 and 1848, but their presence was fleeting. Indeed, Hégésippe Légitimus, who was elected deputy in 1898, may have caused a sensation but he turned out to be almost an absentee member. Candace clearly represents the presence of black politicians for the duration of the parliamentary history. His place in French history is firmly situated within colonialism, though limited to elections and Guadeloupe.[2] However, 'the dichotomy between colonial history, which has become imperial, and the history of the metropole, which became hexagonal in 1962, is no longer relevant'.[3] Relating Candace's story and what enabled his presence within the system of the French colonial republic requires reassembling, like an electrician, imperial interconnections that hitherto have been concealed.[4]

What enabled Candace to succeed?

Universal male suffrage, state schools and networks are the three factors that explain Candace's rise within the French political system. The emergence in France of 'universal' suffrage in the context of the Second Republic that commenced in 1848 is the first explanation for the appointment of someone like Candace in the Third Republic, a regime that can be described by the oxymoron, the 'colonial Republic'. Early 'universal' suffrage for males marked a contrast – in its precocity – in Europe with the late arrival in France of female suffrage in 1944 and the paradox between democratic institutions and the inequality of the colonial system. In a colonial empire marked by the racial paradigm, the election of black parliamentarians was not considered *a priori*. The majority of non-whites in the colonies were of humble background, and the election of a non-white was legally impossible in most of them. Yet it was foreseeable in the old colonies, vestiges of a first colonial empire, where, since 1848, all males were citizens of the Republic. With the advent of the Second Republic (1848–51), France, deprived of most of its first colonial empire from 1760 to 1815, granted civil equality to former slaves without feeling threatened, as it did from 1920 to 1950, with one day becoming a colony of its colonies. This situation allowed blacks to be elected in La Réunion, French Guiana, the West Indies and four Senegalese municipalities in the context of a centralization process that involved parliamentary representation in Paris.[5]

Although Martinique met the legal conditions for sending blacks to the French parliament, this did not happen until the election of Aimé Césaire and Léopold Bissol (1945). Before then, it elected *békés* (Martiniquan white-Creoles) and then mulattos (an intermediary class in Martinique).[6] In Senegal, inhabitants of the Four Communes began by electing whites, then mulattos and finally blacks like Diagne (1914). French Guiana elected white parliamentarians followed by the black deputy Gaston Monnerville (1932), who later became a senator in southwestern France and president of the Senate in 1947–68. In Guadeloupe, the election of a black deputy became possible in 1898 with Légitimus (1898), followed by Candace (1912).

L' école républicaine, the state non-religious school of the secular Republic, was another key factor. For a small number of children of black workers in agriculture, state schools provided a means of escaping from farming as a livelihood and becoming a civil servant. Young Candace received his schooling when the family moved to Basse-Terre, where he attended a study programme that provided instruction to good elementary school students who would not otherwise have advanced to reach a higher level of education. Having qualified as a teacher, he taught in 1892–4 in rural schools on the Guadeloupean Côte-sous-le-Vent, where he came from. He then obtained paid leave to pursue his studies and moved to Toulouse with the financial assistance of an aunt. Thus, in his early life Candace's personal aptitude and family solidarity were interlinked with the developing École de la République. It was in 1895 that Candace discovered the reality of a France which up to then he had idealized. He became a school supervisor to finance his natural science studies. With a degree in natural sciences, he was sent on a mission to Tunisia and then to Trinidad by the Ministry of Colonies before to be able to apply for a teaching position in Toulouse. Such posts were usually sought by teachers who were advanced in their careers. However, the director of public instruction considered that this thirty-year-old Guadeloupe native did not yet have the necessary authority to teach in Toulouse. He appointed him to the post of science teacher in Pau, a smaller town, the capital of the Lower Pyrenees. He was probably the first black teacher there and the first black man ever seen by his Béarnais students; however, no official administrative source directly alluded to his colour – synonymous with race – or to the potential link that would be established between 'race' and ability. In fact, administrative documents convey an attitude to Candace that was more culturally biased than racialist at a time when a rural background was enough to generate openly paternalistic comments. This does not mean that the term 'race' remained unspoken. A report indicates that the young Guadeloupian teacher displayed a certain amount of goodwill in order to be able to make himself useful and 'render greater services' to his 'compatriots'.[7] In a context of racist theories, there is no evidence, however, to show that such goodwill was not, in fact, the result of an unconsciously diminished appraisal of the black student's abilities.[8] Candace is not the only student from a rural background to experience the sociological acculturation process of upward social mobility through the École de la Republique. After only five years of teaching, his colonial mission earned him a Public Instruction medal, a decoration generally awarded to teachers at the end of their careers.

This provided him with a successful introduction to political networks. Additionally, his Masonic initiation in Pau in 1900 seems to have helped this integration into republican circles.

The victory of the left in the 1906 elections brought to power an alliance between the *radical* secular left and moderate socialism unaffiliated with the Second (Socialist) International. This circumstance explains the appointment of socialist René Viviani to the newly created Ministry of Labour and Social Security. His chief of staff, Joseph Paul-Boncour (several times minister and head of government), hired Candace to work on his team. The teacher from Guadeloupe then became one of his direct collaborators, but not chief of staff, as he is described in certain dubious biographical references. He left Pau in the middle of the 1907 school year to take up his post more than 800 kilometres away.[9] Candace was then awarded the Agricultural Merit Award. Without having done his military service, which was not applicable in the colonies at the time, he was not eligible for the Legion of Honour. Working in a ministerial cabinet did not provide him with sufficient means, and he was obliged to supplement his income by teaching in Creil, near Paris, where the young Jacques Doriot was one of his students.[10] The political climate forced him to leave the ministry in 1909, at which time he chose to enter politics by running for legislative elections in Guadeloupe in 1910 against the metropolitan Alfred Gérault-Richard, but he failed to succeed due to fraud and collusion by the authorities.[11] The premature death of his successful opponent in 1912, however, meant he was elected by complying with the conditions of the metropolitan senator Henry Bérenger, the new dominant figure in local political life. Candace then became the other leading political figure in Guadeloupe and remained so for three decades.

Between the left and the right of the political centre

Candace, like Légitimus, stood out from the republicans of the previous generation who came from the mulatto bourgeoisie.[12] He professed socialist policies of emancipation for the local black proletariat that reflected the independent socialism in France represented by Aristide Briand, Alexandre Millerand and René Viviani, supporters of a social variant of republican and secular culture. Resistant to party discipline, these men did not adhere in 1905 to Jean Jaurès's attempt at socialist unification in the French Section of the Workers International affiliated with the Second International.[13] However, they regrouped in the rather loose structures of the Republican Socialist Party

Figure 9.1 Gratien Candace 'en habit', *c.* 1935–7. This formal dress was worn on special days, such as the election of the French president by the Parliament assembled in Versailles. The photo was taken at the peak of Candace's political career in the late 1930s. In 1938–42, he was one of the vice-speakers of the French Chamber of Deputies. Courtesy of Fonds L.-J. Bouge, Musée des Beaux-Arts de Chartres.

from 1913 to 1934. Candace viewed moderation in socialism as going hand in hand with internal assimilation, a sense of belonging to France. Anxious to finally extend military service to the old colonies, he voted with the centre-right and the nationalists in July 1913 for the Three-Year Military Service law, one of those great parliamentary votes that revealed the left–right divide of the day. Splitting the Chamber in two, the vote pushed the moderate socialists towards the centre.[14] Until the 1930s, Candace, by virtue of a reflex typical of French centrism, claimed the term 'left' in line with the standard reference to a political cosmogony dating back to the late nineteenth century, the period of republican infighting and the Dreyfus affair. The term 'right' then applied only to monarchists or Bonapartists, in contrast to a 'left' that was understood as republican.[15] In fact, since 1913 Candace had belonged to the family of so-called moderates, characterized by the centrist utopia of a middle ground supporting the left-wing coalitions of 1924–6 and 1932–4 and the centre-right combinations (national union).[16] He was distrustful of the 1936 Popular Front but was elected and re-elected deputy speaker of the House in 1938 and 1939 with the votes of the socialist left and the communist extreme left.[17] Candace is quite frequently regarded as the puppet of a colonial power pulling the strings in the shadows, a view that reveals a lack of knowledge of the relationship between parliament, the central administration and the old colonies. Not only that, the stereotype of the puppet implies the impossibility that a black man might be an autonomous actor in history, with his own individual agency. Yet this is far from being the case. At the time of the Cartel des Gauches,[18] Édouard Herriot, Prime Minister, was to invite Candace to negotiate the participation of the Socialist Republicans in the 1926 cabinet.[19] The deputy from Guadeloupe had real political power through his participation in important parliamentary committees from the beginning of his career: the merchant Navy, the Navy during the war (vice-president in 1931 and 1928–32), finance and peace treaties, among other matters, at a time when parliamentary committees were more powerful than government ministers, whose average term of office was only six months. This is the paradox of a French system in which ministerial mandate was severely limited by a powerful legislature while everyone was vying for the position of minister to further their *cursus honorum*. By the late 1930s, Candace had garnered a wealth of expertise in national defence, particularly in the field of the Navy, but also in-depth knowledge of the technical workings of parliament. He was a member of the French delegation to the 1932 Geneva Conference and, as noted above, the meetings of the Inter-Parliamentary Union in Berlin (1928) and Madrid (1933).

Candace's discursive strategy was influenced by his moderate political temperament, although it was not the only factor. It may well be one of the keys to his political longevity, which was also facilitated by the most unspeakable political manoeuvres.

Positioned at the centre of the republican camp, Candace had no need to fear accusations of separatist and/or communist radicalism. The colonial endeavour was for him a civilizing and pacification process. Colonial problems were attributable to bad Frenchmen, foreign activities and/or communist subversion. Thus the claim of political radicalism could be applied to all opponents, who were readily accused of separatism – Candace was a victim of it in his early days in 1910 – as an excuse for the lowest political blows, especially electoral fraud, which adversaries were always accused of committing. Since 1912, Candace was bound by a pact of silence with the metropolitan Henry Bérenger, elected senator for Guadeloupe the same year. Candace's longevity in the first electoral constituency of Guadeloupe (Basse-Terre) can be attributed to his acceptance of this arrangement.[20] Moreover, the pact was the result of political instability that prevented the emergence of a major personality in the second electoral district (Pointe-à-Pitre). Elected deputies never exceeded two four-year terms, a period that inevitably ended with a rupture with Candace. This was the case of Achille René-Boisneuf, elected in 1914, whose term was extended until November 1919 due to the war, was later abandoned by Candace, and then beaten in 1924. Candace himself secretly wished to put an end to Bérenger's dominance. His desire for a split dates back to 1929 at least, when he used the Guadeloupian Maurice Satineau (activist, journalist and registered fraudster) as an intermediary with the conservative Jacques Bardoux, suggesting that he go forward as a candidate for the 1929 senatorial elections.[21] Candace was careful to bring about electoral solutions involving a 'union of races' with black and white candidates, in order never to be accused of separatism. His split with Bérenger became public in the mid-1930s in the run-up to the 1938 senatorial elections.[22] He relied on the 1936 election of Satineau in the second electoral division. Massive fraud in a few polling stations allowed the latter to win the election by defeating his opponent in only four communes with 92 to 99.9 per cent of the vote. Candace's support and the smokescreen in the Chamber caused by the fraud (involving thirteen votes) imputed to deputy Jean Chiappe, validated Satineau's election.[23] The Chamber's and successive governors' compliance apparently was motivated by the appeal of stability represented by Candace and his allies as opposed to the unknown prospects of separatism and Communism. They also harboured scepticism with regard to the civic skills of the black population of the French

West Indies. Well acquainted with this kind of violent electoral climate, Candace was able to exercise discipline in the Chamber, and he asserted himself in an area of expertise – the Navy – that was in no way original but became his exclusive domain, reinforced by his seat on the Finance Committee.

Unlike many parliamentarians who were lawyers, doctors or professors with brilliant résumés, Candace had not been schooled in the classical humanities.[24] This was another distinguishing feature, in addition to his skin colour, differentiating him sociologically from a certain section of the political arena. Paradoxically, many of these brilliant parliamentarians were classical orators, such as the professor of philosophy Édouard Herriot, who was accustomed to using Latin quotations but who lacked the ability or flair for technical or economic issues.[25] Candace was no more brilliant than his peers on the question of the gold exchange standard, but his taste for economic and social issues marked a contrast with his contemporaries' lack of appetite for dealing with these problems. The deputy from Guadeloupe sat on the House Finance Committee from 1919 to 1940, a time when parliamentary committees had a major influence on the choice of an executive that changed on average every six months. His geo-economic and geopolitical vision was clearly visible in parliamentary debates and in his two books on the Navy. One of them, prefaced by Aristide Briand,[26] earned him second prize for the best colonial work.[27] In it, Candace advocated introducing new crops, multimodal transport developments, the autonomy of seaports and the establishment of free port zones. On this issue alone, he devoted several reports and draft legislative proposals from 1925 to 1937.[28] All this was closely integrated into an imperial system in which he believed colonies embodied the conditions of a great merchant navy. They also represented salvation in the event of war at the end of the 1930s, when Candace advocated naval rearmament and noted with consternation the failure of the League of Nations in China, Europe and Ethiopia. This conversion to rearmament came only after a long period of trust in international institutions. In foreign policy, like Briand, Candace was firmly attached to the spirit of international institutions. He still supported the reduction of military funding at the end of February 1933.[29]

Assimilation, egalitarianism and black experience

'Between the German of today and the black man I am, I think I am the one who represents civilization'; with these words Candace addressed the International League against racism and anti-semitism,[30] meeting in Paris, along with

Galandou Diouf.[31] Whereas in the previous decade they had counterposed the French identity of the coloured population against the alien nature of racial prejudice, Candace and Diouf were now advocating French civilization and the cohesion of the empire against Nazi barbarism. This was the logical continuation of a discourse that had always called for racial equality.

In June 1912, Candace was only an ordinary deputy whose skin colour prevented him from going unnoticed in the Chamber. However, after a mere few weeks as a deputy, he took the floor to speak about extending conscription to the old colonies, the focus of a campaign in which he was one of the main actors. To vigorous and frequent applause he declared:

> I am a patriot as ardent as I am thoughtful, because I personally am very conscious of all that I owe to France. I know all that my race owes to the great and generous France of 1789 and 1848 … [In] colonies other than those in Africa there are populations that have long aspired to the honour of serving their homeland; it is these old French colonies that are called Guadeloupe, Martinique, Réunion Island, and Guiana … At a time when the Minister of War is about to ask the Chamber for new funding for black troops, I felt it was worthwhile to tell him that good Frenchmen, far from their motherland in distance, but very close to it in their hearts … aspire to the honor of serving their homeland. Every year, poor people in our West Indies make great sacrifices to allow their children to go to France to join the army or the navy … We cannot count on the assistance of local governments in this situation. They have no funds at their disposal … However, nothing can stop the patriotic enthusiasm of our young West Indians … You have turned us into citizens, into free men. We want to be treated like real French people! That will only truly come to pass when you have associated us with all the other sons of the homeland in the healthy work of national defence.[32]

By participating in a budget debate regarding military recruitment in Africa, Candace was deliberately using a related subject as a forum to raise awareness of his demands, which could only be addressed by simple executive decree. He was fully aware that he was relying on the imminence of the German threat to support his request. The strange irony was that black men were being asked to participate in a war of whites even as their skin colour rendered them unable to attain full Frenchness.[33] However, the claims made by Candace and others in no way represent outdated servility to the colonial order; which would mean in these cases that black deputies were merely the objects of history whose driving forces would systematically elude them.

Conscription was part of an assimilationist political culture based on both egalitarianism and identification with the French nation.[34] From the late nineteenth century, politicians in the West Indies had been urging the government to put an end to the humiliating situation by applying the military service law. Adopted in 1889, the law was not applied until 1913. Wealthy white Creoles were concerned about the agricultural workforce and the 'injustice' that would result from forcing men of all 'races' to serve in the same ranks.[35] For its part, military culture was driven by the idea that interbreeding of West Indian societies would produce an indolent Creole race with little talent for war. The international situation was favourable to conscription. In November 1913, in an increasingly tense international context, President Raymond Poincaré signed a decree enforcing national service in the old colonies as a consequence of the Nationality Act. It was not a law per se but a simple decree extending to the old colonies the 1913 law that set military service at three years. This made the vote on the Three-Year Service Law, without which conscription could not take place, virtually compulsory. Candace's assimilationist culture pushed him towards the centre. Diagne, elected in 1914, followed the same assimilationist line when he demanded conscription for the inhabitants of Senegal's Four Elective Communes.[36] Candace and his colleagues demonstrated to their contemporaries that they were capable of acting with latitude and agency, in sharp contrast to the concept of *la Force Noire* promoted by General Mangin, where the only actor would be monolithic white colonizers.[37]

As the empire is fundamentally unequal in fact and in law, the standard practices and institutions that constitute the norm for the colonies can paradoxically appear in metropolitan France as surprising deviations. Thus, while equality seemed inconceivable in the colonies, metropolitan France afforded colonial natives the freedom to denounce racial discrimination. This became the case following discussion on conscription laws in 1913. In January 1915, addressing the Chamber, Candace and the Martiniquan Joseph Lagrosillière denounced the activities of La Morue Française, a company accused of delivering rotten cod, while one of its representatives claimed in defence that the fish was intended for 'the Negroes of Martinique'. Candace, referring to the blood tax represented by conscription implemented in 1913, went on to say: 'When blacks are fighting alongside whites for law and freedom, it is not the moment for certain snipers (*embusqués*), certain war profiteers ... to insult them or attempt to belittle them.'[38] Later on, we find further instances of this kind of discourse which contrasts good French patriots from the colonies with bad French people displaying racial prejudice that demonstrates their ignorance, lack of honesty and an invariably dubious sense of patriotism.

Carole Reynaud-Paligot's work shows how racial thinking permeated the French intelligentsia of the early twentieth century.[39] This is illustrated by the controversy surrounding the 1921 Goncourt Prize. Shortly before the prize was awarded, Candace told the young Guyanese colonial administrator, Félix Éboué, that he wanted the winner to be René Maran from Martinique, which would prove that a black man could do as well as a white. Maran won and the news was initially well received by the press. Even the nationalist and deeply anti-semitic jury member Léon Daudet affirmed in *L'Action Française* that the black race was not inferior.[40] Very soon, however, Maran was criticized for literary incoherence due to his race and was accused of being an indictment of France's colonial undertakings. The jury was blamed for its alleged complaisance towards a black author, as was the colonial administration, which ought to have revoked it.[41] Two months after the prize was awarded, controversy persisted in *Le Temps* with Maran's capacity to reason being challenged on the grounds of race: 'the brain of negroes is still a mechanism that operates intermittently'.[42] Candace publicly condemned such offensive remarks 'for a whole race that is gradually rising, like all other races, towards the total light of the spirit'.[43] He wryly asked what the white writers of *Le Temps* and the Communist Marcel Cachin – in his eyes the French incarnation of Bolshevik barbarism – might have in common: 'It would be too easy for me [to] prove that it is not only in Negroes that the brain is still an intermittently functioning mechanism.' In contrast, Candace underscored the wisdom of blacks who defended humanity against German and Bolshevik barbarism and explained how Maran had earned his respect as a free writer with a distinctly French talent. The response from *Le Temps* remained politely contemptuous, claiming scientific authority. While the French public was ready to recognize the blood that had been shed and to rub shoulders with 'Frenchmen of colour' in the subway, this did not in any way erase their belief in the inferiority of blacks. Many politicians were ready to display sympathy for the people of the colonies at a political level; however, this attitude had its limits when the intelligentsia displayed its unwillingness to recognize the literary prowess of those whom they were willing to welcome as soldiers.

Equality in the Third Republic was officially a male domain. This situation raises even more questions about the Candace case, given the ambiguous relations between suffragists and the African American question in the United States. Like other Republican Socialists (Briand, Viviani), Candace was a supporter of women's suffrage, voted by the House in 1919, 1925, 1935 and 1936. In 1918, he was a rapporteur for the draft law extending certain civil rights to women in the former colonies. He was also one of nineteen French candidates for the 1919 general elections to include women's voting rights in his electoral programme, even though the socialists of the Guadeloupian SFIO (the French section of the Workers' International, a precursor of the French Socialist Party) remained opposed to it until 1945. He defended the suffragist cause in 1925 and 1935 in the Chamber, whose votes in favour of women's franchise were systematically rejected by the Senate, which feared the influence of the Roman Catholic Church on women. For his part, Candace defended women's suffrage (again he was interrupted by applause) by drawing on European examples and the egalitarian principles of the French abolitionist Victor Schœlcher:[44]

> In 1848, in one fell swoop, France broke the chains of slavery and turned blacks into voters and candidates. Can we really let ourselves be stopped by procedural considerations when it comes to giving women the vote and the right to stand for election to municipal councils? ... Like many of my colleagues, I have the honour of being a member of the Inter-Parliamentary Union conference. In all European capitals ... we find women deputies, senators, mayors. We have even seen women ministers in England, America, Finland, and Norway, and yet you would be led by a kind of egotism peculiar to this country – whose ideal of justice is otherwise so laudable – using all kinds of arguments to avoid establishing equality between women and ourselves. Onward, then! ... Let us vote on the proposal ... by acclamation![45]

So, while he never missed an opportunity to declare his love for the France of 1789, Candace helped to highlight the limitations of the republican model put forward by secular liberals in terms of race and gender. However, electoral tactics restrained his actions. Candace was applauded mainly by the moderates, that centre-right, socially conservative grouping, which remained convinced, like the socialist and the secular and liberal left, that the vote for women would be subjected to the conservative influence of the Roman Catholic Church, which readily supported Candace's candidacy in Guadeloupe.[46]

Despite resistance by the literary world to Maran's book, *Batouala: A True Black Novel*, the black experience in politics seemed different in Candace's time than it was in the days of Légitimus. Rather than depicting just any black man, cartoonists drew the image of Candace (or Diagne). Humour became more subtle as black politicians were no longer a novelty for a generation that remembered Légitimus. Accent was no longer the issue it had been when he was a deputy. One still heard dubious jokes when a black speaker took the floor, such as Léon Daudet's 'do not eat him' in 1923, but shouts demanding the abolition of colonial representation were a thing of the past. The tendency for debate to give way to commotion and uproar when colonial issues were discussed, and black speakers took the floor seems to have faded after the Great War.[47] This is similar to the phenomenon observed decades later with female speakers. Despite living in a highly idealized France, Candace was well aware of these prejudices. When he split with Diagne in 1924, he invited him to put up his sword and not entertain the Chamber with the spectacle of a dispute between 'two black deputies'. This did not prevent the conservative Catholic provincial press from drawing the conclusion that black deputies were worthless.[48] Sources do not systematically mention Candace's skin colour, as was borne out by a very comprehensive 1925 parliamentary yearbook and a geography thesis from 1934 on the issue of a free-trade zone in Marseille.[49]

Candace's interventions on equal rights often attracted the approval of the Chamber, particularly in times of war. His denunciation in 1915 of the scandal over rotten cod intended for the 'Negroes of Martinique' was widely applauded. While mention of his name was often racialized in the media, there were many instances where it passed without comment. The word *nègre* was still used to refer to him until about 1910, but from then on there appeared to be growing indifference to his colour, although it was occasionally deemed useful to specify that he was 'coloured'. This was the case when he defended Maran. *Le Temps* had this to say: 'Mr. Gratien Candace is a black man. He is also a graduate of science; he was a teacher … he now sits in Parliament and is President of the Pan-African Association. What was said about *Batouala*, the novel penned by his fellow countryman, Mr. René Maran, offended him and he made us aware of his dissatisfaction.'[50] Nevertheless, there were no racial references when the press announced the composition of the 1932 and 1933 cabinets, in which Candace was appointed under-secretary of state. There are later testimonies relating to the presence of black parliamentarians, but these strongly underscore the biased views of authors who perceived black deputies as having the profession of being black. Referring to Diagne's and Candace's terms of office at the Palais-Bourbon, the journalist André Guérin only remembered light-hearted jokes about how the ancestors of one of them sold the ancestors of the other.[51] It is pointless trying to verify such comments from authors trapped in a stereotypical race-based perspective that eclipsed anything not in keeping with prevailing portrayals of blacks.[52] Racial references sometimes referred to stereotypes about cannibalism and brute force. Despite ostensible statements of sympathy for the 'black race', Léon Daudet's parliamentary memoirs contain numerous caricaturized illustrations. Candace is displayed with a menacing fist, with the repeated reminder that he is not a cannibal – a graphic description that relates back to the idea of a wild African force pacified in the service of France.[53]

In 1933, *Le Charivari* represented Candace as he hummed the hit song 'Yes, we have no bananas', wearing only a girdle of bananas reminiscent of Josephine Baker.[54] Four years earlier, Diagne was depicted as a cannibal wizard (a reference to Freemasonry) by the illustrator Sennep, who in 1935 sketched the Ethiopian Negus on a coconut tree in the company of two monkeys.[55]

Anxious to denounce discrimination against people of colour in France even if it meant denouncing the influence of foreigners – German, American and even British – depending on the circumstances, Candace, like Légitimus before him, often played on his own distinctiveness. He would readily speak of a '*nuit blanche*' (a sleepless night) on a case or his desire to be whitened (cleared) or to whiten his colleague Maurice Satineau, another deputy from Guadeloupe.[56]

Accustomed to travelling throughout France and a familiar figure at colonial exhibitions and conferences, Candace appeared on European film newsreels, at least during his two consecutive ministerial appointments in 1932 and 1933. As a result, he was particularly visible to French people accustomed to a paternalistic view of the colonial world. This visibility interacted with and contributed to building his black identity. There is no doubt that this biased view of colonial parliamentarians in metropolitan France limited their room for manoeuvre. More than their peers, black deputies had to demonstrate their loyalty to France through self-restraint and their status as a civilized people far from the wilderness. Candace made people laugh, but through constant racial self-derision. He was always affable, as if displaying the opposite of savagery in order to counteract the stereotypes of his social environment. Thus, in 1923, he and Diagne denounced racial discrimination in Paris blamed on Americans who had reverted to their savage state or even to their status as foreigners. In *L'Homme libre*, Candace decried the 'savage customs' introduced by Americans whom he invited to leave France. He was offended to see in 'our' Louis XVI salons the bad taste of their imported dances and invited them to be content with the Bois de Boulogne, a Parisian symbol of low-level prostitution.[57] In 1919, Achille René-Boisneuf, deputy from Guadeloupe, and Lagrosillière, from Martinique, protested the violence by American soldiers in France whom they described as savages from the Far West. Candace and Boisneuf joined forces in this tactic of reversing stereotypes aimed at demonstrating the civilized French identity of black colonials in contrast with the savagery of American foreigners. Another illustration of this is to be found in 1928 in Candace's platform for re-election as delegate of French Oceania to the High Council of Colonies.[58] In it he echoed the anti-Chinese themes rife in Tahiti with overtones of the so-called Yellow Peril of the late nineteenth century.

The propensity to attribute racial prejudice to foreigners did not prevent Candace from denouncing facts that he perceived as failings. This was the case in 1923 when he proposed an inquiry into the bullying of French people of colour in the streets of provincial towns by ignorant French or in 1931 when he wrote to Marshal Liautey condemning certain issues relating to the colonial exhibition.[59] The reversal of stereotypes came to the fore once again in his speeches of the 1930s, during the rise of Nazism, at a time when the term 'racism' was generally associated with the Nazi Party. When Candace celebrated his parliamentary jubilee at the Inter-Allied Circle in 1937, he was embraced by Herriot, Speaker of the House and three-time President of the Council. The *Dressdner Anzeiger* then wrote that the former head of government was a traitor to his race.[60] While the German press was targeting Frenchmen who accepted black politicians, racism appeared to be a foreign ideology. As in 1915 against the Germans and in 1923 against the Americans, denunciation of racial prejudice, renamed 'racism', became all the more admissible as it was one of the elements of the anti-Nazi and anti-German argument, with xenophobic overtones reminiscent of the Great War. Like his fellow colonial deputies, having been drawn towards the young International League against Racism and Anti-Semitism (LICA) founded in 1928 by secular and very left-wing Jews,[61] Candace claimed to represent civilization, unlike the Germans.[62] He opposed any possible German claim on the French colonies and described the Germans as barbarians and racists lacking the capacity to engage in colonial endeavours. For Candace and his colleagues, as for the LICA, racism and Hitler's ideology were anti-French. This logic was in line with that of the Marchandeau Decree of 21 April 1939 (the predecessor of the anti-racist law of 1972) against press offences linked to foreign activities in France.[63]

In addition to classic French and European political networks, Candace's originality derived from his contacts with an international black network and his desire to show that 'slower races' could be improved. W. E. B. Du Bois, upon learning in 1929 that the André Tardieu cabinet had included Alcide Delmont, from Martinique, wrote to him: 'I understand that M. Alcide Delmont is Under Secretary of State in Tardieu's cabinet and that he is a coloured man. If this is true, I wish very much to get an original photograph of M. Delmont and an account of his career.'[64]

From 1929 onwards, the post of under-secretary of state for the colonies was successively filled by people from the colonies: Delmont (Martinique) in 1929, Diagne (Senegal) in 1931, Candace in 1932–3 and Monnerville (French Guiana) in 1936.[65] In June 1936, when the anti-semite Xavier Vallat in an address to the Chamber stigmatized the new president of the Council, Léon Blum, for being a

Jew, an admirer wrote to him that entrusting the government to a 'kike' was less grave than leaving it to a black man.[66]

On 11 January 1938, Candace was elected vice-president of the Chamber of Deputies with 81 per cent of the votes, the second highest result and equal to that of the president of the Chamber, Herriot.[67] On 10 January 1939, he again ran for the vice-presidency, but the fragmentation of the left kept him behind Vallat. In the next round, Vallat was at 41 per cent, while Candace, reduced to 14 per cent of the vote, used a point of order to address the Chamber and affirm that his candidacy represented the fraternal union of all French people and that his presence in the chair as vice-president was linked to the concept of the French Empire. Left-wing abstentions allowed him to be elected with 58 per cent of the vote against Vallat, who remained at 41 per cent. Candace later reaffirmed in the LICA newspaper that his election was testimony of the lack of racial differentiation in France.[68] It is clear that defending the imperial cause and racial equality was in keeping with his own career. It is thus understandable that by the late 1930s Candace was seen as a representative of the empire.

In 1935, when Ethiopia was at the heart of a debate that was at the same time French, Guadeloupean and global, affecting the entire black Atlantic space of the 1930s, Candace, always anxious to find middle ground, tried to bring about a compromise. Together with nationalists and moderates he wanted to spare Mussolini, who had been perceived as a potential ally against Hitler since the Stresa conference in April 1935. He wanted a solution based on the transfer to Italy of non-ethnic Ethiopian peripheral land. This conciliatory position towards the *Duce* placed him rather on the right of the political spectrum, but he could not espouse the eminently negrophobic vision of French national-pacifists. Instead, he claimed that 'the black race has a civilization'. This placed him in a difficult situation both in Paris and in Guadeloupe, where tensions had arisen over a small Italian settlement from Campania.[69] Candace was publicly questioned on the Ethiopian issue in Marie-Galante (one of the islands of Guadeloupe) during the 1936 legislative elections.[70] His political milieu had difficulty accepting that one could support the equal rights of black Ethiopia against white Italy. This stance distinguished Candace from the hard right-wing and the anti-fascist anti-Italian left, but the nationalists of *Action Française* seized the opportunity to show that a black man had accepted a change in Ethiopian territory. This was enough to fuel criticism in Guadeloupe, where the theme of Ethiopia, as elsewhere in black America, ignited the 1935 and 1936 election campaigns. Candace was thus jeered at as a traitor to his race.[71]

A survivor of the Third Republic, 1940–53

By 1940, Candace's career had attained an unexpected level for a man from a modest rural household in Guadeloupe for whom the status of teacher embodied the pinnacle of success. However, his position and hegemony in Guadeloupe were threatened by his defeat in October 1938 by Senator Bérenger, against whom he had long been secretly campaigning. This failure reflects the erosion of his client base during the cantonal elections of 1934–7 and the municipal elections of 1935. However, he expected a number of the mayors elected in 1935 to guarantee him favourable ballots in 1937, which in turn had to provide a majority of electors (general and municipal councillors) for the senate elections. His post of vice-president, to which he was appointed in January 1938, became his fallback position, an essential symbol of his power in a strong legislative regime. Nonetheless, while he used his role with vigour, the position itself was weakened. Vice-President Candace was elected on the left thanks to republican discipline threatened by international events and also thanks to the imperative of imperial cohesion that he was supposed to represent. In his own words, Candace was the empire. Not electing him would be an insult to the populations from whom a new war effort would be requested in the event of conflict. His behaviour during the period 1940–4 therefore shows a self-satisfied figure wrapped up in his role as vice-president of the Chamber and systematically posing as the embodiment of the empire at the summit of the Republic. But the Republic itself disappeared and seemed to reject him when it returned four years later.

On 19 June 1940, when the government relocated to Bordeaux as it had done in 1870, Candace handed over a solemn open letter co-signed by colonial deputies Satineau and Diouf to the president of the Republic, Lebrun, urging him to continue the war through the empire. The appeal was in line with the one issued the previous day in London by the young Charles de Gaulle, a provisional brigadier general who had been named ephemeral under-secretary of state for war and national defence just three days earlier. This idea of power wielded through the empire implies the choice between capitulation and armistice. The military act of surrender on mainland France would allow the government to maintain a state of belligerency as an empire without breaking its alliance with the British. Satineau, Diouf and Candace had passports issued for North Africa, with the intention of moving the chambers.[72] For his part, the new head of government, Pétain, supported an armistice that would commit the government to establishing a separate peace while betraying the British alliance and risking the fate of the empire to the *vae victis* of the victor. Finally, armistice was signed on June 22. The two Guadeloupians remained in France, perhaps on the advice of Herriot. Diouf and others sailed on the liner *Massilia*. The parliamentarians who remained in metropolitan France then settled in Vichy.

Four days after the British bombardment of the French fleet in Mers-el-Kebir harbour on 3 July 1940, Candace, Flandin and Mistler formed the parliamentary delegation which arrived in full ceremonial dress to urge President Lebrun to resign.[73] Deputy Pierre Laval promised to give up his constitutional review project in return for Lebrun's resignation, but the matter came to a sudden end.[74] On July 10, at the Vichy casino, both Chambers of the National Assembly voted to give full powers to Pétain. We must resist the anachronistic view of regarding this as an adherence to the Vichy regime and a collaboration that was not yet in place. At the time Candace seemed to be looking for a reasonable solution after Mers-el-Kébir. The latter was bound to have affected him deeply, given his previous involvement with the Navy as a parliamentarian.

The period 1940–3 seemed to be an opportunity to learn from the past. In several publications, Candace lamented mistakes made in the always hoped-for but never achieved development of the colonies, regretting that the 1920 Sarraut plan was never implemented.[75] He is generally viewed as an expert on parliamentary business, acting in the Vichy regime as he did in the Republic. Jules Jeanneney, president of the Senate, was eager to ask for his opinions on important regulatory issues.[76] Police reports of his conversations in cafés show that he continued to refer to political parties and republican routine as if all this still existed in Vichy France. In 1940–2, he fiercely protested to Pétain about racial discrimination at the demarcation line between occupied and southern zones. While in August 1940 it still seemed logical to assume that France did not discriminate among her children, appealing to Pétain appeared increasingly discordant and less universal after the exclusion of Jews by the October 1940 Statute. Loyalty towards Pétain did not protect him from the animosity of pro-German Parisian collaborationists. In February 1942, he was violently attacked in *Au Pilori*, an ultra-collaborationist Parisian newspaper subsidized by the occupying forces.[77] Candace's black identity was presented by his caricatured but clearly identifiable face. As with all the other parliamentarians targeted by the newspaper's eponymous column, the attacks, which are poorly documented, ritually denounced the influence of this Freemason and businessman who was a member of the French League for Human Rights,[78] or featured his own uselessness and his Jewish friends in Parliament. Added to that was his complicity with the fraudster Satineau. The reprove followed in the wake of similar attacks against Monnerville (January 1942) and Diouf (December 1941).

While Pétain was considering the composition of his new government in April 1942,[79] Candace's republican identity came to the fore when a cabinet chief included his name on a draft list of republican personalities.[80] On 31 August 1942, along with the vice-presidents of both chambers, Candace added his name to a protest letter to Pétain against the Vel' d'Hiv roundup and the disappearance of the word *République*.[81] Nevertheless he continued visiting Pétain, putting his pen to articles on colonial France in a Toulouse daily newspaper, and broadcasting on the radio until the beginning of 1944.[82] Despite being perceived as a former republican, he never engaged in any real conflict with the regime.

In September 1943, Candace continued to subscribe to Pétain's legitimacy by virtue of the National Assembly vote on 10 July 1940 granting him full powers.[83] He was privately scandalized when de Gaulle established political institutions in Algiers in direct competition with the legitimacy of the elected representatives of the pre-1940 period. According to him, de Gaulle's approach was unjustified and it was Pétain's responsibility to restore to the representatives of the French people the powers they had given him in July 1940. However, on 21 April 1944, a lengthy *ordonnance* drawn up by de Gaulle relating to post-Liberation powers decreed female suffrage and declared ineligible the 569 'yes' votes of 10 July 1940. We now know that that vote does not serve to identify future resistance fighters and future collaborators, but that was nonetheless the opinion of those around de Gaulle. Returning to liberated Paris in August 1944, Candace again put forward his candidacy but was declared ineligible to hold office. Anxious to be seen as a former elected official of 1936 rather than a former Vichy representative, he continued to maintain a public life but announced his retirement after 1945.[84] His funeral in 1953 in Nogent-le-Roi, a small town near Dreux, was a very republican ceremony attended by local and national elected officials, firemen and gendarmes. This was followed by a 3,500-word tribute in the local newspaper and sixty-eight lines in *Le Monde*, glossing over the fact that he had tried to regain his foothold in 1945.[85]

Candace's long parliamentary career testifies to the possibility, albeit limited, that a black man might reach the pinnacle of French political life during the colonial era. Ostracized on account of his vote on 10 July 1940, Candace became a dissident for the majority of Guadeloupe's population, especially the left, even if a more right-wing section of the public saw him as an illustrious Guadeloupian. Just two out of thirty-six municipalities have named a street after him. He remains unknown today to most French people, some of whom may point to Monnerville, or even Diagne, as the black pioneer in politics. He was remembered in Guadeloupe when the presence of a Guadeloupean woman in the Alain Juppé government of 1995–7 brought back memories of the 1932–3 minister. More recently, on the occasion of the publication of *La France Noire*, an extreme right-wing personality posted on his blog a huge close-up of Candace, recalling his full endorsement of Pétain by underlining his membership in the 'Radical Left' without specifying that it was a centre-right group. The gesture reflected a common view on the far right of the links between the left and Vichy. Candace thus portrayed guilt in a black face. More seriously, his career testifies – with Diagne's shorter term in office and that of Monnerville at a later date – to the existence of precedents for today's debates and controversies regarding the diversity of France and its political figures.

Notes

1   Union interparlementaire, *Compte-rendu de la XXVème conférence tenue à Berlin, 23–28 août 1928* (Geneva: Payot, 1928), 420–3; *CR de la XXIXème conférence tenue à Madrid, 4–10 October 1933* (Geneva: Payot, 1933), 461–6.

2   J.-F. Schaub, 'La catégorie "études coloniales" est-elle indispensable? Do we need "colonial studies"?', *Annales. Histoire, Sciences Sociales*, 3 (August 2008): 625–46.

3   Michelle Zancarini-Fournel, *Une histoire nationale est-elle encore possible?* (Bordeaux: Presses Universitaires de Bordeaux, 2018), 45.

4   We are reminded here of the word employed by Sanjay Subrahmanyam in 'Connected histories: notes towards a reconfiguration of early modern Eurasia', in Victor Lieberman (ed.), *Beyond Binary Histories. Re-Imagining Eurasia to c.1830* (Ann Arbor: University of Michigan Press, 1999), 761.

5   See Eric Garcia-Moral's chapter on Blaise Diagne in this volume.

6   See Abel Alexis Louis's chapter on Cyrille Bissette in this volume.

7   Departmental archives of Haute-Garonne (Toulouse), letter from the academy inspector to the Board of Education in Toulouse (20 January 1904), cited by Émile R. Énoff, *Les parlementaires de la Guadeloupe, 1889–1958* (Le Gosier, Guadeloupe: PLB, 2013), 62.

8   On the dissemination of scholarly racial discourse and colonial imaginaries, see Carole Reynaud-Paligot, *Science, race et politique en Europe et aux États-Unis, XIXe–XXe siècle* (Paris: Presses Universitaires de France, 2011), 87–152; Frédéric Pineau and Élikia M'Bokolo, 'Indigènes: Premières présences et imaginaires coloniaux (1890–1913)', in *La France Noire, Trois siècles de présence*, ed. Pascal Blanchard (Paris: La Découverte, 2011), 66ff.

9   Departmental archives of Pyrénées-Atlantique (formerly Basses-Pyrénées),
     1 February 1907; National archives (Fr.), Instruction publique, CHAN, F17,
     AJ/16/998, G. Candace, professor, Creil, 1912.

10 Jacques Doriot (1898–1945): number two of the French Communist Party and then
     founder of the fascist and collaborationist French People's Party (PPF).

11 Philippe Cherdieu, 'La vie politique en Guadeloupe: L'affrontement Boisneuf-
     Légitimus, 1898–1914', Thèse de 3ᵉ cycle (Paris: IEP, 1981), 591–632.

12 Hégésippe Légitimus, deputy in 1898–1914.

13 SFIO (1905), which became the Socialist Party (French) in 1969.

14 *Journal officiel de la République française (JORF)* (7 July 1913); Yves Billard, 'Le
     Parti républicain socialiste, 1911–1934', PhD diss. (Paris-Sorbonne University,
     France, 1993), 165.

15 André Siegfried, *Tableau des partis en France* (Paris: Grasset, 1930), 172–3; René
     Rémond, *La droite en France de 1815 à nos jours* (Paris: Aubier, 1954), 197.

16 *Les modérés dans la vie politique française, 1870–1965*, ed. François Roth (Nancy:
     Presses Universitaires de Nancy, 2000), 3–18.

17 In the 1880s, the term 'far-left' was applied to the anti-clerical republicans. It referred
     to the Socialists around 1920 and later to the Communists in the mid-1930s.

18 Centre-left alliance without the participation of the Socialist SFIO (1924–6).

19 Serge Berstein, *Herriot ou la République en personne* (Paris: FNSP, 1985), 142.

20 Each deputy is theoretically a deputy for the entire French people.

21 Dominique Chathuant, 'D'une République à l'autre: Ascension et survie politique
     de Maurice Satineau (1891–1945)', *Bulletin de la Société d'histoire de la Guadeloupe*,
     178 (September–December 2017): 24–5.

22 Municipal elections in 1935, cantonal elections (partial renewal of the colony's
     general councillors following the example of the departments of metropolitan
     France) in 1934 and 1937, and legislative elections in 1936; Dominique Chathuant,
     'Gratien Candace, ascension et déclin d'un candidat officiel (1910–1946)', in *Les
     élections législatives et sénatoriales outre-mer, 1848–1981*, ed. Laurent Jalabert,
     Bertrand Joly and Jacques Weber (Paris: Les Indes savantes, 2010), 103–15.

23 This was the Paris *Préfet de police*, Jean Chiappe, who was dismissed from office by
     the centre-left government on 3 February 1934.

24 French National Archives, F17, AJ/16/998.

25 Radical (left), President of the Council (French Premier) 1924, 1926, 1932–3.

26 Briand started out close to the républicains socialistes (left) and then moved
     towards the centre. He was eleven times prime minister and twenty-six times
     minister.

27 Gratien Candace, *La Marine marchande française et son importance dans la vie
     nationale* (Paris: Payot, 1930); *La Marine de la France. Marine militaire, marine
     marchande* (Paris: Payot: 1938); 'Rapport sur le prix Lucien de Reinach', *Travaux de
     l'Académie des sciences morales et politiques* (November–December 1931): 362–4.

28 Legislative proposal for the establishment of free-trade zones I., no. 4679; an., SO (1927), 1121; ibid, 209, an., SO (1928), 220; ibid: discussion and adjournment request from Henry Le Mire, *JORF, Débats parlementaires* (1932): 607, 1193; new proposal from Candace on free-trade zones for sea and inland waterways, I., no. 4958; an., SO (1935), 560.

29 *JORF* (25 February 1933): 1059. For: 305 (left). Against: 205.

30 LICA from 1928 to 1979 then LICRA. Even during the LICA period, the word 'racism' was used.

31 'Pas de colonies pour les racistes' and Galandou-Diouf, 'Un crime: céder nos colonies aux barbares', *Le Droit de vivre* (11 March 1939). Gaston Monnerville, Black Guianan, Under-Secretary of State for the Colonies in 1937–8, Resistance fighter, President of the Senate from 1947 to 1968. In 1962, he denounced the constitutional reform of de Gaulle aimed at electing the President of the Republic by universal suffrage, describing it as a Caesarist temptation, a term which, in the French political culture, refers to the 1851 coup d'état by Louis-Napoleon Bonaparte or even that of his uncle in 1799.

32 *JORF*, Chambre (26 June 1912): 2; 794.

33 Subsequent justification by the collaborator Henri Labroue of his parliamentary attitude in 1915: 'Racisme et service militaire des noirs', *Au pilori*, 10 February 1944; Dick van Galen Last, Ralf Duurt Futselaar and Paul-Louis Van Berg, *Des soldats noirs dans une guerre de blancs, 1914–1922. Une histoire mondiale* (Brussels: Éditions de l'Université, 2015).

34 On these topics, see Jacques Dumont, *L' Amère patrie. Histoire des Antilles françaises au XXe siècle* (Paris: Fayard, 2010), 71ff and 'Conscription antillaise et citoyenneté revendiquée', *Vingtième Siècle. Revue d'histoire*, 92 (October–December 2006): 103; Serge-Mam Lam Fouck, *Histoire de l'assimilation, des 'vieilles colonies' françaises aux départements d'outre-mer. La culture politique de l'assimilation aux Antilles et en Guyane françaises, XIXe et XXe siècle* (Matoury: Ibis Rouge, 2006), 15ff; Dominique Chathuant, 'L'assimilationnisme', in *Études guadeloupéennes*, Special issue, ed. Cyril Serva (Pointe-à-Pitre: Jasor, 2001), 111–22.

35 Jack Corzani, 'Conscription', *Dictionnaire encyclopédique Antilles-Guyane* 3 (Fort-de-France: Désormeaux, 1992), 713–4.

36 Iba Der Thiam, *Le Sénégal dans la guerre 14–18 ou le prix du combat pour l'égalité* (Dakar: Nouvelles éditions africaines du Sénégal, 1992), 42–4; George W. Johnson, *The Emergence of Black Politics in Senegal, The Struggle for Power in the Four Communes, 1900–1920* (Stanford: Stanford University Press, 1971), 178.

37 Recently published on this question: Julie d'Andurain, 'La genèse intellectuelle de la Force noire', in *Combattants de l'empire. Les troupes coloniales et la Grande Guerre*, ed. Philippe Buton and Marc Michel (Paris: Vendémiaire, 2018), 11–28.

38 *JORF*, Chambre (28 January 1915): 51; (17 December 1915): vol. 2, 2174ff; Yves Pourcher, *Pierre Laval vu par sa fille d'après ses carnets intimes* (Paris: Le Cherche-midi, 2002), 31.

39 Paligot, *Identité nationale*, 144.

40 Ibeanachor Egonu, 'Le prix Goncourt de 1921 et la "querelle de Batouala"', *Research in African Literatures* (Winter 1980): 529–45; J. L., 'A propos de Batouala', *Le Temps*, 25 February 1922, 1; Léon Daudet, 'Après le prix Goncourt', *L'Action française*, 16 December 1921, 1; Paul Souday, 'Les livres', *Le Temps*, 15 December 1921, 3; Gilbert Charles, 'Les lauréats d'hier', *Le Figaro*, 15 December 1921, 1. *Le Temps* was the leading daily newspaper of reference; it was later replaced by *Le Monde*.

41 *La Dépêche coloniale*, 8 January 1922; Carl Siger, 'Questions coloniales – Littérature et colonies', *Le Mercure de France*, 15 February 1922, 197–208; Paul Souday, 'Autour du prix Goncourt', *Le Temps*, 16 December 1921.

42 J. L., 'La logique noire', *Le Temps*, 18 February 1922, 1.

43 J. L., 'A propos de Batouala', *Le Temps*, 25 February 1922, 1.

44 Billard, *Parti républicain-socialiste*, 133; 'Barodet' (1919); *JORF*, Chambre (1 March 1935): 792; Christine Vérot, 'La question du vote des femmes devant le parlement dans l'entre-deux guerres', MA thesis (Charles de Gaulle University – Lille III, France, 1987), 100.

45 *JORF* (1935). Votes: 541. For: 305. Against: 236. The applause came from the centre, the right and several benches on the left.

46 'Radical' in the French sense, i.e. republican and lay.

47 *JORF* (22 December 1924): 4733.

48 J. Mollet, 'Un interminable débat sur le budget des colonies', *L'Ouest-Éclair* (23 December 1924): 2.

49 Gilles Normand, *Politiques et hommes politiques, Esquisse d'un recensement des compétences politiques du temps*, vol. 1, *Les avenues du pouvoir* (Paris: Perrin, 1925), 200–1; Gaston Rambert, *Marseille, la formation d'une grande cité moderne. Étude de géographie* (Marseille: Société Anonyme du Sémaphore, 1934), 482.

50 J. L., 'La logique noire'.

51 André Guérin, *La vie quotidienne au Palais-Bourbon sous la Troisième République* (Paris: Hachette, 1978), 73.

52 Maurice Martin du Gard, *Chronique de Vichy, 1940–1944* (Paris: Flammarion, 1948), 353.

53 Léon Daudet, *Député de Paris, 1919–1924* (Paris: Grasset, 1933) and *Paris vécu* (Paris: Gallimard-NRF, 1930), in *Souvenirs et polémiques, Recueil commenté par B. Oudin* (Paris: Robert Laffont, 1992), 819, 1137.

54 A reference to a song by Frank Silver and Irving Cohn, interpreted in 1923 by Eddie Cantor's musical revue in New York.

55 *Le Charivari*, 23 September 1933, 378; Jean Sennep, *Cartel et Cie* (Paris: Bossard, 1926); François Mauriac, *Le Figaro*, 24 September 1935; 'Qu'est-ce qu'un barbare?', *L'Action française*, 26 September 1935.

56 *Le Figaro*, 3 July 1936; *L' Action française*, 3 July 1936; *Le Temps*, 5 June 1938; Chathuant, 'D'une République' (2017), 26. Available online: https://doi.org/10.7202/1045699ar (accessed 5 February 2021).

57 Gratien Candace, 'Préjugé de couleur, il est temps que cela cesse', *L' Homme libre*,
    11 August 1923.

58 Gratien Candace, *Ce qu'il a fait pour les Établissements français de l'Océanie,
    1924–1928*, electoral brochure (Paris: Imprimerie Maulde et Renou, 1928), 4–7.

59 'Discussion of an inquiry into incidents caused daily in Paris and the provinces by a
    number of foreign tourists and French traders who insult and harass French people
    of the black race solely because of the color of their skin', *JORF*, table (13 November
    1923): 3506; Brigitta Kuster, 'Zur Exposition koloniale Internationale, Paris 1931',
    in *Das Unbehagen im Museum: postkoloniale Museologien*, ed. Belinda Kazeem,
    Charlotte Martinz-Turek and Nora Sternfeld (Vienna: Turia + Kant, 2009), 77–109.

60 Gaston Monnerville, *Témoignage. De la France équinoxiale au Palais du
    Luxembourg* (Paris: Plon, 1975), 101.

61 LICRA since 1979 but the term 'racism' has always been employed; see Emmanuel
    Debono, *Aux origines de l'antiracisme: la LICA, 1927–1940* (Paris: CNRS, 2012).

62 'Pas de colonies pour les racistes' and Galandou-Diouf, 'Un crime: Céder nos
    colonies aux barbares', *Le Droit de vivre*, 11 March 1939.

63 Debono, *LICA*, 376ff.

64 Du Bois to Candace (19 December 1929); Candace to Du Bois (14 January 1930)
    (Amherst MA: W. E. B Du Bois Library). Delmont was a mulatto in Martinique,
    went unnoticed in Paris but remained 'coloured' in the United States.

65 Dominique Chathuant, 'Une élite politique noire dans la France du premier 20e
    siècle?', *Vingtième siècle. Revue d'histoire*, 101 (January–March 2009): 133–48.

66 *JORF*, debates, Chambre (7 June 1936): 1327; Laurent Joly, *Xavier Vallat, du
    nationalisme chrétien à l'antisémitisme d'État, 1891–1972* (Paris: Grasset, 2001),
    130, 160.

67 *JORF*, debates, Chambre (12 January 1938): 3.

68 Gratien Candace, 'La leçon d'une élection: union des races!', *Le Droit de vivre*,
    23 January 1939.

69 Dep. Archives of Guadeloupe, C. 6213, Governor's office; Marthe Oulié, *Les
    Antilles, filles de France* (Paris: Fasquelle, 1935), 165.

70 Dominique Chathuant, 'Entre gauches et droites, entre Paris et Guadeloupe:
    polémiques autour du conflit italo-éthiopien (1935)', *Bulletin de la Société d'histoire
    de la Guadeloupe*, 160 (September–December 2011): 40–56.

71 Chathuant, 'Autour du conflit italo-éthiopien'; Governor Bouge's papers,
    GUA V–VI: rapport de gendarmerie (26 May 1936); electoral leaflet (Chartres:
    Art Gallery, 1936); Kevin A. Yelvington, 'The War in Ethiopia and Trinidad,
    1935–1936', in Bridget Brereton and Kevin A. Yelvington, eds., *The Colonial
    Caribbean in Transition: Essays on postemancipation social and cultural history*
    (Kingston, Jamaica: University of the West Indies, 1999), 189; Kevin A. Yelvington,
    'Dislocando la diáspora: la reacción al conflicto italo-etíope en el Caribe, 1935–
    1941', *Estudios Migratorios Latinoamericanos* (2003): 555–77

72 Charles Pomaret, *Le dernier témoin* (Paris: Presses de la Cité, 1968), 204.

73 In certain circumstances, parliamentarians wore top hats and frock coats, in particular for the election of the President of the Republic by the National Assembly, which, at the time, consisted in a joint session of the two Chambers in Versailles.

74 'Interrogatoire de Pierre-Etienne Flandin', *Le Monde*, 13 November 1945; Édouard Barthe, *Le combat d'un parlementaire sous Vichy. Journal des années de guerre, 1940–1943* (Sète: Singulières, 2007), 134; Albert Lebrun, *Témoignage* (Paris: Plon, 1945), 105; Robert Aron, *Histoire de Vichy* (Paris: Plon, 1950), 94; Jules Jeanneney, *Journal politique* (Paris: Armand Colin, 1972), 435.

75 Gratien Candace, 'Les Antilles, berceau de la colonisation française', *Les Cahiers de France, Organe de la Révolution nationale* (Clermont-Ferrand: 1942), 59; Candace, 'Économie franco-coloniale', *La Dépêche de Toulouse*, 17 December 1940.

76 Jeanneney, *Journal politique*, 291.

77 Jean Théroigne, 'Nous clouons au pilori: Gratien Candace', *Au pilori*, 26 February 1942.

78 Ligue des droits de l'Homme (LDH), founded during the Dreyfus affair in 1898.

79 Robert O. Paxton, *Vichy France, 1940–44. Old Guard and New Order* (New York: Columbia University Press, 1972), 131.

80 Henry du Moulin de Labarthète, *Le Temps des illusions. Souvenirs, July 1940–April 1942* (Geneva: Le Cheval Ailé, 1946); François-Georges Dreyfus, *Histoire de Vichy* (Paris: Perrin, 1990), 612; the private papers of Moulin de Labarthète (Arch. Nat. Fr., 474 AP 1–2) were scoured without success.

81 Jeanneney, *Journal politique*, 318; Arch. nat. Fr., Jury d'honneur du Conseil d'État, AL5303: G. Candace, 'Quelques traits de mon action politique de 1939 à 1945' [A few aspects of my political actions from 1939 to 1945], Statement of defense for the Court of Honor of the *Conseil d'État* (14 July 1945).

82 *La Dépêche de Toulouse* (1940-4); INA: État Français (Vichy): National broadcasting, 1942-4.

83 Elected in 1936 by direct universal male suffrage (Chamber) and in 1932, 1935 and 1938 by indirect universal male suffrage (Senate). Center of Contemporary Archives, Fontainebleau, police note (RG) of 19 November 1943, MA 34 JP/AG, 19800280/8/2127.

84 'M. Pierre-Etienne Flandin participera au 34e congrès de l'Alliance démocratique', *Le Monde*, 5 February 1948; Jacques Fauvet, 'M. Pierre-Etienne Flandin condamne la juridiction d'exception et l'inéligibilité', ibid., 10 February 1948; J. F., 'Le dimanche politique: le banquet des Mille ou le retour des Anciens', ibid., 16 March 1948.

85 *Le Monde*, 14 April 1953; 'A Nogent-le-Roi, sous la pluie, les obsèques de M. Gratien Candace, ancien ministre, ancien vice-président de la Chambre des Députés', *L'Écho républicain*, 15 April 1953.

10

Blaise Diagne: French parliamentarian from Senegal

Eric Garcia-Moral

In May 1914 the Senegalese Blaise Diagne became the first African representative elected to the French Chamber of Deputies.[1] From that moment until his death in 1934, Diagne was re-elected in four consecutive legislative elections, was appointed to be general commissioner of black troops during the First World War (a post equivalent to that of governor general) and was Under-Secretary of State for the Colonies in 1931–2. His was an exceptional career in every way, and one that requires explanation.

From Gorée to French Guiana, 1872–1914

At the end of the nineteenth century, the Four Communes of Senegal (Saint-Louis, Gorée, Dakar and Rufisque) had three important local governmental institutions: a parliamentary representative (called a deputy), municipal councils and a General Council. In the mid-century, the local councils had been the only sites effectively controlled by the French. Starting in 1848, Saint-Louis and Gorée had the right to choose a representative to the National Assembly.[2] In 1872 both were given the rights of French municipalities. Rufisque attained that status in 1880, and Dakar did so in 1887. An 1890 decree placed the Four Communes and their outlying territories, along with areas affected by the railway between Saint-Louis and Dakar, under direct administration. The rest of Senegal occupied after the conquest officially remained a protectorate. While inhabitants of directly administered areas gradually won rights, the remaining inhabitants continued being French subjects (*sujets*). So the laws applied to residents of the communes, known as *originaires*, differed little from those in the metropolis, permitting them to participate in local government with similar institutions.[3]

Until the twentieth century the municipal councils were dominated by members of the Creole oligarchy and by Frenchmen working as agents for commercial houses based in Bordeaux and Marseilles. The General Council, given its budgetary powers, was the most important political arena in the colony until the 1910s and was controlled by the Creole aristocracy during its first forty years of existence. The aristocracy controlled the parliamentary seat until 1852, when Louis Napoleon ordered an end to colonial representation in Paris.[4] By the time the Third Republic re-established the seat in 1871, the social and political situation in the communes had changed. The colony of Senegal had expanded and the Creole aristocracy had ceded power to the rising community linked to business and commerce based in France. Dakar and Rufisque, undergoing economic and demographic growth and where the French population had far greater interests than in the old communes of Saint-Louis and Gorée, both voted for the first time after the re-creation of the seat. From 1871 to 1901, the seat was always occupied by Frenchmen, but starting in 1898 it was clear that Creoles were gaining electoral strength; they dominated Saint-Louis and Gorée, had influence in Rufisque and were the most important group in the General Council. François Carpot, a Creole lawyer who enjoyed the support of several leading families, became Senegal's parliamentarian in 1902, the start of an era in which that post became the most important institution. There were significant changes in France's sub-Saharan colonies during Carpot's years in office. The most important of these was the 1902 transfer of the capital of French West Africa to Dakar. Ever since the creation of the federation in 1895, Saint-Louis had been the capital, both of the federation and the colony of Senegal. The change put distance between the Senegalese governor and his superior, the governor general, in Dakar, and complicated his relationship with the metropolis. The deputy, on the other hand, had direct contact with Paris, and it was through him that Senegal deployed influence and power in colonial affairs, a relationship unlike any other between France and its sub-Saharan colonies.

Blaise Diagne was born in Gorée in October 1872. His father was a Serer named Niokhor Diagne, and his mother was a Manjak named Gnagna Preira.[5] He was adopted by Adolph Crespin, a member of one of the most important Creole families in the colony. Crespin took charge of his education until Diagne was in the Duval school in Saint-Louis in 1890. Two years later the young man passed his exams to join the colonial customs service, where he began in November 1892 as a second-class commissioner (*commis*).[6]

From 1892 to 1914 Diagne worked for the customs service in various French colonies: Dahomey (1892–7), French Congo (1897–8), Réunion (1899–1902),

Madagascar (1902–9) and French Guiana (1909–13).[7] During these years, his pragmatic yet combative nature, combined with his clear awareness of prejudice arising from his skin colour, led him to frequently challenge the administration, resulting in disciplinary measures against him. While he was outside Senegal, Diagne joined the Masons, and on 21 September 1899, was accepted into the Amitié lodge on Réunion; he was interested in acquiring a support system to protect his person and actions in a hostile colonial environment. From then on, Diagne made it clear he wished to be stationed in colonies with Masonic lodges. In his correspondence with the Conseil de l'Ordre du Gran Orient de France, he expressed unhappiness with the administration. He also joined two lodges in Madagascar: L' Indépendance Malgache of Tematave, in 1906; and Loge France Australe of Tannanarive, in 1907.[8]

In 1907 his first son was born, to a Frenchwoman named Marie Odette Villain. This was a key moment in his political career because his family was to become an important part of his discourse in his speeches on behalf of the Senegalese people. After a leave of absence in the metropolis, he returned to Madagascar and continued annoying the colonial upper ranks, who soon wished to get rid of him. In 1909 he married, making his unprecedented relationship official. Sending him to an African colony might constitute a bad example, it was thought, so he was sent to French Guiana (in 1909–13), where he joined two different lodges and began establishing contacts with African representatives and with Africans in France. He also discovered his political vocation, becoming a member of the Saint-Laurent council, which actually he was not allowed to do as a civil servant. He gained the support of Governor Fernand Levecque, another Mason, who in 1913 authorized him to go to France to sit for an examination for a higher job, from where Diagne planned his return to Senegal. In 1912 a decree made it illegal for any African who had left the Four Communes to seek the protection of French or Muslim law; rather, they were subject to the summary administrative justice system (the *code de l'indigénat*) just like all the other subjects of the protectorate. The decree set off protests among Africans in the Four Communes, who understood that the rights they had acquired over the past fifty years were now being threatened.[9]

The birth of the deputy: the 1914 elections

Before February 1914 Blaise Diagne was nearly unknown in the Four Communes. One of the politically and intellectually active African electoral groups, the

Jeunes Sénégalais, did not even bother promoting an African candidate. Instead, they supported a French candidate, Jean Théveniaut, an administrator from Baol province who was linked to Senegal's most important newspaper, *La Démocratie du Sénégal*, founded in 1913 by Jean Daramy d'Oxoby, a Frenchman who lived in the colony. But at the end of that same year, Théveniaut and d'Oxoby broke off their friendship, and the former withdrew his financial support for the latter's newspaper. With that, the Jeunes Sénégalais had no viable candidate. At the same time, François Pouye, a former administrator of Gorée, arrived in Senegal, having been sent by Diagne to investigate possible reactions to a new candidate. Among the *jeunes*, only Galandou Diouf, elected in 1909 in Rufisque as a representative to the Colonial Council, showed any interest in Pouye's suggestion to propose Diagne for a post that not even Diagne himself had aspired to.[10] The administration did not think much of Diagne's opportunities and counted on the victory of the outgoing deputy, François Carpot.[11] But in a campaign full of rallies and gatherings that galvanized the electorate against big business and the administration, along with his private contacts and dealings, Diagne won the support of many Lebu people (the majority ethnicity in Dakar and Rufisque and the second-largest group in the Four Communes after the Wolof) as well as that of the Muslim Mouride brotherhood, one of the most influential in Senegal, thanks to the brotherhood's founder, Sheikh Ahmadou Bamba, whom Diagne had known when Bamba was exile in the French Congo. Diagne won over the support of some French colonists and merchants, and, along with Diouf, managed to convince the Jeunes Sénégalais despite the reticence of their leader, Thiécouta Diop. With that he became political director of the newspaper *La Démocratie*, which became the propaganda vehicle for his candidacy.[12]

The elections were held on 26 April, and Diagne won in the first round, with 1,910 votes against 671 for the second-highest candidate, Carpot.[13] The fact that there were seven Creole and French candidates meant that the vote was split among them and Diagne had not obtained a majority of registered voters, leading to a second round on 10 May. All the other candidates, including representatives of the great Bordeaux commercial companies and the Saint-Louis Creole aristocracy, devised a strategy against him. Henri Heimburger, the candidate of the Devès family (which controlled Saint-Louis and the General Council) was chosen to be the opposing bloc's candidate against Diagne.[14] Even so, family rivalries among the Creole aristocrats were such that Carpot rejected their consensus choice and decided to run again in the second round, fearing that Heimburger's victory would signal the definitive rise of the Devès group over his own.[15] And two of the Creole candidates, George Crespin and Louis

Pellegrin, realizing that the alliance was one based on race, decided to support Diagne in the second round. Thus, the Creole community committed political suicide, dividing their support among Heimburger, Carpot and Diagne.[16]

Diagne saw the coalition as an alliance among his rivals with big business and the administration, and believed that it also marked a clear racial line that would push the native population to vote for him, acting in favour of their own survival. Nevertheless, during the campaign he called upon Europeans as well as Africans: 'This country belongs to the three elements that live there, and in equal measure. We want justice and legal rights for all. Claiming rights for the natives never meant that we were intending to take them away from the others.'[17]

Divisions among the Creoles was the key to Diagne's victory in the second round, in which he got 2,424 votes, edging Heimburger by fewer than two hundred votes and soundly defeating Carpot, who received just 472.[18] No one was unaffected by his election. In Paris, the Ministry of the Colonies demanded an explanation, and many Bordeaux merchants complained to the office of the Governor General in Dakar. The possibility of annulling the vote was even considered in the Chamber of Deputies session of 7 July 1914, when a report by G. M. Leredu about the Senegalese elections was presented. The question of the electoral rights of indigenous peoples was discussed, and the report ended up validating Diagne's election as deputy for Senegal.[19]

Citizenship and blood tax: Diagne and the First World War

Just six weeks after Diagne's election and barely twenty days after the Leredu report was presented, the First World War began. The conflict provided Diagne with the opportunity to elucidate the rights of the *originaires*. After numerous efforts in the Chamber and the Four Communes, where Diagne encouraged the *originaires* to refuse to fight in the colonial armies, the deputy managed to get a bill approved that stipulated that recruits from the Four Communes would be incorporated into European armies.[20] The legislation, known as the first Diagne law, quickly drew the attention of Governor Raphaël Antonetti, who pointed to three dangerous results: a divide between the communes and the protectorate because of different types of military service; the complete takeover of local government by urban Africans; and the fact that Diagne had pressured for the law to be applied not only to *originaires* but also to Africans who had an *originaire* father.[21] Though *La Démocratie du Sénégal* tried to encourage recruitment and glorified the role not just of the *originaires* but also of the *tirailleurs* (colonial soldiers recruited in sub-Saharan French possessions), the first Diagne law did not lead to a significant increase in the number of volunteers.[22]

Having returned to Paris, Diagne understood that the 1915 law left two major questions unresolved. The first was the political status of the *originaires*, and the second was the question of French citizenship.[23] The urgency of the war could play in his favour, given that military service could be seen as a toll required to become a citizen. The need for troops and Diagne's persuasiveness were such that on 29 September 1916, the Chamber adopted a bill with just one article: 'The natives of Senegal's established townships and their descendants are and shall remain French citizens subject to the military obligations provided for by the law of 19 October 1915.'[24] From then on there would be no legal doubt that *originaires* and their children, regardless of where they were born, were French citizens. This was a crucial step in the politics of assimilation, and Diagne's allies in Senegal regarded the law as a legislative triumph.[25] It reignited the debate regarding colonial subjects' and citizens' rights and obligations and about the process through which French citizenship could and should be acquired, guaranteed and recognized.[26]

The administration issued several reports about problems arising from the Diagne laws. They pointed to the incompatibility between French civil code and Islam. There was fear that the laws might disturb Africans in the colonies who were not *originaires*.[27] Business circles tried to prevent the bill from being passed, leading to a confrontation between Diagne and the Union Colonial, a merchants organization that, starting in early 1916, was the centre of opposition against him.[28] Even before the second bill was passed, the Union Colonial accused Diagne of using it to register a vast number of people as inhabitants or *originaires* of the communes.[29] The idea that the law was part of an operation devised by Diagne to obtain more votes was common in commercial and colonial circles and also was reflected in the French press. According to Bordeaux, Diagne's growing electoral support was a direct threat to business.[30] In the months following passage of the Diagne laws, the deputy turned his attention to the Senegalese *tirailleurs*, trying to improve the working conditions of colonial soldiers in the war. When another deputy said that Diagne was not the only one concerned about the *tirailleurs*, Diagne replied, 'if they are of interest to us all, they are of double interest to me, and even more than that', reminding his interlocutor of the broken promises made to the families of African soldiers.[31]

The year 1918 was key in Diagne's consolidation as a broker in the metropolis. His laws were his first political efforts and had a certain impact on public opinion, but what lay ahead would provide a true jolt; during his first term in office he obtained not only citizenship for the *originaires* but also carved out areas of power for himself that were unimaginable for an indigenous politician in the colonies. In 1918 the French government organized a military recruitment drive in West Africa, and in order to win African support the colonial minister, Henri Simon, decided to make a significant gesture by putting Diagne in charge of preparing the levy. In exchange, he promised that recruits and their families would get improvements in their living situation and that French West Africa (AOF) infrastructure would also be improved.[32] Diagne received the title of 'commissioner of the Republic in West Africa', similar in rank and privilege to colonial governors.[33] Governor Joost Van Vollenhoven quit in protest soon after Diagne's appointment.[34] From the perspective of the French government, Diagne's mission, which ended in August 1918, was a success; though the goal had been to recruit forty thousand men, in fact sixty thousand joined, and twenty thousand more joined them soon afterwards. Diagne was praised by French officials in France and in Africa, and Prime Minister Georges Clemenceau offered him the Legion of Honour, which Diagne turned down by saying that he regarded his efforts as simply his duty during wartime.[35]

The Union Coloniale, however, did not look upon the mission positively and nor did some members of the administration, who thought Diagne had undertaken the effort solely to increase his own prestige and influence. They accused him of having caused the departure of Van Vollenhoven, who later was killed in the war. A subsequent governor, Gabriel Angoulavant, would also leave. According to his opponents, Diagne was injecting racial hatred into Senegal, setting Africans against Europeans, and his pernicious influence was spreading to all the territories of French West Africa.[36] There also was opposition from within the military hierarchy, where one of the French generals active during the mission, General Bounnier, said Diagne's appointment had been unfortunate. In his opinion, Deputy Diagne represented Senegal, not everyone in the AOF, and had given *originaires* favourable treatment.[37] Some members of the administration shared this viewpoint, saying Diagne wished to expand his own power over the peoples of West Africa.[38] These allegations found their way into the press, which even published criticism by leaders of the *tirailleurs* such as Abd-el-Kader Mademba, who accused Diagne of trying to represent all French Africans and eliminate his political rivals.[39] During the mission some accused Diagne of seeking promotions for his friends and political allies and sympathizers and of removing those opposed to him.[40]

The following year, Diagne changed the name of *La Démocratie* to *L' Ouest Africain Français*, confirming the opinions of African officials and chiefs who said the Senegalese deputy considered himself to be the spokesman and representative of all French Africa. While the mission strengthened his prestige, it also encouraged recriminations against the *originaires'* privileges and the first accusations of collaborationism.[41] Such attitudes only intensified once promises made during the mission were not fulfilled, leading people to think that Diagne had sent his people to die in someone else's war.[42] Even so, the notion that the colonies had paid a blood tax would in the future justify all demands put forward by colonial deputies.[43]

The Diagnist era, 1919–23

By the time of the 1919 elections, Diagne's power was at its peak and he was ready to make his decisive move in the Four Communes. Years before the mission, leading economic figures had already sounded the alarm regarding his possible re-election and the need to prevent it, or at least not favour it.[44] Their greatest fear was that the Senegalese politician and his supporters would end up taking over local political institutions. Because of the Diagne laws, a significant number of people went to the Four Communes to demand recognition as *originaires* and attain French citizenship. The system for doing this was called *judgement supplétif*, in which the petitioner brought witnesses who swore that he had been born in one of the Four Communes or that his parents were *originaires*.[45] There were many doubtful cases, or cases of fraud, encouraging complaints from those who opposed the Diagne laws. According to a report by the governor's office, the electorate grew from 8,710 people in 1914 to 13,572 people in 1919. On election day there were 16,015 people registered.[46]

In their electoral propaganda, the Diagne camp used slogans appealing to the *originaires'* wish for political liberty and independence.[47] Basing his candidacy on the achievements during his tenure in office, Diagne once again confronted the leading merchants.[48] To the voters, he presented himself as a politician who had fulfilled the electoral mandate he received in 1914. He also turned to his 'European compatriots', once again pointing to his close relationship to them through his wife and his children, emphasizing that the rational, not brutish, evolution of Africans would bring glory and honour to France. Finally, he referred implicitly to their sacrifices during the war: 'you will go to the polls for the full and complete emancipation of this proletariat which, in the view of the whole world, has just covered itself in immortal glory'.[49] Meanwhile, Carpot, though his programme was not all that different from Diagne's, presented himself as the candidate of social peace and unity among all sectors of the population. His electoral materials attacked Diagne's activities during the war, saying he had sent many men to their deaths while he himself remained safe. He said Diagne was trying to stir up rivalries between the races and warned *originaires* that if they wished to be citizens they would have to choose between the law of the Koran and the law of France.[50] In reply, Diagne declared: 'French citizens you are! French citizens you will remain, moreover, without your personal status being affected ... One can be French and Muslim!'[51]

During the fierce campaign that began in November, in which the 1918 mission along with the laws of 1915 and 1916 were criticized, Diagne founded the Socialist Republican Party of Senegal and kept a low profile, with few public appearances, leaving his closest aides to manage the debates and rallies. He also announced that *Ouest Africain Français* was no longer the mouthpiece of the Jeunes Sénégalais, as he and the organization's leader, Thiecouta Diop, were enemies, but rather the mouthpiece of his new party.[52] Despite all the attacks, Diagne's victory was overwhelming: he received 7,444 votes, while Carpot got just 1,252.[53] In the December municipal elections, his party won complete control of local governments in the Four Communes. The only Frenchmen elected were his followers; three of his principal associates – Amadou Duguay-Clédor, Galandou Diouf and Jules Sergent – were elected to be mayors. Of Diagne's closest aides, only d'Oxoby did not run for municipal office, though he did present his candidacy for a seat in the General Council in the 4 January 1920 elections.[54] Once again, Diagne's followers were victorious, and the Creole stronghold passed over to Africans. While the 1914 election had quickly been overshadowed by the war, that of 1919 was different. Journalists, politicians and members of the colonial power structure expressed concern over the radical changes occurring in Senegal. If indeed there was a revolution in the colony, understood to be a profound change among those holding political positions, it occurred in 1919, not 1914.

During the campaign Diagne styled himself as the candidate of the Lebus and the Jeanes Sénégalais, while Carpot ran as the candidate of an alliance between Bordeaux and the Creole families. The French press depicted him as the candidate of unity, opposed to what was coming to be known as Diagnism.[55] The term appeared for the first time in the press referring to Diagne's close relationship with Henry Simon, the colonial minister, who was accused of lending official support to the candidacy of a man allegedly threatening colonialism.[56] Efforts to attack the outgoing deputy reached Paris, where newspapers such as *Le Soir* and *La Démocratie Nouvelle* accused him of wishing to replace all the French officials in West Africa with Africans.[57] In the colony, *L'AOF* opened the campaign with a front-page article saying Diagnism wanted to set society against commerce.[58]

Diagne's victory occurred as colonialists were beginning to question the theory of assimilation, which was gradually replaced with so-called association. Political awareness among urban dwellers and Diagne's victory spurred arguments in favour of putting an end to assimilation. In the face of growing numbers of *évolués* asking for political equality and who, under Diagne's leadership, posed a danger, Dakar political circles began arguing that African society would be better off if traditional chiefs maintained power and were consulted and instructed by the French. Thanks to their education, these chiefs could then 'civilize' the rural masses whom they also represented.[59] As Conklin points out, this political adjustment in Dakar was motivated by a desire to contain the *évolués*. Albert Sarraut, the most powerful of the colonial ministers during the interwar years and a firm reformist, said in 1921 that a new era of 'association' was about to begin in the empire, in which old and new elites would be guaranteed some sort of representative assemblies.[60]

A report drawn up by the administration in the early 1920s spoke of 'Diagnism' as a multiform phenomenon with two faces, metropolitan and African. According to that thesis, in Paris Diagne presented himself as a defender of French colonization, while in Senegal he stirred up trouble. The report stated that after 1918, Diagne defeated or forced the withdrawal of many candidates for posts in the colonial administration. The challenge was understood to be a dangerous one that could inspire certain sectors of the population, such as demobilized soldiers, to act similarly:

> In Senegal, there is an increasingly prevalent mentality which views Europeans as exploiters and tyrants, while indigenous people have all the rights and duties, and where above the law, above the Administration, above the direct representative of the Government itself, the sovereign power of the Deputy reigns supreme, whose intervention is sufficient to break all resistance and to conceal all wrongdoings provided they are perpetrated by men of colour, and especially if the victims are the Europeans whom they detest.[61]

This report and other similar ones understood Diagnism to embody, on the one hand, cordial co-operation in Paris and, on the other, racial hatred and war on French authority in Senegal.[62]

Those who supported Diagne also wanted to define the phenomenon. Adrien Allègre, one of his supporters among the Creole families, defined Diagnism as the frame of mind among those who had faith in him. Indeed, many voters did not know exactly what his political ideas were, but they supported him as a person, to the point that some attributed him with supernatural powers often linked to his membership in the Masons.[63] But Diagnism was more than a cult. The French press turned it into a synonym for 'Africanization', and when most people used the term, that is what they meant. There was fear that if Senegalese Africanization continued unstopped, it would spread to other territories. Thus, Diagnism ended up being identified with separatism and radicalism.

The fear and distrust was magnified as a result of Diagne's participation in events perceived to be radical. In January 1920, on a visit to Liberia, where he was named a knight of the Liberian Human Order of African Redemption, he said Africans were just as capable as whites of governing themselves and the country. That phrase, along with speeches by some of his allies in the Four Communes, increased fears within the administration.[64] In February 1919, Diagne had participated in the Pan-African Congress; he played a key role in persuading Clemenceau to allow the meeting and presided over sessions in Paris, where he praised French rule in Africa.[65] Even so, sectors of the administration used the congress to point to the dangers of Diagnism.[66] To his way of thinking, the congress 'was above all a tribute to France for its colonization methods, which my fellow citizens and I would like to see adopted by all colonizing peoples'.[67] While W. E. B. Du Bois was critical of colonialism, Diagne, along with Gratien Candace, the deputy from Guadeloupe, held an assimilationist perspective according to which France would emancipate colonized peoples.[68] In later years, Diagne moved away from Pan-Africanism, believing that American blacks were overly radical while the Senegalese were above all French and only on a secondary plane black.[69] He did not attend the following Pan-Africanist congress, in London in 1921, which gave rise to the London Manifesto. One of that document's points concerned land ownership, causing Diagne to refer to it as 'Bolshevik'. When the congress continued in Brussels from 30 August to 2 September, Diagne did show up, and once again he presided. At the opening session he said the congress's goal was to ensure equal rights and that it was not linked to Communism, and again he said that Africans who had fought in the war should have rights and privileges. But on the afternoon of 2 September, when the London Manifesto was to be discussed, things broke down. According to Diagne, Du Bois's declaration encouraged radicalism and separatism, two things of which he himself was being accused by the colonial press and administration. He distinguished between African Americans, 'with rather dangerous feelings', and French and Belgian Africans who believed in co-operation between blacks and whites. He said the manifesto encouraged Communist theories and that the black race belonged to no party.[70] At the meeting, Africans, African Britons and African Americans all broke definitively with Diagne.[71] Later on, Diagne referred to Marcus Garvey's vision of a multinational black community as a 'dangerous utopia' and called American Pan-Africanists 'damned blacks'.[72] He moved away from Garvey's theses, called them inadmissible and mistaken, and said neither they nor Bolshevism would be accepted in France's African colonies.[73] In Diagne's view, African development required collaboration with whites, not the isolation of blacks.[74] But despite this public stance, a series of incidents (commented upon in government reports) intensified the belief that Diagne's goal was to take control of the colony through local institutions. The most emblematic took place in Kaolack in January 1920, where Diagne, accompanied by members of the General Council and the mayors of Saint-Louis and Rufisque, spoke to a rally against M. Siadous, administrator of the Cercle de Sine-Saloum, one of the colony's districts. The governor of Senegal, Fernand Levecque, who until then had been one of Diagne's allies, wanted to calm down the audience, but the crowd chanted, 'Down with Siadous! Down with the governor!' Levecque, humiliated, broke with Diagne and wrote to Paris that France no longer ruled the country.[75]

The clash between Diagne and the administration reached its high point when the governor general, Martial Merlin, asked for secret reports about Diagne and his impact in the colony.[76] Merlin was convinced that the unrest in the colony was the fault of Diagne having stirred up separatism and resistance. While Diagne was the maximum representative of assimilation, Merlin stood for a politics of association, stressing collaboration with traditional chiefs.[77] One of his main plans was to turn the General Council, the colony's legislative assembly, into a Colonial Council, which instead of only having elected representatives from the communes would also include a considerable number of local chiefs, who would counter the growing power of the political elites led by Diagne. The new Colonial Council was created by decree on 4 December 1920. From then on, elected communal representatives would be joined by chiefs from the protectorate who would have representative powers. In principle, there were twenty elected members and twenty chiefs appointed by the administration. In the first elections after these reforms, Diagne was again victorious. His followers and Merlin were pleased, the former because they had argued that citizens and subjects could work alongside one another in local politics, the latter because he hoped for growing influence through the chiefs. Creation of the Colonial Council marked a decisive blow against the aspirations of the French and Creoles who wished to participate in Senegalese politics.[78]

Diagne and the 1923 Pact of Bordeaux

The early 1920s, when Diagne's fame grew alongside accusations that he was too radical, was also, paradoxically, when he broke with the most radical black intellectual circles of the time owing to his opposition to Pan-Africanism and his defence of French colonization.[79] His attacks against the administration diminished, and in 1923 his attitude toward the leading merchants also shifted. For years he had been trying to make approaches to Bordeaux that never bore fruit. In October 1916 he wrote, 'Bordeaux ... is the metropolis of the African coast. It is from its port that the commercial wealth of old Senegal in the first instance, and then of black Africa, has originated. This is a vast area that can provide immense benefits if we are willing to agree and work at it for ourselves.'[80] He had to wait until February 1923 to begin the conversations. In the negotiations, which the administration followed closely, one can see that the objectives were not simply economic, as Diagne said later, but rather focused on the influence and powers of the Senegalese councils. One of the first moves toward an agreement was to place M. Giraud, general agent of the Maurel & Prom merchant firm, on the Colonial Council.[81] The agreements were signed on 12 June 1923 at the Chamber of Commerce in Bordeaux, with the participation of all the great merchant houses operating in Senegal. At the meeting, Diagne said the pact would allow the administration to improve its responses to shared concerns, adding that in Senegal there was a party that had a numeric majority and another, in the minority, that had financial majority. Together they could work to improve the colony.[82] He justified his position in a letter to his colleagues:

> The pursuit of the common goal required a notion of solidarity on the part of all the elements of the population living in Senegal, indigenous and European. The failure to implement the Treaty of Versailles ... leads us to believe, and to affirm, that the development of its undeniable colonial wealth is still, for France, the most reliable and least discouraging way of ensuring its recovery, and of restoring its economic and financial balance.[83]

And he went on: 'The general impression that emerged from the Bordeaux meeting is – I say this without any false modesty – that, on both sides, we have done a useful job. This is the formal opinion in all political and colonial circles of the metropolis.'[84] The agreement was praised by Albert Sarraut, the colonial minister, and by Governor General Jules Carde. Diagne, once the pact was signed, put aside his old strategy of confrontation: 'in order to reach agreement the first condition ... is, in fact, to replace the spirit of controversy, which created adversaries, with the desire for conciliation that will facilitate the collaboration of all under all circumstances. In a word, it is the removal of the adversarial atmosphere in which any new creation or reform ... inevitably met with resistance.[85] Diagne asked his friends in Senegal to agree to respect the agreement for the general good. He also defined it as a necessary armistice with neither winners nor losers, freely accepted by both sides with an eye to a lasting and productive peace in the national interest. At a meeting at the Dakar mayor's office in November 1923, Diagne insisted on the importance of the agreement not only for the colony but also for France: 'You will judge me later. It is necessary for all of us, enemies and friends, white and black, to collaborate in the common endeavour that has only one purpose: the greatness of France our country.[86] The agreement with Bordeaux, practically speaking, gave Diagne the support of the merchant companies in exchange for their representation on the councils and ushered in a decade of co-operation among the administration, Diagne's party and Bordeaux.

Swimming among sharks: The opposition comes to life, 1923–8

From being a fierce enemy of commerce, Diagne went to being a collaborator, and from being the scourge of the administration, he became its official candidate. Along the way, many of those who had supported him left, and some even became political rivals. His first test during this period were the 1924 legislative elections, the third in a row in which he was a candidate. His language, which had become more moderate during the 1919 campaign, became much less belligerent. And this time, the administration and the merchants were on his side. As his old rival, Carpot, said, 'worshipping what he once would have razed to the ground, he has become the ally of the Bordeaux coffers.[87] The pact of Bordeaux set off the first dissidence. Despite Diagne having said that Diouf supported the initiative, merchants feared that the agreement would provoke disagreements among the Diagnists.[88] One of the first to abandon the party was Lamine Guèye, whose dissertation for his doctorate in law in 1921 was about *originaires* and French citizenship.[89] In 1923 he joined the French Section of the Workers International (SFIO) and in 1924 he supported the candidacy of Paul Defferre, who opposed Diagne in the legislative elections along with Thiécouta Diop, the historical leader of the Jeunes Sénégalais.[90] That same year he bought

L'AOF, the newspaper that traditionally had opposed Diagne. Despite Guèye's support, on 11 May Defferre suffered an overwhelming defeat, and Diagne received 6,133 votes to just 1,891 for his adversary.[91] However in the municipal elections in Saint-Louis in 1925, Guèye's list defeated Diagne's candidate, Duguay-Clédor, and the lawyer became the mayor until 1927.[92]

In a letter written in 1925, Guèye explained his position regarding Diagne and justified having supported Defferre: 'I was faced with two men, one of whom, a friend from the very beginning, treated me almost like a stranger and asked me nothing; and the other, a friend from a more recent date, but who wanted my support.'[93] But the gulf between Guèye and Diagne was neither sudden nor definitive. In June 1925 they met to reach a political agreement for the general interest of the country. Guèye kept the conversations secret so as to protect his reputation with his followers, but he was attacked by a sector of Diagne's supporters who, he said, spread lies about the agreement: 'If I wanted to propose peace with Mr. Diagne after battling against him, I could not have done so except out of self-interest; that was only a step away from considering myself a renegade, a traitor, and a sell-out.'[94] During 1926 the two politicians continued their efforts to find common ground. In February, Guèye was willing to publicly recognize their collaboration if Diagne accepted the theses of an article published by the lawyer in *L'AOF*.[95] Guèye was confident in his supporters though he preferred to not pressure those in Saint-Louis.[96] There were rumours in his camp that Guèye wanted to go with Diagne and sacrifice everyone else. But Guèye committed not only not to oppose Diagne but to support him as long as the deputy respected their agreement.[97]

While the agreement itself depended on the subtleties of the two men's correspondence, in the colony there was growing discontent. In January 1927 the Lebus in Rufisque complained that the deputy was ignoring them and was not responding to the commune mayor's abuses and nepotism.[98] In July of that year, when the agreement with Guèye was almost finalized, the pact led to disagreements among Guèye's party in Saint-Louis.[99] In September, Guèye lamented the fact that Duguay-Clédor, Diagne's right-hand man and the president of the Colonial Council since 1925, had not relied upon him to help choose members of the council's commission. In October, tired of Diagne's followers' politicking, he announced his decision to quit his municipal post in Saint-Louis. After months of failed negotiations, Guèye threw in the towel: 'I truly regret that your detachment has not permitted you to see first-hand the inability and bad faith of some of our colleagues who say they are your friends and who seem to have your full confidence.'[100]

In 1926, Jean d'Oxoby, one of the key players in Diagne's political success and the one-time owner of *La Démocratie*, also left the party. But the most outstanding departure was that of Galandou Diouf, who had fought in the war when Diagne asked him to and who had accompanied the leader on his 1918 mission.[101] He was irritated at how Duguay-Clédor had gradually become Diagne's chief aide in Senegal, and also at the fact that Diagne had picked Louis Guillabert, a member of one of the most influential Creole families, to preside over the Colonial Council, a gesture toward reconciliation with Saint-Louis business circles. Diouf decided to run for election in 1928, with Guèye's support.[102] The latter made his newspaper's opinion page available to Diouf during the campaign and appointed him to be political director, a move similar to Diagne's at *La Démocratie* in 1914.[103]

Thus, in the 1928 elections Diagne for the first time had an African rival, which forced him to go to Senegal in the early part of the year, long before the campaign got under way. The letters he exchanged with his wife during these months reveal the collapse of his relations with Diouf and Guèye. Diagne believed that most voters would continue supporting him and that he would defeat Diouf, whom he described as immoral.[104] Diagne relied upon the monied sectors to undercut his rivals and was pleased that both in Rufisque and, especially, in Saint-Louis, his support grew as his rivals lost steam.[105] He was received triumphantly in Saint-Louis for the first time ever in his political career, and he fully expected to win a majority and get more votes than in previous rounds: 'Galandou and Lamine did not even dare show their faces in Saint-Louis the day I arrived.'[106] Shortly after this, the deputy became aware of internal difficulties among Guèye's family members who thought that Guèye, and not Diouf, should represent them.[107] Back in Dakar, amid the campaign, he accused his rivals of having spread false rumours about him.[108] His optimism about Rufisque and Saint-Louis spread to Gorée, where he enjoyed substantial support.[109]

One week before the elections, having completed his campaign, Diagne was sure of an overwhelming victory. Rufisque was where Diouf had the greatest support, where certain sectors, including civil servants, small businessmen and young people with ambitions, accused Diagne of being too close to the administration and the leading merchants. The deputy's own erstwhile arguments were now being used against him. Galandou's people, meanwhile, took it upon themselves to say that he was the only one who could ensure that the natives of Rufisque controlled their own municipal finances.[110] Even so, just days before the election Diagne believed he would also win in Rufisque.[111] He was also pleased that most Europeans supported him against the 'Communist candidacy of Galandou'.[112] Diouf accused Diagne of theft during his political and administrative career and sullied the memory of Diagne's mother, leading the deputy to file a complaint for defamation.[113]

In his ideological programme, Diagne mentioned collaboration with the administration and commerce and argued that this alliance with his old enemies signalled a transition from the politics of passion to the politics of work, law and order. He also pointed to his growing authority with regard to municipal and colonial power structures and accused Diouf of concealing his Communist tendencies. For Diagne, a vote for him was a vote in favour of the continuation of French colonial progress. He did not conceal his defence of the chambers of commerce, and also pointed to the support from the federation of civil servants. He lamented the failed pact with Guèye, blaming it on Guèye's and Diouf's 'Communist heresies'.[114]

The outcome of the elections signalled a change in Senegalese politics. Diagne won, but his victory was far from overwhelming. He received 5,175 votes against Diouf's 4,396. Diagne won in all the communes, including Rufisque.[115] As he had predicted, Diouf challenged the results, alleging irregularities at the polls in Bargny (people who voted twice, votes cast by the dead and by those who were not there), and he asked that the election be annulled.[116] The authorities denied his request.[117] Afterwards, Diagne recognized that he had lost support in Senegal: 'Some of my compatriots have forgotten all my loyal efforts to safeguard the general interest.'[118] During the campaign, the language that earlier had been used by Diagne was now used by the opposition, which fought the administration and the merchants. The man who had once fought the 'Bordeaux sharks' had become one of them.[119]

Diagne continued increasing his influence in the metropolis, meanwhile, and was appointed to be president of the Colonial Commission.[120] But African intellectuals and the descendants of Africans there waged an incessant campaign against his positions. Several important African organizations were established in Paris starting in 1924, the most important of which was the Ligue Universelle pour la Défense de la Race Noire, led by Kojo Tovalou Houénou, who was from Dahomey. The group's members were radicals from the French colonies who questioned assimilation and wished for deputies such as Diagne and Danace to be replaced by Pan-Africanists. More radical activists in 1926, led by Lamine Senghor, a member of the Communist Party of France, established the Comité de Défense de la Race Nègre.[121] Diagne's opposition to Communism was based on two main principles: the obligation of CPF members to give up their membership in the Masons, and the party's defence of independence for the colonies.[122] The culmination of the face-off between black intellectuals and Diagne came in 1924 when the periodical *Les Continents*, founded by Houénou, published an article titled 'Le Bon Apôtre', in which the paper imprudently maintained that during Diagne's 1918 recruitment mission Clemenceau had promised him a commission for every recruit. Diagne sued for libel and won. The trial featured a face-off among intellectuals such as the Martinique writer René Maran, editor-in-chief of *Les Continents* and Senghor himself, who testified against Diagne and described irregular methods used to recruit African troops.[123] The case received a great deal of coverage in the press; papers including the daily *Les Annales Coloniales*, which until then had opposed Diagne, began praising him and even defending him against Maran.[124] Intellectuals saw Diagne's suit as a political manoeuvre to discredit anticolonialists and other of his opponents in the Ligue. Diagne became the symbol of everything they hated; they disagreed on colonial politics, colonial recruitment, communism and nationalism. According to Langley, the conflict between Diagne and the Ligue was seen as a logical one between two schools of thought regarding French colonial politics: the progressive critics led by Maran and Houénou, and the reactionaries led by Diagne.[125]

'The omnipotent Diagne', 1928–34

During the Great Depression, Diagne advocated protectionist measures and, according to Wesley Johnson, this was one of his most important contributions to Senegal. In what became known as the 'peanut war', he denounced low-priced imports from British India and tried to get the French to buy Senegalese peanuts. The product became the basis for the colony's modern economy for the following thirty years.[126]

In Senegal, the fight against the administration and big commerce became Diouf's watchword.[127] Diagne, who was concerned about his adversaries' progress, managed to remove Guèye and Diouf from the Colonial Council, pointing to their unjustified absences.[128] In the 1930 elections to the Colonial Council, Diagne's candidates won again, though by fewer votes than before.[129] Intellectuals and the educated youth were more firmly than ever opposed to Diagne. Some, such as Ibrahim Sow, ended up in prison, the price for challenging the 'omnipotent Diagne'. At around the same time, the opposition began accusing Diagnists of provoking incidents during the Colonial Council election and using fraudulent and illegal methods.[130] D'Oxoby, his oldest ally but now his rival, called him a 'black dictator'.[131] In response, Diagne used the discourse that the administration had used against him for so long: 'Voting for us means continuing the progress of French colonization. Voting for our opponents means creating an anti-social and anti-French atmosphere and fratricidal hostilities within the Colonial Council.'[132]

If the pact of Bordeaux had brought about a chasm between Diagne and the more radical African intellectuals, his participation as France's representative to the 1930 International Labour Conference in Geneva marked the definitive break. The key factor was Diagne's defence of France's position regarding forced labour, according to which the population of colonies assimilated to the metropolis (citizens of Martinique, Guadaloupe, Réunion, Guiana and North Africa) had achieved a level of economic and social development that made it unnecessary to subject them to forced labour. But more primitive sectors (in Africa and Indochina) must continue being oppressed. At the conference, Diagne wrote several letters to his son Adolphe in which he expressed pride about his role at Geneva.[133] The French government's theses, which Diagne shared, were passed on to the deputy by the colonial minister, François Piétri.[134] France favoured eliminating forced labour in all its forms but demanded the right to decide how long the transition period would be and, given certain regions' labour needs for public works, demanded that obstacles not impede legitimate obligatory forms of labour for public works. At the conference, Diagne complained about proposals by workers groups that emphasized colonial abuses and argued in favour of an end to forced labour within five years. Insisting on the various degrees of evolution of indigenous peoples, he pointed to the dilemma: 'The suppression at all costs of forced labour at the expense of a setback to the process of social civilization, or a delay in the use of the regulatory system.'[135] Despite the attacks, a year later Diagne once again stated that the sorts of labour demanded of people in the French colonies was a necessary step toward their definitive liberation, which had begun with the elimination of slavery.[136]

Diagne's power continued to grow. On 26 April 1931 he achieved his most important post in the metropolis when the Laval government appointed him to be under-secretary of state at the colonial ministry, a post he held until 19 February 1932. This marked the first time that a sub-Saharan African had held a ministerial position.[137] Also, Guèye retired from politics in 1931. Senegalese archival documents show how the Dakar defence attorney left his job and, through Diagne and Duguay-Clédor, sought candidacy with the Colonial Magistrate.[138] Thanks to efforts by Diagne, the attorney was given a post at the appeals court on Réunion Island.[139] Thus Diagne managed to get one of his chief rivals out of the way and arrive at the elections stronger than ever.

Figure 10.1 Blaise Diagne, Under-Secretary of State for the Colonies, leaving the Minister of the Interior with a group of deputies and ministers after the end of the Laval government in February 1932. Courtesy of Bibliothèque nationale de France.

In the elections, set for 1 May 1932, his strongest adversary once again was Diouf. Diagne's programme was a summary of all his accomplishments during the past eighteen years. In the campaign he presented himself not just as Senegal's deputy but also as that of the entire AOF, and he praised the 1918 mission just as he had praised his role in Geneva two years earlier: 'I have very successfully defended French humanitarian doctrine in the vocational education of undeveloped indigenous populations, that is, of those who do not have the status of French citizens. This doctrine, cleverly misrepresented by Geneva's international leaders, only seeks to promote work for the public good, and not the work of indigenous people for the benefit of individuals.'[140] He also praised the Colonial Exposition of 1931, which he had participated in as under-secretary of state for the colonial ministry: 'The unity of our country goes beyond differences of skin, to the stupefied admiration or horror of foreign peoples. Whether Latin or Anglo-Saxon, these have received a lesson in high moral standards of the kind that France alone was capable of giving. This is what the collective sacrifice in defence of the Fatherland has produced.'[141]

For the first time more than two African candidates were running, but it was a tight race between Diagne and Diouf, in which the former won by a substantial margin: 7,250 votes to 3,785.[142] Once again, the defeated candidates demanded that the election be declared null and void, arguing, among other things, that during the campaign Diagne had been appointed by the government to participate on an official mission in the AOF, which was true; the Laval government had asked him to spend three months (March to May) drawing up a study for the administrative, financial and economic reorganization of the AOF, Togo and Cameroon.[143] In the report, Diagne said he had devoted himself fully to the mission, leaving the campaign to his friends.[144] As a result, he was accused of being the administration's official candidate.[145] His campaign was said to have committed violent acts during the campaign and tabulated the votes of the dead. His adversaries filled newspaper columns with incendiary attacks on him, calling him a dictator who controlled the entire administrative machinery in the colony, including the police.[146]

Nonetheless, the electoral commission validated the election, and thus the Senegalese deputy began his last term in office. From the metropolis, the Ligue de Défense de la Race Nègre, which had supported Diouf, admitted that Diagne's re-election was a blow to its objectives in the French Empire: 'From which front could we be seen to reflect the opinion of the black community, since Senegal's almost exclusively black electorate had re-elected, or at least allowed Blaise Diagne, the advocate in Geneva of forced labour, to return to France?'[147]

In 1933 the deputy's health began getting worse. It was thought he might have tuberculosis or pleurisy, and it was recommended that he rest in Africa, owing to the dry climate. He was given another AOF mission and appointed to be president of the committee to inaugurate monuments in honour of the French conqueror of Sudan, Borgnis Desbordes y Archinard.[148] This was the culmination of the notion of assimilation: an African was inaugurating monuments to the man who had conquered the interior of the continent, and praising his accomplishments in Africa.[149] In April, while in French Sudan, his health grew worse. Jules Brevié, the governor general, asked that a doctor accompany Diagne on his trip back to the metropolis.[150] Diagne left for Bordeaux on 25 April and died on 11 May in the French town of Cambo-les-Bains.[151]

His death did not mark the end of his political impact. Duguay-Clédor, still president of the Colonial Council, wrote to his widow that municipal elections would have to be held before the remains could be sent to Senegal. Duguay-Clédor, along with Brevié and other administration officials, wanted to avoid Diagne's remains arriving in Dakar in the heat of the election campaign. Diagne had expressed a wish to be buried next to his mother in Dakar's Muslim cemetery. But the fact that he was not only a Mason but also had been baptized ensured that his burial in the cemetery would give rise to protests. A compromise was found by which Diagne was buried next to the cemetery: 'He will sleep his last sleep just a few steps from his mother and among his fellow countrymen.'[152]

In the municipal elections after his death, Dakar had to pick a new mayor, a post he had occupied since 1920, and also replace one of its councillors. The opposition list led by Diouf won by five hundred votes, but Diagnists continued as the majority on the town council, with twenty-one members, and they elected one of their own as mayor. There was speculation regarding who would succeed Diagne, and the topic was widely written about in police and administrative reports.[153] The end of Diagnism was approaching, the party appeared to be as dead as its leader, and meanwhile two candidates fought to replace him in the National Assembly: Diouf and Guèye.[154]

Diouf defeated Guèye in the 29 July 1934 elections by 6,132 votes to 4,534.[155] Indeed, Diagnism had died with its ideologue. Among his old adversaries celebrating Diouf's election was the Ligue, which affirmed that the dignity of the black race had been reconfirmed.[156]

Governor General Brevié astutely summed up Diagne's political career: 'He had managed to assimilate our French conceptions and ideas in the widest sense without ever renouncing the traditions of the country in which he had been born. His politics never separated Senegal from France and thus his work had a highly national character.'[157] From start to finish, Diagne was the spokesman for the politics of assimilation. Even so, when the colonial administration adopted association instead, he became its ally. His pragmatism first led him to confront the administration and business as the best means for achieving his objectives of being elected by Africans and recognized as a French citizen. That same pragmatism explains his subsequent alliances; once he had attained his goal of being a citizen, he must preserve and defend that. His objective, even in his most 'radical' phase, was never the complete emancipation of Africans but rather recognition as equals within the French Empire. And that, above all, involved the members of Senegal's Four Communes. His position regarding the protectorate's territories was never quite as clear as his defence of the *originaires*' rights.

Notes

1   Until 1914 the colony was represented by members of Senegalese Creole families, descendants of French and Africans. For parallel instances in the French Empire,

see Dominique Chathuant, 'Le émergence d'une élite politique noire dans la France du premier 20 siècle', *Vingtième Siècle. Revue d'histoire*, 101 (2009): 133–47. For a more distant example, see the case of Jean Baptise Belley discussed by David Geggus in this volume.

2 Senegal in this respect joined the *vieilles colonies* that already enjoyed parliamentary representation: Martinique, Guadaloupe, Réunion, Guiana and French India.

3 George Wesley Johnson, *The Emergence of Black Politics in Senegal: The struggle for power in the Four Communes, 1900–1920* (Stanford: Stanford University Press, 1971), 45. See also Robert W. July, *The Origins of Modern African Thought: Its Development in West Africa during the Nineteenth and Twentieth Centuries* (Asmara: African World Press, 2004) 234–53.

4 Johnson, *The Emergence of Black Politics in Senegal*, 31–72.

5 Historians disagree about Blaise Diagne's family tree. Iba Thiam has argued that Diagne's real name was Galaye M'Baye and that his maternal line came from both Portuguese Guinea and the Lebu people of Cape Verde; Iba Thiam, *La Révolution de 1914 au Sénégal, ou l'élection au palais Bourbon du député noir Blaise Diagne (de son vrai nom Galaye Mbaye Diagne)* (Dakar: L'Harmattan-Sénégal, 2014), 144–9. However, the civil registry of Gorée in 1872 shows that his parents called him Blaise Diagne, making it doubtful that his personal name was assigned to him in primary school; Archives Nationales d'Outre Mer (ANOM), État Civil. Sénégal, Gorée 1872, no. 235, 113.

6 For a broader look at the various interpretations of his education and colonial service career, see Thiam, *La Révolution*, 151–60; Johnson, *The emergence of Black Politics in Senegal*, 155; Amady Dieng, *Blaise Diagne, premier député africain* (Paris: Éditions Chaka, 1990), 54; and François Zucarelli, *La vie politique sénégalaise* (Paris: CHEAM, 1987), 35.

7 Thiam, *La Révolution*, 169.

8 Fred Zeller, 'Blaise Diagne: Premier homme politique sénégalais, franc-maçon et humaniste', *Humanisme: Revue des franc-maçons du grand orient de France* (1973): 32–9; Jean-Louis Domergue, 'Blaise Diagne (1872–1934)', *Humanisme: Revue des franc-maçons du grand orient de France* (1994): 56–8.

9 Lamine Guèye, *Itinéraire africain* (Paris: Présence Africaine, 1966), 23–4; Zeller, 'Blaise Diagne', 35; Thiam, *La Révolution*, 176; Johnson, *The Emergence of Black Politics in Senegal*, 84.

10 Johnson, *The Emergence of Black Politics in Senegal*, 161–4.

11 ANOM, Sénégal, VII 81, Le Gouverneur des Colonies Lieutenant-Gouverneur du Sénégal: à Monsieur le Gouverneur Géneral de l'Afrique Occidentale française. A. S. des élections législatives de 1914 au Sénégal. Saint-Louis, 14 January 1914.

12 Johnson, *The Emergence of Black Politics in Senegal*, 168.

13 Ibid., 170–3.

14 Thiam, *La Révolution*, 278.

15 *L'AOF Echo de la côte occidentale d'Afrique*, 2 May 1914.

16 Johnson, *The Emergence of Black Politics in Senegal*, 170.

17 Blaise Diagne, 'Sincérité', *La Démocratie du Sénégal*, 2 May 1914.

18 ANOM SEN VII 81, Colonie du Sénégal. Membre de la Chambre des Députés, election of 10 May 1914, second round.

19 *Journal officiel de la République française*. Débats parlementaires. Chambre des députés, séance de 7 de juillet 1914, M. G. Leredu, rapporteur. Rapport sur l'élection du Sénégal, 2736–7.

20 Catherine Coquery-Vidrovitch, 'Nationalité et citoyenneté en Afrique occidental française; Originaires et citoyens dans le Sénégal colonial', *The Journal of African History*, 42, no.2 (2001): 190; Johnson, *The Emergence of Black Politics in Senegal*, 185.

21 Johnson, *The Emergence of Black Politics in Senegal*, 189–90.

22 'Nos tirailleurs', *La Démocratie du Sénégal*, 3 September 1916; ANOM, 1AFFPOL/597. Le Gouverneur Général de l'Afrique Occidentale Française à Monsieur Le Ministre des Colonies, 21 August 1915; Le Gouverneur Général de l'Afrique Occidentale Française à Monsieur Le Ministre des Colonies, 30 March 1917; Gouvernement Général de l'Afrique Occidental Française. Sénégal. Rapport sur la situation politique et administrative au Sénégal pendant le premier trimestre 1917, 6 July 1917.

23 Johnson, *The Emergence of Black Politics in Senegal*, 191.

24 ANOM, 100APOM/686, Senat, année 1916, no. 270. Proposition de loi adoptée par la Chambre des Députés Etendant aux descendants des originaires des communes de plein exercise du Sénégal les dispositions de la lois militaires du 19 octobre 1915.

25 Johnson, *The Emergence of Black Politics in Senegal*, 191; J. Reynis, 'Loi Diagne', *La Démocratie du Sénégal*, 1 October 1916.

26 Larissa Kopytoff, 'French Citizens and Muslim Law: The Tensions of Citizenship in the Early Twentieth Century', in Richard Marback and Marc W. Kruman (eds.), *The Meanings of Citizenship* (Detroit: Wayne State University Press, 2015), 320–38.

27 ANOM, 100APOM/686, 'Naturalisation des indigènes originaires des quatre communes de plein exercise du Sénégal. 1916'; U.C. Notes sur le projet de loi Diagne (1916). Angoulavant, 1916.

28 ANOM, 100APOM/686, Monsieur le Directeur General à l'Union Coloniale Française, 15 January 1916.

29 ANOM, 100APOM/686, Georges Lesieur et ses fils à Monsieur Le Cesne, Président de la Section de l'Afrique Occidentale Française de l'Union Coloniale, 19 January 1916.

30 'Petite Histoire Sénégalaise', *Le Temps*, 29 January 1915; ANOM, 100APOM/686, Blaise Diagne à Monsieur le Directeur du Le Temps, 29 January 1916; Directeur General de l'Union Coloniale à Monsieur Emile Maurel, Feburary 1, 1916; extrait d'une lettre de Bourdeaux, 2 February 1916; Georges Lesieur et ses fils, à Monsieur Le Cesne; lettre à Monsieur Joseph Chailley, Directeur Général de l'Union Coloniale Française, 2 February 1916.

31 'Chambre des Députés. Séance du samedi 9 décembre', *La Démocratie du Sénégal*, 14 January 1917.

32 ANOM, 100APOM/686, Ministère des Colonies, Documents relatifs à la reprise du recrutement en Afrique Occidentale Française, 14 January 1918.

33 ANOM, 100APOM/686, Ministère des Colonies, Décret portant organization d'une mission chargée d'intensifier le recrutement, 11 January 1918.

34 Marc Michel, *Les Africains et la Grande Guerre: L'appel à l'Afrique (1914–1918)* (Paris: Karthala, 2014), 66–7.

35 Johnson, *The Emergence of Black Politics in Senegal*, 194; Michel, *Les Africains*, 77.

36 ANOM, 100APOM/686, note de l'Union Coloniale sur le Commissariat général aux troupes noires et Blaise Diagne.

37 ANOM, FP37APC/7. Souvenirs du Général Bounnier, cahier 6. La mission de M. le Député Blaise Diagne en A.O.F.

38 Archives Nationales du Sénégal (ANS), 17 G 233 (108). Blaise Diagne, no title or date, though later than 1921, signed by Ch. Dumont.

39 ANS, 17 G 233 (108), notes de presse sur la Mission Diagne, Lieutenant Abd-el-Kader Mademba, *La Démocratie Nouvelle*, 9 October 1919; 'Cuisine Politicienne', Lieutenant Abd-el-Kader Mademba, *La Démocratie Nouvelle*, 16 September 1919.

40 *La Démocratie Nouvelle*, 'M. Diagne, Politicien. Le gachis de l'Afrique occidentale française', 4 October 1919.

41 Dominique Chathuant, 'Connexions et circulations; l'assimilationnisme dans un conflit mondialisé (1914–1919)', *Bulletin de la Societé d'Histoire de la Guadeloupe*, 168 (2014): 105–33; Johnson, *The Emergence of Black Politics in Senegal*, 195.

42 Michael Crowder, *Senegal: A Study of French Assimilation Policy* (London: Methuen, 1967), 30.

43 Chathuant, 'Le émergence d'une élite politique noire dans la France du premier 20 siècle', 139.

44 ANOM, 100APROM/686, Georges Lesieur et ses fils, à Monsieur Le Cesne, 19 January 1916.

45 Johnson, *The Emergence of Black Politics in Senegal*, 196–7.

46 ANOM, 1AFFPOL/595, Le Gouverneur des Colonies, Lieutenant-Gouverneur du Sénégal, à Monsieur le Gouverneur Général de l'Afrique Occidentale Française, 25 December 1919.

47 ANOM, 1AFFPOL/595, 'Sénégalais'.

48 ANOM, 1AFFPOL/595, 'A mes Compatriotes et Concitoyens'.

49 ANOM, 1AFFPOL/595, Elections législatives, 30 November 1919. Profession de foi du citoyen Blaise Diagne.

50 ANOM, 1AFFPOL/595, François Carpot et le Comité d'Union Républicaine Sénégalaise. Saint Louis, Imprimerie O. Lesgourgues; *L'AOF Écho de la côte Occidentale d'Afrique*, 'La Profession de Foi de notre Candidat', 23 November 1919.

51 ANOM, 1AFFPOL/595, Elections législatives, 30 November 1919. Profession de foi du citoyen Blaise Diagne.

52 Johnson, *The Emergence of Black Politics in Senegal*, 200.

53 ANOM, 1AFFPOL/595, Le Gouverneur des Colonies, Lieutenant-Gouverneur du Sénégal, à Monsieur le Gouverneur Général de l'Afrique Occidentale Française, 25 December 1919.

54 Johnson, *The Emergence of Black Politics in Senegal*, 202–3.

55 *Les Annales Coloniales*, 'Elections Sénégalaises', 11 November 1919.

56 Johnson, *The Emergence of Black Politics in Senegal*, 197.

57 Ibid., 198. Other newspapers included *Les Annales Coloniales*, *Le Temps*, *La Grande Revue*, *Le Cri de Paris* and *Parlement et Colonies*.

58 *L'AOF Echo de la Côte Occidentale d'Afrique*, 'Ceux que nos sommes', 1 November 1919.

59 Alice L. Conklin, *A Mission to Civilize: The Republican Idea of Empire in France and West Africa, 1985–1930* (Stanford: Stanford University Press, 1997), 174–211.

60 Alice L. Conklin, '"Democracy" Rediscovered: Civilization through Association in French West Africa (1914–1930)', *Cahiers d'études africains*, 37, no. 145 (1997): 59–84, 61–6.

61 ANS 17 G 233 (108), dossier, no signature, date, or title, 23.

62 Ibid., 24; ANS 17 G 233 (108), 'Politique de M. Diagne au Sénégal: Le Diagnisme'; *La Démocratie Nouvelle*, 'Une dictadure scandaleuse. Diagne, ministre des colonies et proconsul de France en A. O. F', 18 October 1919; *Le Soir*, 'Le Diagnisme. La désorganization économique de l'A. O. F', 16 September 1919. In September and October of 1919, *Le Soir* regularly published columns headlined 'Le diagnisme'.

63 Johnson, *The Emergence of Black Politics in Senegal*, 205. During this period, Diagne was admitted to the Grand Orient de France; Zeller, 'Blaise Diagne', 35.

64 ANS, 17 G 233 (108), 'Politique de M. Diagne au Sénégal – Le diagnisme'; ANS, 1Z 25. Papiers de Blaise Diagne, Republic of Liberia.

65 J. Ayodele Langley, *Pan-Africanism and Nationalism in West Africa, 1900–1945: A study in ideology and social classes* (Oxford: Clarendon Press, 1973), 64.

66 ANOM, 100APOM/686, 'Note sur le Commissariat Général aux Troupes Noires', 5.

67 ANS, 1 Z 25, Blaise Diagne à Monsieur le Directeur de *La Démocratie Nouvelle*, Paris, 17 March 1919.

68 Chathuant, 'Connexions et circulations', 110.

69 Michael C. Lambert, 'From Citizenship to Negritude: "Making a Difference" in Elite Ideologies of Colonized Francophone West Africa', *Comparative Studies in Society and History*, 35, no.2 (1993): 239–62.

70 Langley, *Pan-Africanism and Nationalism in West Africa, 1900–1945*, 71–9.

71 Ibid., 79–80; Babacar M'Baye, *Black Cosmopolitanism and Anticolonialism: Pivotal Moments* (New York: Routledge, 2017), 79–80.

72 Dieng, *Blaise Diagne*, 133–4.

73 *La Dépêche Coloniale*, 'Le mouvement pan-noir: Les théories Johnson-Garvey. L' attitude du Libéria. Pas de menace bolchevik', 20 September 1921.

74 M'Baye, *Black Cosmopolitanism and Anticolonialism*, 100–1.

75 ANS, 17 G 233 (108), 'Politique de M. Diagne au Sénégal: Le diagnisme'.

76 Ibid.; George Wesley Johnson, 'The Rivalry between Diagne and Merlin for Political Mastery of French West Africa', in Charles Becker, Saliou Mbaye and Ibrahima Throub (eds.), *AOF: Réalités et heritages. Sociétés ouest-africaines et ordre colonial, 1895–1960* (Dakar: Direction des Archives du Sénégal, 1997), 303–14.

77 ANOM, 1AFFPOL/536. Gouvernement Général de l'Afrique Occidentale Française, Rapport d'Ensemble, 1923, 9; Conklin, '"Democracy" Rediscovered', 68.

78 Johnson, *The Emergence of Black Politics in Senegal*, 212; ANOM, 1AFFPOL/542, Protestations. Diagne Député, contre Gouverneur Général Merlin, 1922.

79 The most illustrative example, which went beyond French borders, was his public defense of Senegalese boxer Battling Siki after the latter's victory over the French world champion, Georges Carpentier; *Journal Officiel de la République Française*. Débats parlementaires. Chambre des députés: compte rendu in-extenso, 2nd séance, 30 November 1922, 3661; ANOM, 148APOM/1, Le Président à Monsieur Diagne, 5 December 1922; Seth Weeks à Monsieur Diagne, 4 December 1922; Le Rapporteur Frantz-Reichel à Monsieur Diagne, 20 December 1922; *L'Echo des Sports*, 'Le Triomphe', 16 January 1923.

80 *La Démocratie du Sénégal*, 'Le député du Sénégal à la Foire de Bordeaux', 29 October 1916.

81 ANS, 17G 234 (108), Blaise Diagne. Blaise Diagne à Monsieur le Président du Syndicat de Défense des Intérêts Sénégalais, 6 February 1923; F. Vezia à Monsieur Diagne, 16 February 1923; Blaise Diagne à Monsieur François Vezia, Président du Syndicat de Défense des Intérêts Sénégalais, 24 February 1923; Brevié à Monsieur Diagne, 3 March 1923.

82 ANS, 17G 234 (108), Notes sur la Conférence de M. Blaise Diagne, Député du Sénégal, au Palais de la Bourse, 12 June 1923.

83 ANS, 17G 234 (108), letter, no addresse, signed by Diagne, 27 June 1923.

84 Ibid.

85 Ibid.

86 ANS, 17G 234 (108), Le commissaire de Police Dubois à Monsieur le Commissaire Central, 19 November 1923; Service de Sûreté du Sénégal. Objet: Réunion publique organisée par M. Diagne, député, 20 November 1923.

87 Cited in Dieng, *Blaise Diagne*, 148.

88 ANS, 17 G 234 (108), Notes sur la Conférence de M. Blaise Diagne, Député du Sénégal, au Palais de la Bourse.

89 Irving L. Markovitz, 'The Political Thought of Blaise Diagne and Lamine Guèye: Some Aspects of Social Structure and Ideology in Senegal', *Présence Africaine*, 72 (1969): 21–38.

90 ANS 17 G 233 (108), Thiécouta Diop à Monsieur d'Iriart d'Etheparte, Député, Président de la Comission des Colonies, 9 August 1921; Dieng, *Blaise Dieng*, 114.

91 ANOM, 1AFFPOL/1274. Sénégal. Élections législatives 1924, 'Élection d'un membre de la Chambre des Députés. Procès-Verbal du recensement général des votes émis dans les collèges électoraux de la circonscription unique de la Colonie du Sénégal'; 'Colonie du Sénégal. Membre de la Chambre des Députés élu le 11 May 1924, premier tour de scrutin'; 'La Chambre a validé l'élection de M. Diagne'; ANOM, 1AFFPOL/598, 'Colonie du Sénégal. Rapport Politique Année 1924'; Johnson, *The Emergence of Black Politics in Senegal*, 214.

92 Dieng, *Blaise Diagne*, 115–16.

93 ANOM, FP148APOM/1, Lamine Guèye à Maitre Giacomoni, 28 November 1925.

94 Ibid.

95 ANOM, FP148APOM/1, M. Lamine Guèye à Monsieur Blaise Diagne, 27 February 1926.

96 ANOM, FP148APOM/1, M. Lamine Guèye à Monsieur Blaise Diagne, 13 April 1926.

97 ANOM, FP148APOM/1, M. Lamine Guèye à Monsieur Blaise Diagne, 18 May 1926.

98 ANOM, FP148APOM/1, Délégués du Parti lébou Diagnistes à Monsieur Blaise Diagne, 6 January 1927.

99 ANOM, FP148APOM/1, M. Lamine Guèye à Monsieur Blaise Diagne, 3 August 1927.

100 ANOM, FP148APOM/1, M. Lamine Guèye à Monsieur Blaise Diagne, Député du Sénégal, 5 October 1927.

101 George Wesley Johnson, 'The Impact of the Senegalese Elite upon the French, 1900–1940', in George Wesley Johnson (ed.), *Double Impact: France and Africa in the Age of Imperialism* (London: Greenwood Press, 1985), 166–71.

102 Johnson, *The Emergence of Black Politics in Senegal*, 214–15.

103 Dieng, *Blaise Diagne*, 116.

104 ANOM, FP148APOM/1, Blaise Diagne to his daughter, 6 February 1928.

105 ANOM, FP148APOM/1, Blaise Diagne to his daughter, 12 March 1928.

106 ANOM, FP148APOM/1, Blaise Diagne to his daughter, 21 March 1928.

107 ANOM, FP148APOM/1, Blaise Diagne to his daughter, 23 March 1928.

108 ANOM, FP148APOM/1, Blaise Diagne to his daughter, 28 March 1928; ANOM, FP148APOM/1, Blaise Diagne to his daughter, 31 March 1928.

109 ANOM, FP148APOM/1, 'Le Petit Peuple Goréen', à Monsieur le Député du Sénégal, 12 April 1928.

110 ANOM, FP148APOM/1, report on the Rufisque campaign, 1928.

111 ANOM, FP148APOM/1, Blaise Diagne à sa femme, 17 April 1928.

112 ANOM, FP148APOM/1, Blaise Diagne à sa femme, 14 April 1928.

113 ANOM, FP148APOM/1, Télégramme-circulaire, 21 April 1928, Blaise Diagne.

114 ANS, 1Z 25, Proffessions [sic] de foi de 1928 et 1932, Sénégal, M. Diagne.

115 *La France Coloniale*, 'Résultats des élections législatives du 22 Avril 1928', 17 May 1928.

116 ANOM, FP148APOM/1, Blaise Diagne to his wife, 10 April 1928.

117 ANOM, FP148APOM/1, Élections Législatives du 22 avril 1928.

118 ANOM, FP148APOM/1, Blaise Diagne to his wife, 4 May 1928.

119 ANOM, FP148APOM/1, Le Secrétaire de Police Salomon Robert à Monsieur le Commissaire de Police, 16 May 1928.

120 *Les Annales Coloniales*, 'À la Commission des Colonies. M. Blaise Diagne président', 4 July 1924.

121 Langley, *Pan-Africanism and Nationalism in West Africa, 1900–1945*, 287–301.

122 Dieng, *Blaise Diagne*, 135.

123 *Les Annales Coloniales*, 'M. Diagne fait condamner ses diffamateurs', 27 November 1924; Alice L. Conklin, 'Who Speaks for Africa? The René Maran – Blaise Diagne Trial in 1920s Paris', in Sue Peabody and Tyler Stovall (eds.), *The Color of Liberty: Histories of Race in France* (Durham, NC: Duke University Press, 2003), 302–37.

124 *Les Annales Coloniales*, 'M. Diagne a été diffamé', 25 November 1924; *Le Petit Journal*, 'Le procès intenté par M. Diagne député su Sénégal, à un journal colonial, s'ouvre aujourd'hui devant la Cour d'assises de la Seine', 24 November 1924.

125 Langley, *Pan-Africanism and Nationalism in West Africa, 1900–1945*, 300–1.

126 George Wesley Johnson, 'Discours de Monsieur Wesley Johnson', in *Blaise Diagne: Sa vie, son oeuvre*, ed. Obeye Diop (Dakar: Nouvelle Éditions Africaines, 1974); ANS, 1Z 25, Note sur la crise des arachides au Sénégal, 8 October 1930.

127 ANOM, 1AFFPOL/595, Direction des Affaires Politiques et Administratives, Envoi des dossiers relatifs à l'élection législative du 22 avril 1928, 12 May 1928; ANOM, 1AFFPOL/595, Cabinet du Ministre, Bureau du Cabinet, télegramme, 2 April 1928, Galandou Diouf.

128 Dieng, *Blaise Diagne*, 116.

129 ANOM, 1AFFPOL/594, Direction des Affaires Politiques et Administratives, Elections pour le Conseil Colonial, 17 May 1930.

130 *Le Populaire*, 'Au Sénégal le sang a coulé pendant les élections. Toute la responsabilité en incombe à l'Administration', 16 May 1930.

131 Jean d'Oxoby, 'Chronique Électorale. Les élections au Conseil Colonial. Victoire administrative', *L' Ouest Africain Français*, 15 May 1930.

132 'Parti Républicain-Socialiste. Élections Générales au Conseil Colonial du Sénégal. Dimanche 11 mai 1930. Aux Électeurs du Sénégal', *La France Coloniale*, 5 May 1930.

133 ANOM, FP148APOM/1, Blaise Diagne to his son Adolphe, 20 June 1930.

134 ANS, 1Z 25. Le Ministre des Colonies à Monsieur Diagne, Paris, 7 June 1930.

135 ANS, 1Z 25. Papiers de Blaise Diagne. Paris, 8 July 1930, 1–9.

136   Blaise Diagne, preface to Charles J. Fayet, *Travail et Colonisation. Esclavage et Travail Obligatoire* (Paris: Librarie Général de Droit et de Jurisprudence, 1931), 5–7.

137   *Les Annales Coloniales*, 'Le nouveau Ministère', 27 January 1931; 'Blaise Diagne', www2.assemblee-nationale.fr/sycomore/fiche/(num_dept)/2496 (accessed 13 May 2019).

138   ANOM, FP148APOM.1, Lamine Guèye à Monsieur Guguay-Clédor, Président du Conseil Colonial du Sénégal, 21 February 1931; Lamine Guèye à Monsieur Guguay-Clédor, 24 February 1931; Lamine Guèye à Monsieur le Ministre des Colonies, 25 February 1931.

139   Guèye, *Itinéraire*, 57; ANOM, FP148AAPOM.1, Lamine Guèye à Monsieur Guguay-Clédor, 21 April 1931; Le Gouverneur Général de l'Afrique occidentale française à Monsieur le Ministre des Colonies, 17 March 1931; Maurice Sauniere, Sous Directeur au Ministère des Colonies, à Monsieur Blaise Diagne, Sous Secrétaire d'Etat au Ministères des Colonies, 9 Deccember 1931.

140   ANOM, FP148APOM.1, Colonie du Sénégal. Élections Législatives du 1 Mai 1932, Parti Républicain-Socialiste, Blaise Diagne, Député Sortant, Candidat. Profession de Foi.

141   Ibid.

142   ANOM, 1AFFPOL/831, dossier 1. Élections Législatives 1932. Telegram from Governor Bearnier to the Ministry of the Interior, 5 May 1932.

143   ANOM, 1AFFPOL/551, Mission d'Étude de M. Diagne, Député du Sénégal, Ancien Sous-Sécretaire d'Etat des colonies en Afrique occidentale française, au Togo et au Cameroun. Note pour le Ministre; ANS 17G 206 (104), Mission Diagne 1932.

144   ANS 1Z 25. Déclaration de M. Diagne, député du Sénégal, ancien Sous-Secrétaire d'État des Colonies, chargé de mission.

145   Georges Barthélemy, 'L' élection de M. Diagne, au Sénégal, ne peut pas être validée', *La Gazette Coloniale*, 25 May 1932.

146   'Les Élections Sénégalaises vues de Rufisque, Lettre d'un de nos Correspondants', *La Gazette Coloniale*, 2 June 1932; *L' AOF Républicaine*, 1 February 1932.

147   Cited in Langley, *Pan-Africanism and Nationalism in West Africa, 1900–1945*, 321.

148   Dieng, *Blaise Diagne*, 154.

149   'Les Généraux Borgnis-Desbordes et Archinard. Discours prononcé le 25 décembre à Bamako par Blaise Diagne, Député du Sénegal', *L' Africain*, 31 December 1933.

150   ANOM, 1AFFPOL/595, telegram from Brevié to the ministry, 19 April 1934.

151   ANS, 1Z 25. Extraite des Registres de l'État Civil de la Commune de Cambo-les-Bains. Décès (1934). Blaise Diagne (11 May 1934); ANOM, 1AFFPOL/595, telegram from Brevié to the ministry, 26 April 1934.

152   ANOM, FP148APOM.1, Duguay-Clédor à Madame Blaise Diagne, 18 May 1934.

153 ANOM, 4SLOTFOM.9. Sénégal. Élection d'un député en remplacement du député Diagne en 1934. 'La succession de M. Diagne au Sénégal', Le commissaire Divisionnaire de police spéciale, 23 May 1934; 'Les élections prochaines en A.O.F', Le Commissaire Divisionnaire de police spéciale, 6 June 1934.

154 ANOM, 4SLOTFOM.9. Sénégal. Élection d'un député en remplacement du député Diagne en 1934. Le Commissaire Divisionnaire de police spéciale à Monsieur le Directeur de la Sûreté Nationale (Cabinet), 21 June 1934.

155 'Galandou Diouf. Biographie extraite du dictionnaire des parlementaires français de 1889 a 1940', www2.assemblee-nationale.fr/sycomore/fiche/(num_dept)/2523 (accessed 15 May 2019).

156 Langley, *Pan-Africanism and Nationalism in West Africa, 1900–1945*, 321.

157 ANOM, 1AFFPOL/595, telegram from Brévié to the president of the Chamber of Deputies, 12 May 1934.

Conclusion

Adrian Shubert

In the English-speaking world at least, biography is one of the most popular forms of writing about the past. Despite this undeniable popularity, however, the relationship between historians and biography has been ambivalent at best, frequently hostile and reaching at times an almost visceral rejection. This goes back a very long way. Even Thucydides, considered the first historian in the Western tradition, dismissed biography. It became more general in the nineteenth century with the professionalization of history and then in the twentieth with the spread of Marxist historiography, the Annales, quantitative history and social history.

Through most of the past century, historians in France were particularly hostile. Biography was the classic form of the *'histoire événementielle'*, the dust that settled on the surface, that Fernand Braudel sought to displace.[1] Criticism became particularly sharp in the 1960s and 1970s. Enchanted by the possibilities of quantitative methods, Emmanuel Leroy Ladurie sought a 'history without people'.[2] Jacques LeGoff sought to discover *mentalités*, ways of understanding the world that were collective and transcended individuals, what he described as 'the daily and the automatic … that which escapes the subjects of history, that which Columbus shared with the least of his crew'.[3] In the crucial year of 1989, which saw both the bicentenary of the French Revolution and the fall of the Berlin Wall, Marc Ferro spoke of '*cette handicapée de l'histoire*'.[4] Most influentially of all, Pierre Bourdieu denounced what, in a short essay, he called 'The Biographical Illusion'.[5]

English-speaking historians could be equally scathing, expressing themselves in terms that make Henry James's description of a biographer in the *Aspern Papers* as a 'publishing scoundrel' seem mild.[6] As in France, the 1960s and 1970s were crucial. Social history was the growth field in those years. Its practitioners were concerned with social groups and the unknown individuals who left few traces in the historical records whereas the dominant, if not only, subjects of biography were members of the elite. They were also struggling for professional space against political and diplomatic history, the privileged fields of biography.[7] But the suspicion of biography was not the monopoly of progressives. Even so conservative a figure as British historian Geoffrey Elton denounced it. He was prepared to countenance biography as an acceptable 'form of writing', but it was 'not a good way of writing history .... The historian ... should not write biography'.[8] As David Nasaw put it in his introduction to a 2009 roundtable on Historians and Biography in the *American Historical Review*, historians have long considered biography a 'lesser form of history' incapable of providing the 'kind of analytically sophisticated interpretation of the past that academics have long expected'.[9]

The suspicion of biography endures. In 2011, Jonathan Steinberg, the author of a marvellous biography of Bismarck, could ask 'Is biography proper history?' on his publisher's blog. His answer was a qualified yes: 'if it asks the kind of questions which an academic historian can define and offers evidence to support the answer'.[10] As recently as 2014, Daniel Snowman asked a similar question in the popular UK history magazine *History Today*: 'Can biography ever be a serious contribution to history?'[11]

During the last twenty years or so, however, the humanities and the social sciences have experienced what has been called a 'biographical turn'.[12] History has not been exempt and, as Barbara Caine puts it, biography has come 'to occupy more of th[e] centre ground' of the discipline.[13] Indeed, historians' attitudes towards biography have changed so significantly that many who formerly rejected it now actively embrace the genre. For example, by 1996 Jacques Le Goff, who twenty years earlier had advocated *mentalités*, was calling biography a 'privileged observatory' and writing biographies himself.[14] Danish historian Hans Kirchoff went from describing biography as 'an outdated, at best harmless, genre' in 1978 to publishing, in 2013, a biography of G. F. Duckwitz, the German diplomat who tipped off Danish Jews about their upcoming deportation.[15]

At the same time, biography itself has been changing in ways that make it more appealing to historians. In general, there has been new concern for the ways in which, as Lois Banner put it, 'biography interacts with the history of [the subject's] era', and has been recognized as a powerful vehicle for understanding the larger processes of society, culture and politics in a past time and place that are the historian's usual subject.[16] Biography no longer automatically means a straightforward cradle-to-grave narrative of the life of a great man or, much less frequently, woman. There is now a much greater variety of subjects and ways of approaching their lives.

Historians have played a major role in this revitalization. Jo Burr Margadant's 2000 collection, *The New Biography: Performing Femininity in Nineteenth-Century France*, was a landmark here.[17] The collection analysed the lives of eight French women 'from socially elite backgrounds' who became celebrities at a time when there were few possibilities for transcending the private sphere for the public one in a respectable way. What made these biographies 'new', however, was their methodological approach. Rather than seeking to tell 'a coherent story about an identifiably unified, though not necessarily unconflicted, individual', these essays examined the subjects' creation of a 'feminine self, legible to the public and credible to herself that might also win approval in at least some influential circles'. Their real subject, then, is 'self-invention'.[18]

One of the key reasons for this change in attitude has been the interest in new historical subjects prompted by fields such as labour history, social history, women's history and the histories of racial and ethnic minorities. Initially antagonistic to biography, historians working in these fields have come to see that '[a]s questions about the importance of gender, race and class come to the fore, so too has the recognition that the detailed analysis of individual or collective lives offers one of the best ways to explore them'.[19] Or, as Danish historian Birgitte Possing puts it, biography can serve as an 'element of democratization in a globalized community giving increasing numbers of individuals a place in history, a visibility and a contemporary response'.[20]

Introducing a special issue of the *Journal of the Canadian Historical Association*, 'The Biographical (ReTurn)', in 2010 Adele Perry and Brian Lewis spoke for many younger than Le Goff and Kirchoff as they described their journey from social history and gender history to biography and is worth quoting at length.

> We were both schooled in the new social historical tradition, that grand project arising in the sixties and holding sway for a quarter of a century or more. In trying to write history from below, in moving beyond the top-down decision-making of Great Men, the new social historians sought to uncover the experiences and impact of ordinary people. In deploying statistical and economic data to capture the economic and social fortunes of people who had left few other traces, these historians emphasized collectivities over individuals, marching classes, ethnicities and genders up and down the pages of their texts. Biographies seemed old fashioned — retaining their appeal among non-academic writers and to a popular audience, to be sure, but not something able to capture history from below, the longue durée, or the shifting fortunes of ordinary people in a changing world.

The cultural and linguistic turns of the eighties, the rise of poststructuralist and postmodernist analysis and the claiming of a place at the academic table by a new generation of feminist and racially, ethnically and sexually diverse scholars all helped to challenge the grand, teleological narratives. With a renewed interest in the individual and in agency, the contextualized biography as an entry-point to a study of a broader world (and psychoanalysis as a means of exploring the interior self), gained a new lease on life and a greater scholarly credibility.[21]

The nine wonderful studies in this volume further demonstrate the importance of this revitalized biography with its concern for self-invention and a democratization of vision. They span the period from the French Revolution to the Second World War and take us from the Americas, India and Africa to the European metropoles of France, Spain and Great Britain, as well as to the new nations of Colombia and the United States. They cast new light on the making, remaking and unmaking of empires and the evolution of former colonial places. They stress the agency and creativity of individuals and groups in the face of the complexities of their societies and what Josep M. Fradera describes as the determined efforts of imperial or national authorities to 'close off or short circuit or deliberately distort constitutional possibilities'. They tell stories of struggles against exclusion, of 'ambiguous zones', 'narrow spaces' and 'precarious' victories. They describe men who had complex lives and even more complex ancestries: an 'ambiguous and interlaced' one in the case of the Martiniquais Cyrille Bissette and a manufactured one in the case of Peruvian Dionisio Inca Yupanqui. Some, such as Yupanqui, Colombian Pedro José de Ibarra, and South African Mpilo Walter Benson Rubusana, had parliamentary lives, the product of special circumstances, that were fleeting; others, Gratien Candace from Guadeloupe and Blaise Diagne from Senegal, managed to build long careers and, in the case of Candace, wield real influence and attain ministerial office. Some, such as Candace and Dadabhai Naoroji from India, advocated for other progressive causes, especially women's suffrage. On the other hand, Candace never challenged the legitimacy of the collaborationist Pétain regime, even if he did protest the 1942 Vel' d'Hiv' Roundup of French Jews, and was not allowed to run for office after Liberation.

All the protagonists in the book except Naoroji were Christians. As a Parsi, he would have faced another form of exclusion had the requirement for new members of Britain's parliament to swear a Christian oath not been abolished only four years earlier. The Oaths Act 1888, which permitted new MPs to 'solemnly affirm' their loyalty to the monarch rather than swear it before God, was the culmination of a campaign led by Charles Bradlaugh (1833–91), founder of the National Secular Society. In a series of events that echoed the struggle of Lionel de Rothschild to become the first Jewish Member of Parliament in 1858, between 1880 and 1886, Bradlaugh was repeatedly elected, and repeatedly denied the right to take his seat because he refused to swear the oath that mentioned God.[22]

Robert Smalls, the American protagonist in this volume, stands out. Unlike the other eight, he was not an isolated individual, but a part of the ultimately aborted wave of transformational change that swept the US south following the defeat of the Confederacy in the Civil War. A key figure in the South Carolina Republican party, he controlled a political machine in a unique part of the state that allowed him to win five elections to the US House of Representatives even as Reconstruction, and the window of Black political opportunity it had opened, was being undone.

The United States itself stands out as well. The stories in this volume are about empire, but the nature of American empire was different: 'internal colonialism' as opposed to the 'more general case of countries with traditions of both colonialism and liberalism'.[23] The United States was not the only place whose colonies were within its borders, however. France had its own internal settler colony too. Algeria became French after a long and brutal conquest that started in 1830 and took the lives of between 15 and 33 per cent of the total population of three million. The European settlers, known as *colons* and later *pieds noirs*, who included large numbers of Spaniards and Italians, numbered 100,000 in 1847 and 1.1 million a century later. Settlement was accompanied by large-scale dispossession of lands, especially after 1880.

Under the Third and Fourth Republics, Algeria sent deputies to the National Assembly in France: six between 1876 and 1928, nine between 1928 and 1936 and ten thereafter. In theory, all residents, not just Europeans, had the right to vote, but Muslims could do so only if they requested French citizenship. In practice, almost none did so because becoming a citizen required they renounce Muslim law, a form of apostasy. After the Second World War, Algeria had thirty seats in the National Assembly: fifteen elected by 1.5 million French citizens and fifteen by 8 million Muslims *indigens*.

This short-lived system brought a number of Muslims into the chamber, although the French administration made sure there were no radical nationalists among them. These were not the first Muslim deputies, however. That title belonged to Philippe Grenier (1865–1944), a French medical doctor who had converted to Islam in 1894 after a trip to Algeria. Victorious in a by-election in the Jura in December 1896 despite being derided in the press for his Arab dress, as a deputy he was accused of maintaining a harem and frequently washing his

Source: gallica.bnf.fr / Bibliothèque nationale de France

Figure 11.1 *Le Petit Journal*, 24 January 1897. Courtesy of Bibliothèque nationale de France.

feet. *Le Petit Journal* greeted his first appearance as a deputy with the headline 'The Muslim on the Chamber' and a drawing that showed the shocked and puzzled reaction of his colleagues to the burnoose he wore. On the other hand, Grenier's presence was also lauded as an example of republican liberties. 'So what if he's a Muslim?' asked a M. de Kérobant in *Le Soleil.* 'Does freedom of conscience not exist in France? Is one not free to elect a Muslim, or a Jew, or an atheist?'[24]

After his election, the great Socialist leader Jean Jaurès sent Grenier a congratulatory letter urging him to act as the 'deputy of the Arabs'. Grenier took his advice, using his parliamentary platform to promote Algerian and other colonial issues. His most important initiative was to present a bill to raise taxes on alcohol to pay for an army of Algerians to be stationed in France to help counter the country's isolation. 'The actual situation of France', he said in introducing his bill, 'seems to me to be exceptionally grave. Perhaps more than at any time in our history, we find ourselves in a state of manifest inferiority vis a vis a probable coalition of European powers.'[25] Universal service was leaving France with an annual deficit of 120,000 men compared to Germany alone, and much more when compared to the Triple Alliance that also included Austria–Hungary and Italy. Conscripting men from Algeria and the colonies, men 'of a warlike temperament', would overcome that deficit; it would also 'extend the influence of civilization among people who are today stagnant from the point of view of progress'. Grenier's bill was prescient, as France would lean heavily on colonial troops during the First World War, but it did not become law.

Grenier's tenure as a deputy was brief, but it coincided with one of the high points of the Dreyfus Affair. He was in the chamber on 23 January 1898 when a deputy attacked Jean Jaurès while he was speaking, triggering a brawl involving some eighty parliamentarians. According to *The New York Times*, Grenier provided some comic relief. 'During the attitude of prayer, he assumed in the height of the fighting, [he] helplessly waived his white burnous, giving the effect of a huge duck flapping the water with its wings.'[26] Grenier lost his seat in the elections held in May that year, largely because his bill went down badly in his district, which was one of the country's centres of absinthe production. He ran for a third time in 1902 and was again defeated.[27]

Some of Britain's so-called 'White Dominions': Australia, New Zealand and especially Canada had internal colonies too. These places, which were at once both colonies and colonizers, were undergoing the same process of settler colonialism as the United States. Australian anthropologist Patrick Wolfe sees settler colonialism following what he called a 'logic of elimination'. In these places, settlers expropriated the lands of the indigenous inhabitants, who were either exterminated, imprisoned on reservations or forced to assimilate, and built a new society where indigenous ones had stood.[28] Unlike other forms of European imperialism, settler colonialism is difficult, if not impossible, to reverse, although indigenous peoples have increasingly challenged its legacies through land claims, claims for restitution, and truth and reconciliation. The 'national' parliaments of these settler colonial societies could be as, or even more, impermeable to 'unexpected voices' than Westminster itself. This was certainly true of Canada and Australia.

The Dominion of Canada was created by the British North America Act of 1867. Section 91 of this Act of the British parliament, which set out the respective responsibilities of the Parliament of Canada and provincial legislatures, gave 'exclusive Legislative Authority' for 'Indians, and Lands reserved for the Indians' to the former.[29] Nine years later the Dominion government of Alexander Mackenzie passed the Indian Act, which consolidated two previous pieces of legislation: the Gradual Civilization Act of 1857 and the 1869 Gradual Enfranchisement Act.[30] As the names of its predecessors make clear, the purpose this sweeping piece of paternalistic legislation was to drive the assimilation of 'Indians' into white Canadian society. The Act defined who was, and was not, an 'Indian', a European category that turned hundreds of sovereign First Nations into a single homogeneous mass – and gave the federal government control over all significant aspects of their lives. The Department of Indian Affairs

> had the power to determine who was of 'good moral character' and therefore deserve certain benefits, such as deciding if the widow of an enfranchised Indian 'lives respectably' and could therefore keep her children in the event of the father's death. The Act also severely restricted the governing powers of band councils, regulated alcohol consumption and determined who would be eligible for band and treaty benefits. It also marks the beginning of gender-based restrictions to status.

Subsequent amendments would make the Act even more all-encompassing: children were required to attend residential schools; certain religious ceremonies, such as the potlach, were banned; and dancing, whether on reserve or off, was prohibited. One section of the Act, which remained in force until 1961, mandated 'compulsory enfranchisement', that is loss of status as an Indian, to any First Nations person who got a university degree qualified as a doctor or lawyer or became a Christian clergyman.[31]

It is no surprise that, under such a system, one which denied the vote to status 'Indians' until 1960, there were no unexpected 'Indian' voices in Canada's parliament for a very long time. The first was Leonard Marchand, elected in a British Columbia riding in 1968. During his eleven years as an MP, he also became the first 'Indian' to serve as a member of the federal cabinet.[32] No indigenous woman served as an MP until Ethel Blondin-Andrew in 1988. The first indigenous person elected to any legislature in Canada was Frank Calder, who sat in British Columbia's parliament from 1949 to 1979.[33]

The Indian Act did not apply to two groups who are now recognized as First Nations: the Inuit and the Métis. As were status 'Indians', Inuit were denied the vote until 1960 and no Inuk sat in Parliament until Peter Ittinuar was elected in 1979. As a child, Ittinuar had been one of three 'Experimental Eskimos' forcibly removed from their Arctic homes to Ottawa as part of an experiment to determine how Inuit would adapt.[34]

The Métis, a nation born in the eighteenth century from marriages between European fur traders and indigenous women and constitutionally recognized as one of the 'aboriginal peoples of Canada' since 1982, present a more complex picture.[35] Most Métis lived in former Hudson's Bay Company lands ceded to Canada in 1869 as the Northwest Territories. Led by Louis Riel, in 1870 Métis formed a provisional government and sent representatives to negotiate with the government of Canada. This led to the creation of the province of Manitoba, the first new province since Confederation. The special election to choose the province's first MPs in 1871 returned two Métis: Pierre Delorme and Angus Mackay, although both lost their seat in the general election the following year. Louis Riel, the leader of the 1870 rebellion, won the riding of Provencher in a by-election in 1873 and twice in 1874, but he never took his seat in the House of Commons. No Métis would be elected for sixty years, and none in Manitoba until 1980.

Exclusion from Canada's legislative body was not limited to multiple First Nations who were its colonial subjects. It also extended to people of African descent who had lived in what became Canada since the seventeenth century and who have a place in Canada's national mythology, which boasts of its place as the destination for between thirty thousand and forty thousand people escaping slavery on the Underground Railroad.[36] That said, no black was elected to the federal parliament until Lincoln Alexander in 1968.[37]

The story in Australia is, if anything, even grimmer. Senator Neville Bonner became the first Aboriginal ever elected in 1971, but it was only in 2010 that an Aboriginal, Kenneth Wyatt, was elected to the House of Representatives. As to the state legislatures, the first Aboriginal was elected in Queensland and the Northern Territory in 1974, Victoria in 1979, Western Australia in 1980, Tasmania in 1996, New South Wales in 2003 and the Capital Territory in 2011.[38]

New Zealand stands in stark contrast to Canada and Australia. As Fradera points out, the colonial legislature had a small number of designated Maori seats – a testament to the tenacity of their military resistance to the colonial takeover. While Maori were not prohibited from voting under the colony's 1852 constitution, their tradition of collective landholding prevented them from meeting the property qualification, and only a hundred were able to vote in the first election, compared to 5,750 Pakeha, or whites. In 1867, the Māori Representation Act created four designated seats, compared to seventy-two 'European' seats. The Act also gave the vote to all Maori males twenty-one years or older, meaning they enjoyed universal suffrage twelve years before Pakeha men. And when New Zealand became the first place in the world to allow women to vote in national elections in 1893, this applied to the Maori seats as well. As a result, whatever the limitations of the Maori's place in New Zealand's political life, Maori women had a formal political voice twenty-five years before British women were granted one. (Women, white or Maori, could not be candidates for parliament until 1919. The first Pakeha woman elected was Elizabeth McCombs in 1933; the first Maori was Iriaka Matiu Rātana in 1949.) After 1896, any opportunity for Maori to participate outside their own electoral system was abolished; from then until 1975, so-called 'half castes', people with one European and one Maori parent, could choose whether to participate in the Maori or the general system. And until they were allowed the secret ballot in 1938, Maori voted by voice before a white polling official. As part of a broader reform of the electoral system that brought in a version of proportional representation, a 1985 Royal Commission proposed the Maori seats be abolished, but Maori organizations successfully mobilized to protect them.[39]

The first Maori – Irish father and Maori mother – to win a 'European' seat, was James Carroll (1857–1926). He started out in one of the Maori seats but switched to a 'European' one in 1893 and held it until 1919. He was also the last to do so until 1975. An ardent assimilationist, Carroll's political career was based on the idea that Maori needed to wholeheartedly join Pakeha society and work to progress within it. This brought him into conflict with the more radical elements of the Maori political movement, especially over issues regarding land but it never prevented him being 'emphatically and sometimes passionately Māori', as his entry in the *Dictionary of New Zealand Biography* proclaims.[40] In addition to having a lengthy political career, James Carroll served as a cabinet minister and was twice even acting Prime Minister, surely a global first. In all his complexities, his accomplishments and his compromises, he would have been an emblematic case study for this collection of enlightening biographies.

Both the unexpected voices I have mentioned here and the nine described in the other chapters illustrate three important points. The first is the centrality of contingency: the place, the moment, the overall context. The second is the centrality of agency: the ability of certain individuals to work within the constraints – and especially racial constraints – of imperial systems and squeeze their way into sacred political spaces never intended for them. Finally, the fact that they were so few and, beyond the fact of their election, their accomplishments so few, highlight the severe limits to reform within these imperial structures.

Notes

1 Fernand Braudel, 'Histoire et Sciences Sociales: La longue durée', in *Réseaux. Communication – Technologie – Société*, 27 (1987): 7–37. The phrase itself was coined by Francois Simiand.

2 Emmanuel Leroy Ladurie, *Le territoire de l'historien*, vol. 1 (Paris: Gallimard, 1973).

3 Jacques Le Goff, 'Les mentalités; une histoire ambiguë', in Jacques Le Goff and Pierre Nora (eds.), *Faire de l'histoire*, vol. III (Paris: Gallimard, 1974).

4 Marc Ferro, 'La biographie, cette handicapée de l'histoire', *Le Magazine littéraire* (April 1989): 85–8.

5 Pierre Bourdieu, 'L'illusion biographique', *Actes de la recherche en sciences sociales*, 62–3 (1986): 69–72.

6 Henry James, *The Aspern Papers* (London: Macmillan and Co., 1888), 352.

7 Geoff Eley, *A Crooked Line. From Cultural History to the History of Society* (Ann Arbor: University of Michigan Press, 2005).

8 Geoffrey Elton, *The Practice of History* (London: Methuen, 1967), 135.

9 David Nasaw, 'Introduction', *American Historical Review*, 114, no. 3 (2009): 573.

10 Jonathan Steinberg, 'Is Biography Proper History', *OUPblog*, https://blog.oup.com/2011/02/biography/ (accessed 5 February 2021).

11 Daniel Snowman, 'Historical Biography', *History Today*, 64, no. 11 (November 2014). Available online: www.historytoday.com/daniel-snowman/historical-biography (accessed 5 February 2021).

12 Prue Chamberlaine, Joanna Bornat and Tom Wengraf, eds., *The Turn to Biographical Methods in the Social Sciences* (London: Verso, 2000).

13 Barbara Caine, *Biography and History* (London: Palgrave Macmillan, 2010), 1.

14 Jacques Le Goff, *Saint Louis* (Paris: Gallimard, 1996); *Saint Francis of Assisi* (London: Routledge, 2003).

15 Birgitte Possing, *Understanding Biographies: On Biographies in History and Stories in Biography* (Odense, Denmark: University Press of Southern Denmark, 2016), 43.

16 Lois Banner, 'Biography as History', *American Historical Review*, 114, no. 3 (June 2009): 585.

17 Jo Burr Margadant, *The New Biography: Performing femininity in nineteenth-century France* (New York: Berkeley, 2000). The phrase 'new biography' was first used by Virginia Woolf in her article of that name first published in the *New York Herald Tribune* on 20 October 1927.

18 Margadant, *The New Biography*, 1–7.

19 Caine, *Biography and History*, 3.

20 Possing, *Understanding Biographies*. For a fine example of a gender-conscious approach to biography, see Erla Hulda Halldórsdóttir, Tiina Kinnunen, Maarit Leskelä-Kärki and Birgitte Possing, *Biography, Gender and History: Nordic perspectives* (Turku, Finland: Kulttuurihistoria – Turun yliopisto, 2017).

21 Adele Perry and Brian Lewis, Introductory Remarks: Special Issue on 'The Biographical (Re)Turn', *Journal of the Canadian Historical Association*, 21, no. 2 (2010): 3–4.

22 Robert Woodall, 'The Jewish Relief Act', *History Today*, 25, no. 6 (6 June 1975). Available online: www.historytoday.com/archive/jewish-relief-act-1858 (accessed 5 February 2021); Bryan Niblett, *Dare to Stand Alone: The Story of Charles Bradlaugh* (Oxford: Kramedart Press, 2011).

23 Josep M. Fradera, 'The value of political representation in modern empires', in this volume, 5–23.

24 Robert Bichet, *Un Comtois musulman, le docteur Philippe Grenier: Prophète de Dieu, député de Pontarlier* (Paris: R. Bichet, 1976); *Le Petit Journal*, 24 January 1897.

25 Philippe Grenier, *Proposition de loi concernant la défense nationale, Présentée Par M. Philippe Grenier, ... (6 mars 1897)* (Paris: Motteroz, 1897).

26 *The New York Times*, 24 January 1898. See also *Le Figaro*, 23 January 1898.

27 Robert Fernier, *Docteur Philippe Grenier. Ancien Député musulman de Pontarlier* (Paris: Alfabarre, 2016); cited on http://migrations.besancon.fr/histoire/1800-1914/740-philippe-grenier-le-depute-musulman-de-pontarlier-.html?showall=&start=2 (accessed 5 February 2021).

28 Patrick Wolfe, 'Settler Colonialism and the Elimination of the Native', *Journal of Genocide Research*, 8, no. 4 (2006): 387.

29 Ken Coates, 'Gentle Confiscation: The Settlement of Canada and the Dispossession of the First Nations', in Paul Haveman (ed.), *Indigenous Peoples and the Law: Comparative Perspectives* (Auckland: Oxford University Press, 1999), 141–61; 'Constitution Acts, 1867 to 1982', Justice Laws Website, https://laws-lois.justice.gc.ca/eng/const/page-4.html (accessed 5 February 2021).

30 'An Act to amend and consolidate the laws respecting Indians', Indigenous and Northern Affairs Canada, https://www.aadnc-aandc.gc.ca/eng/1100100010252/1100100010254 (accessed 5 February 2021).

31 'The Indian Act', Indigenous Foundations https://indigenousfoundations.arts. ubc.ca/the_indian_act/ (accessed 5 February 2021); 'Indian Act', *The Canadian Encyclopedia*, www.thecanadianencyclopedia.ca/en/article/indian-act (accessed 5 February 2021).

32 Len Marchand and Matt Hughes, *Breaking Trail* (Halfmoon Bay,British Columbia: Caitlin Press, 2000).

33 'Ethel Dorothy Blondin-Andrew', https://lop.parl.ca/sites/ParlInfo/default/en_CA/ People/Profile?personId=6997#comp (accessed 5 February 2021); 'Frank Calder', *The Canadian Encyclopedia*, https://thecanadianencyclopedia.ca/en/article/frank-calder (accessed 5 February 2021).

34 Peter Ittinuar, https://lop.parl.ca/sites/ParlInfo/default/en_CA/People/ Profile?personId=3790 (accessed 5 February 2021); 'You used us unwittingly, you didn't ask our parents, you just took us', *Nunatsiaq News*, 3 July 2008. Available online: https://nunatsiaq.com/stories/article/You_used_us_unwittingly_you_ didnt_ask_our_parents_you_just_took_us/ (accessed 5 February 2021).

35 Constitution Act, 1982. Available online: https://laws-lois.justice.gc.ca/eng/const/ page-15.html#h-38 (accessed 5 February 2021); Metis Nation, https://www. metisnation.ca/index.php/who-are-the-metis (accessed 5 February 2021).

36 See, for example, the *Heritage Minute* devoted to the Underground Railroad: https://www.historicacanada.ca/content/heritage-minutes/underground-railroad (accessed 5 February 2021).

37 The Hon. MacCauley Lincoln Alexander, https://lop.parl.ca/sites/ParlInfo/default/ en_CA/People/Profile?personId=42 (accessed 5 February 2021).

38 'Indigenous parliamentarians, federal and state: A quick guide', Parliament of Australia, www.aph.gov.au/About_Parliament/Parliamentary_ Departments/Parliamentary_Library/pubs/rp/rp1718/Quick_Guides/ IndigenousParliamentarians (accessed 5 February 2021).

39 Neill Atkinson, *Adventures in Democracy: A history of the vote in New Zealand* (Dunedin: University of Otago Press in association with the Electoral Commission, 2003); Philip A. Joseph, *The Maori seats in Parliament* (Wellington: Parliamentary Library, 2008).

40 'James Carroll', *Dictionary of New Zealand Biography*, https://teara.govt.nz/en/ biographies/2c10/carroll-james (accessed 5 February 2021).

Select Bibliography

Artola, Miguel. *La España de Fernando VII*. Madrid: Espasa, 2008.

Barker, Hannah. *Newspapers, Politics, and Public Opinion in Late Eighteenth-century England*. London: Routledge, 2000.

Barkley-Brown, Elsa. 'Negotiating and transforming the public sphere: African American political life in the transition from slavery to freedom'. *Public Culture*, 7 (1994): 107–46.

Bayly, Cristopher A. *Imperial Meridian: The British empire and the world, 1780–1830*. Edinburgh: Longman, 1989.

Bayly, Christopher Alan. *Recovering Liberties: Indian thought in the age of liberalism and empire*. Cambridge: Cambridge University Press, 2011.

Belley, Jean-Baptiste. *Le Bout d'oreille des colons, ou le système de l'Hôtel de Massiac, mis au jour par Gouli; Belley, député noir de Saint-Domingue, à ses collègues*. Paris: Imp. Pain, n.d.

Bénot, Yves. 'Comment la Convention a-t-elle voté l'abolition de l'esclavage en l'an II?'. *Annales Historiques de la Révolution Française*, 293 (1993): 349–61.

Benzaken, Jean-Charles. *Louis Pierre Dufaÿ, conventionnel abolitionniste et colon de Saint-Domingue*. Paris: Éditions SPM, 2015.

Blackburn, Robin. *The Overthrow of Colonial Slavery*. London: Verso, 1988.

Blanchard, Pascal, and Alain Mabanckou, edseds. *La France noire: Trois siècles de présence*. Paris: La Découverte, 2011.

Burton, Antoinette. *At the Heart of Empire: Indians and the colonial encounter in late-Victorian Britain*. Berkeley: University of California Press, 1998.

Cahill, David. 'Becoming an Inca: Juan de Bustamante Carlos Inca and the roots of the Great Rebellion'. *Colonial Latin American Review*, 22 (2013): 259–80.

Carter, Dan T. *When the War Was Over: The failure of Self-Reconstruction in the South, 1865–1867*. Baton Rouge, LA: Louisiana State University Press, 1985.

Chathuant, Dominique. 'Gratien Candace: Une figure de la vie politique française. 1ère partie: La Troisième République (1900–1940)'. *Bulletin de la Société d'histoire de la Guadeloupe*, 134 (2003): 27–102.

Chathuant, Dominique. 'Gratien Candace: Une figure de la vie politique française. 2ème partie: Un vestige de la Troisième République (1940–1953)'. *Bulletin de la Société d'histoire de la Guadeloupe*, 149 (2008): 3–131.

Chathuant, Dominique. 'L'émergence d'une élite politique noire dans la France du premier 20e siècle?'. *Vingtième siècle: Revue d'histoire*, 101 (2009): 133–48.

Chathuant, Dominique. 'D'une République à l'autre: Ascension et survie politique de Maurice Satineau (1891–1945)'. *Bulletin de la Société d'histoire de la Guadeloupe*, 178 (2017): 9–85.

Conklin, Alice L. *A Mission to Civilize: The republican idea of empire in France and West Africa, 1895–1930*. Stanford: Stanford University Press, 1997.

Conklin, Alice L. "'Democracy" rediscovered: Civilization through association in French West Africa (1914–1930)'. *Cahiers d'études africains*, 145 (1997): 59–84.

Coquery-Vidrovitch, Catherine. 'Nationalité et citoyenneté en Afrique occidental française: Originaires et citoyens dans le Sénégal colonial'. *The Journal of African History*, 42 (2001): 285–305.

Darnton, Robert, and Daniel Roche, eds. *Revolution in Print: The Press in France, 1775–1800*. Los Angeles: University of California Press, 1989.

De la Puente Luna, José Carlos. *Andean Cosmopolitans: Seeking justice and reward at the Spanish royal court*. Austin: University of Texas, 2018.

Dieng, Amady. *Blaise Diagne, premier député africain*. Paris: Éditions Chaka, 1990.

Du Bois, W. E. B. *Black Reconstruction in America: An essay toward a history of the part which black folk played in the attempt to reconstruct democracy in America, 1860–1880*. New York: The Free Press, 1992; 1935; repr.

Dubow, Saul. *Racial Segregation and the Origins of Apartheid in South Africa, 1919–36*. New York: Palgrave Macmillan, 1989.

Dumont, Jacques. *L'Amère patrie: Histoire des Antilles françaises au XXe siècle*. Paris: Fayard, 2010.

Fisher, Michael H. *Counterflows to Colonialism: Indian travellers and settlers in Britain, 1600–1857*. Delhi: Permanent Black, 2004.

Foner, Eric. *Reconstruction: America's unfinished revolution*. New York: Harper and Row, 1988.

Foner, Eric. *Freedom's Lawmakers: A directory of black officeholders during Reconstruction*. New York: Oxford University Press, 1993.

Fradera, Josep M. *The Imperial Nation: Citizens and subjects in the British, French, Spanish, and American empires*. Princeton: Princeton University Press, 2018.

Friede, Juan. *La otra verdad: La independencia americana vista por los españoles*. Bogotá: Carlos Valencia Editores, 1979.

Gainot, Bernard. 'La députation de Saint-Domingue au corps législatif du Directoire'. *Revue française d'histoire d'outre-mer*, 84 (1997): 95–110.

Gainot, Bernard. 'Les réseaux d'un conventionnel noir à travers les papiers de Joseph Boisson (1793–1800)'. *Annales Historiques de la Révolution Française*, 388 (2017): 29–51.

Gandhi, Leela. *Affective communities: Anticolonial thought, fin-de-siècle radicalism and the politics of friendship*. Durham, NC: Duke University Press, 2006.

Garrett, David T. *Shadows of Empire: The Indian nobility of Cusco, 1750–1825*. Cambridge: Cambridge University Press, 2005.

Geggus, David. 'The Haitian Revolution in Atlantic perspective'. In *The Atlantic World, c. 1450–c. 1820*, edited by Nicholas Canny and Philip Morgan. New York: Oxford University Press, 2011.

Geggus, David. 'The slaves and free people of color of Cap Français'. In *The Black Urban Atlantic in the Age of the Slave Trade*, edited by Jorge Cañizares-Esguerra, Matt Childs and James Sidbury. Philadelphia: University of Pennsylvania Press, 2013.

Girollet, Anne. *Victor Schoelcher, abolitionniste et républicain: Approche juridique et politique de l'œuvre d'un fondateur de la République*. Paris: Karthala, 2000.

Gopal, Priyamvada. *Insurgent empire: Anticolonial resistance and British dissent*. London, Verso, 2019.

Gutiérrez Ardila, Daniel. *La Restauración en la Nueva Granada (1815–1819)*. Bogotá: Universidad del Externado de Colombia, 2016.

Hayot, Emile. 'Les gens de couleur libres du Fort-Royal, 1679–1823'. *Revue française d'histoire d'outre-mer*, 203 (1969): 5–163.

Higgs, Catherine. *The Ghost of Equality: The public lives of D.D.T. Jabavu of South Africa, 1885–1959*. Athens: Ohio University Press, 1997.

Hirschman, Albert O. *Exit, Voice and Loyalty: Responses to decline in firms, organizations, and states*. Cambridge, MA: Harvard University Press, 1970.

Hinnells, John R., and Alan Williams, eds. *Parsis in India and the diaspora*. London: Routledge, 2007.

Hughes, Heather. *First President: A life of John L. Dube, founding president of the ANC*. Auckland Park, South Africa: Jacana Media, 2011.

Isambert, François-André. *Affaire des déportés de la Martinique*. Paris: Constantin, 1824.

Isambert, François-André. *Mémoire justificatif des hommes de couleur de la Martinique condamnés par arrêt de la cour royale de cette colonie, contenant l'histoire des hommes de couleur dans les colonies françaises*. Paris: Imprimerie E. Duverger, 1826.

Jalabert, Laurent, Bertrand Joly and Jacques Weber, eds. *Les élections législatives et sénatoriales outre-mer (1848–1981)*. Paris: Les Indes savantes, 2010.

James, C. L. R. *The Black Jacobins: Toussaint L'Ouverture and the San Domingo Revolution*. New York: Vintage, 1963.

Jennings, Lawrence C. 'Cyrille Bissette, radical black french abolitionnist'. *French History*, 9 (1995): 48–66.

Jennings, Lawrence C. *French Anti-slavery: The movement for the abolition of slavery in France, 1802–1848*. Cambridge: Cambridge University Press, 2000.

Jennings, Lawrence C. 'Le second mouvement pour l'abolition de l'esclavage colonial français'. *Outre-mers: Revue d'histoire*, 336–7 (2002): 177–91.

Johnson, George Wesley. *The Emergence of Black Politics in Senegal: The struggle for power in the Four Communes, 1900–1920*. Stanford: Stanford University Press, 1971.

Johnson, George Wesley. 'The impact of the Senegalese elite upon the French, 1900–1940'. In *Double impact: France and Africa in the age of imperialism*, edited by G. Wesley Johnson, 166–71. London: Greenwood Press, 1985.

Kopytoff, Larissa. 'French citizens and Muslim law: The tensions of citizenship in early twentieth century Senegal'. In *The Meaning of Citizenship*, edited by Richard Marback and Marc W. Kruman, 320–37. Detroit: Wayne State University Press, 2015.

Langley, J. Ayodele. *Pan-Africanism and Nationalism in West Africa, 1900–1945: A study in ideology and social classes*. Oxford: Clarendon Press, 1973.

Le Cour Grandmaison, Olivier. *De l'indigénat: Anatomie d'un 'monstre' juridique: Le droit coloniale en Algérie et dans l'Empire français*. Paris: La Découverte, 2010.

Louis, Abel Alexis. *Les libres de couleur en Martinique*. Paris: L'Harmattan, 2012.

Louis, Abel Alexis. *Marchands et Négociants de couleur à Saint-Pierre (1777–1830): Milieux socioprofessionnels, fortune et mode de vie*. Paris: L'Harmattan, 2015.

Louis, Abel Alexis. *Jean-Pierre Eugène Clavier: Premier homme de couleur membre du Conseil colonial et de la Cour d'appel de la Martinique (1810–1863): L'homme, l'avocat, le propriétaire d'esclaves et d'habitations sucreries à l'épreuve de la zone grise*. Paris: L'Harmattan, 2016.

Loveland, Ian. *By Due Process of Law? Racial discrimination and the right to vote in South Africa, 1855–1960*. Oxford: Hart Publishing, 1999.

M'Baye, Babacar. *Black Cosmopolitanism and Anticolonialism: Pivotal moments*. New York: Routledge, 2017.

Mam Lam Fouck, Serge. *Histoire de l'assimilation, des 'vieilles colonies' françaises aux départements d'outre-mer. La culture politique de l'assimilation aux Antilles et en Guyane françaises (XIXe et XXe siècle)*. Matoury, French Guiana: Ibis Rouge, 2006.

Masani, Rustom Pestonji. *Dadabhai Naoroji: The Grand Old Man of India*. London: Allen & Unwin, 1939.

McCurry, Stephanie. *Confederate Reckoning: Power and politics in the Civil War South*. Cambridge, MA, and London: Harvard University Press, 2010.

Mehrotra, Sri Ram, and Dinyar Patel, eds. *Dadabhai Naoroji: Selected private papers*. Delhi: Oxford University Press, 2016.

Mesnard, Eric. 'Les mouvements de résistance dans les colonies françaises: L'affaire Bissette (1823–1827)'. In *Les abolitions de l'esclavage de L. F. Sonthonax à V. Schoelcher, 1793, 1794, 1848*, edited by Marcel Dorigny, 293–7. Vincennes, Paris: Presses Universitaires de Vincennes, Éditions UNESCO, 1995.

Miller, Edward A. *Gullah Statesman: Robert Smalls from slavery to Congress, 1839–1915*. Columbia: University of South Carolina Press, 1995.

Ngqongo, Songezo Joel. 'Mpilo Walter Benson Rubusana'. In *African Intellectuals in the 19th and early 20th century: South Africa*, edited by Mcebisi Ndletyana, 45–54. Pretoria: HSRC Press, 2008.

Noel, Érick. *Dictionnaire des gens de couleur dans la France Moderne*. Geneva: Droz, 2011.

O'Phelan, Scarlett. 'Linaje e Ilustración: Don Manuel Uchu Inca y el Real Seminario de Nobles de Madrid (1725–1808)'. In *El hombre y los Andes: Homenaje a Franklin Pease G. Y.*, edited by Javier Flores and Rafael Varón, 841–56. Lima: Instituto Francés de Estudios Andinos, 2002, vol. II.

O'Phelan, Scarlett. 'Los diputados suplentes Dionisio Uchu Inca Yupanqui y Vicente Morales Duárez: Su visión del Perú'. In *Voces americanas en las Cortes de Cádiz: 1810–1814*, edited by Scarlett O'Phelan and Georges Lomné, 83–102. Lima: Instituto Francés de Estudios Andinos, 2014.

Odendaal, Andre. *Black Protest Politics in South Africa to 1912*. Totowa: Barnes and Noble Books, 1984.

Piquet, Jean-Daniel. *L'émancipation des noirs dans la Révolution française (1789–1795)*. Paris: Karthala, 2002.

Queipo del Llano (Conde de Toreno), José María. *Historia del levantamiento, guerra y revolución de Espa*ña. Pamplona: Urgoiti, 2008.

Regan-Lefebvre, Jennifer. *Cosmopolitan Nationalism in the Victorian Empire: Ireland, India and the politics of Alfred Webb*. London: Palgrave Macmillan, 2009.

Régent, Frédéric. *Esclavage, métissage, liberté: La Révolution française en Guadeloupe 1789-1802*. Paris: Grasset, 2004.

Restrepo, José Manuel. *Historia de la revolución de la República de Colombia en la América meridional*. Besançon, France: José Jacquin, 1858.

Rich, Paul B. *White Power and the Liberal Conscience: Racial segregation and South African liberalism, 1921-1960*. Manchester: Manchester University Press, 1984.

Robinson, Donald L. *Slavery in the Structure of American Politics, 1765-1820*. New York: Harcourt Brace Janovich, 1970.

Schermerhorn, Calvin. *Unrequisited Toil: A history of United States slavery*. Cambridge: Cambridge University Press, 2018.

Schneer, Jonathan. *London 1900: The imperial metropolis*. New Haven: Yale University Press, 1999.

Serva, Cyril, eded. *Études guadeloupéennes*. Pointe-à-Pitre, Guadeloupe: Jasor, 2001.

Silvestre, Francisco. *Relación de la provincia de Antioquia*, edited by David J. Robinson. Medellín: Secretaría de Educación y Cultura de Antioquia, 1988.

Stoan, Stephen K. *Pablo Morillo and Venezuela, 1815-1820*. Columbus: Ohio State University Press, 1974.

Switzer, Les. *Power and Resistance in an African Society: The Ciskei Xhosa and the making of South Africa*. Pietermaritzburg: University of Natal Press, 1993.

Switzer, Les., ed. *South Africa's Alternative Press: Voices of protest and resistance, 1880-1960*. Cambridge: Cambridge University Press, 1997.

Thésée, Françoise. *Le Général Donzelot à la Martinique: Vers la fin de l'Ancien Régime colonial (1818-1826)*. Paris: Karthala, 1997.

Thiam, Iba. *La révolution de 1914 au Sénégal, ou L' élection au Palais Bourbon du député noir Blaise Diagne (de son vrai nom Galaye Mbaye Diagne)*. Dakar: L'Harmattan Sénégal, 2014.

Twinam, Ann. *Mineros, comerciantes y labradores: Las raíces del espíritu empresarial en Antioquia, 1763-1810*. Medellín: Fondo Rotatorio de Publicaciones FAES, 1985.

Vanegas, Isidro. *La revolución neogranadina*. Bogotá: Ediciones Plural, 2013.

Villegas, Samuel. '¿Indio o criollo? Identidad étnica del diputado Dionisio Inca Yupanqui en las Cortes de Cádiz'. *Nueva crónica*, 1 (2013): 1–10.

Visram, Rozina. *Ayahs, Lascars and Princes: Indians in Britain, 1700-1947*. London: Pluto Press, 1987.

Walker, Charles. *The Tupac Amaru Rebellion*. Cambridge, MA: Harvard University Press, 2014.

Walshe, Peter. *The Rise of African Nationalism in South Africa*. Berkeley: University of California Press, 1971.

Wasniewski, Matthew, ed. *Black Americans in Congress, 1870–2007*. Washington, DC: Government Printing Office, 2008.

Whiting, Richard. 'The empire and British politics'. In *Britain's Experience of Empire in the Twentieth Century*, edited by Andrew Thompson, 161–210. Oxford: Oxford University Press, 2012.

Wilentz, Sean. *No Property in Man: Slavery and antislavery at the nation's founding*. Cambridge, MA: Harvard University Press, 2018.

Winock, Michel. *Les voix de la liberté*. Paris: Éditions du Seuil, 2001.

Wise, Stephen R., and Lawrence S. Rowland. *Rebellion, Reconstruction, and Redemption, 1861–1893: The history of Beaufort, South Carolina*, vol. 2. Columbia, SC: University of South Carolina Press, 2015.

Wood, Peter. *Black Majority: Negroes in colonial South Carolina from 1670 through the Stono Rebellion*. New York: W. W. Norton and Co., 1974.

Worden, Nigel. *The Making of Modern South Africa: Conquest, Apartheid and democracy*. Chichester, UK: Wiley-Blackwell, 2012.

Zancarini-Fournel, Michelle. *Une histoire nationale est-elle encore possible?* Bordeaux: Presses universitaires de Bordeaux, Presses de l'Université de Pau, 2018.

Zuczek, Richard. *State of Rebellion: Reconstruction in South Carolina*. Columbia: University of South Carolina Press, 1996.

Index

www.ingramcontent.com/pod-product-compliance
Lightning Source LLC
Chambersburg PA
CBHW060152280326
41932CB00012B/1737